Romanticism

Palgrave Sourcebooks

Series Editor: Steven Matthews

Published
Simon Bainbridge: **Romanticism**
Steven Matthews: **Modernism**

Forthcoming
Carolyn Collette and Harold Garrett-Goodyear: **Medieval Literature**
Lena Cowen Orlin: **The Renaissance**
John Plunket, Ana Vadillo, Regenia Gagnier, Angelique Richardson, Rick Rylance
    and Paul Young: **Victorian Literature**
Nigel Wood: **The 'Long' Eighteenth Century**

Palgrave Sourcebooks

ISBN 978–1–4039–4277–7 hardback
ISBN 978–1–4039–4278–4 paperback

You can receive further titles in this series as they are published by placing a standing order. Please contact your bookseller or, in the case of difficulty, write to us at the address below with your name and address, the title of the series, and the ISBN quoted above.

Customer Services Department, Palgave Ltd.
Houndmills, Basingstoke, Hampshire, RG21 6XS, England

Romanticism

A Sourcebook

Edited by Simon Bainbridge

palgrave
macmillan

First published 2008 by
PALGRAVE MACMILLAN
Houndmills, Basingstoke, Hampshire RG21 6XS and
175 Fifth Avenue, New York, N.Y. 10010
Companies and representatives throughout the world

PALGRAVE MACMILLAN is the global academic imprint of the Palgrave
Macmillan division of St. Martin's Press, LLC and of Palgrave Macmillan Ltd.
Macmillan® is a registered trademark in the United States, United Kingdom
and other countries. Palgrave is a registered trademark in the European
Union and other countries.

ISBN-13: 978–0–230–00034–6   hardback
ISBN-10: 0–230–00034–7   hardback
ISBN-13: 978–0–230–00035–3   paperback
ISBN-10: 0–230–00035–5   paperback

This book is printed on paper suitable for recycling and made from fully
managed and sustained forest sources. Logging, pulping and manufacturing
processes are expected to conform to the environmental regulations of the
country of origin.

A catalogue record for this book is available from the British Library.

A catalog record for this book is available from the Library of Congress.

10 9 8 7 6 5 4 3 2 1
17 16 15 14 13 12 11 10 09 08

Printed and bound in China

Short Contents

For Charlie and Grace

Detailed Contents

List of Illustrations

List of Maps

Acknowledgements

I am very grateful to Steven Matthews for inviting me to edit this anthology, for his advice and encouragement throughout the project, and for his helpful comments on the typescript at various stages. At Palgrave Macmillan, Kate Haines has been supportive and helpful from the proposal stage through to the submission of the final version. I have benefited considerably from the professional expertise of Felicity Noble, Valery Rose and Jocelyn Stockley during the production process.

I would like to thank the staff at the following libraries: The British Library; The British Library (Boston Spa); The British Library (Newspaper Reading Room, Colingdale); The John Rylands University Library, University of Manchester; Keele University Library; Lancaster University Library; University of Liverpool Library and University of York Library.

A number of individuals have advised on the contents of the volume, discussed selections of material, helped with the sourcing of texts and images, read and commented on sections of the typescript, and assisted with the production of the book, and I would particularly like to thank the following: David Amigoni; Arthur Bradley; Fred Botting; Eleanor Brown; Cécile Brunner; Sally Bushell; Helen Clish; Georgina French; Keith Hanley; Jacky Hardcastle; Ivor Kerslake; Jim McLaverty; Jennifer Ramkalawon; Nicholas Roe; Jane Stabler; Caroline Sutcliffe; Andrew Tate; Sharon Ruston and Lindsey Walker. Three anonymous readers for Palgrave made many valuable suggestions about the conception and contents of the volume that have strengthened it considerably. In preparing the headnotes and supporting materials for this book I found a number of reference works particularly helpful, and I would like to acknowledge my intellectual debt to the following: *An Oxford Companion to the Romantic Age: British Culture 1776–1832*, ed. Iain McCalman et al (Oxford: Oxford University Press, 1999); Oxford Dictionary of National Biography Online (http://wwww.oxforddnb.com); *Romanticism: An Oxford Guide*, ed. Nicholas Roe (Oxford: Oxford University Press, 2005); and *The Romantic Period: The Intellectual and Cultural Context of English Literature, 1789–1830*, Robin Jarvis (London: Pearson Longman, 2004). I am grateful to the Faculty of Arts and Social Sciences at Lancaster University for research leave to work on this book.

The editor and publishers wish to thank the following for permission to use copyright material:

The Bridgeman Art Library for the copy of the Laocoon on p. 175.

The British Library for the photographs of 'The Head of a Chief of New Zealand' on p. 248, and 'Art of Self Defence' on p. 205.

The trustees of the British Museum for the photographs of 'The Zenith of French Glory' on p. 34, 'Very Slippy Weather' on p. 198, 'Tales of Wonder!' on p. 226, 'Scientific Researches' on p. 278, 'Am I Not a Man and a Brother' on p. 256, 'Copenhagen House' on p. 70, 'Poor Bull & his Burden' on p. 82, 'Fashionable Mamma' on p. 100, 'Keep Within Compass' on p. 93, 'The Established Church' on p. 138, sketch of Illissus on p. 190, 'Four Specimens of the Reading Public' on p. 240, 'The Contrast' on p. 32, and 'The Age of Reason' on p. 146.

Kunsthaus Zürich for 'The Artist Moved by the Grandeur of Antique Fragments' on p. 164.

The Division of Rare and Manuscript Collections, Cornell University Library for *Essai Théoretique et Expérimental sur le Galvanisme*, WC517.A36 E7, Plate 4 on p. 282.

The Rare Books Archive, Lancaster University Library for 'Picturesque Beauty' on p. 184.

Every effort has been made to trace the copyright holders but, if any have been inadvertently overlooked, the editor and publishers will be pleased to make the necessary arrangements at the first opportunity.

Finally, I would like to acknowledge the support of Anne-Julie Crozier and of my children, Charlie and Grace.

Series Editor's preface

For at least twenty-five years, questions about the relation between literature and the historical period in which it was created have formed the central focus and methodology of critics. From the early 1980s, crucially, a range of literary scholars have sought to explore and define the parallels and differences between the representational language deployed in creative texts, and uses of similar rhetorical strategies in other contemporary cultural sources, such as journals, court documents, diaries and religious tracts. This kind of historicist reconsideration of literature has had far-reaching consequences in the academy and beyond, and the drive better to understand the dialogue established between texts and their originating period has brought new dynamism to ideas of context and contextualization.

The *Sourcebooks* series aims to provide a comprehensive and suggestive selection of original cultural sources for each of the major artistic moments from the medieval period onward. Edited by internationally renowned British and American experts in their chosen area, each volume presents within suitable subsections a panoply of materials relating to everything from historical background, to gender, philosophy, science and religion, which will be of use to both students and scholars seeking to contextualize creative work in any given period. It has been a particular ambition of the series to put back into circulation ephemeral original texts from magazines, newspapers, and even private sources, in order to offer a more representative sense of any one period's cultural debates and processes. Literature remains the primary focus of the volumes, but each contains documents relating to the broader artistic and cultural context which will be of interest and use to all those working in the humanities area.

Each volume contains an informative general Introduction giving an overview of pertinent historical and cultural movements and pressures of its time. Each document is edited to a high scholarly standard through the use of headnotes and other supportive apparatus, in order to make the document accessible for further study. This apparatus is not prescriptive in determining the relation between any one literary text and these background resources, although each volume contains instances where documents directly alluded to by major writers are specifically excerpted. Generally, however, the series seeks to further historicist study and research by making available important or intriguing materials which might act to instigate further thought and reflection, so aiding to determine a more substantial picture of any literary work's moment of coming into being.

Steven Matthews

Timeline

1768 Start of Captain James Cook's first voyage to Pacific (until 1771)

1770 Discovery of Botany Bay, Australia, by Cook;
Discovery of source of Blue Nile by James Bruce

1772 Cook's second voyage to Pacific (until 1775)

1773 Boston tea party

1774 Discovery of oxygen by Joseph Priestley;
End of perpetual copyright

1775 Start of American War of Independence;

1776 American Declaration of Independence
Start of Cook's third voyage

1779 Death of Cook

1780 Anti-Roman Catholic Gordon Riots in London

1782 Negotiations for peace in America

1783 Treaty of Paris: Britain recognizes American Independence;
William Pitt the Younger's first ministry (until 1801)

1785 Pitt's Bill for Parliamentary Reform;
Foundation of Sunday School Society

1787 Foundation of Society for Effecting the Abolition of the Slave Trade;
United States Constitution

1788 Celebrations of centenary of 'Glorious Revolution';
George III suffers first attack of mental illness;
Start of trial of Warren Hastings, former Governor-General of India

1789 In France, Louis XVI summons Third Estate, which declares itself a National Assembly;
Storming of Bastille (14 July);
'Declaration of Rights of Man in France';
Mutiny on the *Bounty*;
George Washington becomes first President of United States

1790 Louis XVI accepts new constitution;
Defeat of attempts to change Test and Corporation Acts

1791 'Church and King' riots in Birmingham, destroying Priestley's house;
Louis XVI's failed 'flight to Varennes' and forced return to Paris;
Wilberforce's Bill for Abolition of Slave Trade defeated in Parliament

1792 Foundation of London Corresponding Society;
France becomes a Republic
France defeats invading Austrian and Prussian armies at Valmy;
'September Massacres' in Paris;
Foundation of Association for the Preservation of Liberty and Property against Levellers and Republicans;
Acquittal of Warren Hastings

1793 Execution of Louis XVI (January) and Marie Antoinette (October);
War between France and England;
Start of 'Reign of Terror' in France;
Revolt of French loyalists in La Vendée

1794 Suspension of *Habeas Corpus*;
      Treason trials of Thomas Holcroft,
      John Thelwall, Horne Tooke and
      Thomas Hardy result in their
      acquittal;
      Fall of Robespierre and end of the
      'Terror' in France

1795 Mungo Park in Africa;
      Pitt's 'Two Acts' against treason-
      able practices;
      Speenhamland Act for poor relief;
      Methodism secedes from Church
      of England

1796 French Army victorious in
      northern Italy

1797 Napoleon Bonaparte defeats
      Austrians in Italy, abolishes
      Venetian Republic;
      French threaten invasion of Britain;
      British naval mutinies at Nore and
      Spithead

1798 France invades Switzerland;
      Rebellion in Ireland suppressed;
      Failed French landing in Ireland;
      Suspension of *Habeas Corpus*;
      British navy (under Nelson) defeats
      French at Battle of Nile

1799 Six Acts enforce further suppres-
      sion of radical activity;
      Introduction of income tax (until
      1815);
      Napoleon becomes first Consul

1800 France victorious in Italy;
      Food riots in England;
      Foundation of Robert Owen's New
      Lanark factory;
      Act of Union between Britain and
      Ireland

1801 William Pitt resigns over royal
      opposition to Catholic
      Emancipation;
      Addington Prime Minister (until
      1804);
      Major British naval victory at
      Copenhagen

1802 Peace of Amiens between Britain
      and France (until 1803);
      Napoleon becomes Consul for Life;
      French defeat slave rebellion led by
      Toussaint L'Ouverture on Santo
      Domingo;
      French army invades Switzerland;
      Legislation restricting children's
      working hours in cotton mills

1803 War between Britain and France
      recommences;
      Execution of Robert Emmett in
      Ireland

1804 Napoleon becomes Emperor of
      France;
      Pitt becomes Prime Minister (until
      1806);
      Renewed threat of French invasion

1805 Napoleon becomes King of Italy;
      Nelson dies during naval victory
      over French and Spanish navies at
      Battle of Trafalgar;
      Major French victories at Battles of
      Ulm and Austerlitz

1806 Death of Pitt;
      Grenville becomes Prime Minister
      in 'Ministry of all the Talents';
      Start of Napoleon's Continental
      System intended to reduce British
      trading

1807 Grenville resigns over royal
      opposition to Catholic
      Emancipation;
      Portland becomes Prime Minister;
      Abolition of slave trade;
      French invasion of Portugal signals
      start of Peninsular War

1808 French enter Spain;
      Spanish risings;
      British army arrive in Portugal;
      Convention of Cintra

1809 Failure of British expedition to
      Walcheren;
      British defeat at Corunna (death of
      Sir John Moore);
      Resignation of Portland;
      Perceval becomes Prime Minister

1810   George III suffers further mental illness

1811   Prince of Wales becomes Regent; Economic depression and industrial unrest (Luddite riots)

1812   Assassination of Prime Minister Spencer Perceval;
Lord Liverpool forms government;
Anti-Luddite legislation passed, but continued unrest;
War between Britain and United States (until 1814);
Napoleon invades Russia with huge army but is forced to retreat

1813   'Pious Clause' inserted into India Act, encouraging missionary activity;
Wellington victorious in Peninsular War;
Napoleon defeated at Battle of Leipzig;
End of East India Company's monopoly

1814   Napoleon abdicates and is exiled to Elba;
Congress of Vienna;
George Stephenson builds steam locomotive

1815   Napoleon escapes from Elba, defeated by British under Wellington and Prussians at Battle of Waterloo,
exiled to St Helena;
Restoration of Louis XVIII;
Corn Law passed

1816   Postwar economic depression and unrest;
Spa Fields Riot;
Parliament purchases Elgin Marbles for British Museum

1817   Continued disturbances
Increased support for demands for universal manhood suffrage;
Seditious Meetings Bill;
Habeas Corpus suspended (until 1818)

1818   Defeat of parliamentary motion for universal suffrage

1819   Peterloo Massacre
'Six Acts' restricting meetings and publications;
Children limited to twelve-hour working day

1820   Death of George III, accession of George IV;
Cato Street Conspiracy;
Trial of Queen Caroline

1821   Death of Napoleon;
Start of Greek War of Liberation;
Defeat of motion for parliamentary reform

1822   Suicide of Castlereagh

1824   Repeal of Combination Acts; trade unions now recognized by government

1825   First passenger railway (Stockton–Darlington)

1826   Defeat of motion for parliamentary reform

1828   Wellington becomes Prime Minister;
Test and Corporation Acts repealed, enabling Roman Catholics to take public office

1829   Catholic Emancipation

1830   Death of George IV, succeeded by William IV;
Lord Grey replaces Wellington as Prime Minister;
Whigs gain power;
Revolution in France;
Greece gains independence

1832   Reform Act

1833   Slavery abolished throughout British Empire;
Factory Act

1836   Publication of 'People's Charter' for universal suffrage

1837   Death of William IV, accession of Queen Victoria

Chronological List of Major Literary Texts

The numbers given after some of the entries in this chronology indicate those extracts in the *Sourcebook* which might be particularly helpful in contextualizing a text of the period. The first number given in the brackets denotes the Section of the *Sourcebook*, the second number given denotes the extract (so '(2.2)' indicates Section 2, Extract 2 – the passage from Adam Smith's *The Wealth of Nations*).

NB   These indications are meant to be merely suggestions: the work of contextualizing a literary text is complex, and many potential sources of influence upon any one piece of text are likely to be in play at once. For example, all the women writers (and many of the men) are likely to be responding in different ways to the materials in Section 3. Extracts in this volume not included here nonetheless provide vital background context regarding ideas and issues in the period. Likewise, texts which receive no numerical indication pointing to a specific extract often partly derive from several of the ideas contained in the various sections of this sourcebook.

1783   Hannah Cowley, *A Bold Stroke for a Husband* (drama) (8.5)

1784   Charlotte Smith, *Elegiac Sonnets* (2.4, 8.5)

1785   William Cowper, *The Task* (poetry)

1786   Robert Burns, *Poems, Chiefly in the Scottish Dialect*
Helen Maria Williams, *Poems* (8.5)

1787   Ann Yearsley, *Poems on Various Subjects* (8.5)

1788   Hannah More, *Slavery, A Poem* (8.5, 9.4, 9.5, 9.7)
Ann Yearsley, *A Poem on the Inhumanity of the Slave-Trade* (8.5, 9.4, 9.5, 9.7)
Helen Maria Williams, *A Poem on the Bill Lately Passed for Regulating the Slave Trade* (8.5, 9.4, 9.5, 9.7)
Mary Wollstonecraft, *Mary* (novel) (3.4, 8.5)

1789   William Blake, *Songs of Innocence* (poetry) (5.5)

Erasmus Darwin, *The Loves of the Plants* (poetry)

1790   William Blake, *The Marriage of Heaven and Hell* (poetry/prose) (4.4, 4.7)
Ann Radcliffe, *A Sicilian Romance* (novel) (8.4, 8.9)

1791   Elizabeth Inchbald, *A Simple Story* (novel) (8.1)
Ann Radcliffe, *The Romance of the Forest* (novel) (8.4, 8.5, 8.9)

1792   Robert Bage, *Man as He Is* (novel) (1.1, 1.2, 1.3, 1.4, 1.5, 1.6)
Anna Laetitia Barbauld, *Poems* (8.5)
Thomas Holcroft, *Anna St Ives* (novel)
Samuel Rogers, *The Pleasures of Memory* (poetry)
Charlotte Smith, *Desmond* (novel)

1793   William Blake, *Visions of the Daughters of Albion* and *America* (poetry)

Charlotte Smith, *The Old Manor House* (novel) and *The Emigrants: A Poem in Two Books* (1.1, 1.2, 1.3, 1.4, 1.5, 1.6)
Jane West, *The Advantages of Education* (novel)

1794   William Blake, *Songs of Innocence and of Experience* and *Europe* and *Book of Urizen* (poetry) (4.4, 4.7)
Erasmus Darwin, *Zoonomia* (poetry)
William Godwin, *Caleb Williams* (novel) (1.1, 1.2, 1.3, 1.4, 1.5, 1.6, 1.8, 4.2, 5.8)
Ann Radcliffe, *The Mysteries of Udolpho* (novel) (8.4, 8.5, 8.9)

1795   William Blake, *Book of Los* (poetry)
Ann Batten Cristall, *Poetical Sketches, in Irregular Verse*

1796   Robert Bage, *Hermsprong, or Man as He is Not* (novel)
Frances Burney, *Camilla* (novel)
Mary Hays, *Memoirs of Emma Courtney* (novel)
Samuel Taylor Coleridge, *Poems on Various Subjects*
Matthew Lewis, *The Monk* (novel) (8.4, 8.9)
Charlotte Smith, *Marchmont* (novel)
Robert Southey, *Joan of Arc* (poetry) (8.3, 8.6)
Mary Wollstonecraft, *Letters Written . . . in Sweden, Norway and Denmark*

1797   Ann Radcliffe, *The Italian* (novel) (8.4, 8.5, 8.9)
Robert Southey, *Poems* (8.3, 8.6)
Jane West, *A Gossip's Tale* (novel)

1798   Joanna Baillie, *Plays on the Passions* (drama)
Samuel Taylor Coleridge, *Fears in Solitude . . . France: An Ode and Frost at Midnight* (poetry) (1.10, 1.11)
Elizabeth Inchbald, *Lovers' Vows* (drama)

Matthew Lewis, *The Castle Spectre* (drama)
Mary Wollstonecraft, *Maria* (novel) (8.5, 3.4)
William Wordsworth and Samuel Taylor Coleridge, *Lyrical Ballads* (2.4, 5.1, 5.2, 5.3, 5.5, 8.6)

1799   Thomas Campbell, *The Pleasures of Hope* (poetry)
William Godwin, *St Leon* (novel)
Mary Hays, *The Victim of Prejudice* (novel)
Jane West, *A Tale of the Times* (novel)

1800   Maria Edgeworth, *Castle Rackrent* (novel) (1.9)
Mary Robinson, *Lyrical Tales* (poetry) (8.5)
Wordsworth and Coleridge, *Lyrical Ballads* (2nd edition) (see above)

1801   Maria Edgeworth, *Belinda* (novel)
Thomas More, *Poetical Works of the Late Thomas Little Esq.*
Amelia Opie, *Father and Daughter* (novel)
Robert Southey, *Thalaba the Destroyer* (poetry) (8.3, 8.6)
John Thelwall, *Poems Written Chiefly in Retirement*

1802   Samuel Taylor Coleridge, 'Dejection: An Ode'
Amelia Opie, *Poems*
Walter Scott, *Minstrelsy of the Scottish Border* (poetry) (7.1)

1803   Erasmus Darwin, *The Temple of Nature*
Jane Porter, *Thaddeus of Warsaw* (novel)

1804   William Blake, *Milton* (poetry) (4.4, 4.7)
Maria Edgeworth, *Popular Tales* (fiction)
Amelia Opie, *Adeline Mowbray* (novel)

1805   William Godwin, *Fleetwood, or the New Man of Feeling* (novel) (5.4)

Walter Scott, *The Lay of the Last Minstrel* (poetry)
Robert Southey, *Madoc* (poetry)
Ann and Jane Taylor, *Original Poetry for Infant Minds*
Mary Tighe, *Psyche; or, the Legend of Love* (poetry)
William Wordsworth, *The Prelude* (completed but unpublished until 1850) (1.1, 1.2, 1.3, 1.4, 1.5, 1.6, 1.8, 2.5, 5.1, 5.2, 5.3, 5.4, 5.5, 5.6, 5.8, 6.2, 6.4, 8.6)

1806   Charlotte Dacre, *Zofloya* (novel)
Maria Edgeworth, *Leonora* (novel)
Lady Morgan, *The Wild Irish Girl* (novel)
Amelia Opie, *Simple Tales* (fiction)
Mary Robinson, *The Poetical Works of the Late Mrs Robinson* (8.5)

1807   George Crabbe, *The Parish Register* (poetry)
Charles and Mary Lamb, *Tales from Shakespeare* (prose)
Charles Maturin, *The Fatal Revenge* (novel)
Thomas Moore, *Irish Melodies* (poetry)
Lady Morgan, *Lays of an Irish Harp; or Metrical Fragments* (poetry)
Charlotte Smith, *Beachy Head: With Other Poems* (10.2, 10.8, 10.9)
William Wordsworth, *Poems in Two Volumes*

1808   Felicia Hemans, *Poems* (8.10)
Charles Maturin, *The Wild Irish Boy* (novel)
Hannah More, *Coelebs in Search of a Wife* (novel) (3.6)
Amelia Opie, *The Warrior's Return, and Other Poems*
Walter Scott, *Marmion* (poetry)

1809   Lord Byron, *English Bards and Scotch Reviewers* (poetry)
Lady Morgan, *Woman, or Ida of Athens* (novel)

1810   George Crabbe, *The Borough* (poetry)

Anne Grant, *The Highlanders, and Other Poems*
Walter Scott, *The Lady of the Lake* (poetry)
Anna Seward, *Poetical Works* (8.5)
Robert Southey, *The Curse of Kehama* (poetry)

1811   Jane Austen, *Sense and Sensibility* (novel)
Lady Morgan, *The Missionary: An Indian Tale* (novel) (4.1, 9.1, 9.10)

1812   Anna Laetitia Barbauld, *Eighteen Hundred and Eleven, A Poem*
Lord Byron, *Childe Harold's Pilgrimage*, I and II (poetry) (8.7)
George Crabbe, *Tales in Verse* (poetry)
Maria Edgeworth, *Tales of Fashionable Life* and *The Absentee* (novel)
Felicia Hemans, *Domestic Affections and Other Poems* (8.10)
Amelia Opie, *Temper, or Domestic Scenes* (novel)

1813   Jane Austen, *Pride and Prejudice* (novel) (3.1)
Lord Byron, *The Giaour* and *The Bride of Abydos* (poetry) (8.7, 9.1)
Samuel Taylor Coleridge, *Remorse: A Tragedy in Five Acts*
Percy Shelley, *Queen Mab*

1814   Jane Austen, *Mansfield Park* (novel)
Lord Byron, *The Corsair* (poetry) (8.7)
Fanny Burney, *The Wanderer* (novel)
Leigh Hunt, *Feast of the Poets* (poetry) (8.8)
Lady Morgan, *O'Donnell: A National Tale* (novel)
Walter Scott, *Waverley* (novel)
William Wordsworth, *The Excursion* (poetry) (8.6)

1815   Thomas Love Peacock, *Headlong Hall* (novel)
William Wordsworth, *Poems* (8.6)

1816   Jane Austen, *Emma* (novel)
        Lord Byron, *Childe Harold's
        Pilgrimage* III and *The Prisoner of
        Chillon and Other Poems* (8.7)
        Samuel Taylor Coleridge,
        *Christabel; Kubla Khan: A Vision;
        The Pains of Sleep*
        Leigh Hunt, *The Story of Rimini*
        (poetry) (8.8)
        Lady Caroline Lamb, *Glenarvon*
        (novel) (8.7)
        Thomas Love Peacock, *Headlong
        Hall* (novel)
        Walter Scott, *The Antiquary* (1.10,
        1.11, 7.1) and *Old Mortality*
        (novels)
        Percy Shelley, *Alastor; or, The Spirit
        of Solitude, and Other Poems*
        William Wordsworth,
        'Thanksgiving Ode'

1817   Lord Byron, *Manfred: A Dramatic
        Poem* (6.2, 8.7)
        Samuel Taylor Coleridge,
        Biographia Literaria (prose) and
        Sibylline Leaves (poetry)
        John Keats, *Poems* (8.8)
        Thomas Moore, *Lalla Rookh*
        (poetry)
        Thomas Love Peacock, *Melincourt*
        (novel)

1818   Jane Austen, *Northanger Abbey*
        (8.4) and *Persuasion* (novels)
        Lord Byron, *Beppo* and *Childe
        Harold's Pilgrimage* IV (poetry)
        (8.7)
        Susan Ferrier, *Marriage* (novel)
        John Keats, *Endymion* (poetry)
        (8.8)
        Thomas Love Peacock, *Nightmare
        Abbey* (novel) (8.4, 8.7)
        Walter Scott, *Heart of Midlothian*
        (novel)
        Mary Shelley, *Frankenstein* (novel)
        (1.5, 1.8, 3.4, 4.2, 5.8, 6.2, 9.2, 9.3,
        10.1, 10.3, 10.4, 10.5, 10.6, 10.7)
        Percy Shelley, *The Revolt of Islam*
        (poetry)

1819   Lord Byron, *Don Juan* I and II
        (poetry)
        Felicia Hemans, *Tales, and Historic
        Scenes, in Verse* (8.10)
        John Polidori, 'The Vampyre'
        (short story)
        Walter Scott, *Ivanhoe* (novel)
        William Wordsworth, *Peter Bell*
        and *Benjamin the Waggoner*
        (poetry)

1820   William Blake, *Jerusalem* (poetry)
        John Clare, *Poems Descriptive of
        Rural Life* (poetry)
        John Keats, *Lamia, Isabella, The
        Eve of St Agnes and Other Poems*
        Charles Maturin, *Melmoth the
        Wanderer* (novel)
        Amelia Opie, *Tales of the Heart*
        (fiction)
        Percy Shelley, *The Cenci* (drama),
        Prometheus Unbound (poetic
        drama)
        William Wordsworth, *Sonnets to
        the River Duddon*

1821   Joanna Baillie, *Metrical Legends of
        Exalted Characters*
        Lord Byron, *The Prophecy of Dante,
        Sardanapalus, Don Juan* III–V, *Cain*
        (poetry and poetic dramas) (10.8)
        John Clare, *The Village Minstrel*
        (poetry)
        Thomas De Quincey, *Confessions
        of an English Opium Eater* (prose)
        Percy Shelley, *Adonais: An Elegy on
        John Keats* and *Epipsychidion*
        (poetry)
        Robert Southey, *A Vision of
        Judgement* (poetry)

1822   Lord Byron, *The Vision of
        Judgement* (poetry)
        James Hogg, *Poetical Works*
        Samuel Rogers, *Italy*
        Percy Shelley, *Hellas* (poetry)

1823   Lord Byron, *Don Juan* VI–XIV and
        The Island (poetry)
        Felicia Hemans, *The Siege of*

Map 1   Map of England, Scotland, Wales and Ireland

Introduction

In the opening canto of his comic epic *Don Juan*, Lord Byron characterizes the epoch in which he lived as 'the age of oddities let loose' (I, 128).[1] While illustrating the clear engagement between literature and the kinds of historical, religious, and scientific contexts documented in this *Sourcebook*, Byron's account captures forcefully his sense of the period's sheer excitement, as well as its paradoxes, contradictions, and newness. He declares of the era's developments:

> What opposite discoveries we have seen!
>   (Signs of true genius, and of empty pockets)
> One makes new noses, one a guillotine,
>   One breaks your bones, one sets them in their sockets;
> But vaccination certainly has been
>   A kind antithesis to Congreve's rockets,
> With which the Doctor paid off an old pox
> By borrowing a new one from an ox.
>
> Bread has been made (indifferent) from potatoes;
>   And galvanism has set some corpses grinning,
> But has not answer'd like the apparatus
>   Of the Humane Society's beginning,
> By which men are unsuffocated gratis:
>   What wondrous new machines have late been spinning!
> I said the small-pox has gone out of late,
> Perhaps it may be followed by the great. . . .
>
> This is the patent-age of new inventions
>   For killing bodies, and for saving souls,
> All propagated with the best intentions;
>   Sir Humphrey Davy's lantern, by which coals
> Are safely mined for in the mode he mentions,
>   Timbuctoo travels, voyages to the Poles,
> Are ways to benefit mankind, as true,
> Perhaps, as shooting them at Waterloo.
>
> (I. 129–32)

---

1 Lord Byron, *The Major Works*, ed. Jerome J. McGann (Oxford: Oxford University Press, 2000). *Don Juan* is referenced by canto and stanza number.

Primarily concerned with scientific and medical advances – including Benjamin Charles Perkins's 'metalic tractors' ('new noses'), Sir William Congreve's military rockets, Edward Jenner's development of vaccination, Giovanni Aldini's 'Galvanic' experiments with electricity (see extract 10.5), the technological improvements in cotton-spinning, and Humphry Davy's safety lamp – Byron locates these discoveries within a set of broader contexts whose events were similarly extraordinary. These contexts included the momentous historical upheavals of the French Revolution (alluded to in the reference to 'a guillotine'), the prolonged war with France (which culminated with the Battle of Waterloo), the significant religious developments (particularly the evangelical revival, with its emphasis on 'saving souls'), and the global explorations of the sort undertaken by James Grey Jackson to Timbuktu and Sir William Edward Parry to the North Pole. This sense of living in a time of extraordinary events is heard throughout the period. In the year often pointed to as the start of the Romantic period, 1789, Richard Price declared: 'What an eventful period is this! I am thankful that I have lived to it' (extract 1.2). In 1832, at the end of the period, J. S. Mill looked back on the era as 'an age of transition' during which individuals 'have outgrown old institutions and old doctrines, and have not yet acquired new ones' (extract 5.10). However, such claims do need to be set against other texts, such as Percy Shelley's poem 'England in 1819', which present the historical moment as stagnant, with transformation as something deeply desired but by no means certain.

The Romantic era was an exciting time for literature too. Characterized by *Blackwood's Edinburgh Magazine* in 1824 as an 'Age of Genius',[2] the period also witnessed a considerable growth in the number of publications, with improvements in literacy and changes in the book trade meaning that a much greater proportion of the population participated in writing and reading than ever before (with an increased involvement from women and the 'lower orders' being a significant feature of this expanded literary marketplace (see Section 8)). For many living in this period, literature was both shaped by, and contributed to, the political and social developments of the day. Percy Shelley commented that 'Poets, not otherwise than philosophers, painters, sculptors and musicians, are in one sense the creators, and in another the creations, of their age,' and stridently declared that 'Poets are the unacknowledged legislators of the World.'[3] In an era of political revolution and enormous social upheaval, literature was even seen by some as the primary force for the maintenance or destruction of society. T. J. Mathias argued (making the most of the typographical resources available to him) that 'LITERATURE, *well or ill conducted*, is THE GREAT ENGINE *by which*, I am fully persuaded, ALL CIVILIZED STATES *must ultimately be*

---

2 *Blackwood's Edinburgh Magazine*, 16 (1824), p. 162.
3 *Shelley's Poetry and Prose*, ed. Donald H. Reiman and Neil Fraistat (London and New York: W. W. Norton, 2002), pp. 208 and 535.

supported or overthrown.'[4] Yet if these writers located literature within a historical context, the period also witnessed several powerful attempts to redefine literature as outside or beyond history. Some writers sought to create a new and elevated role for the poet as a figure who transcended the historical, operating in a realm of the imagination far removed from the political or social conflicts of the era. Similarly, literature was sometimes defined against other forms of knowledge or disciplines, as in Wordsworth's opposition of the Poet to the Man of Science, the Chemist, the Botanist, the Mineralogist, the Mathematician, the Biographer, and the Historian in his 'Preface' to *Lyrical Ballads*.

This *Sourcebook* makes available a substantial number of extracts from the writings of the Romantic period on a wide range of subjects, enabling readers to experience at first hand the excitement of contemporary debates and providing them with the materials necessary to locate literary texts within a variety of contexts. Underpinning such a collection is the critical assumption that these contexts helped shape the literary output of the period, even when writers sought to escape, transcend, or define themselves against them. Literary texts in turn contributed to these contexts, during the period itself and in later ones (for example, Byron and Shelley became important writers for the Chartist movement while Wordsworth's poetry influenced the forms of religious belief in Victorian Britain). The extracts from the 'Revolution debate' included in Section 1 indicate how much was felt to be at stake in contemporary representations of historical events, while many of the materials in Section 8 reveal the highly politicized nature of the literary scene. I have used the Section introductions and the individual head-notes to indicate some of the ways in which this symbiotic relationship between texts and contexts might be explored, in addition to supplying biographical and historical information. Here, I want to provide a broader framework for these extracts and for the volume as a whole by considering some of the different ways in which Romanticism and the writing of the Romantic period have been thought about over the last two centuries.

Critical Versions of 'Romanticism'

Central to any discussion of Romanticism must be the terms 'Romanticism' and 'Romantic' themselves.[5] The key question here is whether they should be used to designate a coherent literary, artistic or cultural movement or whether they

---

4 T. J. Mathias, *The Pursuits of Literature: A Satirical Poem in Dialogue. Part the Fourth*, 2nd edition (London, 1797), p. i.

5 Valuable discussions of these terms, and of the critical history of 'Romanticism', are provided by Nicholas Roe in *Romanticism: An Oxford Guide* (Oxford: Oxford University Press, 2005), pp. 1–12, and Peter J. Kitson, *Coleridge, Keats and Shelley: New Casebooks* (Basingstoke: Macmillan, 1996), pp. 1–24.

should be used to refer to a period of time during which a diverse number of writers, artists and musicians practised. Certainly none of the British writers of what is termed 'the Romantic period' would have considered themselves part of a coherent movement, much less of a Romantic one. For them the word 'Romantic' was derived from the genre of romance and associated with ideas of chivalry, adventure, idealized love, and the supernatural. In Britain it was only in the 1880s that the term began to gain real currency as a way of describing a particular kind of writer – a Romantic poet – or a particular kind of writing – Romantic literature.

The most famous definition of 'Romanticism' as a coherent movement was given in the late 1940s by René Wellek, who argued that across Europe 'romantic' literature was characterized by 'imagination for the view of poetry, nature for the view of the world, and symbol and myth for poetic style'.[6] While these are certainly major features in much of the writing of the period (as is evident from a number of the extracts in this book), Wellek based his characterization of British Romanticism on the work of only a few exceptional writers working in a single genre, what he elsewhere termed 'the great poets of the English Romantic movement' (p. 178). (At the time Wellek was writing, critics such as Northrop Frye and David Erdman were in the process of recovering the work of William Blake and adding him to the canon of other poets – Wordsworth, Coleridge, Byron, Shelley and Keats – to make up the so-called 'Big Six' male poets of the day.) Indeed, rather than characterizing the majority of the writing of the period, for Wellek the 'English romantic movement' was not only a break from the literature of the past but out of keeping with the literary tastes and standards of its own age:

> The great poets of the English romantic movement constitute a fairly coherent group, with the same view of poetry and the same conception of imagination, the same view of nature and mind. They share also a poetic style, a use of imagery, symbolism, and myth, which is quite distinct from anything that had been practised by the eighteenth century, and which was felt by their contemporaries to be obscure and almost unintelligible.　(p. 178)

Wellek's model of 'Romanticism' as a coherent movement created by 'great poets' provided the major focus for literary study of the period, in the three decades after the end of the Second World War in 1945. During this time it was refined and developed in various ways but with an underlying assumption about the key themes of the writing, which included: the creative powers of the artist and poet; the role of the imagination; the idea of genius; the elevated role of the poet as prophet; the development of the self; the beneficent and shaping role of

---

6 René Wellek, 'The Concept of Romanticism in Literary History', reprinted in *Concepts of Criticism* (New Haven, CT: Yale University Press, 1963), p. 161. Further references are cited within the text.

the natural world; the possibilities of transcendence; an organic understanding of human psychology and the creative process, in opposition to a mechanical one; and limitless aspiration.

In the late 1970s and 1980s, this model of 'Romanticism' came under increasing pressure on a number of counts, including its ideas about language, its focus on a very limited number of writers (all of whom were men), and its critical replication of 'Romantic' assumptions that privileged the poet and his imaginative power at the expense of historical or political issues. Linked to these critiques of the dominant critical model of 'Romanticism', the 1980s witnessed the beginning of a recovery of a remarkable number of writers who, it appeared, had been almost entirely forgotten, many of whom were women, together with an increased focus on a range of forms beyond poetry, including the novel, non-fictional prose, and more recently, drama. In the context of these developments, a number of critics have argued that it is pointless to use the word 'Romanticism' to designate what was always a shifting and contested construct, preferring to use the word 'Romantic' to indicate a particular period. A significant illustration of this usage was the title of Jerome J. McGann's anthology *The New Oxford Book of Romantic Period Verse* of 1993, which also indicates how the critical focus on the period has expanded. McGann includes work by 80 poets in addition to several anonymous poems, whereas in their *Romantic Poetry and Prose* of 1973, Harold Bloom and Lionel Trilling presented work by the six poets Blake, Wordsworth, Coleridge, Byron, Shelley and Keats (accounting for 550 of their 590 pages on poetry), followed by brief selections from 11 other (male) poets. McGann's anthology also reshaped conceptions of the period in a number of ways, ordering its selections on a year-by-year basis (thus playing down the importance of the canonical writers) and including only material published at the time (and so excluding what had been the key text in studies of 'Romanticism', Wordsworth's *The Prelude*, which wasn't published until after the poet's death in 1850).

The general shift in the critical usage of the word 'Romanticism' away from meaning a coherent movement and towards a more inclusive sense of the writing of a particular period is also seen in the titles of books such as Nicholas Roe's *Romanticism: An Oxford Guide* of 2005, which includes essays on 'The novel', 'Gothic', and 'Letters, journals, and diaries', and Duncan Wu's third edition of his anthology *Romanticism* (2006), the opening pages of which include pieces of political prose by Richard Price, Edmund Burke, Thomas Paine and William Godwin, alongside poetry by Thomas Warton, William Cowper, Anna Seward, Anna Laetitia Barbauld, Hannah More, Charlotte Smith, George Crabbe and Ann Yearsley, before the first canonical writer, William Blake, is reached on page 169. In using the word 'Romanticism' in this way, these editors are following the argument made as early as 1924 by Arthur Lovejoy that 'the word "romantic" has come to mean so many things that, by itself, it means nothing. It has ceased to perform the functions of a verbal sign.' Lovejoy contended that instead 'we should learn to use the word "Romanticism" in the plural. . . . What is needed is that any study of the subject should begin with a recognition of a *prima-facie* plurality of Romanticisms, of possibly quite distinct thought-complexes, a number of which may appear in one country.'[7]

This general (though not universal) shift to an inclusive model of 'Romanticism' to signify the wide-ranging and frequently diverse writing of a particular age is not without its own problems, not least the question of when that period was. The temporal span of the 'Romantic period' is obviously not as clear-cut as that of 'eighteenth-century literature' or the 'nineteenth-century novel', or even of terms such as 'Victorian literature' or 'Jacobean tragedy' which imply the reign of a particular monarch. To define the Romantic period, many critics turn to historical events, often choosing 1789 – the year of the French Revolution – for its commencement and 1832 – the year of the great Reform Act – for its conclusion. Others opt for literary landmarks, with the publication of Blake's *Songs of Innocence* in 1789 and the death of Coleridge in 1834 often cited as key dates. It should be noted, however, that these choices can influence a sense of the period itself. For example, the choices of 1789 and 1832 lend considerable weight to characterizations of the period and its literature as revolutionary, though much recent work has argued that it was an age of counter-revolution as Britain reacted to the threats of revolution, war, and domestic unrest, and that the literature previously thought of as revolutionary was a conservative culmination of Enlightenment trends. Similarly, the death of Byron in 1824 (following those of Keats in 1821 and Shelley in 1822) used to be frequently pointed to as the moment when the fire of Romanticism was extinguished, though it is now generally recognized that such a construction of the period excludes much important work of late-Romantic writers, not least that of two of the most important women poets of the period, Felicia Hemans and Letitia Elizabeth Landon.

As the materials in Section 8 on 'Literary Production and Reception' show, during the Romantic period itself writers were frequently grouped together in a number of separate 'Schools' (a practice and term drawn from art history) rather than being seen as part of a unified movement. The main groupings were: the 'Lake School' of William Wordsworth, Robert Southey and Samuel Taylor Coleridge, so called because they were associated with the Lake District in the North-West of England (see extract 8.6); the 'Cockney School', the London-based circle that gathered around Leigh Hunt, the poet and editor of the *Examiner* newspaper, which included John Keats, William Hazlitt and the painter Benjamin Robert Haydon (and sometimes Mary and Percy Shelley and Lord Byron); and the 'Satanic School' of Lord Byron and Percy Shelley, named by Robert Southey in response to what he saw as the immorality of the writers' lives and works. Novelists too were grouped into 'Schools', such as the 'Radcliffe

---

7 A. O. Lovejoy, 'On the Discrimination of Romanticisms', reprinted in *English Romantic Poets: Modern Essays in Criticism*, 2nd edition, ed. M. H. Abrams (Oxford: Oxford University Press, 1975), pp. 6 and 8.

School' of those whose writing we now think of as Gothic novels (see extract 8.4). The labels 'Lake School' and 'Cockney School' were propagated by the critics Francis Jeffrey and John Gibson Lockhart in the increasingly influential literary periodicals and were pejorative: 'Lake School' suggesting provinciality and geographical remoteness from the centres of literary power and 'Cockney School' implying its members were of low origin and lacked the classical education and gentlemanly credentials necessary to be a true poet. There was a sense of rivalry between these schools too, exacerbated by a mutual antagonism that was frequently politicized, with both the 'Cockney' and 'Satanic' Schools hostile towards what they perceived as betrayal of the liberal cause by the 'Lakers' and their increasing conservatism, exemplified by Southey becoming Poet Laureate in 1813 and Wordsworth accepting the position of Distributor of Stamps for Westmorland in the same year. The critical tendency to assign writers to rival groupings also applies to the female writers of the period, as illustrated by Richard Polwhele's notorious satirical poem *The Unsex'd Females* of 1798 (extract 8.5), in which he sets a 'female band despising Nature's law' (Mary Wollstonecraft, Anna Laetitia Barbauld, Mary Robinson, Charlotte Smith, Helen Maria Williams, Ann Yearsley, Mary Hays, Angelica Kauffman and Emma Crewe) against a number of writers who embodied for him a more acceptable model of female authorship (Elizabeth Montague, Elizabeth Carter, Hester Chapone, Anna Seward, Hester Thrale Piozzi, Frances Burney, Ann Radcliffe, Diana Beauclerk, Princess Elizabeth and Hannah More). Perhaps rather ironically, Polwhele's poem indicates not only how many women were publishing poetry in the period but also their increasingly important role in the literary marketplace.

While a map of the writing of the Romantic period in terms of the 'Lake', 'Cockney' and 'Satanic' Schools bears some correspondence to accounts of Romanticism which present the 'Big Six' as two generations flourishing at different historical moments (the first of Blake, Shelley and Wordsworth producing their best work in the 1790s and early 1800s, the second of Byron, Shelley and Keats writing in the years after the Battle of Waterloo), it too can misrepresent the ways in which contemporaries saw the literary scene at any particular time. A good example of how unfamiliar such a contemporary view may appear to us now is given by Lord Byron in a journal entry of 1813, in which he describes Walter Scott as the 'Monarch of Parnassus' and continues 'I should place Rogers next in the living list – (I value him more as the last of the *best* school) – Moore and Campbell both *third* – [then] Southey and Wordsworth and Coleridge.'[8] Byron was writing prior to the emergence of Percy Shelley and John Keats (both of whom Leigh Hunt would fanfare in December 1816 as part of 'a new school of poetry rising of late' in his essay 'Young Poets' for the *Examiner*), but what might surprise us in 1813 is his relegation of the Lakers to a fourth division of

8 *Lord Byron's Letters and Journals*, 12 vols, ed. Leslie Marchand (London: John Murray, 1973–82), III, 219–20.

poetry below Walter Scott, Samuel Rogers, Thomas Moore and Thomas Campbell (whose major publications are listed in the 'Chronological List of the Major Literary Works of the Romantic Period'). But Byron was not alone in seeing Walter Scott as 'the Monarch of Parnassus'. Prior to Byron's own sensational success in 1812 with *Childe Harold's Pilgrimage*, Scott had been by far the most popular poet of the day, selling phenomenal numbers of his metrical romances *The Lay of the Last Minstrel*, *Marmion*, and *The Lady of the Lake*. Though Byron would become the best-selling poet of the Romantic period (prompting Scott to change genres and gain further success as the key figure in the development of the Historical Novel), the poet who achieved the greatest sales in the nineteenth century was Felicia Hemans (extract 8.10), a figure in whom there has been a significant renewal of critical interest since the 1990s.

It was during the nineteenth century that Wordsworth moved from Byron's fourth division to become regarded as the figure who exemplified Romanticism and even a Romantic revolution in literature. There were a number of elements in this transformation, including: the championing of his poetry by influential figures, including Coleridge (in *Biographia Literaria*), William Hazlitt (in essays such as 'My First Acquaintance with Poets' and 'Mr Wordsworth'), John Wilson, John Keble, John Stuart Mill, Matthew Arnold, Stopford Brooke, and Edmund Gosse; the changing selections of poems in anthologies such as Palgrave's *Golden Treasury* and editions such as the influential one published by Matthew Arnold in 1879; and the rise of English Literature as a university discipline. As Nicholas Roe has commented, quoting C. H. Herford's *Age of Wordsworth* of 1897, 'by the start of the twentieth century . . . Wordsworth stood as the "most original and commanding figure" of the new, Romantic canon'.[9]

Central to Wordsworth's growing critical stature had been the publication in 1850 of the epic autobiographical poem he had begun in 1798, which became crucial for most twentieth-century accounts of the poet. In 1926, Helen Darbishire gave a lucid illustration of what critics found important in *The Prelude*:

> The inspiration of Wordsworth's poetry had its vitalizing source in the power with which he realized a particular experience. . . . The core of the experience was an intense consciousness of Nature passing through his sense to his mind; and the growth of that consciousness, its action and reaction upon his inner life, is the central theme of *The Prelude*. The experience was peculiar simply in its intensity. So pure and strong was the life his senses led that it passed, on a tide of feeling, into the life of his spirit. . . .
>
> Wordsworth's creed may be said in three words: God, Man, Nature. . . . When he confessed his faith in *The Prelude* he had only to use these words,

---

9 Roe, *Romanticism: An Oxford Guide*, p. 7. On 'the establishment of Wordsworth as the most significant and representative voice of Romanticism', see also Kitson, *Coleridge, Keats and Shelley*, pp. 2–3.

simply and passionately, and all his meaning was conveyed. He had only to speak . . . of the soul that 'passing through all Nature rests with God', and he had uttered the first article of his creed. The words were charged with power. What greater things can be said than God, Man, Nature?[10]

Building on nineteenth-century readings of Wordsworth as a religious poet, or at least of what Stephen Gill has termed 'Spiritual Power',[11] Darbishire's account includes a number of elements that would become central to constructions of 'Romanticism', including the interaction with the natural world, the importance of the poet's 'inner life', and the narrative of the 'growth of [the poet's] consciouness'. It was these elements that would increasingly provide the focus for the study of the other poets in the emerging canon of Romanticism: Coleridge, Byron, Keats and Shelley.

With the rediscovery and incorporation into this canon of the 'visionary' William Blake in the late 1940s and early 1950s, the critical focus on the poet's inner life was further developed through an emphasis on his creative powers and particularly on the 'imagination'. Maurice Bowra makes this case boldly in the opening sentence of his study written in 1950, *The Romantic Imagination*: 'If we wish to distinguish a single characteristic which differentiates the English Romantics from the poets of the eighteenth century, it is to be found in the importance which they attached to the imagination and in the special view which they held of it.'[12] Bowra expands on this statement, providing a useful definition of the 'Romantic imagination' itself:

This belief in the imagination was part of the contemporary belief in the individual self. The poets were conscious of a wonderful capacity to create imaginary worlds, and they could not believe that this was false or idle. On the contrary, they thought that to curb it was to deny something vitally necessary to their whole being. They thought that it was just this which made them poets. . . . They saw that the power of poetry is strongest when the creative imagination works untrammelled, and they knew that in their own case this happened when they shaped fleeting visions into concrete forms and pursued wild thoughts until they captured and mastered them . . . the Romantics, brought to a fuller consciousness of their own powers, felt a . . . need to exert these powers in fashioning new worlds of the mind.[13]

Bowra's model of Romanticism was given considerable support three years later by the publication of M. H. Abrams's monumental study *The Mirror and the*

---

10 Helen Darbishire, 'Wordsworth's *Prelude*', in *Wordsworth: The Prelude*, ed. W. J. Harvey and Richard Gravil (London: Macmillan, 1972), pp. 83–91.

11 Stephen Gill, *Wordsworth and the Victorians* (Oxford: Clarendon Press, 1998, pp. 40–80.

12 Maurice Bowra, *The Romantic Imagination* (Oxford: Oxford University Press, 1950), p. 1.

13 Ibid., pp. 1–2.

Lamp: Romantic Theory and the Critical Tradition, in which he traced a shift in aesthetics from the mimetic (art as a 'mirror' which reflects the world) to the expressive (art as the projection of the artist, the shining light of the lamp, which contributes to the objects it perceives). As Abrams shows, many of the key definitions of the period emphasized the idea of the expression of the poet's own feelings; Wordsworth defined poetry as 'the spontaneous overflow of powerful feelings' while Byron described it as 'the lava of the imagination whose eruption prevents an earthquake'.[14] Similarly, Abrams drew attention to the characteristic imagery of overflow in Romantic poetry, seen in the fountain of Coleridge's 'Kubla Khan' and the volcanoes and skylarks of Shelley's poetry. He also emphasized the development of an 'organic' model of artistic creativity and psychological development, particularly in the writing of Coleridge, opposed to the empirical or mechanistic models dominant in much of the philosophical writing in the early eighteenth century (see extract 5.9). As this would suggest, *The Mirror and the Lamp* is part of a tradition of scholarship that seeks to locate the poetry of the Romantic period within broader philosophical contexts (see Section 5: Philosophy).

While M. H. Abrams and others were reading Romantic literature in relation to philosophy, other critics were beginning to locate it within the historical contexts of its time. A major pioneering work here was David Erdman's *Blake: Prophet Against Empire* of 1954, in the introduction to which Erdman gives a valuable description of the methodology of the critical approach now known as 'Old Historicism' (to differentiate it from 'New Historicism', which will be described below):

> In order to get close to the eye-level at which Blake witnessed the drama of his own times – the level at which history is 'nothing else but improbabilities and impossibilities, what we should say was impossible if we did not see it always before our eyes' – I have read the newspapers and looked at the prints and paintings and sampled the debates and pamphlets of Blake's time. As Blake would say, I have 'walked up & down' in the history of that time.[15]

Like Bowra and Abrams, Erdman elevated the Romantic poet who becomes a 'Prophet', but unlike them his Blake is fully engaged in 'the drama of his own times' rather than creating 'new worlds of the mind' through his imagination.

It was M. H. Abrams who brought together these seemingly opposed ways of reading Romanticism in relation to history and the imagination, though his highly influential account ultimately reasserted imagination as its crucial and defining concept. In his essay of 1963 entitled 'English Romanticism: the Spirit of the Age', Abrams argued that the crucial occurrence of the period had been the French Revolution but that no significant link had been made between this

---

14 M. H. Abrams, *The Mirror and the Lamp: Romantic Theory and the Critical Tradition* (Oxford: Oxford University Press, 1953), pp. 47, 49.

15 David Erdman, *Blake: Prophet Against Empire* (Princeton, NJ: Princeton University Press, 1954), p. viii.

key historical event and the literature of the period: 'when critics and historians turn to the general task of defining the critical qualities of "Romanticism," or of the English Romantic movement, they usually ignore its relationship to the revolutionary climate of the time'.[16] Abrams begins, then, by asserting the importance of history for Romanticism: 'the Romantic period was eminently an age obsessed with the fact of violent and inclusive change, and Romantic poetry cannot be understood, historically, without awareness of the degree to which this preoccupation affected its substance and form' (ibid.). However, Abrams argues that the increasingly violent course of events during the 1790s (outlined in the 'Introduction' to 'Section 1') caused the poets he examines to turn away from history and towards the imagination. While the early stages of the Revolution had led many to hope that it would bring about a secular version of the apocalypse (see extracts 1.2 and 4.3), Abrams contends that the disappointments of the 1790s caused the Romantic poets to recognize that their millennial hopes could only be realized through what he terms 'the apocalypse of the imagination' (p. 62). For example, Abrams identifies a secularized Judeo-Christian narrative of fall and redemption in Wordsworth's poetry, and writes of his 'Prospectus' to *The Recluse* that 'the restoration of paradise, as in the Book of Revelation, is still symbolized by a sacred marriage. But the hope has been shifted from the history of mankind to the mind of the single individual, from militant external action to an imaginative act' (p. 66). Abrams extends this argument to his other chosen writers of the period:

> In the other Romantic visionaries, as in Wordsworth, naive millennialism produced mainly declamation, but the shattered trust in premature political revolution and the need to reconstitute the grounds of hope lay behind the major achievements. And something close to Wordsworth's evolution – the shift to a spiritual and moral revolution which will transform our experience of the old world – is also the argument of a number of the later writings of Blake, Coleridge [and] Shelley.   (pp. 66–7)

Abrams developed this argument in his second monumental and highly influential book on the literature of the period, *Natural Supernaturalism* of 1971, which represents the central statement of what for many years was a dominant model of Romanticism (and one that still persists), that it was structured by a turn away from history, as writers sought to realize their internalized political hopes in the realm of the imagination.

Abrams's model of Romanticism as a turn away from history has been contested in a number of ways, not least by work which has continued the 'Old Historicist' tradition of critics such as David Erdman and which operates

---

16 M. H. Abrams, 'English Romanticism: the Spirit of the Age', in *The Correspondent Breeze: Essays on English Romanticism* (New York and London: W. W. Norton, 1984), p. 46. Further references are cited within the text.

through the location of texts within contexts. Such a contextualizing approach, in which the critic seeks to elucidate the historical references of a text and locate it within the various contemporary debates in which it is seen to partake, has become a major strand in studies of Romantic writing, the most influential example being Marilyn Butler's *Romantics, Rebels and Reactionaries: English Literature and its Background, 1760–1830* of 1981. The issues relating to the canon of writers and texts discussed above are often central to these projects; for example, by focusing on Wordsworth's political sonnets, his tract on the Convention of Cintra, and his Waterloo poetry, it becomes possible to reconstruct him as a writer who remained closely engaged with European political events and as one who saw himself playing a continuing role in them. Similarly, Marilyn Butler argued in the 1980s that Wordsworth's centrality to the canon was a reflection of an American critical tradition that privileged the private and intellectual over the public and politically engaged. She called for an expansion of the canon, and specifically for a greater acknowledgement of the important role of Robert Southey, her model of the public, politically-committed poet.[17] In the years since Butler made this appeal, not only Southey but a large number of other writers have become the focus of critical study, revealing the complexity and diversity of the relationship between the literature and the history of the period and calling into question any overarching narrative of 'Romanticism'.

Another challenge to Abrams's account of the relationship between Romanticism and history was offered in 1983 by Jerome McGann in his book *The Romantic Ideology*, the first and still a central text of what has become known as 'New Historicism'. In this polemical work, McGann argued that critics of Romanticism were themselves too Romantic, reproducing uncritically the values and beliefs of the texts they studied. McGann outlines his preferred methodology as follows:

> the past and its works should be studied by a critical mind in the full range of their pastness – in their differences and their alienations (both contemporary and historical). To foster such a view of past works of art can only serve to increase our admiration for their special achievements and our sympathy for what they have created within the limits which constrained them – as it were, for their grace under pressure. . . . I have tried . . . on the one hand, to situate Romanticism and its works in the past in order to make them present resources by virtue of their differential; and, on the other, to free present criticism from the crippling illusion that such a past establishes the limits, conceptual and practical, of our present and our future.[18]

---

17 Marilyn Butler, 'Repossessing the Past: the Case for an Open Literary History', in Marjorie Levinson et al., *Rethinking Historicism: Critical Readings in English Romanticism* (Oxford: Basil Blackwell, 1989), pp. 64–84.

18 Jerome J. McGann, *The Romantic Ideology: A Critical Investigation* (Chicago: University of Chicago Press, 1985), pp. 2–3. Further references are contained within the text.

McGann argues that this position of historical distance from the text enables the critic to identify its 'ideology' or 'false consciousness' (p. 90). The Romantic celebration of the poet, the imagination, and the natural world was achieved at the cost of the writers' failure to engage with the historical, political, or social problems of the age. He explains:

> In moments of crisis the Romantic will turn to Nature or the creative Imagination as his places of last resort. Amidst the tottering structures of early-nineteenth century Europe, poetry asserted the integrity of the biosphere and the inner, spiritual self, both of which were believed to transcend the age's troubling doctrinal conflicts and ideological shifts. (pp. 67–8)

Drawing on a combination of Marxist and psychoanalytic theory, McGann and other 'new historicist' critics like Marjorie Levinson and Alan Liu argue that history is 'displaced', 'annihilated', 'erased' and 'elided' by the Romantic text. Abrams and McGann both see Romanticism as transcending history through the imagination, then, but they assess this process very differently. While for Abrams the realization of the powers of the imagination is the culmination of a heroic quest, McGann argues that 'Wordsworth lost the world merely to gain his own immortal soul' (p. 82).

Whether seeking to use historical materials to contextualize a literary work or to reveal its ideological function, much historical criticism has focused on the areas covered in Sections 1 and 2 of this *Sourcebook*: the French Revolution, the war with France, and British economic and social conditions. Partly inspired by the publication of Edward Said's *Orientalism* in 1985, there has also been an important focus on the relationship between literature and Britain's colonial and imperial identity, examining areas such as the representation of the 'East' in the very popular poetry of the period (such as that by Byron and Moore), the role of literature in the campaign for the abolition of the slave trade, the figure of the explorer, and the genre of travel writing (see Section 9). The current sense of ecological crisis has also prompted a major reinvestigation of the relationship between the writers of the period and the natural world (a long-standing theme in the study of Romanticism, as we have seen). Works such as Jonathan Bate's *Romantic Ecology: Wordsworth and the Environmental Tradition* (1991), Karl Kroeber's *Ecological Literary Criticism: Romantic Imagining and the Biology of Mind* (1994) and James McKusick's *Green Writing: Romanticism and Ecology* (2000) have shown that the interest in what McGann described as 'the integrity of the biosphere' is no longer seen as an escape from the political but is an important anticipation of present-day concerns. (Extracts relating to the understanding of the natural world can be found in a number of sections of this book; see especially Section 2 for materials on the rural and the urban; Section 6 for ideas about landscape; Section 9 for the relationship with the nation; and Section 10 for the interaction of science and nature.)

A significant element in the shift from the examination of 'Romanticism' to the consideration of the writing of the Romantic period has been the increased focus on women's writing and on related issues, including: the position of women in the literary marketplace and the ideological and economic pressures on them; the changes in the distribution and circulation of books, which made more texts available to women readers; the representation of women in literary texts; the relationship of women's writing to that by men; and the re-evaluation of previously little studied forms and genres in the production of which, women played a major role, such as the novel and drama. An important early publication in this area was the collection of essays edited by Anne K. Mellor in 1988, *Romanticism and Feminism*, which indicated a number of the directions that would be taken by work in this field, offering a reassessment of the gender politics of canonical Romanticism while also recovering the work of several women writers. A key essay in this volume was Stuart Curran's 'The I Altered', which drew attention to the centrality of women writers in the period, powerfully illustrated by Mary Robinson's description in 1799, which is well worth repeating here:

> The best novels that have been written, since those of Smollett, Richardson, and Fielding, have been produced by women: and their pages have not only been embellished with the interesting events of domestic life, portrayed with all the refinement of sentiment, but with forcible and eloquent, political, theological, and philosophical reasoning. To the genius and labours of some enlightened British women posterity will also be indebted for the purest and best translations from the French and German languages. I need not mention Mrs. Dobson, Mrs. Inchbald, Miss Plumtree, &c. &c. Of the more profound researches in the dead languages, we have many female classicks of the first celebrity: Mrs. Carter, Mrs. Thomas, (late Miss Pankhurst;), Mrs. Francis, the Hon. Mrs. Damer, &c. &c.
>
> Of the Drama, the wreath of fame has crowned the brows of Mrs. Cowley, Mrs. Inchbald, Miss Lee, Miss Hannah More, and others of less celebrity. Of Biography, Mrs. Dobson, Mrs. Thickness, Mrs. Piozzi, Mrs. Montagu, Miss Helen Williams, have given specimens highly honourable to their talents. Poetry has unquestionably risen high in British literature from the productions of female pens; for many English women have produced such original and beautiful compositions, that the first critics and scholars of the age have wondered, while they applauded.[19]

As Robinson suggests, women were active as writers in a number of genres, including the novel, translation, the classics, drama, and poetry, to which we

---

19 Quoted in Stuart Curran, 'The I Altered', *Romanticism and Feminism*, ed. Anne K. Mellor (Bloomington and Indianapolis: Indiana University Press, 1988), p. 186. Further references are cited within the text.

could add political and historical essays, religious tracts, theories of education, travel writing, literary criticism, as well as journals and letters. In his essay, Curran is particularly concerned with poetry, which he sees as characterized by an interest in the quotidian or everyday and by the expression of 'sensibility', the latter constituting 'an independent and shared woman's poetic' and providing 'a locus for an encoded treatment of the female condition' (p. 197). The process of the recovery of women poets has led to an ongoing reassessment of what characterizes their verse (and, as with 'Romanticism', an increasing acknowledgement of its diversity and of the dangers inherent in grouping it under one heading). For example, in her pioneering anthology of 1992, *Woman Romantic Poets*, Jennifer Breen highlighted domesticity as a key subject, but this strand of verse is almost entirely absent from Andrew Ashfield's *Romantic Women Poets, 1770–1838: An Anthology* of 1995. Ashfield emphasizes instead the poetry of the sublime and of sensibility while also including a significant amount of political verse (in his second volume, Ashfield would extend his selection of women's political poetry, opening it with 30 pages of verse on the slave trade).[20]

The recovery and analysis of women's writing in the period has also produced a re-evaluation of men's writing. One element of this has been the analysis of the gender politics of canonical Romanticism, which a number of critics have seen as inherently masculine with its emphasis on the creative powers of the self, often troped as the conquest of feminine nature (see, for example, Marlon Ross's *The Contours of Masculine Desire*, 1989). Reading works by men and women alongside each other, Anne Mellor has argued that it is possible to distinguish between 'masculine' and 'feminine' Romanticism, at least as a way of beginning to explore these issues. In Mellor's account, 'masculine Romanticism' is defined in terms of the 'egotistical sublime' (Keats's term for Wordsworth) and the conquest of nature, and 'feminine Romanticism' in terms of a 'relational self' and an 'ethic of care'.[21] Some works by women writers can certainly be read as critiques of their male counterparts. A good example of the feminist critique of 'masculine Romanticism' is Mary Shelley's novel *Frankenstein* (1818), which has been analysed as an attack on the masculine figure of the scientist, an egotist who takes no responsibility for what he has created, and as an exposure of the human cost of the creative project undertaken by the two poets who were part of Mary's circle, Percy Shelley and Lord Byron. This interest in gender has also shown how many of the central aesthetic concepts of the period are defined in masculine and feminine terms, as is the case with the key categories of the sublime (equated with power and grandeur) and the beautiful (linked to smallness and smoothness).

---

20 Jennifer Breen (ed.), *Women Romantic Poets, 1785–1832, An Anthology* (London: Everyman, 1992); Andrew Ashfield, *Romantic Women Poets, 1770–1838: An Anthology* (Manchester: Manchester University Press, 1995) and *Romantic Women Poets, 1788–1848*, Volume II (Manchester: Manchester University Press, 1998).
21 See Anne K. Mellor, *Romanticism and Gender* (London and New York: Routledge, 1993).

Much of the historical and feminist criticism of Romantic period literature described above shares a commitment to the location of texts within broader contexts. This practice has been continued in a number of recent developments in the field, which have illustrated the importance of areas such as science and religion to the era's writing. In the case of the latter, for example, there is a long tradition of reading Romantic poetry for its religious and spiritual power, but recent work has sought to study the literature within a much more carefully delineated picture of the historical forms and practices of religion and belief (and, of course, disbelief). The central methodological question for all such historicizing projects remains a version of that which differentiated 'Old' from 'New Historicism'. Should critics aim to locate themselves at the 'eye-level at which [a writer] witnessed the drama of his [or her] own times', as David Erdman argued, believing that by doing so they will enhance the understanding of a text's meaning? If we do not engage with these contexts, we risk falling into what recent critics have called a 'presentist' bias: we judge the past by our own standards, and praise writers for anticipating our own values or castigate them for not being enough like us. A contextualizing approach seeks to make available to readers a body of knowledge with which they are unlikely to be familiar, even though it was widely available during the period itself. In this way, for example, important recent work in the field of Romanticism and science has shown how engaged writers were with the 'vitality debate', how they participated in it, and how the debate linked to political and theological controversies (see Section 10). Or should critics aim to use their historical distance from a text to identify its 'ideology', its historical 'blindnesses' or 'oversights', to use key 'new historical' terms? This approach involves reinserting into the text the information or contexts that have been erased by psychological or historical processes. The most famous such 'new historical' readings of a literary text are those by McGann and Levinson of Wordsworth's 'Tintern Abbey', arguing that 'the French Revolution . . . and the impoverished and dislocated country poor' are 'displaced out of the narrative'. [22]

A Romantic Text in Context: Wordsworth's *The Prelude*

It might be helpful at this stage to clarify these different methodologies by considering them in relation to a specific text, Wordsworth's *The Prelude*. In the first completed version of this poem, the '1799 Prelude', the poet gives an account of his early life growing up in the Lake District. Reading the poem alongside a number of the extracts in this *Sourcebook* would certainly enhance an understanding and appreciation of it. For example, Wordsworth engages with the philosophical ideas of John Locke and David Hartley (extracts 5.1 and 5.2)

---

22 McGann, *The Romantic Ideology*, p. 85.

in his analysis of the growth of his own mind and his relationship with the external world, while his description of his 'natural' childhood and his decision to write autobiographically can be compared with the work of Jean-Jacques Rousseau (5.3, 5.5 and 5.6). In terms of these ideas, Wordsworth's description of himself as a 'naked savage' (I. 25)[23] in the poem's opening passage opens up a global dimension to the poem that could be explored by examining contemporary accounts of 'savages', such as the inhabitants of Tahiti described by John Hawkesworth (extract 9.2). Similarly, it is difficult fully to understand the poet's account of the role of the natural world in his education without knowledge of the theory of the sublime, as outlined by Edmund Burke (extract 6.2). Thomas West's *A Guide to the Lakes* (extract 6.4) also provides valuable material on the development of ideas of the natural environment in relation to the specific place of the Lake District, the setting for Wordsworth's poem. In all these cases, a reading of these contextual materials will illumine particular references and help establish the broader overall frameworks of philosophical and aesthetic ideas within which the poem is operating. It will show the extent to which the poem draws on, and develops, the ideas of its time.

But in the poem's closing section, Wordsworth makes a sudden reference to the historical moment in which he is writing:

> . . . . if in these times of fear,
> This melancholy waste of hopes o'erthrown,
> If, 'mid indifference and apathy
> And wicked exultation, when good men
> On every side fall off we know not how
> To selfishness, disguised in gentle names
> Of peace and quiet and domestic love –
> Yet mingled, not unwillingly, with sneers
> On visionary minds – if, in this time
> Of dereliction and dismay, I yet
> Despair not of our nature, but retain
> A more than Roman confidence, a faith
> That fails not, in all sorrow my support,
> The blessing of my life, the gift is yours
> Ye mountains, thine O Nature.
>
> (II. 478–92)

Suddenly, a poem celebrating the relationship between the individual and the natural world is interrupted by a sense of historical crisis. How should we read such a passage in relation to history, or the historical materials included in

---

23 The '1799 Prelude' is quoted from William Wordsworth, *The Prelude, 1799, 1805, 1850*, ed. Jonathan Wordsworth, M. H. Abrams and Stephen Gill (New York and London: W. W. Norton, 1979).

Section 1 of this *Sourcebook*? I think the passage can be read in either of the ways I have outlined in the previous section. On the one hand, the lines can be contextualized by reference to the French Revolution and the British reaction. For example, the editors of the Norton edition point to the figure of Sir James Mackintosh as the most notorious of the 'good men' who have renounced their support of the French Revolution. On the other hand, the lines could be taken to exemplify McGann's argument in *The Romantic Ideology* that in 'moments of crisis the Romantic will turn to Nature or the creative Imagination as his places of last resort'. While acknowledging the historical crisis, Wordsworth offers no sustained analysis of the French Revolution or of his own involvement in it, choosing instead to celebrate nature's gift to him. To the New Historicist critic, the Revolution remains the central blindspot in the text and the critic's role is to reinsert it into the poem as the real but unaddressed crisis. In either case, we can read these lines in relation to the extracts in Section 1, but it is a matter of critical emphasis whether these historical debates are seen as specifically invoked or transcended by the poet. And the critic might also want to take into account the fact that in later versions of the poem the events of the French Revolution and the poet's involvement in them *do* become the central crisis, occupying Books IX and X. (Indeed, Wordsworth comments that 'Like others I had read, and eagerly / Sometimes, the master Pamphlets of the day' (IX. 96–7), showing a knowledge of the materials in Section 1.) Is this the natural development of the earlier reference, or the poet at last confronting the history that he had been denying in the earlier version? Or does he confront history only to try to escape it again, asserting the power of the imagination? Whichever critical position is adopted, we must look to the historical context to resolve this matter.

As the section titles to this *Sourcebook* indicate, the study of writing of the Romantic period is now interdisciplinary and diverse. The limited canon of Romanticism has been enlarged to include a much greater number of writers and range of genres, and distinctions that were developing during the period, between literature and other forms of writing, and between 'high' and 'popular' culture, have been questioned and, by some critics at least, abandoned (see Section 7). In many such accounts, literature no longer occupies a hierarchical position in relation to context, drawing upon but somehow elevating itself beyond what used to be termed 'background'. Indeed, some critics have pointed to the textuality of history as well as the historicity of texts. Literature is seen as one of a number of interrelated forms of writing, or as part of a more generally defined field of culture, albeit often utilizing certain formal properties tradition-ally identified with notions of 'literariness'. Yet for other critics it is precisely this issue of form that illustrates the inadequacy of reading in context, at least in trying to gain a full understanding of the special achievement of a work of art. For Formalist critics, for example, it is the internal organization of a piece of writ-ing and its relationship with other pieces whose formal properties it redeploys that constitute the primary value of a literary work, rather than its relationship to non-literary contexts: a literary text is not a historical document and cannot be properly judged or explained in historical terms. (Historicist critics will often respond to such claims by arguing that literary forms and genres are themselves shaped by the historical moments in which they are produced and read.)

The aim of this *Sourcebook* is to make available in a single volume a range of materials that articulate what are currently seen to be the key debates in the Romantic period. Of course, these materials are of interest in themselves, while also providing a sense of the specific possibilities, controversies and challenges which confronted the era's poets, novelists and dramatists. I have chosen pieces which were felt to be particularly important in their own time as well as materials that represent trends and developments focused on in current discussions. In this way, the book is as much a picture of Romanticism today as it is of Romanticism two hundred years ago.

Note on the texts selected

Unless otherwise indicated, the earliest available published editions of the works excerpted have been used. I have not modernized spelling or punctuation and, where possible, I have tried to preserve the typographical features of the original texts (such as the use of capitals and half-capitals, as well as italics). Where three dots appear in an extract (. . .), it is signified that there is a silent break made in the given text, and that some material from the original has been omitted. A longer break is signified by a gap of a line following the three dots. As the focus of the volume is contextual, and given the inevitable limitations on space, I have not included extracts from literary works that are well represented by the major anthologies or are easily available elsewhere, such as Wordsworth's 'Preface' to *Lyrical Ballads* or Percy Shelley's *Defence of Poetry*, which ideally would have been included in Section 8. The book's ten-section structure is in line with other volumes in the Palgrave *Sourcebook* series. Of course, many of the extracts are relevant to more than one section and could often have been placed under a different heading. For example, James Fordyce's critique of the novel in his *Sermons to Young Women* is included in 'Section 3: Women', while Richard Polwhele's attack on women writers in *The Unsex'd Females* can be found in 'Section 8: Literary Production and Reception'. Their assignment could be credibly reversed. Similarly, extracts from Godwin's *Political Justice* appear in three different sections while a number of authors have extracts in more than one section.

1
Historical Events

Introduction

In 1816 the poet Percy Shelley described the French Revolution as 'the master theme of the epoch in which we live'.[1] The events in France were enormously important for all aspects of life in Britain during the Romantic period, though whether the age was one of 'Revolution' or 'Counter-Revolution' continues to be debated by historians. To many contemporaries, the Revolution (often symbolized by the storming of the Bastille on 14 July 1789, though actually a complex series of events that lasted until at least 1795 – see Timeline on pp. xvii–xix), initially appeared not only to be bringing French government into line with the British model of constitutional monarchy established by the 'Glorious Revolution' in 1688 but also to be transforming the world into a paradise on earth. William Wordsworth, who visited France in 1790, commented in his epic poem *The Prelude* that during this stage of the Revolution: 'Bliss was it in that dawn to be alive, / But to be young was very heaven!' (X. 692–3).[2] However, many who had initially supported the Revolution became increasingly disillusioned by the bloody and increasingly imperialistic nature of events in France, including the September Massacres of 1792, the execution of the king and queen in 1793, the outbreak of war between Britain and France in the same year, the Jacobin 'Reign of Terror' of 1793–4, and the invasions of Italy in 1796–8 and Switzerland in 1798. These events provide the subject matter as well as the context for many of the literary works of the period, including Charlotte Smith's *The Emigrants*, Samuel Taylor Coleridge's 'France, an Ode', and Wordsworth's *The Prelude*. The historical pattern of hope and disappointment stimulated by events in France has been seen to shape much of the literary output of the period, while a number of influential accounts have argued that it was Revolutionary disillusionment that turned many of the writers of the 1790s away from politics and towards the natural world and the self (accounts which have been challenged, as the general 'Introduction' to this *Sourcebook* shows).

---

1 *The Letters of Percy Bysshe Shelley*, ed. Frederick L. Jones, 2 vols (Oxford: Clarendon Press, 1964), I. 504.

2 William Wordsworth, *The Major Works*, ed. Stephen Gill (Oxford: Oxford World's Classics, 2000), p. 550.

In *The Prelude*, Wordsworth describes how 'Like others I had read, and eagerly / Sometimes, the master Pamphlets of the day' (IX. 96–7) and this section begins with extracts from the 'pamphlet war' that raged in Britain in response to the French Revolution between 1789 and 1795. This debate was important not only because it analysed key issues about the nature of government and society but because it addressed a much larger proportion of the population than had been previously involved in any such discussion. Edmund Burke's *Reflections on the Revolution in France* (1790; extract 1.4) and Thomas Paine's *Rights of Man* (1791–2; extract 1.6) were the two key texts in this 'Revolution Debate', establishing the conservative and radical positions in relation not only to events in France but to the principles of government more generally. While Burke's melodramatic accounts of the horrors of the Revolution and his advocacy of tradition and prejudice were influential in turning many readers against France, Paine's clearly expressed insistence on natural rights and the prerogative of society to change its government made *Rights of Man* a compelling text for the radical cause and for groups like the London Corresponding Society. Repressive government legislation such as the Treasonable Practices Act of 1795, prompted in part by a fear of revolution in Britain, effectively silenced the public debate, though these measures also coincided with the disillusionment over events in France described above. Literature played an important part in this debate, in 'Jacobin' and 'Anti-Jacobin' novels of the 1790s, which consciously manipulated fictional form to present a political argument, and also in post-Waterloo works such as Jane Austen's novels and Mary Shelley's *Frankenstein*, which can be seen to continue the enquiry into the best structure for society and the potential dangers of 'improvement' (be it in the fields of landscape gardening or biological science).

While Romanticism is often thought about in terms of revolution, it is important to remember that for much of the Romantic period Britain was a nation at war. The conflict with France that began in 1793 lasted for another twenty-two years (with only two short periods of peace in 1802–3 and 1814), with Britain fighting first the Revolutionary state and, after 1803, Napoleon Bonaparte, the French General turned Emperor who was finally defeated at the Battle of Waterloo in 1815. The Revolutionary and Napoleonic conflicts have been described as 'total' rather than 'limited' wars, fought on a global scale and involving whole populations rather than just professional armies. They were also seen to be wars of ideas, fought for political principles rather than simply for territorial gain (though Britain's colonial power increased considerably during them, as Section 9 shows). During these years, and particularly at times of invasion threat, a vicious and witty propaganda war was conducted in Britain against France and Napoleon. Much of the most popular literature of this period, such as the romances of the war's best-selling poet Walter Scott, contributed to this morale-boosting and bellicose project, though other writers did criticize the war (see, for example, Anna Laetitia Barbauld's *Eighteen Hundred and Eleven* and the first canto of Lord Byron's *Childe Harold's Pilgrimage*, 1812).

While the victory over France at Waterloo in 1815 was enthusiastically cele-brated in Britain, the restoration of deposed European monarchs to their thrones that followed the Congress of Vienna (1814–15) seemed to many liberals to mark a return to the pre-revolutionary age and to initiate a period of political reaction. The conservative yet volatile atmosphere of the post-Waterloo years so power-fully conveyed in the poetry of Byron and Shelley was exacerbated by economic hardship that stimulated both renewed demands for reform, and repressive government legislation such as the suspension of *Habeas Corpus* in 1817. The notorious culmination of these conflicting forces was the Peterloo Massacre (extract 1.14), which led to further repressive legislation, but continued agitation ultimately resulted in the limited measures introduced by the Reform Act of 1832.

1.1 'Declaration of the Rights of Man and of Citizens', by the National Assembly of France (1789)

A key document of the French Revolution, the 'Declaration of the Rights of Man and of Citizens', was drafted by the Marquis de Lafayette and approved by the National Assembly of France on 26 (or 27) August 1789. It draws on the European and American Enlightenment thinking of figures such as the philosopher Jean-Jacques Rousseau and the politician Thomas Jefferson, and is partly modelled on the latter's 'United States Declaration of Independence' of 1776, which declared as 'self-evident' the 'truths' that 'all men are created equal' and 'that they are endowed by their Creator with certain unalienable Rights'. The 'Declaration' achieved wide circulation in Britain when Thomas Paine incorporated it into his Rights of Man *(1791; extract 1.6), the source for the text printed below (which reproduces Paine's italics). Paine's comment on the opening paragraph illustrates the significance that came to be attached to this piece of legislation as a symbol of the Revolution: 'we see the solemn and majestic spectacle of a Nation opening its commission, under the auspices of its Creator, to establish a Government; a scene so new, and so transcendently unequalled by anything in the European world, that the name of a Revolution is diminutive of its character, and it rises into a Regeneration of man'.*

The Representatives of the people of FRANCE, formed into a National Assembly, considering that ignorance, neglect, or contempt of human rights, are the sole causes of public misfortunes and corruptions of government, have resolved to set forth, in a solemn declaration, these natural, imprescriptible, and unalienable rights: that this declaration being constantly present to the minds of the members of the body social, they may be ever kept attentive to their rights and their duties: that the acts of the legislative and executive powers of Government, being capable of being every moment compared with the end of political insti-tutions, may be more respected: and also, that the future claims of the citizens, being directed by simple and incontestible principles, may always tend to the maintenance of the Constitution, and the general happiness.

For these reasons, the NATIONAL ASSEMBLEY doth recognize and declare, in the presence of the Supreme Being, and with the hope of his blessing and favour, the following *sacred* rights of men and of citizens:

I.   *Men are born, and always continue, free, and equal in respect of their rights. Civil distinctions, therefore, can be founded only on public utility.*

II.   *The end of all political associations, is, the preservation of the natural and imprescriptible rights of man; and these rights are liberty, property, security, and resistance to oppression.*

III.   *The nation is essentially the source of all sovereignty; nor can any* INDIVIDUAL, *or* ANY BODY OF MEN, *be entitled to any authority which is not expressly derived from it.*

IV.   Political Liberty consists in the power of doing whatever does not injure another. The exercise of the natural rights of every man, has no other limits than those which are necessary to secure to every *other* man the free exercise of the same rights; and these limits are determinable only by the law.

V.   The law ought to prohibit only actions hurtful to society. What is not prohibited by the law, should not be hindered; nor should any one be compelled to that which the law does not require.

VI.   The law is an expression of the will of the community. All citizens have a right to concur, either personally, or by their representatives, in its formation. It should be the same to all, whether it protects or punishes; and *all being equal in its sight, are equally eligible to all honours, places, and employments, according to their different abilities, without any other distinction than that created by their virtues and talents.*

VII.   No man should be accused, arrested, or held in confinement, except in the cases determined by the law, and according to the forms which it has prescribed. All who promote, solicit, execute, or cause to be executed, arbitrary orders, ought to be punished; and every citizen called upon, or apprehended by virtue of the law, ought immediately to obey, and render himself culpable by resistance.

VIII.   The law ought to impose no other penalties than such as are absolutely and evidently necessary: and no one ought to be punished, but in virtue of a law promulgated before the offence, and legally applied.

IX.   Every man being presumed innocent till he has been convicted, whenever his detention becomes indispensable, all rigour to him, more than is necessary to secure his person, ought to be provided against by the law.

X.   No man ought to be molested on account of his opinions, not even on account of his *religious* opinions, provided his avowal of them does not disturb the public order established by the law.

XI.   The unrestrained communication of thoughts and opinions being one of the most precious rights of man, every citizen may speak, write, and publish freely, provided he is responsible for the abuse of this liberty in cases determined by the law.

XII.   A public force being necessary to give security to the rights of men and of citizens, that force is instituted for the benefit of the community, and not for the particular benefit of the persons with whom it is entrusted.

XIII.   A common contribution being necessary for the support of the public force, and for defraying the other expences of government, it ought to be divided equally among the members of the community, according to their abilities.

XIV.   Every citizen has a right, either by himself or his representative, to a free voice in determining the necessity of public contributions, the appropriation of them, and their amount, mode of assessment, and duration.

XV.   Every community has a right to demand of all its agents, an account of their conduct.

XVI.   Every community in which a separation of powers and a security of rights is not provided for, wants a constitution.

XVII.   The right to property being inviolable and sacred, no one ought to be deprived of it, except in cases of evident public necessity, legally ascertained, and on condition of a previous just indemnity.

1.2   Richard Price, *A Discourse on the Love of our Country, delivered on Nov. 4, 1789, at the Meeting-House in the Old Jewry, to the Society for Commemorating the Revolution in Great Britain* (1789)

In 1789 the Welsh Dissenting minister Richard Price (1723–91) addressed the Society that had been founded to commemorate the British 'Glorious Revolution' of 1688. Price's sermon was the first major British response to events in France and the text which initiated the 'pamphlet war'. It illustrates some of the most important political and religious frameworks within which the Revolution was understood, presenting it as a French re-enactment of the 'Glorious Revolution', as a continuation of the spread of Liberty following the American War of Independence, and as an apocalyptic event that was bringing a new world into being. Price's powerful imagery of illumination, fire and fetters was echoed in much pro-revolutionary writing of the period and his highly rhetorical style and pro-French sentiment made him the initial target of Edmund Burke's Reflections on the Revolution in France *(extract 1.4), in which Burke attacked what he saw as the dangerous 'zeal' and lack of moderation of Price's 'pulpit style'.*

What an eventful period is this! I am thankful that I have lived to it; and I could almost say, *Lord, now lettest thou thy servant depart in peace, for mine eyes have seen thy salvation.*[3] I have lived to see a diffusion of knowledge, which has under-

---

3 The opening of the canticle the 'Nunc Dimittis', which draws on Luke 2:29–32.

mined superstition and error – I have lived to see the rights of men better understood than ever; and nations panting for liberty, which seemed to have lost the idea of it. – I have lived to see THIRTY MILLIONS of people, indignant and resolute, spurning at slavery, and demanding liberty with an irresistible voice; their king led in triumph, and an arbitrary monarch surrendering himself to his subjects.[4] – After sharing in the benefits of one Revolution, I have been spared to be a witness to two other Revolutions, both glorious.[5] – And now, methinks, I see the ardor for liberty catching and spreading; a general amendment beginning in human affairs; the dominion of kings changed for the dominion of laws, and the dominion of priests giving way to the dominion of reason and conscience.

Be encouraged, all ye friends of freedom, and writers in its defence! The times are auspicious. Your labours have not been in vain. Behold kingdoms, admonished by you, starting from sleep, breaking their fetters, and claiming justice from their oppressors! Behold, the light you have struck out, after setting AMERICA free, reflected to FRANCE, and there kindled into a blaze that lays despotism in ashes, and warms and illuminates EUROPE!

Tremble all ye oppressors of the world! Take warning all ye supporters of slavish governments, and slavish hierarchies! Call no more (absurdly and wickedly) REFORMATION, innovation. You cannot now hold the world in darkness. Struggle no longer against increasing light and liberality. Restore to mankind their rights; and consent to the correction of abuses, before they and you are destroyed together.

1.3   Helen Maria Williams, *Letters from France* (1790, 1793 and 1795)

The liberal poet and novelist Helen Maria Williams (1761/2–1827) journeyed to France in July 1790 and July 1791 (returning only briefly to England in 1792) and wrote three sets of Letters, *published in 1790, 1793 and 1795, which offered an eyewitness chronicle of Revolutionary events. The* Letters *were well received in Britain, at least initially, though in the increasingly reactionary atmosphere of the 1790s Williams became the target of attacks and was included among Richard Polwhele's 'unsex'd females' (see extract 8.5). Though Williams remained an advocate of Revolutionary ideals throughout the 1790s, the history of her response embodies a trajectory characteristic of many liberals during the first half of the decade, shifting from the wild excitement and enthusiasm seen in her account of the Fédération to the anxiety and disappointment resulting from the Revolutionary violence exemplified by the September Massacres and the 'Terror' (when she herself was imprisoned), described in the second and third extracts below.*

---

4 The events of the French Revolution and particularly of 6 October 1789, when the Parisian crowd marched on the palace of Versailles and brought the royal family back to the capital.

5 Respectively, the 'Glorious', American and French Revolutions.

[1790][6]

I Promised to send you a description of the federation: but it is not to be described![7] One must have been present, to form any judgment of a scene, the sublimity of which depended much less on its external magnificence than on the effect it produced on the minds of the spectators. 'The people, sure, the people were the sight!' I may tell you of pavilions, of triumphal arches, of altars on which incense was burnt, of two hundred thousand men walking in procession; but how am I to give you an adequate idea of the behaviour of the spectators? How am I to paint the impetuous feelings of that immense, that exulting multitude? Half a million of people assembled at a spectacle, which furnished every image that can elevate the mind of man; which connected the enthusiasm of moral sentiment with the solemn pomp of religious ceremonies; which addressed itself at once to the imagination, the understanding, and the heart! . . .

The procession, which was formed with eight persons abreast, entered the Champ de Mars beneath the triumphal arches, with a discharge of cannon. The deputies placed themselves round the inside of the amphitheatre. Between them and the seats of the spectators, the national guard of Paris were ranged; and the seats round the amphitheatre were filled with four hundred thousand people. The middle of the amphitheatre was crouded with an immense multitude of soldiers. The National Assembly walked towards the pavilion, where they placed themselves with the King, the Queen, the royal family, and their attendants; and opposite this group, rose in perspective the hills of Passy and Chaillot, covered with people. The standards, of which one was presented to each department of the kingdom, as a mark of brotherhood, by the citizens of Paris, were carried to the altar to be consecrated by the bishop. High mass was performed, after which Monsieur de la Fayette, who had been appointed by the King Major General of the Federation, ascended the altar, gave the signal, and himself took the national oath. In an instant every sword was drawn, and every arm lifted up. The King pronounced the oath, which the President of the National Assembly repeated, and the solemn words were re-echoed by six hundred thousand voices; while the Queen raised the Dauphin in her arms, shewing him to the people and the army. At the moment the consecrated banners were displayed, the sun, which had been obscured by frequent showers in the course of the morning, burst forth, while the people lifted their eyes to heaven, and called upon the Deity to look down and witness the sacred engagement into which they entered. A respectful silence was succeeded by the cries, the shouts, the acclamations of the multitude: they wept, they embraced each other, and then dispersed.

---

6 Source: *Letters Written in France, in the Summer 1790, to a Friend in England; Containing, Various Anecdotes relative to the French Revolution* (1790).

7 Fête de la Fédération, held on the first anniversary of the storming of the Bastille.

You will not suspect that I was an indifferent witness of such a scene. Oh no! this was not a time in which the distinctions of country were remembered. It was the triumph of human kind; it was man asserting the noblest privileges of his nature; and it required but the common feelings of humanity to become in that moment a citizen of the world. For myself, I acknowledge that my heart caught with enthusiasm the general sympathy; my eyes were filled with tears; and I shall never forget the sensations of that day. . . .

[1792][8]

Surounding nations, who might perhaps have been animated by the example of a country which has long served as a model to the rest of Europe, have heard of the second of September [1792], and have shrunk back into the torpor of slavery.[9] They have beheld, in the room of the pure and sublime worship of liberty, the grim idol of anarchy set up, and have seen her altar smeared with sanguinary rites. They have beheld the inhuman judges of that night wearing the municipal scarf which their polluting touch profaned, surrounded by men armed with pikes and sabres dropping with blood – while a number of blazing torches threw their glaring light on the ferocious visages of those execrable judges, who, mixing their voices with the shrieks of the dying, passed sentence with a savage mockery of justice, on victims devoted to their rage. They have beheld the infernal executioners of that night, with their arms bared for the purposes of murder, dragging forth those victims to modes of death at which nature shudders. – – Ah! ye slaughtered heroes of the immortal 14th of July, was it for this ye overthrew the towers of the Bastile, and burst open its gloomy dungeons? – was it for this, ye generous patriots, that with heroic contempt of life, ye shed your blood to give liberty and happiness to your enslaved country?[10] – Ah! had ye foreseen that the fanatics of liberty, fierce as the fanatics of superstition, would have their day of St. Bartholomew,[11] would not your victorious arms have been unnerved? Would not the sacred glow of freedom have been frozen in your veins? Ah! what is become of the delightful visions, which elevated the enthusiastic heart? – What is become of the transport which beat high in every bosom, when an assembled million of the human race vowed on the altar of their country, in the name of the represented nation, inviolable fraternity and union – an eternal

---

8 Source: *Letters from France: Containing a Great Variety of Interesting and Original Information Concerning the Most Important Events that have lately Occurred in that Country, and particularly respecting the Campaign of 1792* (1793).

9 The 'September Massacres', when over 1,400 Parisian prisoners were murdered on suspicion of being counter-revolutionaries.

10 It is with the repeated phrase 'was it for this' that Wordsworth would begin his composition of *The Prelude* in 1798.

11 A religious massacre in France beginning on 24 August 1572 when a Catholic mob slaughtered thousands of Huguenots.

federation! This was indeed the golden age of the revolution. – But it is past! – the enchanting spell is broken, and the fair scenes of beauty and of order, through which imagination wandered, are transformed into the desolation of the wilderness, and clouded by the darkness of the tempest. If the genius of Liberty – profaned Liberty! does not arise in his might, and crush those violators of freedom, whose crimes have almost broken the heart of humanity, the inhabitants of Paris may indeed 'wish for the wings of the dove, that they may fly away and be at rest – for there is violence and strife in the city.'[12]

[1793–4][13]

But the law of the 22d Prairial[14] tore away every illusion of the imagination or the heart, and displayed the general proscription of the prisoners in all its extent of horror. It was no longer a solitary individual who was called to death; multitudes were summoned at once. Every returning night, long covered carts drawn by four horses entered successively the courtyards of the different prisons. Whenever the trampling of the horses' feet was heard, the prisoners prepared themselves for their doom. The names of the victims marked for execution the following day were called over, and they were instantly hurried into these gloomy hearses. The husband was scarcely allowed time to bid his wife a last farewell, or the mother to recommend her orphan children to the compassion of such of the prisoners as might survive the general calamity. At the prison of the Luxembourg, an hundred and sixty-nine victims were in one night torn from their beds, and led to the grated dungeons of the Conciergerie, that prison over the gates of which might with equal propriety have been written, the same as over that of the infernal region of Dante, 'Lasciate speranza voi ch'entrate;'[15] for here it might literally be said, 'hope never came, that comes to all.'[16] I have seen the Conciergerie, that abode of horror, that anti-chamber of the tomb. I have seen those infectious cells, where the prisoners breathed contagion, where the walls are in some places stained with the blood of the massacres of September, and where a part of the spacious courtyard, round which the grated dungeons are built, remains unpaved since that period, when the stones were taken up for the purpose of burying the dead. I have seen the chamber where the persons condemned by the revolutionary tribunal submitted to the preparatory

---

12 Psalm 55.
13 Source: *Letters containing a Sketch of the Politics of France, from the Thirty-first of May 1793, till the Twenty-eighth of July 1794, and of the Scenes which have Passed in the Prisons in Paris* (1795).
14 This law of 10 June 1794 was enacted during the 'Reign of Terror', increasing the power of the Committee of Public Safety and making it more difficult for those accused of counter-revolutionary activities to defend themselves.
15 Williams's note: 'Let him lose all hope who enters here.'
16 Milton, *Paradise Lost*, I, 66–7.

offices of the executioner; where his scissars cut off the lavish tresses of the youthful beauty, and where he tied her tender hands behind her waist with cords. Merciful Heaven! and among those who have thus suffered were persons to whom my heart was bound by the ties of friendship and affection. – But though I have survived such scenes, they have left upon my heart that settled melancholy which never can be dissipated. – For me, the world has lost its illusive colouring; its fairy spells, its light enchantments have vanished; and death, the idea most familiar to my imagination, appears to my wearied spirit the only point of rest.

The usual pretext for those murders *in mass*, which were practised at this period, was that of a conspiracy in the prisons; a vague and wide term which the tyrants might interpret at their pleasure, and which gave them the power of including whatever persons and whatever numbers they thought proper.

1.4   Edmund Burke, *Reflections on the Revolution in France, and on the Proceedings in Certain Societies in London Relative to that Event* (1790)

Born in Dublin to an Anglican father and Roman Catholic mother, the political and aesthetic theorist Edmund Burke (1729–97) had strongly supported the colonies in Parliament during the American war, making his attack on the French Revolution in his Reflections *all the more forceful for many readers. Replying initially to Richard Price's* Discourse on the Love of our Country *(extract 1.2), Burke's lengthy and highly rhetorical polemic presented the Revolution as a violent and theatrical spectacle, with its author exploiting his understanding of the aesthetics of sensibility and the sublime to capture and terrify the imaginations of his readers (see extract 6.2). Against what he presents as the dangerous abstractions of revolutionary principles such as 'rights', which will lead only to chaos and tyranny, Burke advocates an organic model of government based on tradition, hierarchy, and prejudice.* Reflections *sold 30,000 copies in two years, prompting over a hundred published replies including those by Thomas Paine, Mary Wollstonecraft and William Godwin extracted below. For many readers Burke's arguments gained increased authority from the way they seemed to anticipate the increasingly violent development of the Revolution during the first half of the 1790s. Burke continued to contribute to the pamphlet war until his death in 1797, presenting the conflict with the 'Republick of Regicide' as a war against 'an armed doctrine' in his* Two Letters Addressed to a Member of the Present Parliament *(1796).*

All circumstances taken together, the French revolution is the most astonishing that has hitherto happened in the world. The most wonderful things are brought about in many instances by means the most absurd and ridiculous; in the most ridiculous modes; and, apparently, by the most contemptible instruments. Every thing seems out of nature in this strange chaos of levity and ferocity, and of all sorts of crimes jumbled together with all sorts of follies. In viewing this monstrous tragi-comic scene, the most opposite passions necessarily succeed, and sometimes mix with each other in the mind; alternate contempt and indignation; alternate laughter and tears; alternate scorn and horror.

It cannot however be denied, that to some this strange scene appeared in quite another point of view. Into them it inspired no other sentiments than those of exultation and rapture. They saw nothing in what has been done in France, but a firm and temperate exertion of freedom; so consistent, on the whole, with morals and with piety, as to make it deserving not only of the secular applause of dashing Machiavelian politicians, but to render it a fit theme for all the devout effusions of sacred eloquence.[17] . . .

You will observe, that from Magna Charta to the Declaration of Right, it has been the uniform policy of our constitution, to claim and assert our liberties, as an *entailed inheritance* derived to us from our forefathers, and to be transmitted to our posterity; as an estate specially belonging to the people of this kingdom, without any reference whatever to any other more general or prior right. By this means our constitution preserves an unity in so great a diversity of its parts. We have an inheritable crown; an inheritable peerage; and an house of commons and a people inheriting privileges, franchises, and liberties, from a long line of ancestors.

This policy appears to me to be the result of profound reflection; or rather the happy effect of following nature, which is wisdom without reflection, and above it. A spirit of innovation is generally the result of a selfish temper and confined views. People will not look forward to posterity, who never look backward to their ancestors. Besides, the people of England well know, that the idea of inheritance furnishes a sure principle of conservation, and a sure principle of transmission; without at all excluding a principle of improvement. . . . In this choice of inheritance we have given to our frame of polity the image of a relation in blood; binding up the constitution of our country with our dearest domestic ties; adopting our fundamental laws into the bosom of our family affections; keeping inseparable, and cherishing with the warmth of all their combined and mutually reflected charities, our state, our hearths, our sepulchres, and our altars. . . .

History will record, that on the morning of the 6th of October 1789,[18] the king and queen of France, after a day of confusion, alarm, dismay, and slaughter, lay down, under the pledged security of public faith, to indulge nature in a few hours of respite, and troubled melancholy repose. From this sleep the queen was first startled by the voice of the centinel at her door, who cried out to her, to save herself by flight – that this was the last proof of fidelity he could give – that they

---

17 Burke has Richard Price's *Discourse* (extract 1.2) particularly in mind here.
18 Burke offers an alternative account to Price's of the Parisian crowd's march on the palace of Versailles and their forced transport of the royal family back to Paris (see extract 1.2).

Figure 1 Thomas Rowlandson, 'The Contrast 1793. British Liberty. French Liberty. Which is Best?', January 1793; © Copyright the Trustees of the British Museum.

A version of a print first published in 1792, 'The Contrast' was sponsored by John Reeves's Association for the Preservation of Liberty and Property against Republicans and Levellers and became one of the most widely circulated images of the propaganda war. Working through an opposition of Britannia and the French Medusa, the image illustrates the interrelation of ideas of nationhood and womanhood during the conflict.

were upon him, and he was dead. Instantly he was cut down. A band of cruel ruffians and assassins, reeking with his blood, rushed into the chamber of the queen, and pierced with an hundred strokes of bayonets and poniards the bed, from whence this persecuted woman had but just time to fly almost naked, and through ways unknown to the murderers had escaped to seek refuge at the feet of a king and husband, not secure of his own life for a moment.

This king, to say no more of him, and this queen, and their infant children (who once would have been the pride and hope of a great and generous people) were then forced to abandon the sanctuary of the most splendid palace in the world, which they left swimming in blood, polluted by massacre, and strewed with scattered limbs and mutilated carcases. Thence they were conducted into

---

19 I.e. the execution of the king and queen.

the capital of their kingdom. Two had been selected from the unprovoked, unre-sisted, promiscuous slaughter, which was made of the gentlemen of birth and family who composed the king's body guard. These two gentlemen, with all the parade of an execution of justice, were cruelly and publickly dragged to the block, and beheaded in the great court of the palace. Their heads were stuck upon spears, and led the procession; whilst the royal captives who followed in the train were slowly moved along, amidst the horrid yells, and shrilling screams, and frantic dances, and infamous contumelies, and all the unutterable abominations of the furies of hell, in the abused shape of the vilest of women. After they had been made to taste, drop by drop, more than the bitterness of death, in the slow torture of a journey of twelve miles, protracted to six hours, they were, under a guard, composed of those very soldiers who had thus conducted them through this famous triumph, lodged in one of the old palaces of Paris, now converted into a Bastile for kings.

Is this a triumph to be consecrated at altars? to be commemorated with grate-ful thanksgiving? to be offered to the divine humanity with fervent prayer and enthusiastick ejaculation? – These Theban and Thracian Orgies, acted in France, and applauded only in the Old Jewry, I assure you, kindle prophetic enthusiasm in the minds but of very few people in this kingdom: although a saint and apos-tle, who may have revelations of his own, and who has so completely vanquished all the mean superstitions of the heart, may incline to think it pious and decorous to compare it with the entrance into the world of the Prince of Peace, proclaimed in an holy temple by a venerable sage, and not long before not worse announced by the voice of angels to the quiet innocence of shep-herds. . . .

Although this work of our new light and knowledge, did not go to the length, that in all probability it was intended it should be carried;[19] yet I must think, that such treatment of any human creatures must be shocking to any but those who are made for accomplishing Revolutions. But I cannot stop here. Influenced by the inborn feelings of my nature, and not being illuminated by a single ray of this new-sprung modern light, I confess to you, Sir, that the exalted rank of the persons suffering, and particularly the sex, the beauty, and the amiable qual-ities of the descendant of so many kings and emperors, with the tender age of royal infants, insensible only through infancy and innocence of the cruel outrages to which their parents were exposed, instead of being a subject of exul-tation, adds not a little to my sensibility on that most melancholy occasion.

I hear that the august person, who was the principal object of our preacher's triumph, though he supported himself, felt much on that shameful occasion. As a man, it became him to feel for his wife and his children, and the faithful guards of his person, that were massacred in cold blood about him; as a prince, it

The Zenith of French Glory; – The Pinnacle of Liberty.
Religion, Justice, Loyalty, & all the Bugbears of Unenlighten'd Minds, Farewell!

Figure 2   James Gillray, 'The Zenith of French Glory; – The Pinnacle of Liberty. Religion, Justice, Loyalty, & all the Bugbears of Unenlighten'd Minds, Farewell!', 12 February 1793; © Copyright the Trustees of the British Museum.

Gillray's caricature presents the execution of Louis XVI in the Place de la Révolution in Paris on 21 January 1793. Something of a visual parallel to Burke's *Reflections on the Revolution in France* in the theatricality and extremity of its presentation of events across the Channel, the satire contains many of the elements that were repeated in anti-French propaganda throughout the 1790s, including the figure of the *sans culotte*, the guillotine, the mob (here presented through their *bonnets rouges*), and the hanged figures of a judge, a priest and two monks.

became him to feel for the strange and frightful transformation of his civilized subjects, and to be more grieved for them, than sollicitous [sic] for himself. It derogates little from his fortitude, while it adds infinitely to the honour of his humanity. I am very sorry to say it, very sorry indeed, that such personages are in a situation in which it is not unbecoming to praise the virtues of the great.

I hear, and I rejoice to hear, that the great lady, the other object of the triumph, has borne that day (one is interested that beings made for suffering should suffer well) and that she bears all the succeeding days, that she bears the imprisonment of her husband, and her own captivity, and the exile of her friends, and the insulting adulation of addresses, and the whole weight of her accumulated wrongs, with a serene patience, in a manner suited to her rank and race, and becoming the offspring of a sovereign distinguished for her piety and her courage; that like her she has lofty sentiments; that she feels with the dignity of a Roman matron; that in the last extremity she will save herself from the last disgrace, and that if she must fall, she will fall by no ignoble hand.

It is now sixteen or seventeen years since I saw the queen of France, then the dauphiness, at Versailles; and surely never lighted on this orb, which she hardly seemed to touch, a more delightful vision. I saw her just above the horizon, decorating and cheering the elevated sphere she just began to move in, – glittering like the morning-star, full of life, and splendor, and joy. Oh! what a revolution! and what an heart must I have, to contemplate without emotion that elevation and that fall! Little did I dream that, when she added titles of veneration to those of enthusiastic, distant, respectful love, that she should ever be obliged to carry the sharp antidote against disgrace concealed in that bosom; little did I dream that I should have lived to see such disasters fallen upon her in a nation of gallant men, in a nation of men of honour and of cavaliers. I thought ten thousand swords must have leaped from their scabbards to avenge even a look that threatened her with insult. – But the age of chivalry is gone. – That of sophisters, œconomists, and calculators, has succeeded; and the glory of Europe is extinguished for ever. Never, never more, shall we behold that generous loyalty to rank and sex, that proud submission, that dignified obedience, that subordination of the heart, which kept alive, even in servitude itself, the spirit of an exalted freedom. The unbought grace of life, the cheap defence of nations, the nurse of manly sentiment and heroic enterprise is gone! It is gone, that sensibility of principle, that charity of honour, which felt a stain like a wound, which inspired courage whilst it mitigated ferocity, which ennobled whatever it touched, and under which vice itself lost half its evil, by losing all its grossness.

This mixed system of opinion and sentiment had its origin in the antient chivalry; and the principle, though varied in its appearance by the varying state of human affairs, subsisted and influenced through a long succession of generations, even to the time we live in. If it should ever be totally extinguished, the loss I fear will be great. It is this which has given its character to modern Europe. It is this which has distinguished it under all its forms of government, and distinguished it to its advantage, from the states of Asia, and possibly from those states which flourished in the most brilliant periods of the antique world. It was this, which, without confounding ranks, had produced a noble equality, and handed it down through all the gradations of social life. It was this opinion which mitigated kings into companions, and raised private men to be fellows with kings. Without force, or opposition, it subdued the fierceness of pride and power; it obliged sovereigns to submit to the soft collar of social esteem, compelled stern authority to submit to elegance, and gave a dominating vanquisher of laws, to be subdued by manners.

But now all is to be changed. All the pleasing illusions, which made power gentle, and obedience liberal, which harmonized the different shades of life, and which, by a bland assimilation, incorporated into politics the sentiments which beautify and soften private society, are to be dissolved by this new conquering empire of light and reason. All the decent drapery of life is to be rudely torn off. All the superadded ideas, furnished from the wardrobe of a moral imagination, which the heart owns, and the understanding ratifies, as necessary to cover the defects of our naked shivering nature, and to raise it to dignity in our own esti-mation, are to be exploded as a ridiculous, absurd, and antiquated fashion.

On this scheme of things, a king is but a man; a queen is but a woman; a woman is but an animal; and an animal not of the highest order. All homage paid to the sex in general as such, and without distinct views, is to be regarded as romance and folly. Regicide, and parricide, and sacrilege, are but fictions of superstition, corrupting jurisprudence by destroying its simplicity. The murder of a king, or a queen, or a bishop, or a father, are only common homicide; and if the people are by any chance, or in any way gainers by it, a sort of homicide much the most pardonable, and into which we ought not to make too severe a scrutiny. . . .

Society is indeed a contract. Subordinate contracts for objects of mere occa-sional interest may be dissolved at pleasure – but the state ought not to be considered as nothing better than a partnership agreement in a trade of pepper and coffee, callico or tobacco, or some other such low concern, to be taken up for a little temporary interest, and to be dissolved by the fancy of the parties. It is to be looked on with other reverence; because it is not a partnership in things subservient only to the gross animal existence of a temporary and perishable nature. It is a partnership in all science; a partnership in all art; a partnership in every virtue, and in all perfection. As the ends of such a partnership cannot be obtained in many generations, it becomes a partnership not only between those who are living, but between those who are living, those who are dead, and those who are to be born. Each contract of each particular state is but a clause in the great primæval contract of eternal society, linking the lower with the higher natures, connecting the visible and invisible world, according to a fixed compact sanctioned by the inviolable oath which holds all physical and all moral natures, each in their appointed place. This law is not subject to the will of those, who by an obligation above them, and infinitely superior, are bound to submit their will to that law. The municipal corporations of that universal kingdom are not morally at liberty at their pleasure, and on their speculations of a contingent improvement, wholly to separate and tear asunder the bands of their subordinate community, and to dissolve it into an unsocial, uncivil, unconnected chaos of elementary principles. It is the first and supreme necessity only, a necessity that is not chosen but chooses, a necessity paramount to deliberation, that admits no discussion, and demands no evidence, which alone can justify a resort to anarchy. This necessity is no exception to the rule; because this necessity itself is a part too of that moral and physical disposition of things to which man must be obedient by consent or force; but if that which is only submission to necessity should be made the object of choice, the law is broken, nature is disobeyed, and the rebellious are outlawed, cast forth, and exiled, from this world of reason, and order, and peace, and virtue, and fruitful penitence, into the antagonist world of madness, discord, vice, confusion, and unavailing sorrow.

1.5   Mary Wollstonecraft, *A Vindication of the Rights of Men, in a Letter to the Right Honourable Edmund Burke; occasioned by His Reflections on the Revolution in France* (1790)

Best known for her A Vindication of the Rights of Woman *(extract 3.4), Mary Wollstonecraft (1759–97) published one of the first responses to Burke's* Reflections, *though as she stated in her opening paragraph, 'I war not with an individual when I contend for the rights of men and the liberty of reason.' Wollstonecraft had been part of the same Dissenting circle as Richard Price (see extract 1.2) and she produced her pamphlet on 29 November, within the same month as* Reflections *(published on the 1st), with a second, enlarged edition following in December (from which the text below is taken). In the extract, Wollstonecraft identifies and criticizes a number of characteristic features of* Reflections – *its use of rhetoric, its seeming lack of reason, its appeal to emotion, its attachment to tradition – while offering her own succinct definition of the rights of man, displaying her own ability to employ rhetorical figures and emotional appeal in support of her 'reasoned' argument.*

. . . [A]s you have informed us that respect chills love, it is natural to conclude, that all your pretty flights arise from your pampered sensibility; and that, vain of this fancied pre-eminence of organs, you foster every emotion till the fumes, mounting to your brain, dispel the sober suggestions of reason. It is not in this view surprising, that when you should argue you become impassioned, and that reflection inflames your imagination, instead of enlightening your understanding.

   Quitting now the flowers of rhetoric, let us, Sir, reason together; and, believe me, I should not have meddled with these troubled waters, in order to point out your inconsistencies, if your wit had not burnished up some rusty, baneful opinions, and swelled the shallow current of ridicule till it resembled the flow of reason, and presumed to be the test of truth.

I shall not attempt to follow you through 'horse-way and foot-path;' but, attacking the foundation of your opinions, I shall leave the superstructure to find a centre of gravity on which it may lean till some strong blast puffs it into air; or your teeming fancy, which the ripening judgment of sixty years has not tamed, produces another Chinese erection, to stare, at every turn, the plain country people in the face, who bluntly call such an airy edifice – a folly.

The birthright of man, to give you, Sir, a short definition of this disputed right, is such a degree of liberty, civil and religious, as is compatible with the liberty of every other individual with whom he is united in a social compact, and the continued existence of that compact.

Liberty, in this simple, unsophisticated sense, I acknowledge, is a fair idea that has never yet received a form in the various governments that have been established on our beauteous globe; the demon of property has ever been at hand to encroach on the sacred rights of men, and to fence round with awful pomp laws that war with justice. But that it results from the eternal foundation of right – from immutable truth – who will presume to deny, that pretends to rationality – if reason has led them to build their morality and religion on an everlasting foundation – the attributes of God?

I glow with indignation when I attempt, methodically, to unravel your slavish paradoxes, in which I can find no fixed first principle to refute; I shall not, therefore, condescend to shew where you affirm in one page what you deny in another; and how frequently you draw conclusions without any previous premises: – it would be something like cowardice to fight with a man who had never exercised the weapons which his opponent chose to combat with.

I know that you have a mortal antipathy to reason; but, if there is any thing like argument, or first principles, in your wild declamation, behold the result: – that we are to reverence the rust of antiquity, and term the unnatural customs, which ignorance and mistaken self-interest have consolidated, the sage fruit of experience: nay, that, if we do discover some errors, our *feelings* should lead us to excuse, with blind love, or unprincipled filial affection, the venerable vestiges of ancient days. These are gothic notions of beauty – the ivy is beautiful though it insidiously destroys the trunk from which it receives support.

1.6   Thomas Paine, *Rights of Man: Being an Answer to Mr. Burke's Attack on the French Revolution* (1791 and 1792)

Thomas Paine (1737–1809) had played a significant role as a supporter of the American side during the War of Independence, particularly through his pamphlet Common Sense *(1776). His* Rights of Man, *published in two volumes in 1791 and 1792, was the most important and influential of the responses to Edmund Burke's* Reflections *(extract 1.4), seeking to expose the 'flagrant misrepresentations' of Burke's version of the Revolution by drawing attention to his rhetorical strategies ('I cannot consider Mr Burke's book in scarcely any other light than a dramatic performance') and presenting his 'frenzy of passion' as close to madness. Against this, Paine's own style is 'clear' and 'concise' (the terms he uses for that of Lafayette in the extract below), designed to appeal to a much wider readership than his adversary. Part I sold 50,000 copies in its first year of publication, and the two volumes together are thought to have sold at least 100,000 copies between 1791 and 1792. Authorizing his arguments through reference to reason, progress, and efficiency, Paine rejects Burke's emphasis on tradition, making the nation the source of all sovereignty and asserting the right of the community to change their form of government. Paine, who had left for Paris prior to the publication of* Rights of Man, *was tried and convicted in absentia for seditious libel by the British government.*

Among the incivilities by which nations or individuals provoke and irritate each other, Mr. Burke's pamphlet on the French Revolution is an extraordinary instance. Neither the People of France, nor the National Assembly, were troubling themselves about the affairs of England, or the English Parliament; and why Mr. Burke should commence an unprovoked attack upon them, both in parliament and in public, is a conduct that cannot be pardoned on the score of manners, nor justified on that of policy.

There is scarcely an epithet of abuse to be found in the English language, with which Mr. Burke has not loaded the French Nation and the National Assembly. Every thing which rancour, prejudice, ignorance or knowledge could suggest, are poured forth in the copious fury of near four hundred pages. In the strain and on the plan Mr. Burke was writing, he might have written on to as many thousands. When the tongue or the pen is let loose in a frenzy of passion, it is the man, and not the subject, that becomes exhausted.

Hitherto Mr. Burke has been mistaken and disappointed in the opinions he had formed of the affairs of France; but such is the ingenuity of his hope, or the malignancy of his despair, that it furnishes him with new pretences to go on. There was a time when it was impossible to make Mr. Burke believe there would be any revolution in France. His opinion then was, that the French had neither spirit to undertake it, nor fortitude to support it; and now that there is one, he seeks an escape, by condemning it.

Not sufficiently content with abusing the National Assembly, a great part of his work is taken up with abusing Dr. Price (one of the best-hearted men that lives), and the two societies in England known by the name of the Revolution Society, and the Society for Constitutional Information.

Dr. Price had preached a sermon on the 4th of November, 1789, being the anniversary of what is called in England, the Revolution which took place [in] 1688. Mr. Burke, speaking of this sermon, says: 'The Political Divine proceeds dogmatically to assert, that, by the principles of the Revolution, the people of England have acquired three fundamental rights:

1. To chuse our own governors.
2. To cashier them for misconduct.
3. To frame a government for ourselves.'

Dr. Price does not say that the right to do these things exists in this or in that person, or in this or in that description of persons, but that it exists in the *whole*; that it is a right resident in the nation. – Mr. Burke, on the contrary, denies that such a right exists in the nation, either in whole or in part, or that it exists any where; and, what is still more strange and marvellous, he says, 'that the people of England utterly disclaim such a right, and that they will resist the practical assertion of it with their lives and fortunes.' That men should take up arms, and spend their lives and fortunes, *not* to maintain their rights, but to maintain they have *not* rights, is an entire new species of discovery, and suited to the paradoxical genius of Mr. Burke. . . .

There never did, there never will, and there never can exist a parliament, or any description of men, or any generation of men, in any country, possessed of the right or the power of binding and controuling posterity to the *'end of time,'* or of commanding for ever how the world shall be governed, or who shall govern it: and therefore all such clauses, acts or declarations, by which the makers of them attempt to do what they have neither the right nor the power to do, nor the power to execute, are in themselves null and void. – Every age and generation must be as free to act for itself, *in all cases*, as the ages and generations which preceded it. The vanity and presumption of governing beyond the grave, is the most ridiculous and insolent of all tyrannies. Man has no property in man; neither has any generation a property in the generations which are to follow. The parliament or the people of 1688, or of any other period, had no more right to dispose of the people of the present day, or to bind or to controul them *in any shape whatever*, than the parliament or the people of the present day have to dispose of, bind or controul those who are to live a hundred or a thousand years hence. Every generation is, and must be, competent to all the purposes which its occasions require. It is the living, and not the dead, that are to be accommodated. When man ceases to be, his power and his wants cease with him; and having no longer any participation in the concerns of this world, he has no longer any authority in directing who shall be its governors, or how its government shall be organised, or how administered. . . .

We now come more particularly to the affairs of France. Mr. Burke's book has the appearance of being written as instruction to the French nation; but if I may permit myself the use of an extravagant metaphor, suited to the extravagance of the case, It is darkness attempting to illuminate light.

While I am writing this, there are accidentally before me some proposals for a declaration of rights by the Marquis de la Fayette (I ask his pardon for using his former address, and do it only for distinction's sake) to the National Assembly, on the 11th of July 1789, three days before the taking of the Bastille; and I cannot but be struck by observing how opposite the sources are from which that Gentleman and Mr. Burke draw their principles. Instead of referring to musty records and mouldy parchments to prove that the rights of the living are lost, 'renounced and abdicated for ever,' by those who are now no more, as Mr. Burke has done, M. de la Fayette applies to the living world, and emphatically says, 'Call to mind the sentiments which Nature has engraved in the heart of every citizen, and which take a new force when they are solemnly recognised by all: – For a nation to love liberty, it is sufficient that she knows it; and to be free, it is sufficient that she wills it.' How dry, barren, and obscure, is the source from which Mr. Burke labours! and how ineffectual, though gay with flowers, are all his declamation and his argument, compared with these clear, concise, and soul-animating sentiments! Few and short as they are, they lead on to a vast field of generous and manly thinking, and do not finish, like Mr. Burke's periods, with music in the ear, and nothing in the heart. . . .

I know a place in America called Point-no-Point; because as you proceed along the shore, gay and flowery as Mr. Burke's language, it continually recedes and presents itself at a distance before you; but when you have got as far as you can go, there is no point at all. Just thus it is with Mr. Burke's three hundred and fifty-six pages. It is therefore difficult to reply to him. But as the points he wishes to establish, may be inferred from what he abuses, it is in his paradoxes that we must look for his arguments.

As to the tragic paintings by which Mr. Burke has outraged his own imagination, and seeks to work upon that of his readers, they are very well calculated for theatrical representation, where facts are manufactured for the sake of show, and accommodated to produce, through the weakness of sympathy, a weeping effect. But Mr. Burke should recollect that he is writing History, and not *Plays*; and that his readers will expect truth, and not the spouting rant of high-toned exclamation.

When we see a man dramatically lamenting in a publication intended to be believed, that, '*The age of chivalry is gone!* that *The glory of Europe is extinguished for ever!* that *The unbought grace of life* (if anyone knows what it is), *the cheap defence of nations, the nurse of manly sentiment and heroic enterprise, is gone!*' and all this because the Quixote age of chivalry nonsense is gone, What opinion can we form of his judgment, or what regard can we pay to his facts? In the rhapsody of his imagination, he has discovered a world of wind-mills, and his sorrows are, that there are no Quixotes to attack them. But if the age of aristocracy, like that of chivalry, should fall, and they had originally some connection, Mr. Burke, the trumpeter of the Order, may continue his parody to the end, and finish with exclaiming: – '*Othello's occupation's gone!*'[20]

---

20 Shakespeare, *Othello*, III. iii. 357.

Notwithstanding Mr. Burke's horrid paintings, when the French Revolution is compared with that of other countries, the astonishment will be, that it is marked with so few sacrifices; but this astonishment will cease when we reflect that *principles*, and not *persons*, were the meditated objects of destruction. . . .

Not one glance of compassion, not one commiserating reflection, that I can find throughout his book, has he bestowed on those who lingered out the most wretched of lives, a life without hope, in the most miserable of prisons. It is painful to behold a man employing his talents to corrupt himself. Nature has been kinder to Mr. Burke than he is to her. He is not affected by the reality of distress touching his heart, but by the showy resemblance of it striking his imagination. He pities the plumage, but forgets the dying bird. Accustomed to kiss the aristocratical hand that hath purloined him from himself, he degenerates into a composition of art, and the genuine soul of nature forsakes him. His hero or his heroine must be a tragedy-victim expiring in show, and not the real prisoner of misery, sliding into death in the silence of a dungeon. . . .

What is government more than the management of the affairs of a Nation? It is not, and from its nature cannot be, the property of any particular man or family, but of the whole community, at whose expense it is supported; and though by force or contrivance it has been usurped into an inheritance, the usurpation cannot alter the right of things. Sovereignty, as a matter of right, appertains to the Nation only, and not to any individual; and a Nation has at all times an inherent indefeasible right to abolish any form of Government it finds inconvenient, and establish such as accords with its interest, disposition, and happiness. The romantic and barbarous distinction of men into Kings and subjects, though it may suit the condition of courtiers, cannot that of citizens; and is exploded by the principle upon which Governments are now founded. Every citizen is a member of the Sovereignty, and, as such, can acknowledge no personal subjection; and his obedience can be only to the laws.

When men think of what Government is, they must necessarily suppose it to possess a knowledge of all the objects and matters upon which its authority is to be exercised. In this view of Government, the republican system, as established by America and France, operates to embrace the whole of a Nation; and the knowledge necessary to the interest of all the parts, is to be found in the center, which the parts by representation form: But the old Governments are on a construction that excludes knowledge as well as happiness; Government by Monks, who know nothing of the world beyond the walls of a Convent, is as consistent as government by Kings.

What were formerly called Revolutions, were little more than a change of persons, or an alteration of local circumstances. They rose and fell like things of course, and had nothing in their existence or their fate that could influence beyond the spot that produced them. But what we now see in the world, from the Revolutions of America and France, are a renovation of the natural order of things, a system of principles as universal as truth and the existence of man, and combining moral with political happiness and national prosperity.

1.7 Hannah More, *Village Politics. Addressed to all the Mechanics, Journeymen and Day Labourers, in Great Britain. By Will Chip, a Country Carpenter* (1792)

Village Politics was written by the Evangelical Hannah More (1745–1833, see also extract 3.6) for the Association for the Preservation of Liberty and Property Against Republicans and Levellers, an organization established by John Reeves in 1792 which distributed such loyalist tracts to counter the popular radicalism stimulated by writers such as Paine (see extract 1.6). The pamphlets were usually cheap and sometimes bought en masse to be distributed for free, as is suggested by the price of '2d. [pence] or 25 for 3s. [shillings]' on the second edition of Village Politics. *More writes carefully for her intended semi-literate readership, using a dialogue between two working men to present her critique of Revolutionary France and her (at times qualified) celebration of the conservative British values and system of government. More continued the project initiated by* Village Politics *with a series of similar pieces, the* Cheap Repository Tracts *(1795–8), to which other writers also contributed. The* Tracts *sold two million copies between 1795 and 1796, which Marilyn Butler has described as 'the most remarkable feat of circulation of the decade'.[21] While these pieces were distributed by Evangelicals and backed by the Church of England, they were also criticized by* The Anti-Jacobin *(extract 8.3) for encouraging literacy among the working classes.*

A DIALOGUE *between* JACK ANVIL *the Blacksmith, and* TOM HOD *the Mason.*

Jack. WHAT's the matter, Tom? Why dost look so dismal?
Tom. Dismal indeed! Well enough I may.
Jack. What's the old mare dead? or work scarce?
Tom. No, no, work's plenty enough, if a man had but the heart to go to it.
Jack. What book art reading? Why dost look so like a hang dog?
Tom (looking on his book.) Cause enough. Why I find here that I'm very unhappy, and very miserable; which I should never have known if I had not had the good luck to meet with this book. O 'tis a precious book!
Jack. A good sign tho'; that you can't find out you're unhappy without looking into a book for it. What is the matter?
Tom. Matter? Why I want liberty.

---

21 Marilyn Butler, *Burke, Paine, Godwin, and the Revolution Controversy* (Cambridge: Cambridge University Press, 1984), p. 179.

Jack. Liberty! What has anyone fetched a warrant for thee? Come man, cheer up, I'll be bound for thee. – Thou art an honest fellow in the main, tho' thou dost tipple and prate a little too much at the Rose and Crown.

Tom. No, no, I want a new constitution.

Jack. Indeed! Why I thought thou hadst been a desperate healthy fellow. Send for the doctor then.

Tom. I'm not sick; I want Liberty and Equality, and the Rights of Man.

Jack. O now I understand thee. What thou art a leveller and a republican I warrant.

Tom. I'm a friend to the people. I want a reform.

Jack. Then the shortest way is to mend thyself.

Tom. But I want a *general reform*.

Jack. Then let every one mend one.

Tom. Pooh! I want freedom and happiness, the same as they have got in France.

Jack. What, Tom, we imitate them? We follow the French! Why they only begun all this mischief at first, in order to be just what *we* are already. Why I'd sooner go to the Negers to get learning, or to the Turks to get religion, than to the French for freedom and happiness.

Tom. What do you mean by that? ar'n't the French free?

Jack. Free, Tom! aye, free with a witness. They are all so free, that there's nobody safe. They make free to rob whom they will, and kill whom they will. If they don't like a man's looks, they make free to hang him without judge or jury, and the next lamp-post does for the gallows; so then they call themselves free, because you see they have no king to take them up and hang them for it.

Tom. Ah, but Jack, didn't their KING formerly hang people for nothing too? and besides, wer'n't they all papists before the Revolution?

Jack. Why, true enough, they had but a poor sort of religion, but bad is better than none, Tom. . . .

Tom. But have you read the Rights of Man?

Jack. No, not I. I had rather by half read the *Whole Duty of Man*. I have but little time for reading, and such as I should therefore only read a bit of the best.

Tom. Don't tell me of those old fashioned notions. Why should not we have the same fine things they have got in France? I'm for a *Constitution*, and *Organization*, and *Equalization*. . . .

Jack. I'll tell thee a story. When Sir John married, my Lady, who is a little fantastical, and likes to do every thing like the French, begged him to pull down yonder fine old castle, and build it up in her frippery way. No, says Sir John; what shall I pull down this noble building, raised by the wisdom of my brave ancestors; which outstood the civil wars, and only underwent a little needful repair at the Revolution;[22] and which all my neighbours come to take a pattern by – shall I pull it all down, I say, only because there may be a dark

---

22 The 'Glorious Revolution' of 1688.

closet or an inconvenient room or two in it? My lady mumpt and grumbled; but the castle was let stand, and a glorious building it is, though there may be a trifling fault or two, and tho' a few decays may want stopping; so now and then they mend a little thing, and they'll go on mending, I dare say, as they have leisure, to the end of the chapter, if they are let alone. But no pull-me-down works. What is it you are crying out for, Tom.

Tom. Why for a perfect government.

Jack. You might as well cry for the moon. There's nothing perfect in this world, take my word for it.

Tom. I don't see why we are to work like slaves, while others roll about in their coaches, feed on the fat of the land, and do nothing.

Jack. My little maid brought home a story-book from the Charity-School t'other day, in which was a bit of a fable about the Belly and the Limbs. The hands said, I won't work any longer to feed this lazy belly, who sits in state like a lord, and does nothing. Said the feet, I won't walk and tire myself to carry him about; let him shift for himself; so said all the members; just as your levellers and republicans do now. And what was the consequence? Why the belly was pinched to be sure; but the hands and the feet, and the rest of the members suffered so much for want of their old nourishment, that they fell sick, pined away, and wou'd have died, if they had not come to their senses just in time to save their lives, as I hope all you will do. . . .

Tom. And thou art very sure we are not ruined?

Jack. I'll tell thee how we are ruined. We have a king so loving, that he wou'd not hurt the people if he cou'd: and so kept in, that he cou'd not hurt the people if he wou'd. We have as much liberty as can make us happy; and more trade and riches than allows us to be good. We have the best laws in the world, if they were more strictly enforced; and the best religion in the world, if it was but better followed. While old England is safe, I'll glory in her and pray for her, and when she is in danger, I'll fight for her and die for her.

Tom. And so will I too, Jack, that's what I will. *(sings)*
'O the roast beef of old England!'

Jack. Thou art an honest fellow, Tom.

Tom. This is Rose and Crown night, and Tim Standish is now at his mischief; but we'll go and put an end to that fellow's work.

Jack. Come along.

Tom. No; first I'll stay to burn my book, and then I'll go and make a bonfire and –

Jack. Hold, Tom. There is but one thing worse than a bitter enemy, and that is an imprudent friend. If thou woud'st show thy love to thy King and country, let's have no drinking, no riot, no bonfires; but put in practice this text, which our parson preached on last Sunday, 'Study to be quiet, work with your own hands, and mind your own business.'

Tom. And so I will, Jack – Come on.

1.8   William Godwin, *Enquiry Concerning Political Justice, and its Influence on Morals and Happiness* (1793)

In Political Justice *William Godwin (1756–1836), who had assisted in the publication of Paine's* Rights of Man, *aimed to produce a wide-ranging analysis of the fundamental principles of society and government. His book was influential across several fields (see also 'Religion and Belief', extract 4.2, and 'Philosophy', extract 5.8) and the extracts below focus on issues of government and revolution. Although Godwin viewed events in France positively, he rejected the idea of revolution in general, advocating instead, reason, 'science' and the 'illumination of public understanding', which, he argued, would produce 'gradual' change until it ultimately rendered government unnecessary. This combination of rationalism and Utopianism, which drew on an Enlightenment faith in the individual and a millennial vision of the future (of the sort seen in the extracts from Richard Price (1.2) and Joseph Priestley (4.3)), was highly influential on a number of writers and thinkers at various stages in their development, including Wordsworth, Coleridge, and Shelley (who popularized Godwin's thinking in his notes to* Queen Mab). *Though* Political Justice *sold well (4,000 copies), it was expensive and addressed an educated readership. Shortly after completing it, Godwin began writing his novel* Caleb Williams *(published 1794), in which he sought to bring his arguments to the attention of a wider readership. As he argues in the novel's 'Preface': 'It is now known to philosophers that the spirit and character of government intrudes itself into every rank of society. But this is a truth highly worthy to be communicated to persons whom books of philosophy and science are never likely to reach. Accordingly it was proposed in the invention of the following work, to comprehend, as far as the progressive nature of a single story would allow, a general review of the modes of domestic and unrecorded despotism, by which man becomes the destroyer of man.'*[23]

Man is in a state of perpetual mutation. He must grow either better or worse, either correct his habits or confirm them. The government under which we are placed, must either increase our passions and prejudices by fanning the flame, or by gradually discouraging tend to extirpate them. In reality, it is impossible to conceive a government that shall have the latter tendency. By its very nature positive institution has a tendency to suspend the elasticity and progress of mind. Every scheme for embodying imperfection must be injurious. That which is to-day a considerable melioration, will at some future period, if preserved unaltered, appear a defect and disease in the body politic. It is earnestly to be desired, that each man should be wise enough to govern himself without the intervention of any compulsory restraint; and, since government even in its best

---

23 William Godwin, *Caleb Williams*, ed. David McCracken (Oxford: Oxford University Press, 1982), p. 1.

state is an evil, the object principally to be aimed at is, that we should have as little of it as the general peace of human society will permit. . . .

Revolution is engendered by an indignation against tyranny, yet is itself evermore pregnant with tyranny. The tyranny which excites its indignation can scarcely be without its partisans; and, the greater is the indignation excited, and the more sudden and vast the fall of the oppressors, the deeper will be the resentment which fills the minds of the losing party. . . .

Revolution is instigated by a horror against tyranny, yet its own tyranny is not without peculiar aggravations. There is no period more at war with the existence of liberty. The unrestrained communication of opinions has always been subjected to mischievous counteraction, but upon such occasions it is trebly fettered. At other times men are not so much alarmed for its effects. But in a moment of revolution, when every thing is in crisis, the influence even of a word is dreaded, and the consequent slavery is complete. Where was there a revolution in which a strong vindication of what it was intended to abolish was permitted, or indeed almost any species of writing or argument that was not for the most part in harmony with the opinions which happened to prevail? An attempt to scrutinise men's thoughts and punish their opinions is of all kinds of despotism the most odious; yet this attempt is peculiarly characteristic of a period of revolution. . . .

To the remark that revolutions can scarcely be unaccompanied with the shedding of blood, it may be added that they are necessarily crude and premature. Politics is a science. The general features of the nature of man are capable of being understood, and a mode may be delineated which, in itself considered, is best adapted to the condition of man in society. If this mode ought not every where and instantly to be sought to be reduced into practice, the modifications that are to be given it in conformity to the variation of circumstances, and the degrees in which it is to be realized, are also a topic of scientifical disquisition. Now it is clearly the nature of science to be progressive in its advances. How various were the stages of astronomy, before it received the degree of perfection which was given it by Newton? How imperfect were the lispings of intellectual science, before it attained the precision of the present century? Political knowledge is, no doubt, in its infancy; and, as it is an affair of life and action, will, in proportion as it gathers vigour, manifest a more uniform and less precarious influence upon the concerns of human society. It is the history of all science to be known first to a few, before it descends through the various descriptions and classes of the community. . . .

The only method according to which social improvements can be carried on with sufficient prospect of an auspicious event, is when the improvement of our institutions advances in a just proportion to the illumination of the public understanding. . . . Imperfect institutions, as has already been shown, cannot long support themselves, when they are generally disapproved of, and their effects truly understood. There is a period at which they may be expected to decline and expire almost without an effort. Reform, under this meaning of the term, can scarcely be considered as of the nature of action. Men feel their situation; and the restraints that shackled them before, vanish like a deception. When such a crisis has arrived, not a sword will need to be drawn, not a finger to be lifted up in purposes of violence. The adversaries will be too few and too feeble, to be able to entertain a serious thought of resistance against the universal sense of mankind.

Under this view of the subject then it appears that revolutions, instead of being truly beneficial to mankind, answer no other purpose than that of marring the salutary and uninterrupted progress which might be expected to attend upon political truth and social improvement. They disturb the harmony of intellectual nature. They propose to give us something for which we are not prepared, and which we cannot effectually use. They suspend the wholesome advancement of science, and confound the process of nature and reason.

1.9   Theobald Wolfe Tone, *An Address to the People of Ireland on the Present Important Crisis* (1796)

In 1791, Dublin-born (Theobald) Wolfe Tone (1763–98) was inspired by events in France and his reading of Paine's Rights of Man *to found the Society of United Irishmen. The Society initially aimed to bring together Protestants and Roman Catholics in support of reform but ultimately came to demand full independence of Ireland from Britain. Following the outbreak of war between England and France in 1793, Tone assisted the French in a number of attempts to invade Ireland (1796, 1797 and twice in 1798), none of which succeeded. Captured during the last of these attempts in October 1798, Tone committed suicide in prison while awaiting execution for high treason.*

At length the time is arrived when a friend to the Liberty and Independence of Ireland, may venture to speak the truth, and examine into the situation and interest of his country, without fear of being stopped short by that most unanswerable of all arguments, an information in the Court of King's Bench, at the suit of his Majesty's Attorney General.

It is long since every honest Irishman has mourned in secret over the misery and degradation of his native land, without daring to murmur a syllable in the way of complaint. Not even our groans were free! Six hundred years of oppression and slavery have passed in melancholy succession over our father's [sic] heads and our own, during which period we have been visited by every evil, which tyranny could devise and cruelty execute; we have been scattered, like chaff, over the land, and our name has been forgotten among the nations; we have been massacred and plundered, insulted and despised; we have been reduced to that lowest state of human degradation; we have almost ceased to respect ourselves; we have doubted whether the opinion of our oppressors was not just, and whether we were not in fact, framed for that submission, to which we have been bent by the pressure of so many centuries of hard, unremitting, unrelenting tyranny.

But if the judgments of Providence be slow, they are certain. The villain must not hope to walk in credit to his grave, nor the tyrant to insult for ever, with impunity, the misery, he has caused. The pride and arrogance of England have at length called down upon her head the tardy and lingering justice, which her manifold crimes have so long provoked; the sufferings of Ireland, prostrate and humble as she has been, even to the dust, seem to have awakened the attention of him, who rules the destiny of nations; in his goodness and compassion he has at length regarded us, and placed in our hands the means, if we have the courage to be free.

Without being too much of an enthusiastic visionary, I think I may say I see a new order of things commencing in Europe. The stupendous revolution, which has taken place in France; the unparalleled succession of events, which have, in defiance of the united efforts of all the despots of Europe, established that mighty republic on the broad and firm basis of equal rights, liberties and laws; the abasement, contrary to all human probability, of her enemies, every one of whom has, in his turn, been forced to yield to her ascendant genius, with the exception thus far, of Austria, and especially England, whose fall has only been delayed, to make her degradation more terrible, and the triumph of her victorious rival the more complete; all this, I say, has satisfied my mind, that the ancient system of tyranny must fall. In many nations it is already extinct, in others, it has received its death wound, and though it may for some time trail a feeble and lingering existence, its duration is ascertained, and its days already numbered. I do not look upon the French revolution as a question subject to the ordinary calculation of politics; *it is a thing which is to be*; and as all human experience has verified that the new doctrine ever finally subverts the old; as the Mosaic law subverted idolatry, as Christianity subverted the Jewish dispensation, as the Reformation subverted Popery, so, I am firmly convinced, the doctrine of Republicanism will finally subvert that of Monarchy, and establish a system of just and rational Liberty, on the ruins of the Thrones of the Despots of Europe.

But whether this opinion be well or ill founded, the question I mean to examine will not be affected by the result. Fortunately or unfortunately for Ireland, her cause is independent of the theory. The object for her immediate consideration, is not whether she shall adopt this or that form of Government, but whether she shall be independent under any. She has too many solid, substantial, heavy, existing grievances, to require much ingenuity, or subtle argument, to convince her of her interest and her duty, and the question on which we must take an instant determination will, if I mistake not, be decided as soon as it is stated.

The alternative which is now submitted to your choice, with regard to England is, in one word, UNION OR SEPARATION! You must determine, and that instantly, between slavery and independence, there is no third way. I will not insult you, by doubting what will be your decision. I anticipate your immediate and unanimous declaration, which establishes for ever Liberty to yourselves, and Independence to your country.

To a magnanimous people it is unnecessary to prove that it is *base*, to an enlightened people it is unnecessary to prove that it is *ruinous*, to exist in dependance on the will of a foreign power, and that power an ambitious rival. To you this is not matter of mere speculation – you feel it in your government, in your laws, in your manners, in your principles, in your education; with all the great moral and physical advantages of which you are possessed, you are unnoticed and unknown as a nation in Europe; your bodies and your minds are bent down by the incumbent pressure of your tyrant; she, to maintain whose avarice and ambition you are forced to spill your best blood, in whose cause you fight without glory, and without profit, where victory but rivets your chains the faster, and where defeat adds to slavery, mortification and disgrace. In vain are you placed in the most advantageous position for unlimited commerce, in vain are you blessed with a fruitful soil, with every requisite for trade and manufactures, with inexhaustible mines, with navigable rivers, and with the noblest harbours in Europe. All these advantages are blasted by the contagious presence of your imperious rival, before whose influence your strength is withered, your resources crushed, and the rising spirit of emulation strangled in the birth. It is England, who debauches and degrades your gentry; it is England, who starves your manufacturers, to drive them into her fleets and armies; it is England, who keeps your wretched peasantry half-fed, half-clothed, miserable and despised, defrauded of their just rights, as human beings, and reduced, if the innate spirit of your country did not support them, as it were, by a miracle, below the level of the beasts of the field; it is England who buys your legislators, to betray you, and pays them by money levied on yourselves; it is England, who foments and perpetuates, as far as in her lies, the spirit of religious dissension among you, and that labours to keep asunder Irishman from Irishman, because that in your cordial Union among yourselves, she sees clearly the downfall of her usurpation, and the establishment of your liberties; it is England, who supports that rotten, aristocratic faction among you, which, though not the tenth part of your population, has arrogated to itself five-sixths of the property, and the whole of the patronage and power of your nation; a faction which to maintain itself by the power of England, is ready to sacrifice, and does daily sacrifice your dearest rights to her insatiable lust of gold and power.

1.10 William Thomas Fitzgerald, 'Britons, to Arms', *The Gentleman's Magazine* (1803)

Fitzgerald's poem is part of the huge outpouring of patriotic verse prompted by the French invasion threat. This threat was at its most intense in 1796–8 and 1803–5; during the latter period a French force of 140,000 men designated the 'Army of

England' were encamped along the north coast of France, equipped with 2,000 vessels. Part of the British response was the development of a volunteer force, which grew to 400,000 men in 1803. According to some estimates, during the invasion crisis as many as one in five of all male adults was a member of the armed forces in either a voluntary or an enrolled position. William Thomas Fitzgerald (1759–1829) was a prolific producer of patriotic and anti-Napoleonic poetry throughout the war, culminating in a popular poem on the Battle of Waterloo (perhaps one reason for Byron's attack on him in English Bards and Scotch Reviewers*). 'Britons, to Arms' gained a wide circulation as a broadside and was reprinted in* The Anti-Gallican *in 1804 (the source for the current text). Fitzgerald had himself recited it to a meeting of the Literary Fund, an organization supporting impoverished writers, of which he was vice-president. 'Britons, to Arms' diplays many of the characteristic tropes of patriotic poetry, including: the call to arms; the linking of nation, church and monarch; the invocation of great national victories and heroes of the past and present; the derogation of the French 'other'; the celebration of Britain's island geography; the enlistment of fate; the stress on Britain's divinely sanctioned role; and the prophecy of ultimate victory.*

BRITONS, to ARMS! of apathy beware,
And let your COUNTRY be your dearest care;
Protect your ALTARS! guard your monarch's Throne,
The Cause of GEORGE and Freedom is your own!
What! shall that ENGLAND want her SONS' support,
Whose HEROES fought at CRESSY[24] – AGINCOURT?[25]
And when GREAT MARLB'ROUGH[26] led the English van,
In FRANCE, o'er FRENCHMEN, triumph'd to a man!
By ALFRED's[27] great and ever honour'd name!
By EDWARD's prowess, and by HENRY's fame!
By all the gen'rous blood for freedom shed,
And by the Ashes of the patriot dead!
By the bright glory Britons lately won
On EGYPT's plains,[28] beneath the burning sun,

---

24 Fitzgerald's note: 'In the year 1346, Edward, Prince of Wales (commonly called the Black Prince), son of our King Edward III, gained the famous battle of Cressy, in which thirty thousand of the French were killed upon the field.'

25 Fitzgerald's note: 'In the year 1415, Henry V. King of England invaded France, and gained the memorable battle of Agincourt, when ten thousand of the French were slain, and fourteen thousand were taken prisoners. The prisoners were more in number than the victorious English army!'

26 Fitzgerald's note: 'In Queen Anne's reign, A.D. 1706, the great Duke of Marlborough gained the renowned battle of Blenheim. 12,000 French were slain and 13,000 taken prisoners, together with the French general, Marshal Tallard.'

27 Alfred the Great (c.849–99), King of Wessex and England who defeated an invading Viking force.

28 Britain's campaign against France in Egypt, 1798–1801.

> BRITONS, to ARMS! defend your Country's cause,
> Fight for your KING! your LIBERTIES! and LAWS!
> Be France defied, her slavish YOKE abhorr'd,
> And place your safety only on your Sword.
> The Gallic DESPOT, sworn your mortal FOE,
> Now aims his last, but his most deadly blow;
> With ENGLAND's PLUNDER tempts his hungry Slaves,
> And dares to brave you on your native waves!
> If Britain's rights be worth a Briton's care,
> To shield them from the son of Rapine – *swear*!
> Then to INVASION be defiance given,
> Your Cause is just, approv'd by earth and heaven!
> Should adverse winds our gallant Fleet restrain,
> To sweep his 'bawbling'[29] vessels from the main;
> And Fate permit him on our shores t'advance,
> The TYRANT never shall return to FRANCE;
> Fortune herself shall be no more his Friend,
> And *here* the history of his crimes shall end –
> His slaughter'd Legions shall manure our shore,
> And ENGLAND never know Invasion more.

1.11   Anon., 'The British Heroes', *The Anti-Gallican* (1804)

Women played a major role in the conflict against France, participating in patriotic events, fund raising, donating money, and making flags and banners for militia and volunteer units. This poem celebrates this female participation in the war, presenting women in chivalric terms as the inspiration for fighting.

> The war's begun, the British fair
>   All weakness overcome;
> The harp and lyre beneath their care,
>   Now hail the sprightly drum.
>
> Like Sparta's matrons nobly great,
>   Wives, mothers, daughter vie
> Who most shall heroes animate
>   To conquer or to die.

---

29 Shakespeare, *Twelfth Night*, V.i.33.

Sound the trumpet loud!
  Bid the minstrel join
The prayer of yonder lovely crowd;
  For our sons of fame,
In sounds divine,
Invoking each auspicious name
  In battle to defend them.
Hail! they exclaim, rending the air,
  O listen to our fervent prayer,
May victory attend them!

See, with delight, some lovely fair
  Her parting hero deck,
A laurel wreath adorn his hair,
  Her portrait grace his neck.

Thus armed, he pants to join th'attack;
  She firmly bids him go,
And warns him soon to bring her back
  Some trophy from the foe.

Sound the trumpet loud, &c.

A mother cries, 'My love's first joy,
  Go, fame and honour bring;
From me thou hold'st thy life, dear boy,
  In trust, to serve thy king:

Yet, from the reeking slaughter come,
  Whatever chance betide,
In safety bring thy father home,
  Or perish by his side.'

Sound the trumpet loud, &c.

Thus shall the lovely British dame
  To latest times be sung;
Great, brave, and noble, as the fame,
  And honour whence she sprung.

Thus heroes perils shall survive,
  Shall love and glory share;
And, angel-guarded, shall derive
  Protection from the fair.

Sound the trumpet loud, &c.

1.12   Robert Southey, *The Life of Nelson* (1813)

Vice-Admiral Horatio Nelson (1758–1805) was killed at the Battle of Trafalgar in October 1805, a British victory over the French and Spanish fleets that ended the invasion threat and ensured British naval supremacy for the rest of the war (significantly strengthening Britain's colonial power). Nelson's death was the culmination of a high-profile (and at times controversial) career that had already turned him into a cult figure and embodiment of Britishness. He was given a state funeral at St Paul's Cathedral and Benjamin West's painting The Death of Nelson *drew large crowds when it was exhibited in 1806.* The Life of Nelson *by the former 'Jacobin Poet' turned Poet Laureate, Robert Southey (1774–1843; on Jacobin poetry, see also extract 8.3), was published in 1813 and crystallized the heroic image of the national martyr at a time when England was still at war with France. Southey himself described the book as 'the eulogy of our great Naval Hero'.[30] Immediately popular, it contributed to the period's increasing glorification of military and naval heroes, which sought to bolster British morale. Even Byron, supporter of Napoleon and future antagonist of Southey, praised the* Life of Nelson *as 'beautiful'.[31] The extract below is taken from the close of the biography.*

The death of Nelson was felt in England as something more than a public calamity; men started at the intelligence, and turned pale, as if they had heard of the loss of a dear friend. An object of our admiration and affection, of our pride and of our hopes, was suddenly taken from us; and it seemed as if we had never, till then, known how deeply we loved and reverenced him. What the country had lost in its great naval Hero – the greatest of our own, and of all former times, was scarcely taken into the account of grief. So perfectly, indeed, had he performed his part, that the maritime war, after the battle of Trafalgar, was considered at an end: the fleets of the enemy were not merely defeated, but destroyed: new navies must be built, and a new race of seamen reared for them, before the possibility of their invading our shores could again be contemplated. It was not, therefore, from any selfish reflection upon the magnitude of our loss that we mourned for him: the general sorrow was of a higher character. The people of England grieved that funeral ceremonies, public monuments, and posthumous rewards, were all which they could now bestow upon him, whom the king, the legislature, and the nation, would alike have delighted to honour; whom every tongue would have blessed; whose presence in every village through which he might have passed would have wakened the church bells, have given schoolboys a holiday, have drawn children from their sports to gaze upon him, and 'old men

30 Quoted in W. A. Speck, *Robert Southey: Entire Man of Letters* (New Haven, Conn., and London: Yale University Press, 2006), p. 151.
31 Lord Byron, *Byron's Letters and Journals*, 12 vols, ed. Leslie Marchand (London: John Murray, 1973–82), III, 214.

from the chimney corner,'[32] to look upon Nelson ere they died. The victory of Trafalgar was celebrated, indeed, with the usual forms of rejoicing, but they were without joy; for such already was the glory of the British navy, through Nelson's surpassing genius, that it scarcely seemed to receive any addition from the most signal victory that ever was achieved upon the seas: and the destruction of this mighty fleet, by which all the maritime schemes of France were totally frustrated, hardly appeared to add to our security or strength; for, while Nelson was living, to watch the combined squadrons of the enemy, we felt ourselves as secure as now, when they were no longer in existence.

There was reason to suppose, from the appearances upon opening the body, that in the course of nature he might have attained, like his father, to a good old age. Yet he cannot be said to have fallen prematurely whose work was done; nor ought he to be lamented who died so full of honours, at the height of human fame. The most triumphant death is that of the martyr; the most awful, that of the martyred patriot; the most splendid, that of the hero in the hour of victory: and if the chariot and horses of fire had been vouchsafed for Nelson's translation, he could scarcely have departed in a brighter blaze of glory. He has left us, not indeed his mantle of inspiration, but a name and an example, which are at this hour inspiring thousands of the youth of England: a name which is our pride, and an example which will continue to be our shield and our strength. Thus it is that the spirits of the great and the wise continue to live and to act after them.

1.13   Richard Whately, *Historic Doubts Relative to Napoleon Buonaparte* (1819)

The Battle of Waterloo in 1815 brought to an end the military and political career of Napoleon Bonaparte (1769–1821), the dominating figure of the Romantic period, who had risen from being a general in the French campaigns of the 1790s to become Emperor of France in 1804. He would die imprisoned on the island of St Helena in 1821. British reactions to Napoleon were polarized; Hazlitt acclaimed him as 'the greatest man in modern history',[33] Byron adopted him as a personal idol and declared himself 'the grand Napoleon of the realms of rhyme' (Don Juan, XI. 55), while Wordsworth saw his coronation in 1804 as symbolizing the French return to absolute monarchy. To the majority of Britons he was best known as the comic 'Little Boney' of Gillray's caricatures or the terrifying monster of the propaganda war. This essay by Archbishop Richard Whately (1787–1863), a critique of David Hume's 'Essay on Miracles', was written two years before Napoleon died and juxtaposes the various highly contradictory contemporary opinions of Napoleon (as Whately comments:

---

32 Sir Philip Sidney, *Defense of Poesy*: 'and with a tale forsooth he cometh unto you, with a tale which holdeth children from play, and old men from the chimney corner'.
33 William Hazlitt, *The Complete Works of William* Hazlitt, 21 vols, ed. P. P. Howe (London: J. M. Dent, 1930–4), XX, 57.

'According to some, he was a wise, humane, magnanimous hero; others paint him as a
monster of cruelty, meanness, and perfidy'). Whately gives a lively account of
Napoleon's career, and illustrates how its extraordinary scale seemed comprehensible
only through reference to fictional narrative.

If it be doubtful whether any history (exclusive of such as is avowedly fabulous)
ever attributed to its hero such a series of wonderful achievements compressed
into so small a space of time, it is certain that to no one were ever assigned so
many dissimilar characters. . . . This obscure Corsican adventurer, a man, according to some, of extraordinary talents and courage, according to others, of very
moderate abilities, and a rank coward, advanced rapidly in the French army,
obtained a high command, gained a series of important victories, and, elated by
success, embarked in an expedition against Egypt, which was planned and
conducted, according to some, with the most consummate skill, according to
others, with the utmost wildness and folly: he was unsuccessful however, and leaving the army of Egypt in a very distressed situation, he returned to France, and
found the nation, or at least the army, so favourably disposed towards him, that
he was enabled, with the utmost ease, to overthrow the existing government, and
obtain for himself the supreme power; at first under the modest appellation of
Consul, but afterwards with the more sounding title of Emperor. While in possession of this power, he overthrew the most powerful coalitions of the other
European States against him, and though driven from the sea by the British fleets,
overran nearly the whole continent triumphant; finishing a war, not unfrequently
in a single campaign, he entered the capitals of most of the hostile potentates,
deposed and created Kings at his pleasure, and appeared the virtual sovereign of
the chief part of the continent, from the frontiers of Spain to those of Russia. Even
those countries we find him invading with prodigious armies, defeating their
forces, penetrating to their capitals, and threatening their total subjugation: but at
Moscow his progress is stopped: a winter of unusual severity, cooperating with the
efforts of the Russians, totally destroys his enormous host; and the German sovereigns throw off the yoke, and combine to oppose him. He raises another vast army,
which is also ruined at Leipsic: and again another, with which, like a second
Antæus, he for some time maintains himself in France, but is finally defeated,
deposed, and banished to the island of Elba, of which the sovereignty is conferred
on him: thence he returns in about nine months at the head of 600 men, to
attempt the deposition of King Lewis, who had been peaceably recalled; the French
nation declare in his favour, and he is reinstated without a struggle. He raises
another great army to oppose the allied powers, which is totally defeated at
Waterloo: he is a second time deposed, surrenders to the British, and is placed in
confinement at the island of St. Helena. Such is the outline of the eventful history
presented to us; in the detail of which, however, there is almost every conceivable
variety of statement; while the motives and conduct of the chief actor are involved
in still greater doubt, and the subject of still more eager controversy. . . .

Let us then consider what sort of a story it is that is proposed to our acceptance. How grossly contradictory are the reports of the different authorities, I have already remarked: but consider by itself the story told by any one of them; it carries an air of fiction and romance on the very face of it: all the events are great, and splendid, and marvellous; great armies, great victories, great frosts, great reverses, 'hair-breadth 'scapes,'[34] empires subverted in a few days; every thing happening in defiance of political calculations, and in opposition to the *experience* of past times; every thing upon that grand scale, so common in epic poetry, so rare in real life; and thus calculated to strike the imagination of the vulgar, – and to remind the sober-thinking few of the Arabian nights. Every event too has that *roundness* and completeness which is so characteristic of fiction; nothing is done by halves; we have *complete* victories, – *total* overthrows, – *entire* subversion of empires, – *perfect* re-establishments of them, – crowded upon us in rapid succession. . . . In vain will [any judicious man] seek in history for something similar to this wonderful Buonaparte; 'nought but himself can be his parallel.'

1.14   Richard Carlile, 'On Peterloo', *Sherwin's Weekly Political Register* (1819)

The period after Waterloo in Britain was one of considerable economic hardship and political unrest, caused by a series of related factors including postwar unemployment, a fall in wages, a series of bad harvests, increased bread prices, the 1815 Corn Laws, disillusionment over the results of the war, and anxiety about the mechanization of production (the Luddite riots of 1811–12 had already produced large-scale destruction of machinery used in wool and cotton manufacture in Lancashire and Yorkshire). The most notorious event of these years was the so-called 'Peterloo Massacre' of 16 August 1819, when a peaceful gathering of about 60,000 people in support of parliamentary reform at St Peter's Field in Manchester was charged by the yeoman cavalry, resulting in at least ten fatalities and several hundred injured. The event became known as Peterloo in mocking reference to the British victory at Waterloo. Percy Shelley famously expressed his outrage at the event in his poem 'The Mask of Anarchy', though signifi-cantly this was not published until 1832. The radical writer Richard Carlile (1790–1843) wrote an eyewitness account of the event for the newspaper Sherwin's Weekly Political Register, *published on 18 August.*

Mr. Hunt began his discourse by thanking [the assembled crowd] for the favour conferred on him, and made some ironical observations on the conduct of the Magistrates, when a cart, which evidently took its direction from that part of the

---

34 Shakespeare, *Othello*, I.iii.154.

field where the police and magistrates were assembled in a house, was moved through the middle of the field to the great annoyance and danger of the assembled people, who quietly endeavoured to make way for its procedure. The cart had no sooner made its way through, when the Yeomanry Cavalry made their appearance from the same quarter as the cart had gone out. They galloped furiously round the field, going over every person who would not get out of their way, to the spot where the police were fixed, and after a moment's pause, they received the cheers of the police as a signal for attack. The meeting at the entrance of the cavalry, and from the commencement of business was one of the most calm and orderly that I ever witnessed – Hilarity was seen on tbe countenance of all, whilst the Female Reformers crowned the assemblage with a grace, and excited a feeling particularly interesting. The Yeomanry Cavalry made their charge with a most infuriate frenzy; they cut down men, women, and children, indiscriminately, and appeared to have commenced a premeditated attack with the most insatiable thirst for blood and destruction. They merit a medallion on one side of which should be inscribed 'The slaughter-men of Manchester', and a reverse bearing a description of their slaughter of defenceless men, women and children, unprovoked and unnecessary. As a proof of premeditated murder on the part of the magistrates, every stone was gathered fom the ground, on the Friday and Saturday previous to the meeting, by scavengers sent there by the express command of the magistrates, that the populace might be rendered more defenceless.

1.15   Thomas Babington Macaulay, *A Speech Delivered in the House of Commons, in the Debate of Wednesday, March 2, 1831, on Lord John Russell's Motion for Leave to Bring in a Bill to Amend the Representation of the People in England and Wales* (1831)

The Reform Act of 1832 was the culmination of the various campaigns that had agitated for parliamentary reform since the Battle of Waterloo in 1815. Many activists were disappointed by the limited reforms introduced by the Bill, which abolished a number of boroughs with only a small number of voters and increased representation for urban areas, but only extended the franchise to 20 to 30 per cent of the adult male population. However, the Bill has also been seen as a key stage in the development of modern democracy. Thomas Babington Macaulay (1800–59) made the following passionate speech in support of the Reform Bill during its passage through the House of Commons in 1831, locating the call for reform within the contexts of other recent reforms in Britain (Catholic emancipation and the repeal of the Test and Corporation Acts, see extract 4.10) and the 1830 revolutions in Europe.

All history is full of revolutions produced by causes similar to those which are now operating in England. A portion of the community which had been of no account, expands and becomes strong. It demands a place in the system, suited, not to its former weakness, but to its present power. If this is granted, all is well. If this is refused, then comes the struggle between the young energy of one class and the ancient privileges of another. . . . [This] is the struggle which the middle classes in England are maintaining against an aristocracy of mere locality – against an aristocracy, the principle of which is to invest a hundred drunken pot-wallopers in one place, or the owner of a ruined hovel in another, with powers which are withheld from cities renowned to the furthest ends of the earth for the marvels of their wealth and of their industry. . . .

Since that declaration[35] was made nearly four years have elapsed; and what is now the state of the three questions that chiefly agitated the minds of men? What is become of the Test and Corporation acts? They are repealed. By whom? By the late administration. What has become of the Catholic disabilities? They are removed? By whom? By the late administration. The question of Parliamentary Reform is still behind. But signs, of which it is impossible to misconceive the import, do most clearly indicate, that, unless that great question also be speedily settled, property and order, and all the institutions of this great monarchy, will be exposed to fearful peril. Is it possible that gentlemen long versed in high political affairs cannot read these signs? Is it possible that they can really believe that the representative system of England, such as it now is, will last till the year 1860? If not, for what would they have us wait? Would they have us wait merely that we may show to all the world how little we have profited by our own recent experience? Would they have us wait that we may once again hit the exact point where we can neither refuse with authority nor concede with grace? Would they have us wait that the numbers of the discontented party may become larger, its demands higher, its feelings more acrimonious, its organization more complete? Would they have us wait till the whole tragi-comedy of 1827 has been acted over again; till they have been brought into office by a cry of 'No Reform!' to be reformers, as they were once before brought into office by a cry of 'No Popery!' to be emancipators? Have they obliterated from their minds – gladly perhaps would some among them obliterate from their minds – the transactions of that year? And have they forgotten all the transactions of the succeeding year? Have they forgotten how the spirit of liberty in Ireland, debarred from its natural outlet, found a vent by forbidden passages? Have they forgotten how we were forced to indulge the Catholics in all the licence of rebels, merely because we chose to withhold from them the liberties of subjects? Do they wait for associations more formidable than that of the Corn Exchange, – for contributions larger

---

35 By Sir Robert Peel, in May 1827, that he would not resist the repeal of the Test and Corporation Acts and the reform of Parliament.

than the rent, – for agitators more violent than those who, three years ago, divided with the King and the Parliament the sovereignty of Ireland? Do they wait for that last and most dreadful paroxysm of popular rage – for that last and most cruel test of military fidelity? . . .

Turn where we may, – within, – around, – the voice of great events is proclaiming to us, Reform, that you may preserve.

Now, therefore, while everything at home and abroad forebodes ruin to those who persist in a hopeless struggle against the spirit of the age, – now, while the crash of the proudest throne of the Continent is still resounding in our ears, – now, while the roof of a British palace affords an ignominious shelter to the exiled heir of forty kings, – now, while we see on every side ancient institutions subverted and great societies dissolved, – now, while the heart of England is still sound, – now, while the old feelings and the old associations retain a power and a charm which may too soon pass away, – now in this your accepted time, – now in this your day of salvation, – take counsel, – not of prejudice, – not of party-spirit, – not of the ignominious pride of a fatal consistency, – but of history, – of reason, – of the ages which are past, – of the signs of this most portentous time. Pronounce in a manner worthy of the expectation with which this great debate has been anticipated, and of the long remembrance which it will leave behind. Renew the youth of the state. Save property divided against itself. Save the multitude, endangered by their own ungovernable passions. Save the aristocracy, endangered by its own unpopular power. Save the greatest, and fairest, and most highly civilised community that ever existed, from calamities which may in a few days sweep away all the rich heritage of so many ages of wisdom and glory. The danger is terrible. The time is short. If this bill should be rejected, I pray to God that none of those who concur in rejecting it may ever remember their votes with unavailing regret, amidst the wreck of laws, the confusion of ranks, the spoliation of property, and the dissolution of social order.

2
Society, Politics and Class

Introduction

Many accounts of the writing and culture of the Romantic period have stressed the link with the complex and much debated set of economic, social and demographic developments grouped together under the term 'the Industrial Revolution'. While historians have debated the nature and duration of this 'revolution' (some arguing for 'evolution' and others that the whole idea is a 'myth'), to many of those living at the time it certainly felt like an age of rapid change and social upheaval, as the extracts contained within this section illustrate. These extracts comment on the major features which have been seen to characterize the onset of this process of transformation, including: rapid overall population growth; rural depopulation, caused in part by the acceleration of the enclosure movement; expansion in the number and size of large towns and cities; the acceleration and mechanization of production (driven by the harnessing of steam power, creating the 'factory system' with what was seen to be its dehumanizing effects on the workforce); the despoliation of the landscape; and the widening gap in wealth between the upper and (emerging) middle classes and the poor.

The period was certainly one of dramatic growth in population, which increased in England from 6.4 million in 1771 to 13 million in 1831.[1] While this provided the supply of cheap labour that contributed to the accelerating economy, it also placed enormous stress on social formations and infrastructures, such as the various provisions made for poor relief (extract 2.1). The issue of the spiralling population prompted one of the most controversial yet influential texts of the period, Thomas Malthus's *Essay on the Principle of Population* (extract 2.5), the pessimistic predictions of which prompted many (including the Prime Minister, William Pitt) to rethink their ideas about scarcity and poverty. A number of the extracts in this section (2.1, 2.4, 2.7) highlight the issue of poverty, especially rural poverty, which became a major literary theme in the period, seen in the impoverished vagabonds, beggars and widows of

---

1 *An Oxford Companion to the Romantic Age: British Culture, 1776–1832*, ed. Iain McCalman et al. (Oxford: Oxford University Press, 1999), p. 654.

Wordsworth's poetry (e.g. 'Simon Lee, the Old Huntsman', 'The Old Cumberland Beggar' and Margaret of 'The Ruined Cottage') and central to the writing of John Clare, whose poetry powerfully conveys the sense of social disorientation and dislocation felt by many who experienced the changes in the rural environment, particularly those brought about by enclosure. Enclosure was the process in which common land and wastelands available to all for cultivation, grazing, wood-gathering and game-hunting were converted into private property and divided by boundaries (the origin of many of the dry-stone walls associated with the English landscape). Enclosure increased the efficiency of land use and contributed significantly to the growth in agricultural productivity characteristic of the eighteenth century. It reached its peak during the Revolutionary and Napoleonic Wars, which witnessed the passing of nearly half of all English enclosure Acts. Enclosure benefited larger farmers or landholders but at the cost of cottagers as a result of lost common grazing land and the decreased demand for labour. Clare, who himself experienced the dislocation frequently caused by enclosure, compared its devastating effect to that of a foreign invasion in his poem 'Remembrances', writing: 'Inclosure like a Buonaparte let not a thing remain / It levelled every bush and tree and levelled every hill / And hung the moles for traitors.'[2]

The increase in population and the problem of social impoverishment have frequently been linked to what has been seen as another of the major societal changes in the period, the shift from a predominantly rural and agricultural nation to an urban and manufacture-based one. Again, such an argument involves a generalization, and historians have emphasized the gradual nature of this change, but 'the encreasing accumulation of men in cities' was one of the developments that characterized for Wordsworth the age in which he lived.[3] The population of London doubled to over a million people between 1700 and 1810, making it the largest city in the world (and inspiring both wonder and horror in its residents and visitors), while the fastest growing cities were Liverpool, Manchester, Birmingham, Leeds and Sheffield.[4] These developments not only changed the shape of the nation, they distorted the already highly unrepresentative political system; by 1801 Manchester had grown to a population of 89,000 but it remained without a Member of Parliament until the Great Reform Act of 1832 (section 2.8, see also 1.15). These newer cities of the industrial north and midlands were growing up around the 'factory system', which saw the mechanization of production, most notably in the textile mills of Lancashire and Yorkshire. Significant technological advances during the eighteenth century, perhaps most importantly James Watt's adaptation of his steam-engine for use in the textile industry, made possible vastly increased production, but the

---

2 *John Clare*, ed. Eric Robinson and David Powell (Oxford: Oxford University Press, 1984), p. 260.
3 'Preface' to *Lyrical Ballads*, *William Wordsworth: The Major Works*, ed. Stephen Gill (Oxford: Oxford University Press, 1984), p. 599.
4 *Oxford Companion*, p. 137.

demands placed on the workforce by the new methods of labour and forms of living became an issue of public concern and political activism. These ranged from the campaigns for legislative factory reform of the sort led by Richard Oastler (extract 2.9), through schemes for improved living and working conditions such as those introduced by Robert Owen (extract 2.6), to the Luddite destruction of machinery in 1811 (which resulted in government legislation that made frame-breaking punishable by death, legislation against which the poet Lord Byron spoke in the House of Lords). Literary writers of the period commented directly on industrialization, perhaps most famously William Blake, who denounced the 'dark Satanic mills' that were despoiling 'England's green and pleasant land'. Colebrookdale, the location of the iron works that cast the world's first iron bridge, was the subject of both a famous painting by Phillipe-Jacques de Loutherbourg which captures the sublimity of the new industrial processes, and of a poem by Anna Seward which presents industrialization as the violation of the countryside:

> . . . red the countless fires,
> With umbered flames, bicker on thy hills,
> Darkening the Summer's sun with columns large
> Of thick, sulphureous smoke, which spread, like palls,
> That screen the dead, upon the sylvan robe
> Of thy aspiring rocks; pollute thy gales,
> And stain thy glassy waters.
>
> ('Colebrook Dale')[5]

More generally, critics have debated the extent to which the intensified literary interest in 'Nature' and the landscape in the period was a nostalgic and idealizing reaction to the broader social changes that, to contemporaries at least, appeared to be transforming the world in which they lived.

2.1 Philip Thicknesse, *An Account of the Four Persons Found Starved to Death, at Datchworth in Hertfordshire* (1769)

Philip Thicknesse (1719–92) was a soldier and author whose pamphlet illustrates the problems, abuses and potentially tragic outcomes of the Poor Law system which was in operation in England until the Poor Law Amendment Act of 1834. This system dated back to the Poor Law Act of 1601 and made each parish responsible for the care of its poor. Under this system, Justices of the Peace and leading members of the church and parish (known as the 'vestry') decided on the level of assistance to be given to the poor,

---

5 Andrew Ashfield, *Romantic Women Poets, 1770–1838: An Anthology* (Manchester: Manchester University Press, 1995), p. 7.

and their judgements were carried out by overseers and parish officers. As Thicknesse suggests, poor rate was frequently paid not to the incapacitated but as temporary relief to the able-bodied who provided the source of low-cost labour (that, in much economic theory, would help the growth of the nation's wealth). Thicknesse, who was one of the Jurymen who investigated the incident described below, published his account for the benefit of the surviving child, 'a boy of eleven years of age, [who] was found crawling on the floor amidst the dead bodies of his father, mother, brother and sister, cramp'd and emaciated'.

The following Narrative of an affair so shocking to humanity, and so alarming in this country, (famed throughout the World for charity and benevolence) however simply told, cannot but make a deep impression on the mind of every reader, who possesses one spark of humanity or feeling for the woes of his fellow creatures. I have neither abilities nor inclination to work upon the passions of the reader; nor any motive to publish this account, but the hopes that it may not only prove to have a good effect with those *in this parish who may have neglected their duty*; but that in every parish throughout the kingdom, those, whose more immediate care it is to provide for the Poor, may be roused to a sense of their duty.

To succour and relieve the distressed, is a great and God-like act; and it is undoubtedly the duty, and in the power of every individual to do it: And yet in no kingdom are the Poor more hardly dealt with than in this; especially in extensive, but obscure parishes, where scarce any gentlemen reside. In these it is usual for three or four *upstart* necessitous freeholders to combine to form a vestry, and engross the whole power of every kind into their own hands. I need not go *far from my own house to find such a parish*, and I fear many hundred persons in this kingdom can say the same. Where this is the case, and such low *upstart* people get the lead, the Poor of every denomination become greater slaves, and stand more in awe of the churchwardens, overseers, and all parish officers, than a *Guinea* slave does of an overseer in any of our plantations in America; and the money *which is raised for the Poor*, is in general most shamefully applied, for it is not given to the REAL objects of compassion, but to such who are most ABLE and WILLING to make *their lords and masters* some kind of return.

Having said thus much, I shall proceed to relate, from the evidence of my own eyes, and the testimony of many witnesses examined on oath, the condition, illness, and death of the four persons, namely, *James Eaves*, his wife, and two children.

On the 23d of January, 1769, a day-labourer, who lately lived in a poor-house belonging to this parish, told me, that four or five persons were found dead in a poor-house on the green, and that they perish'd for want of food, rayment, attendance, and a habitable dwelling. Unable and unwilling to believe it, I set out with an intention to examine into the truth of so alarming a report; a report which the extreme severity of the weather alone induced me to give any credit to. However, I immediately went to the place, where I found a small hut, consisting of one room, without floor or ceiling, 14 feet long and 12 feet broad, unthatch'd in some places, a window frame without any glass at one end, and on the opposite side a large hole in the plaistering, through which I could have got, and in at which I look'd. There I beheld the four dead bodies, emaciated beyond any conception, lying on a very small quantity of dirty peas straw, spread on the bare earth. The man had on a piece of a shirt, the woman was quite naked, as were the children; nor had they any other cloaths or covering but the remnant of an old blanket and a sack. So that I cannot conceive, had every table in the parish provided them with meat and drink, and the Almighty with health, but they must have perish'd with cold in such a house, and in such a naked condition.

Upon a strict enquiry amongst the neighbours, I found they had been so ill, as to be confined from last Saturday three weeks; and that this day fortnight one of *the overseers of the parish poor* came and left half a crown for them, directing a neighbour to get them *some tea*, or other sustenance; and this neighbour did ask them what should be brought with it: The woman replied, imperfectly, *a faggot, some brown sugar, and a candle*, which were bought accordingly; and put, together with the change of the half crown, in the house near them. From this time, however, till eleven days after, (when they were by a shepherd's boy accidentally discov'd to be dead) it does not appear, that either parish officer, or neighbour, had the humanity to enter the house, to look in at the holes, or window, or to take the least notice of their well-known wretched, and starving condition: For they perceived, and acknowledge that no fire was made with the purchased faggot; and that they had seen no smoke to issue from their chimney for a fortnight before they were found dead; at which time the same faggot, the change, and the candle lay, as they were left by the neighbour who fetch'd them.

2.2 Adam Smith, *An Inquiry into the Nature and Causes of the Wealth of Nations* (1776)

Adam Smith (1723–90) has became best known as the advocate of free trade in The Wealth of Nations, *though his economic ideas were part of a more general theory of moral philosophy that placed considerable emphasis on the role of 'sentiments' (see extract 5.4 from* The Theory of Moral Sentiments). *The extract below includes Smith's famous definition of the 'invisible hand', central to his account of the free market, which works through the laws of supply and demand to benefit the poor as well as the rich. Though individuals are driven to act by their 'private interests and passions', the 'invisible hand' ensures that these economic actions promote the best interests of society. Smith's argument challenged the established 'mercantile system' that operated in Britain, whereby government intervention sought to ensure a strong balance of trade with other countries, and it has remained highly influential in the discipline of economics, of which Smith is often seen as the founding father.*

Every individual is continually exerting himself to find out the most advantageous employment for whatever capital he can command. It is his own advantage, indeed, and not that of the society, which he has in view. But the study of
his own advantage naturally, or rather necessarily leads him to prefer that
employment which is most advantageous to the society. . . .

. . . [T]he annual revenue of every society is always precisely equal to the
exchangeable value of the whole annual produce of its industry, or rather is
precisely the same thing with that exchangeable value. As every individual,
therefore, endeavours as much as he can both to employ his capital in the
support of domestick industry, and so to direct that industry that its produce
may be of the greatest value; every individual necessarily labours to render the
annual revenue of the society as great as he can. He generally, indeed, neither
intends to promote the publick interest, nor knows how much he is promoting
it. By preferring the support of domestick to that of foreign industry he intends
only his own security; and by directing that industry in such a manner as its
produce may be of the greatest value, he intends only his own gain, and he is in
this, as in many other cases, led by an invisible hand to promote an end which
was no part of his intention. Nor is it always the worse for the society that it was
no part of it. By pursuing his own interest he frequently promotes that of the
society more effectually than when he really intends to promote it. I have never
known much good done by those who affected to trade for the publick good. It
is an affectation, indeed, not very common among merchants, and very few
words need be employed in dissuading them from it. . . .

It is thus that the private interests and passions of individuals naturally dispose
them to turn their stock towards the employments which in ordinary cases are
most advantageous to the society. But if from this natural preference they should
turn too much of it towards those employments, the fall of profit in them and
the rise of it in all others immediately dispose them to alter this faulty distribution. Without any intervention of law, therefore, the private interests and
passions of men naturally lead them to divide and distribute the stock of every
society, among all the different employments carried on in it, as nearly as possible in the proportion which is most agreeable to the interest of the whole society.

All the different regulations of the mercantile system, necessarily derange
more or less this natural and most advantageous distribution of stock.

2.3 Jeremy Bentham, *An Introduction to the Principles of Morals and Legislation* (1789)

*A major writer in a number of fields (especially law and philosophy), Jeremy Bentham
(1748–1832) is particularly associated with Utilitarianism, the branch of philosophy*

which finds value in what Bentham terms the 'principle of utility', an idea most commonly expressed as 'the greatest happiness of the greatest number'. This 'principle of utility' provided the basis for Bentham's analysis of government, law and social institutions and was enormously influential on many of those involved in the major social reforms of the nineteenth century. Bentham's two major associates were James Mill (1773–1836), who applied utilitarian principles to his History of British India *(extract 9.10), and John Stuart Mill (1806–73). The severely rational nature of Utilitarianism (note, for example, Bentham's rejection of 'metaphor and declamation', below) has often been seen to be in conflict (or at least dialogue) with many of the values championed by literary writing of the period, such as the importance of feeling and imagination.*

I.   Nature has placed mankind under the governance of two sovereign masters, *pain* and *pleasure*. It is for them alone to point out what we ought to do, as well as to determine what we shall do. On the one hand the standard of right and wrong, on the other the chain of causes and effects, are fastened to their throne. They govern us in all we do, in all we say, in all we think: every effort we can make to throw off our subjection, will serve but to demonstrate and confirm it. In words a man may pretend to abjure their empire: but in reality he will remain subject to it all the while. The *principle of utility*[6] recognizes this subjection, and assumes it for the foundation of that system, the object of which is to rear the fabric of felicity by the hands of reason and of law. Systems which attempt to question it, deal in sounds instead of sense, in caprice instead of reason, in darkness instead of light.

But enough of metaphor and declamation: it is not by such means that moral science is to be improved.

II.   The principle of utility is the foundation of the present work: it will be proper therefore at the outset to give an explicit and determinate account of what is meant by it. By the principle of utility is meant that principle which approves or disapproves of every action whatsoever, according to the tendency which it appears to have to augment or diminish the happiness of the party whose interest is in question: or, what is the same thing in other words, to promote or to oppose that happiness. I say of every action whatsoever; and therefore not only of every action of a private individual, but of every measure of government.

---

6 In 1822, Bentham added the following footnote: 'To this denomination has of late been added, or substituted, the *greatest happiness* or *greatest felicity* principle: this for shortness, instead of saying at length that principle which states the greatest happiness of all those whose interest is in question, as being the right and proper, and only right and proper and universally desirable, end of human action: of human action in every situation, and in particular in that of a functionary or set of functionaries exercising the powers of Government.'

III.   By utility is meant that property in any object, whereby it tends to produce benefit, advantage, pleasure, good, or happiness (all this in the present case comes to the same thing) or (what comes again to the same thing) to prevent the happening of mischief, pain, evil, or unhappiness to the party whose interest is considered: if that party be the community in general, then the happiness of the community: if a particular individual, then the happiness of that individual.

IV.   The interest of the community is one of the most general expressions that can occur in the phraseology of morals: no wonder that the meaning of it is often lost. When it has a meaning, it is this. The community is a fictitious *body*, composed of the individual persons who are considered as constituting as it were its *members*. The interest of the community then is, what? the sum of the interests of the several members who compose it.

V.   It is in vain to talk of the interest of the community, without understanding what is the interest of the individual. A thing is said to promote the interest, or to be *for* the interest, of an individual, when it tends to add to the sum total of his pleasures: or, what comes to the same thing, to diminish the sum total of his pains.

VI.   An action then may be said to be conformable to the principle of utility, or, for shortness sake, to utility, (meaning with respect to the community at large) when the tendency it has to augment the happiness of the community is greater than any it has to diminish it.

VII.   A measure of government (which is but a particular kind of action, performed by a particular person or persons) may be said to be conformable to or dictated by the principle of utility, when in like manner the tendency which it has to augment the happiness of the community is greater than any which it has to diminish it.

VIII.   When an action, or in particular a measure of government, is supposed by a man to be conformable to the principle of utility, it may be convenient, for the purposes of discourse, to imagine a kind of law or dictate, called a law or dictate of utility: and to speak of the action in question, as being conformable to such law or dictate.

IX.   A man may be said to be a partizan of the principle of utility, when the approbation or disapprobation he annexes to any action, or to any measure, is determined by and proportioned to the tendency which he conceives it to have to augment or to diminish the happiness of the community: or in other words, to its conformity or unconformity to the laws or dictates of utility.

2.4   John Thelwall, 'The Second Lecture on the Causes of the Present Dearness and Scarcity of Provisions, delivered Friday, May 1st, 1795', from *The Tribune, A Periodical Publication, consisting chiefly of the Political Lectures of J. Thelwall* (1796)

John Thelwall (1764–1834) was a major figure in the radical circles of the 1790s, having joined the Society for Constitutional Information in 1790 and helped form the London Corresponding Society in 1792. Along with fellow radicals Thomas Hardy and John Horne Tooke, he was tried for treason in 1794 and acquitted. Though Thelwall's exoneration was seen as a victory for the radical cause, in the following year the government passed the repressive 'gagging acts', which are often taken to signal the start of the decline of the radical movement. Following his acquittal, John Thelwall continued to lecture (despite harassment) and published his speeches in his periodical The Tribune. *His account of the poverty caused by the rise in prices of basic foodstuffs (oats and barley) and by employers' exploitation of the labour force was part of an attack on the 'mad and ridiculous war' which, he argued, had swallowed up the resources of the country while seeking 'the annihilation of freedom'. It also exemplifies what Gregory Claeys has identified as Thelwall's increasing conception of justice 'in terms of fair wages rather than solely the accession of political rights'.*[7]

Citizens, I have had some opportunities, also, of observing the dependent situation of these lower orders of society. Some years ago, before my mind had taken that strong bias in favour of political pursuits, to which it is now attached, going into the native country of my parents, I took the opportunity – being generally desirous to see as much as I could, and, not like those poor wretches condemned to the ignorant confines of the office of a Secretary of State, to know no difference between truth and falsehood, right and wrong, but what was taught me by the lying documents of spies and their employers, which it is the duty of those poor ignorant beings to copy – my employment not being of that description, I took the opportunity of seeing, as far as I could, the condition of those orders of society, about whose happiness in the country I had heard so many romantic stories, while I was an inhabitant of the town, and took my ideas of rural felicity from novels and pastorals. I beheld there poor women, doubled with age, toiling, from morning to night, over their wheels, spinning their flax and hemp; and I found that their condition was so miserable, that many of them were positively obliged to take their work once or twice a day home to the persons who employed them, in order to get the scanty pittance that was to purchase the meal by which they were to sustain their emaciated frames.

---

7 *The Politics of English Jacobinism: Writings of John Thelwall*, ed. Gregory Claeys (Pennsylvania: Pennsylvania State University Press, 1995), p. xxxix.

Figure 3 James Gillray, 'Copenhagen House', 16 November 1795; © Copyright the Trustees of the British Museum.

Gillray's caricature depicts a mass meeting organized by the London Corresponding Society and held at Copenhagen Fields in London (such meetings occurred on 26 October and 12 November 1795). John Thelwall is shown addressing the crowd from the right-hand platform, backed by a Dissenting minister and a figure holding a list of the Society's 'Resolutions'. Joseph Priestley can also be seen among the crowd (centre with arms crossed), and note the three chimney-sweeps signing the 'Remonstrance' in the bottom left corner.

I was astonished, I own, at this picture of misery. I had read a good deal in poems and romances about rural felicity. I did not know that rural felicity consisted in sitting over a wheel till one is double, and getting neither comforts nor conveniencies – no, nor the necessaries of life, to sustain and prop one's declining years, by this eternal drudgery.

This made, I own, a deep impression on my mind; which, though it did not operate immediately, stimulated me to a train of enquiry, which could not fail of its ultimate effect. – I had hitherto been a high government man, a supporter of prerogatives, and an advocate for venerating the powers that be. – O! that some way could but be invented to keep mankind (all but the chosen few) in utter ignorance! Then might placemen, pensioners, and the usurping proprietors of rotten boroughs, enjoy, indeed, a golden age, and the *swinish multitude*[8] (driven as their *swineherds* list, and slaughtered at their will) should grunt forth sedition no more! – But it will not be. Enquiry will some how or other be awakened; and, when it is awakened, the mists of delusion melt before the rising sun of truth, and the midnight hags of despotism bind us in their spells no more.

I soon found myself compelled to acknowledge that, where such was the condition of so large a portion of society, all could not be right – that 'there was something rotten in the state of Denmark;'[9] and every fact which, in the progress of investigation, came under my observation, tended to confirm the opinion.

Among other abuses, I soon found that one of the causes of this calamitous situation was the unfeeling manner in which these poor beings were left to the arbitrary discretion of their employers, who took the liberty, when these poor creatures took home their work, to scotch them as they thought fit; so that, under various pretences, for every pound that was spun by the poor individual, she never got paid for above three quarters, when it came to be estimated by the masters and employers. So much was to be considered as waste, so many deductions were to be made; and the poor individuals, where they are not numerous enough to associate, have no appeal – none at least that they have any hopes from; for you know but little of Justices of the Peace, if you believe a country magistrate will listen to the complaints of a poor friendless being, against the tradesman who has arrived at opulence by his oppression.

Thus then we find, if we regard the facts which history furnishes, that the inevitable consequence must be, from the increased price of the articles consumed, and the want of a proportionate increase in the wages paid to the industrious poor, that within twenty-five years the condition of the latter has been so reduced, that they cannot obtain half the necessaries of life they formerly used to obtain; while their opulent oppressors, the placemen, pensioners,

---

8 Edmund Burke's term for the lower orders in *Reflections on the French Revolution*, which prompted many responses, such as Thomas Spence's ironic title for his radical newspaper, *Pig's Meat or Lessons for the Swinish Multitude*.
9 Shakespeare, *Hamlet*, 1.iv.90.

and contractors of the day, enjoy more than twice the luxuries and extravagance with which they formerly debased their nature.

I have stated to you, also, that oats and barley, which, in many parts of the country, be it remembered, are used as substitutes for wheat, have still more extravagantly increased; and that oats, in particular, have increased *75 per cent.* since the year 1790.

Perhaps the *honourable Clerks of the Treasury* will not be inclined to contradict this. They will have had some opportunity of knowing the truth of it. – But, Citizens, since I met you before, I have had an opportunity of getting possession of some other facts, relative to this very important part of the question. I find, from a person who has been many years in a very considerable way of dealing in those articles, that twenty-seven or twenty-eight years ago, the common price of oats, in the retail market, was from 9s. to 10s. 6d. per quarter; that, till within these twelve years, 12s. was the common price, and that they were never higher than 14s. – But now, what is the price of them? Thirty-five shillings! an increase nearly four-fold, in so small a distance of time, as that which I have stated to you.

Now, remember what a very important article of consumption these are for the labouring poor in certain parts of the country. Remember, that throughout the whole of the country parts of Scotland, wheat is a luxury which the poor man never tastes; that oats, that barley, field peas, and other pulse of this description, constitute the whole sustenance of large proportions of the people there: and I could instance a poor being, of the name of Crawford, who emigrated to America on account of this miserable situation, and who has now, merely from the profits of his own manual labour, been able to take a little farm of his own, and to become a master Farmer, in his turn; but whose sole sustenance, for himself and family, while he resided in Scotland, was one meal a day of meagre potatoes; and that, in the horrors and excesses of their hunger, they gnawed the peelings and fragments for their supper, having no other sort of sustenance whatever to keep themselves from absolute starvation.

2.5   Thomas Malthus, *An Essay on the Principle of Population, as it Affects the Future Improvement of Society. With Remarks on the Speculations of Mr. Godwin, M. Condorcet, and Other Writers* (1798)

As its title suggests, the clergyman Thomas Malthus's (1766–1834) pessimistic account of population (and of human nature more generally) was in part a critique of the optimistic Enlightenment theories of the French philosopher and revolutionary the Marquis de Condorcet and of William Godwin (extracts 1.8, 4.2 and 5.8). Malthus is particularly critical of Godwin's concept of the 'perfectibility of mankind' and his belief that social institutions were responsible for vice and misery. Malthus argues that population growth will outstrip food supply and that, unless this growth is restricted by human measures (such as sexual abstinence), it will be checked by the 'dreadful resources of

nature': war, disease, and famine. Malthus's theory had important political dimen-
sions, particularly in relation to poor relief, to which he himself was opposed, prompt-
ing a change in Pitt's policy and influencing the reform of the Poor Law in 1834.
Malthus's theory prompted a number of replies in the period and has come to be seen
as increasingly important in the shaping of the rhetoric of Romanticism.

Famine seems to be the last, the most dreadful resource of nature. The power of
population is so superior to the power in the earth to produce subsistence for
man, that premature death must in some shape or other visit the human race.
The vices of mankind are active and able ministers of depopulation. They are the
precursors in the great army of destruction; and often finish the dreadful work
themselves. But should they fail in this war of extermination, sickly seasons,
epidemics, pestilence, and plague, advance in terrific array, and sweep off their
thousands and ten thousands. Should success be still incomplete; gigantic
inevitable famine stalks in the rear, and with one mighty blow, levels the population with the food of the world.

Must it not then be acknowledged by an attentive examiner of the histories
of mankind, that in every age and in every State in which man has existed, or
does now exist,

That the increase of population is necessarily limited by the means of subsistence.

That population does invariably increase when the means of subsistence
increase. And,

That the superior power of population it repressed, and the actual population
kept equal to the means of subsistence by misery and vice? . . .

The great error under which Mr. Godwin labours throughout his whole work, is,
the attributing almost all the vices and misery that are seen in civil society to
human institutions. Political regulations, and the established administration of
property, are with him the fruitful sources of all evil, the hotbeds of all the
crimes that degrade mankind. Were this really a true state of the case, it would
not seem a hopeless task to remove evil completely from the world; and reason
seems to be the proper and adequate instrument for effecting so great a purpose.
But the truth is, that though human institutions appear to be the obvious and
obtrusive causes of much mischief to mankind; yet, in reality, they are light and
superficial, they are mere feathers that float on the surface, in comparison with
those deeper seated causes of impurity that corrupt the springs, and render
turbid the whole stream of human life. . . .

Man cannot live in the midst of plenty. All cannot share alike the bounties of
nature. Were there no established administration of property, every man would
be obliged to guard with force his little store. Selfishness would be triumphant.
The subjects of contention would be perpetual. Every individual mind would be

under a constant anxiety about corporal support, and not a single intellect would be left free to expatiate in the field of thought. . . .

If we are not yet too well convinced of the reality of this melancholy picture [when 'a quantity of food equal to the frugal support of twenty-one millions, would be to be divided among twenty-eight millions'], let us but look for a moment into the next period of twenty-five years; and we shall see twenty-eight millions of human beings without the means of support; and before the conclusion of the first century, the population would be one hundred and twelve millions, and the food only sufficient for thirty-five millions, leaving seventy-seven millions unprovided for. In these ages want would be indeed triumphant, and rapine and murder must reign at large: and yet all this time we are supposing the produce of the earth absolutely unlimited, and the yearly increase greater than the boldest speculator can imagine.

This is undoubtedly a very different view of the difficulty arising from population, from that which Mr. Godwin gives, when he says, 'Myriads of centuries of still increasing population may pass away, and the earth be still found sufficient for the subsistence of its inhabitants.'

I am sufficiently aware that the redundant twenty-eight millions, or seventy-seven millions, that I have mentioned, could never have existed. It is a perfectly just observation of Mr. Godwin, that, 'There is a principle in human society, by which population is perpetually kept down to the level of the means of subsistence.' The sole question is, what is this principle? Is it some obscure and occult cause? Is it some mysterious interference of heaven, which at a certain period, strikes the men with impotence, and the women with barrenness? Or is it a cause, open to our researches, within our view, a cause, which has constantly been observed to operate, though with varied force, in every state in which man has been placed? Is it not a degree of misery, the necessary and inevitable result of the laws of nature, which human institutions, so far from aggravating, have tended considerably to mitigate, though they never can remove.

2.6   Robert Owen, *A New View of Society, Or, Essays on the Principle of the Formation of the Human Character, and the Application of the Principle to Practice: Essay Second* (1813)

Often hailed as the founder of Socialism, Robert Owen (1771–1858) was a successful industrialist particularly notable for his concern for his workers' welfare. He eventually became opposed to the factory system that was central to the Industrial Revolution. In this extract from A New View of Society, *Owen outlines some of the reforms he introduced when he became manager of the New Lanark cotton mills in 1800. Underpinning these reforms were Owen's interest in education and his beliefs that 'the character of man is, without a single exception, always formed for him; that it may be, and is, chiefly created by his predecessors; that they give him, or may give him, his ideas and*

*habits, which are the powers that govern and direct his conduct. Man, therefore, never
did, nor is it possible he ever can, form his own character.'*

The practice of employing children in the mills, of six, seven, and eight years of
age, was prevented, and their parents advised to allow them to acquire health
and education until they were ten years old.

The children were taught reading, writing, and arithmetic, during five years,
that is, from five to ten, in the village school, without expense to their parents.
All the modern improvements in education have been adopted, or are in process
of adoption.[10] Some facilities in teaching arithmetic have been also introduced,
which were peculiar to this school, and which have been found very advantageous. . . . [The children] may therefore be taught and well-trained before they
engage in any regular employment. Another important consideration is, that all
their instruction is rendered a pleasure and delight to them. . . .

During the period these changes were going forward, attention was given to
the domestic arrangements of the community. Their houses were rendered
comfortable, their streets were improved, the best provisions were purchased,
and sold to them at low rates, yet covering the original expense; and under such
regulations as taught them how to proportion their expenditure to their income.
Fuel and clothes were obtained for them in the same manner; no advantage was
attempted to be taken of them, or means used to deceive them.

In consequence, their animosity and opposition to a stranger subsided, their
full confidence was given, and they became satisfied that no evil was intended
them: on the contrary, they were convinced that a real desire existed to increase
their happiness, upon those grounds on which alone it could be permanently
increased. All difficulties in the way of future improvement vanished. They were
taught to be rational, and they acted rationally; and thus both parties experienced the incalculable advantages of the system which had been adopted. Those
employed, became industrious, temperate, healthy; faithful to their employers,
and kind to each other; while the proprietors were deriving services from their
attachment, almost without inspection, far beyond those which could be
obtained by any other means, without those mutual principles of confidence
and kindness existing between the parties. Such was the effect of these principles
on the adults, on those whose previous habits had been as ill formed as habits
could be; and certainly the application of the principles to practice was made
under the most unfavourable circumstances. . . .

I have thus, at the urgent request of many respected friends and individuals,
proceeded to give a more detailed account of this experiment than I should

---

10 Owen's note: 'To avoid the inconveniences which must ever arise from the introduction of a particular creed into a school, the children are taught to read in such books as inculcate those leading
doctrines of the Christian religion, which are common to all denominations.'

otherwise have deemed necessary; because these details of the application of the principles to any local situation, are of far less importance than to give a clear and accurate knowledge of the principles themselves; that they may be so well understood as to be easily rendered applicable to practice, in any community, and under any circumstances. Without this being done, particular facts may indeed amuse or astonish, but they would not contain that high degree of substantial value which the principles will be found to possess. But if it shall forward this object, the experiment cannot fail to prove the certain means of renovating the moral and religious principles of the world; by showing whence arise the various opinions, manners, vices, and virtues of mankind, and how the best or the worst of them may be, with mathematical precision, taught to the rising generations.

Let it not, therefore, be longer said that evil or injurious actions cannot be prevented; or that the most rational habits in the rising generation cannot be universally formed. In those characters which now exhibit crime, the fault is most obviously not in the individual, but the defect proceeds from the system in which those individuals have been trained. Withdraw those circumstances which tend to create crime in the human character, and crime will not be created. Replace them with such as are calculated to form habits of order, regularity, temperance, industry, and upon the most certain data these qualities may be formed. Adopt measures of fair equity and justice, and you will readily acquire the full and complete confidence of the lower orders: nay, more; proceed systematically on principles of undeviating persevering kindness, yet retaining and using, with the least possible severity, the means of restraining full formed crime from immediately injuring society; and by degrees, even the crimes now existing in the adults will also gradually disappear; for the worst formed disposition, short of incurable insanity, will not long resist a firm, determined, well directed, persevering kindness. Such a proceeding, whenever practised, will be found the most powerful and effective corrector of crime, and of all injurious and improper habits.

The experiment narrated shows that this is not hypothesis and theory; the whole *has* been done, and can be again done. The principles may be with confidence stated to be universal, and applicable to all times, persons, and circumstances. . . .

These principles, applied to the community at New Lanark, at first under many of the most discouraging circumstances, but persevered in for thirteen years, effected a complete change in the general character of the village, containing upwards of two thousand inhabitants, and into which, also, there was a constant influx of newcomers.

2.7 William Cobbett, *Cobbett's Weekly Political Register* (1813 and 1824)

William Cobbett (1763–1835) was a political journalist and spokesperson for the rural labouring class. Having worked as a farm labourer and served as a soldier in Canada,

Cobbett had lived in America, writing pro-British and anti-French journalism and pamphlets under the name of 'Peter Porcupine'. Within a few years of his return to England in 1799, Cobbett's political views became increasingly radical and opposi-tional and he expressed them forcefully in his periodical the Political Register *(to the extent that in 1810 he was imprisoned for two years for sedition and in 1817 fled the country for another two years fearing a second arrest). Responding to the high tax on newspapers, in 1816 Cobbett published the* Political Register *as a pamphlet, thus avoiding the tariff and enabling him to reach the working-class readership he sought to address. His* Rural Rides, *published in the* Political Register *between 1820 and 1830, gives a detailed portrait of rural conditions in England during the period.*

'The General Enclosure Bill', 31 July 1813[11]

Those who are so eager for new enclosures always seem to argue as if the *waste land*, in its present state, *produced nothing at all*. But is this the fact? Can any one point me out a single inch of it which does not produce something, and the produce of which is not made use of? It goes to the feeding of sheep, of cows, of cattle of all descriptions; and what is of great consequence in my view of the matter, it helps to rear, in health and vigour, numerous families of the children of labourers, which children, were it not for these wastes, must be crammed into the stinking suburbs of towns, amidst filth of all sorts, and congregating together in the practice of every species of idleness and vice. A family reared by the side of a common or a forest is as clearly distinguishable from a family bred in the pestiferous stench of the dark alleys of a town, as one of the plants of Mr Braddick's wheat is distinguishable from the feeble-stemmed, single-eared, stunted stuff that makes shift to rear its head above the cockle, and poppies, and couch-grass, in nine-tenths of the broad-cast fields in the kingdom.

This is with me a consideration of great importance. In the beggarly stinking houses of towns, the labourers' children cannot have health. If they have not health, that greatest of all blessings, they must be miserable in themselves and a burden to the parish. It has been observed that when bred on the side of the commons and forests, they are more saucy and more daring. There may be some inconvenience in this perhaps; but, for my part, give me the saucy daring fellow in preference to the poor, crawling, feeble wretch, who is not saucy, only, perhaps, because he feels that he has not the power to maintain himself. I am not in love with saucy servants any more than other people. But I know how to tackle them. A poor, feeble, heartless, humble, crawling creature I can do noth-ing with; and of this description I have observed are almost all those who are bred up, under a gossiping mother, in the stinking holes, called houses, in coun-try-towns or large villages.

---

11 The aim of the General Enclosure Bill was to make possible the enclosure of land without applica-tion to Parliament.

If this scheme of a general enclosure were to take place, (the scheme is a mad one, and physically impracticable); the whole race of those whom we in Hampshire call foresters, would be extirpated in a few years; and my sons, I dare say, would live to see the day when there would be scarcely a man to be found capable of wielding a felling axe. . . . [I am] a person entitled, in case of a general enclosure, to, perhaps, fifty, sixty, or a hundred acres of waste land, and that, as it happens, very good land too. But, though I make no use of this waste, and it is very likely that I never shall, I will never give my consent to the enclosure of it, or any part of it, except for the purposes of the labourers. All around this great tract of land, which is called waste, the borders are studded with cottages of various dimensions and forms, but the more beautiful for this diversity. The greater part of these are encroachments, as they are called; but the Bishop of Winchester, who is the Lord of the Manors, has never had a very harsh Steward, and the tenants have had too much compassion to attempt to pull down and lay open any of these numerous dwellings. For my part, rather than see them destroyed and their inhabitants driven into towns, I would freely resign all the claim that I have either to the land or to the herbage. These wastes, as they are called, are the blessing and the ornament of this part of the kingdom; and, I dare say, that they are the same in every other part of the kingdom where they are to be found.

These are my reasons for being glad that the general Enclosure Bill has failed; and, until I see them satisfactorily confuted, I shall, of course, retain my present opinion on the subject.

'To the Landowners. On the evils of collecting Manufacturers into great masses', 20 November 1824

[W]hile the country is going on becoming more and more depopulated, and more and more miserable, the great towns, and particularly the manufacturing districts, are daily increasing in numbers. If the people, thus drawn together in masses, were happily situated there might be less ground for lamentation; but, so far from this being the case, these masses are still more miserable than the wretches left behind them in the agricultural districts.

Some of these lords of the loom have in their employ thousands of miserable creatures. In the cotton-spinning work these creatures are kept, fourteen hours in each day, locked up, summer and winter, in a heat of from EIGHTY TO EIGHTY-FOUR DEGREES. . . .

Observe, too, that these poor creatures have no cool room to retreat to, not a moment to wipe off the sweat, and not a breath of air to come and interpose itself between them and infection. The 'door of the place wherein they work, is *locked*, except *half an hour*, at tea-time; the workpeople are not allowed to send for water to drink, in the hot factory; even the *rain-water is locked up*, by the master's order, otherwise they would be happy to drink even that. If any spinner be found with his *window open,* he is to pay a fine of a shilling'![12] Mr. MARTIN of Galway has procured Acts of Parliament to be passed to prevent *cruelty to animals.*[13] If horses or dogs were shut up in a place like this they would certainly be thought worthy of Mr. MARTIN's attention.

Not only is there not a breath of sweet air in these truly infernal scenes; but, for a large part of the time, there is the abominable and pernicious stink of the GAS to assist in the murderous effects of the heat. In addition to the heat and the gas; in addition to the noxious effluvia of the gas, mixed with the steam, there are the *dust,* and what is called the *cotton-flyings* or *fuz,* which the unfortunate creatures have to inhale: and, the fact is, the notorious fact is, that well-constitutioned men are rendered old and past labour at forty years of age, and that children are rendered decrepit and deformed, and thousands upon thousands of them slaughtered by consumptions, before they arrive at the age of sixteen. And are these establishments to boast of? If we were to admit the fact, that they compose an addition to the population of the country; if we were further to admit, that they caused an addition to the pecuniary resources of the Government, ought not a government to be ashamed to derive resources from such means? . . .

[O]bserve, the canting scoundrels of Methodists, who are making such a clamour about the slavery of the blacks, are amongst the most efficient tools of the Cotton-Lords in the upholding of this abominable slavery. They preach content and patience to these suffering mortals; they bid them be *grateful* that they have the comforts of what these rascals call the Gospel. They tell them they will be damned to all eternity if they listen to those who would take them out of eighty-four degrees of heat and the cotton fuz. . . .

Nine hundred and ninety-nine thousandths of the people of England have not the most distant idea that such things are carried on, in a country calling itself free; in a country whose Minister for Foreign Affairs is everlastingly teasing and bothering other Powers to emulate England in 'her *humanity'*, in abolishing the slave trade in the blacks. The blacks, when carried to the West Indies, are put into a paradise compared with the situation of these poor white creatures in Lancashire, and other factories of the North. And yet the Editor of the Morning Chronicle is incessantly singing forth the blessings of the manufacturing districts. Bad as is the situation of the labourers in the agricultural counties, it is heaven itself compared with that of these poor creatures.

---

12 Cobbett is quoting from a statement issued in Manchester in 1823.
13 Richard Martin (1754–1834) was an animal rights activist whose campaigning led to the 'Ill Treatment of Cattle' Bill of 1822.

2.8   William Hone, *The Political Litany, Diligently Revised; to be Said or Sung, until the Appointed Change Come, throughout the Dominion of England and Wales, and the Town of Berwick Upon Tweed* (1817)

William Hone (1780–1842) was a radical writer and publisher whose popular satirical pamphlets reached a huge audience. The best known of his pamphlets, 'The Political House that Jack Built' (1819), sold 100,000 copies in the weeks after its publication. To engage this large readership, Hone employed and parodied forms that were widely familiar (such as nursery rhymes and chapbooks). His 1817 parodies of religious texts (such as the 'Litany' extracted below) led to his three trials (one for each publication) for blasphemy and seditious libel. Following his acquittal, Hone resumed his publication of satirical pamphlets. The form of the litany parodied below is a type of prayer in which the congregation repeat the petitions of the minister, and Hone uses it to satirize the political structures and abuses of the period and to present his reformist agenda.

Here followeth the LITANY, *or General Supplication, to be said or sung at all times when thereunto especially moved.*

O PRINCE, ruler of the people, have mercy upon us, thy miserable subjects,

O Prince, Ruler, &c.

O House of Lords, hereditary legislators, have mercy upon us, pension-paying subjects:

O House of Lords, &c.

O House of Commons, proceeding from corrupt borough-mongers, have mercy upon us, your should-be constituents.

O House of Commons, &c.

O gracious, noble, right honorable, and learned rulers of our land, three estates in one state, have mercy upon us, a poverty-stricken people:

O gracious, noble, &c.

Remember not, most gracious, most noble, right honourable, and honourable gentlemen, our past riches, nor the riches of our forefathers; neither continue to tax us according to our long lost ability – spare us, good rulers, spare the people who have supported ye with their labour, and spilt their most precious blood in your quarrels; – O consume us not utterly:

Spare us, good Prince!

From an unnational debt; from unmerited pensions and sinecure places; from an extravagant civil list; and from utter starvation,

Good Prince, deliver us!

From the blind imbecility of ministers; from the pride and vain glory of warlike establishments in time of peace,

Good Prince, deliver us!

From all the deadly sins attendant on a corrupt method of election; from all the deceits of the pensioned hirelings of the press,

Good Prince, deliver us!

From taxes levied by distress; from jails crowded with debtors; from poor-houses overflowing with paupers,

Good Prince, deliver us!

From a Parliament chosen only by one tenth of the tax-payers; from taxes rasied to pay wholesale human butchers their subsidies[;] from the false doctrines, heresy, and schism, which have obscured our once glorious constitution; from conspiracies against the liberty of the people; and from obstacles thrown in the way of the exertion of our natural and constitutional rights,

Good Prince[,] deliver us!

By your feelings as men; by your interests as members of civil society; by your duty as Christians,

O Rulers, deliver us!

By the deprivations of millions – by the sighs of the widow – by the tears of the orphan – by the groans of the aged in distress – by the wants of all classes in the community, except your own and your dependants,

O Rulers, deliver us!

In this time of tribulation – in this time of want of labour of thousands, and of unrequited labour to tens of thousands – in this time of sudden death from want of food,

Figure 4 George Cruikshank, 'Poor Bull & his Burden – or the Political Murraion!!!', 15 December 1819; © Copyright the Trustees of the British Museum.

Cruikshank's cartoon shows a hierarchy of crown, bishops, lawyers, soldiers and tax collectors crushing the Bull of the nation, who is muzzled with a 'Gagging Bill' and threatened with execution by the Duke of Wellington (who as Master-General of the Ordnance in Lord Liverpool's Tory Government was seen as symbolically responsible for the taxation required to fund the army). Cruikshank's subtitle, '"And the land stank – so num'rous was the fry" – what will become of these Vermin, *if* the Bull *should Rise* – ?!!!!!!!!!!!!', draws on Cowper's poem *The Task* to hint at the possibility of a dramatic upheaval in the structure of British society.

O Rulers, deliver us!

We people do beseech ye to hear us, O Rulers; and that it may please ye to rule and govern as constitutionally in the right way;

We beseech ye to hear us, O Rulers!

That it may please ye to keep yourselves in all sobriety, temperance, and honesty of life – that ye spend not extravagantly the money raised from the production of our labours, nor take for yourselves that which ye need not,

We beseech ye to hear us, O Rulers!

That it may please ye to keep your hearts in fear of oppression, and in love of justice; and that ye may evermore have affiance in our affection, rather than in the bayonets of a hired soldiery,

We beseech ye to hear us, O Rulers! . . .

That it may please ye to bless all the people with equal representation, and to keep them safe from borough-mongering factions,

We beseech ye to hear us, O Rulers!

That it may please ye so to govern us, that unity, peace, and concord, may prevail throughout the nation; and the voice of tumult and dissatisfaction be no more heard in our streets;

We beseech ye to hear us, O Rulers!

That it may please ye to give unto all people all their rights as citizens, what-ever may be the mode in which their consciences may impel them to worship their Creator, and whatever the creed to which their judgments assent;

We beseech ye to hear us, O Rulers!

That it may please ye to bring into the way of truth those apostates, who have erred therefrom, and have deceived us;

We beseech ye to hear us, O Rulers!

That it may please ye to strengthen all such as do stand up for the legal and constitutional rights of the people; to comfort and help the weak-hearted, who want courage in our behalf; to raise up such as do fall; and finally to beat down corruption under our feet;

We beseech ye to hear us, O Rulers!

That it may please ye not to tax 'until the brow of labour sweats in vain;' but to succour and comfort all that are in necessity and tribulation,

We beseech ye to hear us, O Rulers! . . .

That it may please ye to turn the hearts of our enemies, persecutors, and slanderers, by withdrawing their pensions and emoluments, that they may no longer call us a 'rabble,' the 'swinish multitude,' or 'ragamuffins,' but once more style us, 'the real strength of the natio[n'], – 'the body, without which a head is useless,'

We beseech ye to hear us, O Rulers!

That it may please ye to give and preserve to our use the kindly fruits of the earth, untaxed by men in black, whom those who wish for their instruction ought alone to support:

We beseech ye to hear us, O Rulers!

That it may please ye to abolish and destroy all sinecure places, and worthless pensions; to utterly purge and root out all wrong doers; to thoroughly correct the present misrepresentation of the people, by an effectual Reform in Parliament; or otherwise to do, or cause to be done, such further and other acts and deeds, as shall or may conduce to the true interest and benefit of the whole commonwealth;

We beseech ye to hear us, O Rulers!

That it may please ye to lead and strengthen GEORGE, Prince of Wales, our present REGENT, in the true fear and knowledge of the principles whereon the people of this commonwealth placed their crown on the head of his ancestors, and continue it towards him; and that it may please ye, as much as in ye lie, to keep and to defend him from battle and murder, and sudden death, and from fornication and all other deadly sin;

We beseech ye to hear us[,] O Rulers! . . .

Son of George, we beseech thee to hear us.

Son of George, we beseech thee, &c.

O house of Lords, that taketh away so many tens of thousands of pounds in pensions,

Have mercy upon us!

O House of Commons, that votest away the money of the whole nation, instead of that of those only who elect you,

Have mercy upon us!

O Prince[,] hear us.

O Prince[,] hear us!

George[,] have mercy upon us.

George[,] have mercy upon us!

O House of Lords, have mercy upon us.

O House of Lords, have mercy upon us!

O House of Commons, have mercy on us.

O House of Commons, have mercy on us!

Here endeth the Litany.

2.9   Richard Oastler, 'Slavery in Yorkshire', *Leeds Mercury* (1830)

Richard Oastler (1789–1861) was a major figure in the movement for factory reform whose efforts finally resulted in the 1847 Factory Act, which limited to ten the daily hours that could be worked by women and children in the textile industry. His 1830 letter to the Leeds Mercury *drew attention to the fact that the legislation covering the cotton industry did not protect children working in worsted (woollen) mills, and, like Cobbett (extract 2.7), he drew a parallel between the British industrial worker and the African slave. The letter prompted the MP John Cam Hobhouse to introduce a bill preventing the use of children under nine years of age and restricting the hours of older children in textile mills. An amended version of the bill was passed in 1831.*

To the editors of the *Leeds Mercury*

'It is the pride of Britain that a slave cannot exist on her soil; and if I read the genius of her constitution aright, I find that slavery is most abhorrent to it – that the air which Britons breathe is free – the ground on which they tread is sacred to liberty'. *Rev.* R. W. *HAMILTON's Speech at the Meeting held in the Cloth-hall Yard, September 22d, 1830.*[14]

Gentlemen, – No heart responded with truer accents to the sounds of liberty which were heard in the Leeds Cloth-hall Yard, on the 22d inst., than did mine, and from none could more sincere and earnest prayers arise to the throne of Heaven, that hereafter slavery might only be known to Britain in the pages of her history. One shade alone obscured my pleasure, arising not from any difference in principle, but from the want of application of the general principle *to the whole Empire.* The pious and able champions of *Negro* liberty and *Colonial* rights should, if I mistake not, have gone farther than they did; or perhaps, to speak more correctly, before they had travelled so far as the West Indies, should, at least for a few moments, have sojourned in our own immediate neighbourhood, and have directed the attention of the meeting to scenes of misery, acts of oppression, and victims of Slavery, even on the threshold of our homes!

Let truth speak out, appalling as the statement may appear. The fact is true. Thousands of our fellow-creatures and fellow-subjects, both male and female, the miserable inhabitants of a *Yorkshire town,* (Yorkshire now represented in Parliament by the giant of anti-slavery principles,[15]) are this very moment existing in a state of Slavery *more horrid* than are the victims of that hellish system – *'Colonial Slavery'.* These innocent creatures drawl out unpitied their short but miserable existence, in a place famed for its profession of religious zeal, whose inhabitants are ever foremost in *professing* 'Temperance' and 'Reformation,' and are striving to outrun their neighbours in Missionary exertions, and would fain send the Bible to the farthest corner of the globe – aye in the very place where the anti-slavery fever rages most furiously, her *apparent charity,* is not more admired on earth, than her *real cruelty* is abhorred in heaven. The very streets which receive the droppings of an 'Anti-Slavery Society' are every morning wet by the tears of innocent victims at the accursed shrine of avarice, who are *compelled* (not by the cart-whip of the negro slave-driver) but by the dread of the equally appalling thong or strap of the over-looker, to hasten, half-dressed, *but not half-fed,* to those magazines of British Infantile Slavery – *the Worsted Mills in the town and neighbourhood of Bradford*!!!

Would that I had Brougham's eloquence, that I might rouse the hearts of the nation, and make every Briton swear 'These innocents shall be free!'

Thousands of little children, both male and female, *but principally female,* from SEVEN to fourteen years of age, are daily *compelled* to *labour* from six o'clock in the morning to seven in the evening, with only – Britons, blush while you read it! *with only thirty minutes allowed for eating and recreation*!! – Poor

---

14 This was a meeting supporting the abolition of slavery.
15 The anti-slavery campaigner Henry Brougham had become MP for Knaresborough, Yorkshire, in February 1830.

infants! ye are indeed sacrificed at the shrine of avarice, *without even the solace of the negro slave*; – ye are no more than he is, *free agents*; ye are compelled to work as long as the *necessity* of your needy parents may require, or the cold-blooded avarice of your worse than barbarian masters *may demand*! Ye live in the boasted land of freedom, and *feel* and mourn that *ye are Slaves*, and slaves without the only comfort which the Negro has. He knows it is his sordid, mercenary master's INTEREST that he should *live*, be *strong* and *healthy*. *Not so with you*. Ye are doomed to labour from morning to night for one who cares not how soon your weak and tender frames are stretched to breaking!' . . .

The blacks may be fairly compared to beasts of burden, *kept for their master's use*. The whites to those *which others keep and let for hire*! If I have succeeded in calling the attention of your readers to the horrid and abominable system on which the worsted mills in and near Bradford is conducted, I have done some good. Why should not children working in them be protected by legislative enactments, as well as those who work in cotton mills? Christians should feel and act for those whom Christ so eminently loved, and declared that 'of such is the Kingdom of Heaven.'

RICHARD OASTLER
Sept. 29th, 1830

3

Women

Introduction

'It is time to effect a revolution in female manners – time to restore to them their lost dignity – and make them, as a part of the human species, labour by reforming themselves to reform the world.' Mary Wollstonecraft's famous rallying cry in the most important book about women of the period, *A Vindication of the Rights of Woman* (1792; extract 3.4), makes obvious through its terminology her sense that the ongoing debate about political rights for men, heightened by the French Revolution (see Section 1), needed to be extended into an examination of the position and role of women in society. This section begins with extracts from two works that Wollstonecraft criticized in the *Vindication* as illustrations of, and reasons for, women's loss of dignity: James Fordyce's *Sermons to Young Women* and John Gregory's *A Father's Legacy to his Daughters*. These were popular and frequently reprinted examples of the conduct-book, a form of advice manual which sought to instil within its readership of girls and young women an ideal of femininity characterized by passivity, meekness, and submission. But it was not only in such obviously conservative texts that Wollstonecraft and fellow radical thinkers confronted the ideological subordination of women. Catharine Macaulay Graham described the foremost philosopher of republicanism, Jean-Jacques Rousseau, as 'among the most strenuous asserters of sexual difference' (extract 3.3). Similarly, in Chapter 5 of the *Vindication*, Wollstonecraft provided a detailed critical analysis of Rousseau's highly-limited programme of female education outlined in *Émile* (1762), arguing that it assumed 'woman to have been formed only to please, and be subject to man'.

During the 1790s, conservative writers like Hannah More as well as radical writers like Wollstonecraft, Catharine Macaulay Graham and Mary Hays, called for the reform of education for women, repeatedly criticizing a number of the social and cultural forms which they felt contributed to the women's debasement. These included: the emphasis in education on 'accomplishments' (drawing, singing, playing music, speaking modern languages), the potential dangers of the association of women with sensibility, and the false understanding of the world gained from novels. These writers differed, however, on the ultimate aims of this education – whether it should make women better wives and mothers or equip them for a wider role in society – and, fundamentally, on whether or not there were natural differences between men and women. While Catharine Macaulay Graham argued that there was 'no characteristic difference in sex' and that what was perceived as women's weaknesses of mind and body was a result of their 'situation and education' (extract 3.3), Hannah More asserts that 'Each sex has its proper excellencies, which would be lost were they melted down into the common character by the fusion of the new philosophy' (extract 3.6).

The increasingly reactionary political climate of the 1790s and the continuation of the war with France into the 1800s made it progressively more controversial to advocate women's rights, especially once they were conflated with Jacobinism by anti-feminist and anti-Gallic writers (see Polwhele's 'The Unsex'd Females' of 1798 – extract 8.5). However, within the patriotic atmosphere of wartime Britain, in which the family was frequently equated with the nation (along Burkean lines), the figure of woman was given increased importance, as the extracts from More (3.6) and Jane West show, the latter claiming that as a result of their moral authority, women 'become *legislators* in the most important sense of the word, by impressing on the minds of all around us the obligation which gives force to statute' (extract 3.7). This model of womanhood was given further legitimization by the Evangelical emphasis on the piety of the domestic sphere, defined against the masculine and public world of commerce. While this model restricted women's roles to those of wife, mother, and housekeeper, it simultaneously gave them increasing symbolic authority as the guarantors of the nation's health and political strength. Politically and legally, women remained subordinate to men: no woman could vote; once married a woman lost control of her property; and it was almost impossible for a wife to divorce her husband. In the reformist decades of the 1820s and 1830s, there was a new focus on the issue of women's political representation, with William Thompson and Anna Wheeler (extract 3.8) arguing that women's social and legal subordination made their need of political rights all the more urgent (though, of course, it was not until the Married Women's Property Act of 1882 that a wife gained any rights over property merged with her husband's and not until 1918 that women over 30 were given the right to vote).

During the Romantic period, women played an increasing role in the literary marketplace, as both writers and readers (see Section 8). While conduct-books warned readers about the dangers of the relatively new form of the novel (see extract 3.1, which equates novel reading with prostitution) and discouraged women from publishing, increased literacy rates, the rise of circulating libraries, and new forms of publication intended specifically for women readers (such as the gift-book and annual) all contributed to the emergence of women as a major part of the market for literature. As poets, novelists, playwrights, and authors of a wide range of other kinds of texts (such as reviews, histories, biographies, travel guides, children's literature, political essays, letters and diaries), women contributed significantly to the literary culture of the period, despite a number of adverse factors, including: the periodic attacks on women writers and intellectuals as 'unsex'd females' or 'bluestockings'; the attempts by some male writers and critics to reclaim literature as masculine at a time when they feared it was becoming feminized; and the gendering of aesthetic categories such as the sublime and beautiful.

3.1   James Fordyce, *Sermons to Young Women* (1765)

Mary Wollstonecraft provides evidence of the size and nature of the readership for Fordyce's Sermons *in* A Vindication of the Rights of Woman *when she comments, 'Dr Fordyce's sermons have long made a part of a young woman's library; nay, girls at school are allowed to read them.' However, Wollstonecraft continues, 'I should instantly dismiss them from my pupil's [library] if I wished to strengthen her under-standing, by leading her to form sound principles on a broad basis; or, were I only anxious to cultivate her taste, though they must be allowed to contain many sensible observations' (Chapter 5). The picture Fordyce presents of the ideal woman, Wollstonecraft concludes, is 'the portrait of a house slave'. The continuing role of Fordyce's* Sermons *in the teaching of conduct to women is illustrated by Jane Austen's* Pride and Prejudice *(1813), in which the tedious clergyman Mr Collins selects it to read to the assembled Bennet sisters (only to be interrupted after three pages by Lydia). Fordyce (1720–96) was a Scottish Presbyterian pastor, famous for the theatrical nature of his sermons, and his* Sermons to Young Women *were frequently reprinted during the period.*

A masculine woman must be naturally an unamiable creature. I confess myself shocked, whenever I see the sexes confounded. An effeminate fellow, that, desti-tute of every manly sentiment, copies with inverted ambition from your sex, is an object of contempt and aversion at once. On the other hand, a young woman of any rank, that throws off all the lovely softness of her nature, and emulates the daring and intrepid temper of a man – how terrible! The transformation on either side must ever be monstrous. Is not this shadowed out to us in that partic-ular prohibition of the Jewish law, which says, 'The woman shall not wear that which pertaineth unto a man: neither shall a man put on a woman's garment. For all that do so are abomination unto the Lord?' Such confusion of apparel was to be considered as renouncing, in effect, the distinction of form, which the Almighty had established in the creation. To this unnatural mode do we not sometimes observe a visible tendency in our days? But what though the dress be kept ever so distinct, if the behaviour be not; in those points, I mean, where the character peculiar to each sex seems to require a difference? There, a metamor-phosis in either will always offend an eye that is not greatly vitiated. It will do so particularly in your sex. By dint of assiduity, flattery, fortune and show, a Female Man shall sometimes succeed strangely with the women: but to the men an Amazon, I think, never fails to be forbidding. Are none of you, my sisters, in danger of roughening into this ungracious figure? How readily it is assumed, in those scenes where the ignorance of youth co-operates with the magic of fashion, many of you perhaps will not suspect. . . .

Beside the beautiful productions of that incomparable pen,[1] there seem to me to be very few, in the style of Novel, that you can read with safety, and yet fewer that you can read with advantage. – What shall we say of certain books, which we are assured (for we have not read them) are in their nature so shameful, in their tendency so pestiferous, and contain such rank treason against the royalty of Virtue, such horrible violation of all decorum, that she who can bear to peruse them must in her soul be a prostitute, let her reputation in life be as it will. But can it be true – say, ye chaste stars, that with innumerable eyes inspect the midnight behaviour of mortals – can it be true, that any young woman, pretending to decency, should endure for a moment to look on this infernal brood of futility and lewdness?

Nor do we condemn those writings only, that, with an effrontery which defies the laws of God and men, carry on their very forehead the mark of the beast. We consider the general run of Novels as utterly unfit for you. Instruction they convey none. They paint scenes of pleasure and passion altogether improper for you to behold, even with the mind's eye. Their descriptions are often loose and luscious in a high degree; their representations of love between the sexes are almost universally overstrained. All is dotage, or despair; or else ranting swelled into burlesque. In short, the majority of their lovers are either mere lunatics, or mock-heroes. A sweet sensibility, a charming tenderness, a delightful anguish, exalted generosity, heroic worth, and refinement of thought; how seldom are these best ingredients of virtuous love mixed with any judgment or care in the composition of their principal characters! . . .

I scruple not to declare my opinion, that Nature appears to have formed the faculties of your sex for the most part with less vigour than those of ours; observing the same distinction here, as in the more delicate frame of your bodies. Exceptions we readily admit, and such as do the individuals great honour in those particular walks of excellence, wherein they have been distinguished. But you yourselves, I think, will allow that war, commerce, politics, exercises of strength and dexterity, abstract philosophy, and all the abstruser sciences, are most properly the province of men. I am sure those masculine women, that would plead for your sharing any part of this province equally with us, do not understand your true interests. There is an influence, there is an empire which belongs to you, and which I wish you ever to possess: I mean that which has the heart for its object, and which is secured by meekness and modesty, by soft attraction and virtuous love.

---

1 The novels of Samuel Richardson.

But now I must add, that your power in this way will receive a large accession from the culture of your minds, in the more elegant and polished branches of knowledge. When I say so, I would by no means insinuate, that you are not capable of the judicious and the solid, in such proportion as is suited to your destination in life. This, I apprehend, does not require reasoning or accuracy, so much as observation and discernment. Your business chiefly is to read Men, in order to make yourselves agreeable and useful. It is not the argumentative but the sentimental talents, which give you that insight and those openings into the human heart, that lead to your principal ends as Women. . . .

3.2 John Gregory, *A Father's Legacy to His Daughters* (1774)

Along with James Fordyce's Sermons to Young Women *(extract 3.1), Gregory's* A Father's Legacy to His Daughters *was the most widely read and frequently reprinted of the instruction books for girls and young women. Gregory (1724–73) was professor of philosophy and medicine at Aberdeen and Edinburgh Universities respectively. He died in 1773 and his* Legacy *was published the following year, presented in the editorial introduction as 'written by a tender father, in a declining state of health, for the instruction of his daughters, and not intended for the Public'. Gregory's influence is illustrated by Wollstonecraft's critique of his ideas in* A Vindication of the Rights of Woman, *where she writes: 'I may be accused of arrogance; still I must declare what I firmly believe, that all writers who have written on the subject of female education and manners, from Rousseau to Dr Gregory, have contributed to render women more artificial, weak characters, than they would otherwise have been; and consequently, more useless members of society' (Chapter 2).*

One of the chief beauties in a female character is that modest reserve, that retiring delicacy, which avoids the public eye, and is disconcerted even at the gaze of admiration. – I do not wish you to be insensible to applause. If you were, you must become, if not worse, at least less amiable women. But you may be dazzled by that admiration, which yet rejoices your hearts.

When a girl ceases to blush, she has lost the most powerful charm of beauty. That extreme sensibility which it indicates, may be a weakness and incumbrance in our sex, as I have too often felt; but in yours it is peculiarly engaging. Pedants, who think themselves philosophers, ask why a woman should blush when she is conscious of no crime. It is a sufficient answer, that Nature has made you to blush when you are guilty of no fault, and has forced us to love you because you do so. – Blushing is so far from being necessarily an attendant on guilt, that it is the usual companion of innocence.

This modesty, which I think so essential in your sex, will naturally dispose you to be rather silent in company, especially in a large one. – People of sense and discernment will never mistake such silence for dulness. One may take a

Figure 5 Anon., 'Keep within Compass', *c*.1790; © Copyright the Trustees of the British Museum.

This print provides a visual embodiment of the perceived ideal of the restriction of a woman's role (though the figure of the compasses is traditional and was also used for men). The inscriptions on the compasses instruct women to 'Fear God', 'Bridle thy Will', 'Know thyself' and 'Remember thy End', while supporting verses illustrate the potential dangers of prostitution and prison ('Bridewell') for those who fail to 'Keep within Compass'.

share in conversation without uttering a syllable. The expression in the countenance shews it, and this never escapes an observing eye.

I should be glad that you had an easy dignity in your behaviour at public
places, but not that confident ease, that unabashed countenance, which seems
to set the company at defiance. – If, while a gentleman is speaking to you, one
of superior rank addresses you, do not let your eager attention and visible preference betray the flutter of your heart. Let your pride on this occasion preserve
you from that meanness into which your vanity would sink you. Consider that
you expose yourselves to the ridicule of the company, and affront one gentleman, only to swell the triumph of another, who perhaps thinks he does you
honour in speaking to you.

Converse with men even of the first rank with that dignified modesty which
may prevent the approach of the most distant familiarity, and consequently
prevent them from feeling themselves your superiors.

Wit is the most dangerous talent you can possess. It must be guarded with
great discretion and good-nature, otherwise it will create you many enemies. Wit
is perfectly consistent with softness and delicacy; yet they are seldom found
united. Wit is so flattering to vanity, that they who possess it become intoxicated, and lose all self-command.

Humour is a different quality. It will make your company much solicited; but
be cautious how you indulge it. – It is often a great enemy to delicacy, and a still
greater one to dignity of character. It may sometimes gain you applause, but will
never procure you respect.

Be even cautious in displaying your good sense. It will be thought you assume
a superiority over the rest of the company. – But if you happen to have any
learning, keep it a profound secret, especially from the men, who generally look
with a jealous and malignant eye on a woman of great parts, and a cultivated
understanding.

A man of real genius and candour is far superior to this meanness. But such a
one will seldom fall in your way; and if by accident he should, do not be anxious
to shew the full extent of your knowledge. If he has any opportunities of seeing
you, he will soon discover it himself; and if you have any advantages of person
or manner, and keep your own secret, he will probably give you credit for a great
deal more than you possess. – The great art of pleasing in conversation consists
in making the company pleased with themselves. You will more readily hear
[than] talk yourselves into their good graces.

3.3   Catharine Macaulay Graham, *Letters on Education. With Observations on Religious and Metaphysical Subjects* (1790)

Catharine Sawbridge Macaulay Graham (1731–91) was best known for her 8-volume
History of England from the Accession of James I to that of the Brunswick Line
(1763–83), which was informed by her own republican values (Edmund Burke called

her 'our Republican Virago'). Her Letters on Education *was an important and early statement in the debate over women, education, and rights that would rage through the 1790s (intersecting with the 'Revolution Debate' – see Section 1). Macaulay was a major influence on Mary Wollstonecraft, who in* A Vindication of the Rights of Woman *(published the year after Macaulay's death) declared her to have been 'the woman of the greatest abilities, undoubtedly, that this country has ever produced' and commented that her 'judgment, the matured fruit of profound thinking, was a proof that a woman can acquire judgment in the full extent of the word' (Chapter 5).* Letters on Education *is a wide-ranging text, as its subtitle suggests, and is written as a series of letters addressed to the fictional figure Hortensia. The following extract comes from the chapter boldly entitled 'No characteristic Difference in Sex'.*

The great difference that is observable in the characters of the sexes, Hortensia, as they display themselves in the scenes of social life, has given rise to much false speculation on the natural qualities of the female mind. – For though the doctrine of innate ideas, and innate affections, are in a great measure exploded by the learned, yet few persons reason so closely and so accurately on abstract subjects as, through a long chain of deductions, to bring forth a conclusion which in no respect militates with their premises.

It is a long time before the crowd give up opinions they have been taught to look upon with respect; and I know many persons who will follow you willingly through the course of your argument, till they perceive it tends to the overthrow of some fond prejudice; and then they will either sound a retreat, or begin a contest in which the contender for truth, though he cannot be overcome, is effectually silenced, from the mere weariness of answering positive assertions, reiterated without end. It is from such causes that the notion of a sexual difference in the human character has, with a very few exceptions, universally prevailed from the earliest times, and the pride of one sex, and the ignorance and vanity of the other, have helped to support an opinion which a close observation of Nature, and a more accurate way of reasoning, would disprove.

It must be confessed, that the virtues of the males among the human species, though mixed and blended with a variety of vices and errors, have displayed a bolder and a more consistent picture of excellence than female nature has hitherto done. It is on these reasons that, when we compliment the appearance of a more than ordinary energy in the female mind, we call it masculine; and hence it is, that Pope has elegantly said *a perfect woman's but a softer man.*[2] And if we take in the consideration, that there can be but one rule of moral excellence for beings made of the same materials, organized after the same manner, and subjected to similar laws of Nature, we must either agree with Mr. Pope, or we must reverse the proposition, and say, that *a perfect man is a woman formed after*

---

2 Alexander Pope, 'Of the Characters of Women', *Moral Essays.*

a coarser mold. The difference that actually does subsist between the sexes, is too flattering for men to be willingly imputed to accident; for what accident occasions, wisdom might correct; and it is better, says Pride, to give up the advantages we might derive from the perfection of our fellow associates, than to own that Nature has been just in the equal distribution of her favours. These are the sentiments of the men; but mark how readily they are yielded to by the women; not from humility I assure you, but merely to preserve with character those fond vanities on which they set their hearts. No; suffer them to idolize their persons, to throw away their life in the pursuit of trifles, and to indulge in the gratification of the meaner passions, and they will heartily join in the sentence of their degradation.

Among the most strenuous asserters of a sexual difference in character, Rousseau is the most conspicuous, both on account of that warmth of sentiment which distinguishes all his writings, and the eloquence of his compositions: but never did enthusiasm and the love of paradox, those enemies to philosophical disquisition, appear in more strong opposition to plain sense than in Rousseau's definition of this difference. He sets out with a supposition, that Nature intended the subjection of the one sex to the other; that consequently there must be an inferiority of intellect in the subjected party; but as man is a very imperfect being, and apt to play the capricious tyrant, Nature, to bring things nearer to an equality, bestowed on the woman such attractive graces, and such an insinuating address, as to turn the balance on the other scale. Thus Nature, in a giddy mood, recedes from her purposes, and subjects prerogative to an influence which must produce confusion and disorder in the system of human affairs. Rousseau saw this objection; and in order to obviate it, he has made up a moral person of the union of the two sexes, which, for contradiction and absurdity, outdoes every metaphysical riddle that was ever formed in the schools. In short, it is not reason, it is not wit; it is pride and sensuality that speak in Rousseau, and, in this instance, has lowered the man of genius to the licentious pedant.

But whatever might be the wise purpose intended by Providence in such a disposition of things, certain it is, that some degree of inferiority, in point of corporal strength, seems always to have existed between the two sexes; and this advantage, in the barbarous ages of mankind, was abused to such a degree, as to destroy all the natural rights of the female species, and reduce them to a state of abject slavery. What accidents have contributed in Europe to better their condition, would not be to my purpose to relate; for I do not intend to give you a history of women; I mean only to trace the sources of their peculiar foibles and vices; and these I firmly believe to originate in situation and education only: for so little did a wise and just Providence intend to make the condition of slavery an unalterable law of female nature, that in the same proportion as the male sex have consulted the interest of their own happiness, they have relaxed in their tyranny over women; and such is their use in the system of mundane creation, and such their natural influence over the male mind, that were these advantages properly exerted, they might carry every point of any importance to their honour and happiness. However, till that period arrives in which women will act wisely, we will amuse ourselves in talking of their follies.

The situation and education of women, Hortensia, is precisely that which must necessarily tend to corrupt and debilitate both the powers of mind and body. From a false notion of beauty and delicacy, their system of nerves is depraved before they come out of their nursery; and this kind of depravity has more influence over the mind, and consequently over morals, than is commonly apprehended. But it would be well if such causes only acted towards the debasement of the sex; their moral education is, if possible, more absurd than their physical. The principles and nature of virtue, which is never properly explained to boys, is kept quite a mystery to girls. They are told indeed, that they must abstain from those vices which are contrary to their personal happiness, or they will be regarded as criminals, both by God and man; but all the higher parts of rectitude, every thing that ennobles our being, and that renders us both innoxious and useful, is either not taught, or is taught in such a manner as to leave no proper impression on the mind. This is so obvious a truth, that the defects of female education have ever been a fruitful topic of declamation for the moralist; but not one of this class of writers have laid down any judicious rules for amendment. Whilst we still retain the absurd notion of a sexual excellence, it will militate against the perfecting a plan of education for either sex.

3.4   Mary Wollstonecraft, *A Vindication of the Rights of Woman: with Strictures on Political and Moral Subjects* (1792)

*By the time she published her most famous work in 1792, Mary Wollstonecraft (1759–97) had established a school for girls, worked as a governess, published on the subject of education for women (*Thoughts on the Education of Daughters, *1787), written a novel (*Mary: A Fiction, *1788), and contributed to the debate over the 'Rights of Man' (extract 1.5). Wollstonecraft's grand ambition in* A Vindication of the Rights of Woman *is seen in the proclamation she makes in Chapter 3: 'It is time to effect a revolution in female manners – time to restore to them their lost dignity – and make them, as a part of the human species, labour by reforming themselves to reform the world.' She argues that the characteristics associated with women are not natural but the result of society's 'mistaken notions of female excellence' which encourage women to behave in what she sees as debased ways. She advocates educational reform and enabling women to gain independent status through a wider range of professional opportunities. In 1797 Wollstonecraft married William Godwin, author of* Political Justice, *and died following the birth of her daughter Mary (the future Mary Shelley and author of* Frankenstein).

After considering the historic page, and viewing the living world with anxious solicitude, the most melancholy emotions of sorrowful indignation have depressed my spirits, and I have sighed when obliged to confess, that either nature has made a great difference between man and man, or that the civilization which has hitherto taken place in the world has been very partial. I have turned over various books written on the subject of education, and patiently observed the conduct of parents and the management of schools; but what has been the result? – a profound conviction that the neglected education of my fellow-creatures is the grand source of the misery I deplore; and that women, in particular, are rendered weak and wretched by a variety of concurring causes, originating from one hasty conclusion. The conduct and manners of women, in fact, evidently prove that their minds are not in a healthy state; for, like the flowers which are planted in too rich a soil, strength and usefulness are sacrificed to beauty; and the flaunting leaves, after having pleased a fastidious eye, fade, disregarded on the stalk, long before the season when they ought to have arrived at maturity. – One cause of this barren blooming I attribute to a false system of education, gathered from the books written on this subject by men who, considering females rather as women than human creatures, have been more anxious to make them alluring mistresses than rational wives; and the understanding of the sex has been so bubbled by this specious homage, that the civilized women of the present century, with a few exceptions, are only anxious to inspire love, when they ought to cherish a nobler ambition, and by their abilities and virtues exact respect. . . .

My own sex, I hope, will excuse me, if I treat them like rational creatures, instead of flattering their *fascinating* graces, and viewing them as if they were in a state of perpetual childhood, unable to stand alone. I earnestly wish to point out in what true dignity and human happiness consists – I wish to persuade women to endeavour to acquire strength, both of mind and body, and to convince them that the soft phrases, susceptibility of heart, delicacy of sentiment, and refinement of taste, are almost synonymous with epithets of weakness, and that those beings who are only the objects of pity and that kind of love, which has been termed its sister, will soon become objects of contempt. . . .

[T]he most perfect education, in my opinion, is such an exercise of the understanding as is best calculated to strengthen the body and form the heart. Or, in other words, to enable the individual to attain such habits of virtue as will render it independent. In fact, it is a farce to call any being virtuous whose virtues do not result from the exercise of its own reason. This was Rousseau's opinion respecting men: I extend it to women, and confidently assert that they have been drawn out of their sphere by false refinement, and not by an endeavour to acquire masculine qualities. Still the regal homage which they receive is so intoxicating, that till the manners of the times are changed, and formed on more reasonable principles, it may be impossible to convince them that the illegitimate power which they obtain, by degrading themselves, is a curse, and that they must return to nature and equality, if they wish to secure the placid satisfaction that unsophisticated affections impart. But for this epoch we must wait – wait, perhaps, till kings and nobles, enlightened by reason, and, preferring the real dignity of man to childish state, throw off their gaudy hereditary trappings: and if then women do not resign the arbitrary power of beauty – they will prove that they have *less* mind than man. . . .

Women, as well as despots, have now, perhaps, more power than they would have if the world, divided and subdivided into kingdoms and families, was governed by laws deduced from the exercise of reason; but in obtaining it, to carry on the comparison, their character is degraded, and licentiousness spread through the whole aggregate of society. The many become pedestal to the few. I, therefore, will venture to assert, that till women are more rationally educated, the progress of human virtue and improvement in knowledge must receive continual checks. And if it be granted that woman was not created merely to gratify the appetite of man, nor to be the upper servant, who provides his meals and takes care of his linen, it must follow, that the first care of those mothers or fathers, who really attend to the education of females, should be, if not to strengthen the body, at least, not to destroy the constitution by mistaken notions of beauty and female excellence; nor should girls ever be allowed to imbibe the pernicious notion that a defect can, by any chemical process of reasoning, become an excellence. . . .

But should it be proved that woman is naturally weaker than man, from whence does it follow that it is natural for her to labour to become still weaker than nature intended her to be? Arguments of this cast are an insult to common sense, and savour of passion. The *divine right* of husbands, like the divine right of kings, may, it is to be hoped, in this enlightened age, be contested without danger, and, though conviction may not silence many boisterous disputants, yet, when any prevailing prejudice is attacked, the wise will consider, and leave the narrow-minded to rail with thoughtless vehemence at innovation. . . .

I wish to sum up what I have said in a few words, for I here throw down my gauntlet, and deny the existence of sexual virtues, not excepting modesty. For man and woman, truth, if I understand the meaning of the word, must be the same; yet the fanciful female character, so prettily drawn by poets and novelists, demanding the sacrifice of truth and sincerity, virtue becomes a relative idea, having no other foundation than utility, and of that utility men pretend arbitrarily to judge, shaping it to their own convenience.

Women, I allow, may have different duties to fulfil; but they are *human* duties, and the principles that should regulate the discharge of them, I sturdily maintain, must be the same.

To become respectable, the exercise of their understanding is necessary, there is no other foundation for independence of character; I mean explicitly to say that they must only bow to the authority of reason, instead of being the *modest* slaves of opinion.

In the superiour ranks of life how seldom do we meet with a man of superiour abilities, or even common acquirements? The reason appears to me clear, the state they are born in was an unnatural one. The human character has ever been

The Fashionable Mamma, – or – The Convenience of Modern Dress ·Vide The Pocket Holz. &c

Figure 6 James Gillray, 'Fashionable Mamma, – or – *The Convenience of Modern Dress'*, 15 February 1796; © Copyright the Trustees of the British Museum.

Gillray's image illustrates some of the tensions within ideas of womanhood in the 1790s, juxtaposing the idealized picture of 'Maternal Love' on the wall with the 'Fashionable Mamma' who, while breastfeeding her baby in line with the theories of Rousseau and his followers, appears more concerned with the social world beyond the home, symbolized by the waiting carriage outside the window. The crown on the carriage illustrates the mother's aristocratic rank of viscountess and the image satirizes the fashion for revealing dress.

formed by the employments the individual, or class, pursues; and if the faculties are not sharpened by necessity, they must remain obtuse. The argument may fairly be extended to women; for, seldom occupied by serious business, the pursuit of pleasure gives that insignificancy to their character which renders the society of the *great* so insipid. The same want of firmness, produced by a similar cause, forces them both to fly from themselves to noisy pleasures, and artificial passions, till vanity takes place of every social affection, and the characteristics of humanity can scarcely be discerned. Such are the blessings of civil governments, as they are at present organized, that wealth and female softness equally tend to debase mankind, and are produced by the same cause; but allowing women to be rational creatures, they should be incited to acquire virtues which they may call their own, for how can a rational being be ennobled by any thing that is not obtained by its *own* exertions? . . .

Women, in particular, all want to be ladies. Which is simply to have nothing to do, but listlessly to go they scarcely care where, for they cannot tell what.

But what have women to do in society? I may be asked, but to loiter with easy grace; surely you would not condemn them all to suckle fools and chronicle small beer![3] No. Women might certainly study the art of healing, and be physicians as well as nurses. And midwifery, decency seems to allot to them. . . .

They might, also, study politics, and settle their benevolence on the broadest basis; for the reading of history will scarcely be more useful than the perusal of romances, if read as mere biography; if the character of the times, the political improvements, arts, &c. be not observed. . . .

Business of various kinds, they might likewise pursue, if they were educated in a more orderly manner, which might save many from common and legal prostitution. Women would not then marry for a support, as men accept of places under government, and neglect the implied duties; nor would an attempt to earn their own subsistence, a most laudable one! sink them almost to the level of those poor abandoned creatures who live by prostitution. For are not milliners and mantua-makers[4] reckoned the next class? The few employments open to women, so far from being liberal, are menial; and when a superiour education enables them to take charge of the education of children as governesses, they are not treated like the tutors of sons, though even clerical tutors are not always treated in a manner calculated to render them respectable in the eyes of their pupils, to say nothing of the private comfort of the individual. But as women educated like gentlewomen, are never designed for the humiliating situation which necessity sometimes forces them to fill; these situations are considered in the light of a degradation; and they know little of the human heart, who need to be told, that nothing so painfully sharpens the sensibility as such a fall in life. . . .

---

3 Iago in Shakespeare's *Othello*, II.i.160.
4 Hat-makers and dress-makers.

It is a melancholy truth; yet such is the blessed effect of civilization! the most respectable women are the most oppressed; and, unless they have understandings far superiour to the common run of understandings, taking in both sexes, they must, from being treated like contemptible beings, become contemptible. How many women thus waste life away the prey of discontent, who might have practised as physicians, regulated a farm, managed a shop, and stood erect, supported by their own industry, instead of hanging their heads surcharged with the dew of sensibility, that consumes the beauty to which it at first gave lustre; nay, I doubt whether pity and love are so near akin as poets feign, for I have seldom seen much compassion excited by the helplessness of females, unless they were fair; then, perhaps, pity was the soft handmaid of love, or the harbinger of lust.

How much more respectable is the woman who earns her own bread by fulfilling any duty, than the most accomplished beauty! – beauty did I say! – so sensible am I of the beauty of moral loveliness, or the harmonious propriety that attunes the passions of a well-regulated mind, that I blush at making the comparison; yet I sigh to think how few women aim at attaining this respectability by withdrawing from the giddy whirl of pleasure, or the indolent calm that stupefies the good sort of women it sucks in. . . .

Another instance of that feminine weakness of character, often produced by a confined education, is a romantic twist of the mind, which has been very properly termed *sentimental*.

Women subjected by ignorance to their sensations, and only taught to look for happiness in love, refine on sensual feelings, and adopt metaphysical notions respecting that passion, which lead them shamefully to neglect the duties of life, and frequently in the midst of these sublime refinements they plump into actual vice.

These are the women who are amused by the reveries of the stupid novelists, who, knowing little of human nature, work up stale tales, and describe meretricious scenes, all retailed in a sentimental jargon, which equally tend to corrupt the taste, and draw the heart aside from its daily duties. I do not mention the understanding, because never having been exercised, its slumbering energies rest inactive, like the lurking particles of fire which are supposed universally to pervade matter.

Females, in fact, denied all political privileges, and not allowed, as married women, excepting in criminal cases, a civil existence, have their attention naturally drawn from the interest of the whole community to that of the minute parts, though the private duty of any member of society must be very imperfectly performed when not connected with the general good. The mighty business of female life is to please, and restrained from entering into more important concerns by political and civil oppression, sentiments become events, and reflection deepens what it should, and would have effaced, if the understanding had been allowed to take a wider range.

But, confined to trifling employments, they naturally imbibe opinions which the only kind of reading calculated to interest an innocent frivolous mind, inspires. Unable to grasp any thing great, is it surprising that they find the reading of history a very dry task, and disquisitions addressed to the understanding intolerably tedious, and almost unintelligible? Thus are they necessarily dependent on the novelist for amusement. Yet, when I exclaim against novels, I mean when contrasted with those works which exercise the understanding and regulate the imagination. – For any kind of reading I think better than leaving a blank still a blank, because the mind must receive a degree of enlargement and obtain a little strength by a slight exertion of its thinking powers; besides, even the productions that are only addressed to the imagination, raise the reader a little above the gross gratification of appetites, to which the mind has not given a shade of delicacy. . . .

Asserting the rights which women in common with men ought to contend for, I have not attempted to extenuate their faults; but to prove them to be the natural consequence of their education and station in society. If so, it is reasonable to suppose that they will change their character, and correct their vices and follies, when they are allowed to be free in a physical, moral, and civil sense.

Let woman share the rights and she will emulate the virtues of man; for she must grow more perfect when emancipated, or justify the authority that chains such a weak being to her duty.

3.5 Mary Hays, *Appeal to the Men of Great Britain in Behalf of Women* (1798)

Mary Hays (1760–1843) grew up in a context of Rational Dissent and knew the members of the publisher Joseph Johnson's circle, including Paine, Godwin and Wollstonecraft. She was strongly influenced by the latter's A Vindication of the Rights of Woman, *which she defended in her feminist and radical* Letters and Essays, Moral, and Miscellaneous *(1793). She published her* Appeal to the Men of Great Britain *anonymously in 1798, a year after Wollstonecraft's death, by which time there was an increasingly strong reaction against demands for women's rights and education (see, for example, Richard Polwhele's attack on women writers,* The Unsex'd Females, *of the same year – extract 8.5). In this context, Hay's self-representation in the* Appeal *is striking: 'I come not in the garb of an Amazon, to dispute the field right or wrong; but rather in the humble attire of a petitioner, willing to submit the cause, to him who is both judge and party. Not as a fury flinging the torch of discord and revenge amongst the daughters of Eve; but as a friend and companion bearing a little taper to lead them to the paths of truth, of virtue, and of liberty.' Like Wollstonecraft, Hays called for improved education for women, seeing their current degradation as the product of the environment in which they are raised: 'Of all the systems, – if indeed a bundle of contradictions and absurdities may be called a system, – which human nature in its moments of intoxication has produced; that which men have contrived with a view to forming the minds, and regulating the conduct of women, is perhaps the most completely absurd'. Hays developed her list of the great women of history (extracted below) in her pioneering six-volume* Female Biography; or, Memoirs of Illustrious and Celebrated Women, of all Ages and Countries *of 1803.*

No work [has] been attempted with a view to ascertain the pretensions of the sexes upon fair and rational principles; and by drawing just and clear inferences, from these principles. I fear, as I said before, that such an undertaking is almost unconquerably difficult. But we have materials to which we can appeal, though they are too numerous and cumbersome to bring forward; and these are to be found in the works of historians and biographers of credit, ancient and modern, assisted by daily observation and experience.

And here Semiramises of the North and East, Deborahs, Boadiceas, Joan D'Arcs, Elisabeths, Margarets, Catherines, and Christinas, croud upon the 'aching sight.' Nor are the niches of poetry and literature unfurnished with female ornaments, from the muse of fire of Sappho, down to the more chastened flame which beams in the compositions of the female poets, and prose writers, of the present day. But, heaven defend me from drudging in the mines of history and antiquity, and dragging forth to adorn, and swell out my slender pages, all the precious jewels of ancient, middle, and modern times! Life is too short for such an undertaking. It is enough for my purpose that we know, that such things as we allude to, have been, 'and are, and are most true.'

Appealing therefore, on the one hand, to men of reading and information, who are able to decide the question upon the evidence of well-known and established facts, which must readily occur to their memory; and appealing on the other to the mass of mankind, who are fully competent to judge, upon the principles of common sense, and from daily observation; I ask those of both classes, who have sufficient strength of mind to cast prejudice aside, whether, taking into account the very few women, who have received a suitable education; the numbers who have shone, as sovereigns, as legislators, in politicks, in literature, and in common life; are not out of all proportion great? . . .

While then, we wish to exhonor men, with respect to the motives, which prompt their conduct towards women; – while we cannot upon any fair principles of reasoning, doubt, that they are desirous, and even satisfied, that good consequences may follow from their absolute government of women; – we cannot with any degree of sincerity profess, that we consider as well established, but on the contrary, – as false; – or at best but as uncertain; – that principle upon which they build their whole system, viz. THAT MEN ARE SUPERIOR BEINGS, WHEN COMPARED WITH WOMEN; AND THAT CONSEQUENTLY, NATURE AND REASON, INVEST THEM WITH AUTHORITY OVER THE WEAKER SEX. This, – divested of all ambiguity of language, and all attempts, to impose on the understandings, or compound with the vanity of women, – is beyond a doubt, not the opinion only, of the generality of men; – but the leading principle upon which the laws by which we are governed, are founded, – the grand pivot upon which social and domestic politicks turn, – And the language of prejudice all over the world. For, alas for poor human nature! it yet remains to be proven, that it is the language of truth. What is it indeed after all, but an opinion taken up at random, and which perhaps if fairly examined, and cross examined, may be found to be, – the essence, nay the very quintessence, of prepossession, of arrogance, and of absurdity!

But it must be confessed, that even those who consider the human species, in a more liberal and extensive point of view, – who do not see sufficient grounds for those claims so haughtily advanced on the part of the men, – yet suppose the necessity of subordination on one side unavoidable. They therefore fear, that women, were their eyes opened to their natural equality and consequence, would not so tamely submit to the cruel injustice with which they are treated, in many of the leading points in life. And they know that nothing would tend so much to this *eclaircissement*,[5] as an education, which by exercising their reason, and unfolding their talents, should point out to themselves, how they might exert them to the utmost. Such a developement of mind would undoubt-edly enable them to see and reason upon what principles, all the other regula-tions of society were formed, – which however they may deviate in execution, are evidently founded on justice and humanity, – and would consequently enable them to bring home and apply those principles to the situation of their sex in general. Thus awakened to a sense of their injuries, they would behold with astonishment and indignation, the arts which had been employed, to keep them in a state of PERPETUAL BABYISM. . . .

Women then, I must take it upon me to say, ought to be considered as the companions and equals, not as the inferiors, – much less as they virtually are, – as the slaves of men. In every station they are entitled to esteem, as well as love, when deserving, and virtuous, in the different connections of life, – They were originally intended, to be the helpmates of the other sex, as the Scripture most emphatically and explicitly calls them; and not their drudges in the common ranks, and the tools of their passions and prejudices in the higher. . . .

3.6   Hannah More, *Strictures on the Modern System of Female Education. With a View of the Principles and Conduct Prevalent Among Women of Rank and Fortune* (1799)

The Evangelical and conservative writer and poet Hannah More (1745–1833; see also extract 1.7) had a keen practical and theoretical interest in the education of girls and

---

5 Enlightenment; clearing up of something puzzling.

young women. She was the daughter of a headmaster, worked as a teacher and ulti-
mately principal of a girls' school, and played a major role in the Evangelical develop-
ment of the Sunday school system, herself establishing more than a dozen schools from
1789 onwards. Like Macaulay, Wollstonecraft and Hays in Strictures, *More advocates*
educational reform for women, and though she limits their roles much more than those
three writers did, in placing women at the centre of the family, and indeed of the nation,
she grants them considerable importance and authority. Strictures *sold very well, and*
More wrote further on female education in her conduct-book aimed at Princess
Charlotte, Hints Towards Forming the Character of a Young Princess *(1805), and*
in her only novel, Coelebs in Search of a Wife *(1808).*

It is a singular injustice which is often exercised towards women, first to give
them a most defective Education, and then to expect from them the most undeviating purity of conduct; – to train them in such a manner as shall lay them
open to the most dangerous faults, and then to censure them for not proving
faultless. Is it not unreasonable and unjust, to express disappointment if our
daughters should, in their subsequent lives, turn out precisely that very kind of
character for which it would be evident to an unprejudiced by-stander that the
whole scope and tenor of their instruction had been systematically preparing
them? . . .

Among the talents for the application of which women of the higher class will
be peculiarly accountable, there is one, the importance of which they can
scarcely rate too highly. This talent is influence. . . .

   The general state of civilized society depends more than those are aware, who
are not accustomed to scrutinize into the springs of human action, on the
prevailing sentiments and habits of women, and on the nature and degree of the
estimation in which they are held. Even those who admit the power of female
elegance on the manners of men, do not always attend to the influence of
female principles on their character. In the former case, indeed, women are apt
to be sufficiently conscious of their power, and not backward in turning it to
account. But there are nobler objects to be effected by the exertion of their
powers. . . .

   In this moment of alarm and peril,[6] I would call on them with a 'warning
voice,' which should stir up every latent principle in their minds, and kindle
every slumbering energy in their hearts; I would call on them to come forward,
and contribute their full and fair proportion towards the saving of their country.
But I would call on them to come forward, without departing from the refinement of their character, without derogating from the dignity of their rank, without blemishing the delicacy of their sex: I would call them to the best and most

---

6 More is writing during a period of invasion threat (see extracts 1.10 and 1.12).

appropriate exertion of their power, to raise the depressed tone of public morals, to awaken the drowsy spirit of religious principle, and to re-animate the dormant powers of active piety. They know too well how imperiously they give the law to manners, and with how despotic a sway they fix the standard of fashion. But this is not enough; this is a low mark, a prize not worthy of their high and holy calling. For, on the use which women of the superior class may be disposed to make of that power delegated to them by the courtesy of custom, by the honest gallantry of the heart, by the imperious controul of virtuous affections, by the habits of civilized states, by the usages of polished society; on the use, I say, which they shall hereafter make of this influence, will depend, in no low degree, the well-being of those states, and the virtue and happiness, nay perhaps the very existence of that society.

At this period, when our country can only hope to stand by opposing a bold and noble *unanimity* to the most tremendous confederacies against religion and order, and governments, which the world ever saw; what an accession would it bring to the public strength, could we prevail on beauty, and rank, and talents, and virtue, confederating their several powers, to come forward with a patriotism at once firm and feminine for the general good! I am not sounding an alarm to female warriors, or exciting female politicians: I hardly know which of the two is the most disgusting and unnatural character. Propriety is to a woman what the great Roman critic[7] says action is to an orator; it is the first, the second, the third requisite. A woman may be knowing, active, witty, and amusing; but without propriety she cannot be amiable. Propriety is the centre in which all the lines of duty and of agreeableness meet. It is to character what proportion is to figure, and grace to attitude. It does not depend on any one perfection; but it is the result of general excellence. It shows itself by a regular, orderly, undeviating course; and never starts from its sober orbit into any splendid eccentricities; for it would be ashamed of such praise as it might extort by any aberrations from its proper path. . . .

Not a few of the evils of the present day arise from a new and perverted application of terms; among these perhaps, there is not one more abused, misunderstood, or misapplied, than the term *accomplishments*. This word in its original meaning, signifies *completeness, perfection*. But I may safely appeal to the observation of mankind, whether they do not meet with swarms of youthful females, issuing from our boarding schools, as well as emerging from the more private scenes of domestic education, who are introduced into the world, under the broad and universal title of *accomplished young ladies*, of *all* of whom it cannot very truly and correctly be pronounced, that they illustrate the definition by a completeness which leaves nothing to be added, and a perfection which leaves nothing to be desired.

---

7 Demosthenes, the Greek orator.

This phrenzy of accomplishments, unhappily, is no longer restricted within the usual limits of rank and fortune; the middle orders have caught the contagion, and it rages with increasing violence, from the elegantly dressed but slenderly portioned curate's daughter, to the equally fashionable daughter of the little tradesman, and of the more opulent, but not more judicious farmer. And is it not obvious, that as far as this epidemical mania has spread, this very valuable part of society declines in usefulness, as it rises in its unlucky pretensions to elegance. And this revolution of the manners of the middle class has so far altered the character of the age, as to be in danger of rendering obsolete the heretofore common saying, 'that most worth and virtue are to be found in the middle station.' For I do not scruple to assert, that in general, as far as my little observation has extended, this class of females, in what relates both to religious knowledge and to practical industry, falls short both of the very high and the very low. Their new course of education, and the habits of life, and elegance of dress connected with it, peculiarly unfits them for the active duties of their own very important condition; while, with frivolous eagerness and second-hand opportunities, they run to snatch a few of those showy acquirements which decorate the great. This is done apparently with one or other of these views; either to make their fortune by marriage, or if that fail, to qualify them to become teachers of others: hence the abundant multiplication of superficial wives, and of incompetent and illiterate governesses. The use of the pencil, the performance of exquisite but unnecessary works, the study of foreign languages and of music, require (with some exceptions, which should always be made in favour of great natural genius) a degree of leisure which belongs exclusively to affluence. . . .

But, to return to that more elevated, and, on account of their more extended influence only, that more important class of females, to whose use this little work is more immediately dedicated. Some popular authors, on the subject of female instruction, had for a time established a fantastic code of artificial manners. They had refined elegance into insipidity, frittered down delicacy into frivolousness, and reduced manner into *minauderie*. But 'to lisp, and to amble, and to nick-name God's creatures,'[8] has nothing to do with true gentleness of mind; and to be silly makes no necessary part of softness. Another class of cotemporary authors turned all the force of their talents to excite *emotions*, to inspire *sentiment*, and to reduce all moral excellence into *sympathy* and *feeling*. These softer qualities were elevated at the expence of principle; and young women were incessantly hearing unqualified sensibility extolled as the perfection of their nature; till those who really possessed this amiable quality, instead of directing, and chastising, and restraining it, were in danger of fostering it to their hurt, and began to consider themselves as deriving their excellence from its excess; while those less interesting damsels, who happened not to find any of

---

8 Shakespeare, *Hamlet*, III.i.146–7.

this amiable sensibility in their *hearts*, but thought it creditable to have it some-where, fancied its seat was in the *nerves*; and here indeed it was easily found or feigned; till a false and excessive display of feeling became so predominant, as to bring in question the actual existence of that true tenderness, without which, though a woman may be worthy, she can never be amiable. . . .

The chief end to be proposed in cultivating the understandings of women, is to qualify them for the practical purposes of life. Their knowledge is not often like the learning of men, to be reproduced in some literary composition, nor ever in any learned profession; but it is to come out in conduct. A lady studies, not that she may qualify herself to become an orator or a pleader; not that she may learn to debate, but to act. She is to read the best books, not so much to enable her to talk of them, as to bring the improvement she derives from them to the rectifi-cation of her principles, and the formation of her habits. The great uses of study are to enable her to regulate her own mind, and to be useful to others. . . .

But *they* little understand the true interests of woman who would lift her from the important duties of her allotted station, to fill with fantastic dignity a loftier but less appropriate niche. Nor do they understand her true happiness, who seek to annihilate distinctions from which she derives advantages, and to attempt innovations which would depreciate her real value. Each sex has its proper excel-lences, which would be lost were they melted down into the common character by the fusion of the new philosophy. Why should we do away distinctions which increase the mutual benefits and satisfactions of life? Whence, but by carefully preserving the original marks of difference stamped by the hand of the Creator, would be derived the superior advantage of mixed society? Have men no need to have their rough angles filed off, and their harshnesses and asperities smoothed and polished by assimilating with beings of more softness and refine-ment? Are the ideas of women naturally so *very* judicious, are their principles so *invincibly* firm, are their views so *perfectly* correct, are their judgments so *completely* exact, that there is occasion for no additional weight, no superadded strength, no increased clearness, none of that enlargement of mind, none of that additional invigoration which may be derived from the aids of the stronger sex? What identity could advantageously supersede an enlivening opposition and interesting variety of character? Is it not then more wise as well as more honourable to move contentedly in the plain path which Providence has obvi-ously marked out to the sex, and in which custom has for the most part ratio-nally confirmed them, rather than to stray awkwardly, unbecomingly, and unsuccessfully, in a forbidden road? to be the lawful possessors of a lesser domes-tic territory, rather than the turbulent usurpers of a wider foreign empire? to be good originals, rather than bad imitators? to be the best thing of one's own kind, rather than an inferior thing even if it were of an higher kind? to be excellent women rather than indifferent men?

Is the author then undervaluing her own sex? – No. It is her zeal for their true *interests* which leads her to oppose their imaginary *rights*. It is her regard for their happiness which makes her endeavour to cure them of a feverish thirst for fame. A little Christian humility and sober-mindedness are worth all the wild meta-physical discussion, which has unsettled the peace of vain women, and forfeited the respect of reasonable men. And the most elaborate definition of their ideal rights, and the most hardy measures for attaining them, are of less value in the eyes of a truly amiable woman, than 'that meek and quiet spirit, which is in the sight of God of great price.'[9]

3.7 Jane West, *Letters to a Young Lady, in which the Duties and Character of Women are Considered, Chiefly with a Reference to Prevailing Opinions* (1806)

Jane West (1758–1852) was a wide-ranging writer whose works included two conduct-books, Letters to a Young Man *(1801) and* Letters to a Young Lady *(1806). In the latter, she argues that middle-class women should be subordinate to men and that their role should be limited to the domestic sphere, though she stresses that they should be informed and knowledgeable. However, like Hannah More (extract 3.6), she gives women in this limited role considerable authority and importance, making them crucial to the moral well-being of the nation, and so, central to its political health.*

To these domestic duties and obligations, may be added what belongs to us in the aggregate, as the refiners of manners, and the conservators of morals; and in these cases every judicious statesman readily allows our relative importance. No nation has preserved its political independence for any long period after its women become dissipated and licentious. When the hallowed graces of the chaste matron have given place to the bold allurements of the courtezan, the rising generation always proclaims its base origin. Luxurious self-indulgence; frivolous or abandoned pursuits; indifference to every generous motive; mean attachment to interest; disdain of lawful authority, yet credulous subservience to artful demagogues; the blended vice of the savage, the sybarite, and the slave, proclaim a people ripe for ruin, and inviting the chains of the conqueror. As far as the records of past ages permit us to judge, female depravity preceded the downfal of those mighty states of Greece and Italy which once gave law to the world. We have inspired testimony, that the licentiousness, pride, and extrava-gance of 'the daughters of Sion,' during the latter part of her first monarchy, accelerated the divine judgments, and unsheathed the sword of the Babylonish destroyer.[10] The events that we have witnessed in our own times confirm this

---

9 1 Peter, 3:4.
10 West's note: 'See various passages in the prophetical parts of Scripture; especially Isaiah.'

position: in most of the realms that have been overcome by the arms of France, a notorious dereliction of female principle prevailed; and the state of manners in France itself, as far as related to our sex, had obtained such dreadful publicity, as allows us to ascribe the fall of that country in a great measure to the dissipated indelicate behaviour and loose morals of its women. Thus, though we are not entitled to a place in the senate, we become *legislators* in the most important sense of the word, by impressing on the minds of all around us the obligation which gives force to the statute. Were we but steadily united in resisting the corruption of the times, the boastful libertine, the professed man of gallantry, the vapid coxcomb, the profane scoffer, the indecent jester, and all the reptile swarm which perverted pride and false wit produce, would disappear. It is us that they seek to please, or rather to astonish; and if we were but steadily resolved to repay their vanity with contempt, and to bestow our smiles only on what was meritorious, or really brilliant, the habits of the gay world would undergo a most happy transformation.

3.8   William Thompson [and Anna Wheeler], *Appeal of One Half the Human Race, Women, Against the Pretensions of the Other Half, Men, to Retain Them in Political, and Thence in Civil and Domestic, Slavery; In Reply to a Paragraph of Mr. Mill's Celebrated 'Article on Government'* (1825)

William Thompson (1775–1833) was an influential writer on economics, socialism, and the position of women, collaborating on the latter with Anna Wheeler (1785–1848). Though the Appeal *was published under Thompson's name, he acknowledged Wheeler's collaborative authorship in his 'Introductory Letter to Mrs Wheeler'. The* Appeal *is particularly concerned with women's political representation, and had been prompted by James Mill's argument in his 'Essay on Government' that women did not require representation. Wheeler quotes Mill's offending paragraph on his title-page: 'One thing is pretty clear, that all those individuals whose interests are indisputably included in those of other individuals may be struck off from political rights without inconvenience. In this light may be viewed all children up to a certain age, whose interests are involved in those of their parents. In this light also women may be regarded, the interests of almost all of whom is involved either in that of their fathers, or in that of their husbands.'*

Political rights are necessary to women as a check on the almost inveterate habits of exclusion of men. It is in vain to sanction by law a civil right, or to remove an exclusion, if the law affords no means to those whom it designs to benefit of causing the right or permission to be enforced. Women may be eligible by law to the situation of professors; the law may protect them when married from the personal violence or constraint of any kind of their husbands, as fully as it protects husbands against them; but if none but men are to be the electors, if none but men are to be jurors or judges when women complain against men of partiality and injustice, is it in human nature that a sympathy from old habit, from similarity of organization and trains of thought, from love of domination, should not have a tendency to make men swerve from the line of justice and strict impartiality, should not make them underrate the pretensions of women, and be lenient to the errors of men? When to this are joined the superior strength, the *secrecy* of domestic wrongs, and thence the means of transgression and impunity, who can doubt the necessity of an equally mixed, as resulting from equal political laws, in order to be an impartial, tribunal, in all cases where women are the parties as against men, or men as against women? . . .

A second reason why women, in addition to equal laws and an equal system of morals, should also possess equal political rights and be eligible to all offices, (if so disposed, and not by rotation or compulsion,) like men, is, that exclusive legislators, particularly men as exclusive legislators for women, though ever so sincerely inclined to promote the happiness of those whom they exclude equally with their own, must be liable to errors from want of knowledge, from *false judgements*. How can exclusive legislators know the interests of those who are not their constituents, of those whom they never consult, who have no control over them? . . .

Women of England! women, in whatever country ye breathe – wherever ye breathe, degraded – awake! Awake to the contemplation of the happiness that awaits you when all your faculties of mind and body shall be fully cultivated and developed; when every path in which ye can exercise those improved faculties shall be laid open and rendered delightful to you, even as to them who now ignorantly enslave and degrade you. If degradation from long habitude have lost its sting, if the iron have penetrated so deeply into your frame that it has been gradually taken up into the system and mingles unperceived amidst the fluids of your life; if the prostration of reason and the eradication of feeling have kept pace within you, so that you are insensible alike to what you suffer and to what you might enjoy, – your case were all but hopeless. Nothing less, then, than the sight presented before your eyes, of the superior happiness enjoyed by other women, under arrangements of perfect equality with men, could arouse you. Such a sight, even under such circumstances, would excite your envy and kindle up all your extinct desires. But you are not so degraded. The unvaried despotism of so many thousand years, has not so entirely degraded you, has not been able to extinguish within you the feelings of nature, the love of happiness and of equal justice. The united exertions of law, superstition, and pretended morals of past ages of ignorance, have not entirely succeeded. There is still a germ within you, the love of happiness, coeval with your existence, and never to cease but when 'life itself shall please no more,' which shall conduct you, feeble as it now is, under the guidance of wisdom and benevolence, to that perfect equality of knowledge, sympathy, and enjoyment with men, which the greatest sum of happiness for the whole race demands.

Sleeps there an infant on your bosom, to the level of whose intellect the systematic despotism and pitiful jealousy of man have not sought, and for the most part successfully sought, to chain down yours? Does no blush rise amongst you – swells no breast with indignation, at the enormous wrong? Simple as ye are, have ye become enamoured of folly? do you indeed believe it to be a source of power and of happiness? Look to your masters: does knowledge in their hands remain idle? is it with them no source of power and happiness? Think ye then indeed that it is of the use of what are called your personal charms alone that man is jealous? There is not a quality of mind which his animal propensities do not grudge you: not one, those only excepted which, like high-seasoned or far-fetched sauces, render you, as objects of sense, more stimulating to his purely selfish desires. Do ye pretend to enjoy with him, at this banquet of *bought* or *commanded* sensuality, the sensuality of prostitution or of marriage? He has a system of domineering hypocrisy, which he calls morals, which brands with the name of vice your enjoyment, while it lauds with the name of virtue, or gilds with that of innocent gratification, his. What quality, worth the possession, and capable of being applied to useful purposes for your own independence and happiness, do you possess, of which ignorant man is not jealous? Strength is his peculiar prerogative; it is *unfeminine* to possess it: hence every expedient is used in what is called your education, to enervate your bodies, by proscribing that activity which is as necessary to health as to preservation from inevitable casualties. Muscular weakness, what is called delicacy of health approaching to disease, helplessness, are by a strange perversion of language denominated rather perfections than defects in women, in order to increase their dependence, even their *physical* dependence on man; gratifying by one operation his two ruling animal propensities, sexual desire and love of domination.

4

Religion and Belief

Introduction

The previous three sections have shown how volatile the Romantic age was politically, socially, and in the debate over women. This volatility was no less characteristic of the age in terms of religion. As Robert M. Ryan has argued:

> For a period of approximately three decades, the decades in which Romantic poetry flourished, religion in England seemed to abandon its character as a guarantor of social stability and to become, as it had during the sixteenth and seventeenth centuries, a force for potentially revolutionary change.[1]

It was through the protestant Church of England, linked legally and ideologically to the state and monarch, that religion traditionally performed its stabilizing role. In a famous passage, the historian J. C. D. Clark writes that for the average person in the period, the 'agency of the State' confronted him not politically through Parliament but religiously through the Church:

> The ubiquitous agency of the State was the Church, quartering the land not into a few hundred constituencies but into ten thousand parishes, impinging on the daily concerns of the great majority, supporting its black-coated army of a clerical intelligentsia, bidding for a monopoly of education, piety and political acceptability.[2]

During our period, however, the theological and political power of the Established Church was challenged by a variety of conflicting belief systems and organized groupings, ranging from the atheistic denial of the existence of God to the High Church Catholicism of the nascent Oxford Movement.

One major challenge to the Anglican monopoly came from the Dissenters or Non-conformists, collective terms for the Protestant groupings who refused to

---

1 Robert M. Ryan, *The Romantic Reformation: Religious Politics in English Literature, 1789–1824* (Cambridge: Cambridge University Press, 1997), p. 18.
2 J. C. D. Clark, *English Society, 1688–1832: Ideology, Social Structure and Political Practice during the Ancien Régime* (Cambridge: Cambridge University Press, 1985) p. 277.

conform to the doctrines or practices of the Church of England. During the eighteenth century, the main Dissenting sects were the Presbyterians, the Congregationalists, the Baptists, and the Quakers, with Unitarianism (whose members included Joseph Priestley, Samuel Taylor Coleridge, and Charles Lamb) developing during the final third of the century. Traditionally, Dissent was Calvinistic, characterized by a belief in predestination and divine salvation, though the various sects differed on who would be saved and the Unitarians did not believe in the divinity of Christ. While able to worship, Dissenters were restricted by the Test and Corporation Acts from holding public office or from attending grammar schools or the universities of Oxford and Cambridge. One outcome of these educational restrictions was the development of Dissenting academies, at which a number of the major cultural figures of the period were either teachers (e.g. Joseph Priestley) or pupils (e.g. William Hazlitt). Dissent was a significant intellectual force in the period, providing a context for much of its cultural output (such as the works of Anna Laetitia Barbauld, whose father taught at the famous Warrington Dissenting Academy), and its political dimensions became particularly evident in the 1790s. The majority of Dissenters welcomed the French Revolution, famously in the case of Richard Price (extract 1.2). Enthusiastic responses such as Joseph Priestley's (extract 4.3) contributed to the widespread millenarianism of the 1790s, seen also in the popular prophecies of Richard Brothers (extract 4.4) and, in the following decades, of Joanna Southcott (4.7). Non-conformists themselves linked what they saw as the progress of the Revolution with their own demands for the restrictions on them to be lifted, but the perceived alliance of Dissent and Jacobinism scotched any chance of them achieving these reforms, and it was not until 1828 that the Test and Corporation Acts were repealed. The following year also saw the culmination of the movement for Catholic Emancipation with the passing of the Roman Catholic Relief Act, lifting many of the restrictions on Roman Catholics (for further details, see headnote to extract 4.10).

A second major challenge to the orthodox, Christian theology of the Church of England came from Deism or 'natural religion', a varied set of beliefs which reflected the influence of the increasing rationalism of the eighteenth century. Deism found evidence for the existence of God in the natural world, rather than through revelation or supernatural occurrences. Paine's *The Age of Reason* (1795; extract 4.5) was the period's major statement of Deism, and the vehement reaction prompted by Paine's provocative critique of Christian doctrine was heightened by his political reputation. Paine's views were frequently taken for atheism and the subversive threat of *The Age of Reason* was illustrated over two decades after its initial publication when Richard Carlile was imprisoned for reprinting it (see Figure 8). Carlile was outspoken in his atheistic denial of God in a period when such ideas could be prosecuted for blasphemy; indeed, Carlile and his family and employees were jailed for alleged atheism and the young Percy Shelley was expelled from Oxford following his distribution of his pamphlet *The Necessity of Atheism* (extract 4.11). Carlile's *Address to Men of Science* (extract 4.12) also illustrates the challenge that scientific advances were beginning to pose to what he terms 'Priestcraft', though in this pre-Darwinian period it was more usual to see a reconciliation of science and Christian belief. William Paley managed such a reconciliation in his influential *Natural Theology* (extract 5.8), in which his detailed biological enquiries provided support for his 'argument from design' for a beneficent God.

Many commentators have seen the most significant religious development of the Romantic period to be the growth of Evangelical Christianity, which was influential both inside and outside the Church of England. Evangelicalism had its roots in the beliefs and practices of John Wesley and associates in the 1730s, whose commitment to faith and piety saw them nicknamed 'Methodists'. Though Wesley himself remained a member of the Church of England, Methodism seceded from it in 1795, becoming a branch of Dissent. As Leigh Hunt's critique of Methodism illustrates (extract 4.9), the movement was based on a non-rational and highly emotional sense of personal faith and salvation with preaching and conversion as central practices; the Bible (rather than the natural world) was the authoritative text, with considerable emphasis placed on the importance of Christ's crucifixion. The Evangelical movement also exerted a strong influence within the Church of England, most notably through the 'Clapham Sect' grouped around William Wilberforce. Wilberforce's *A Practical View* (extract 4.6) argues strongly that faith rather than works must be the basis of true Christianity, though he and other Evangelicals recognized that their faith could provide the foundation for social reform, as it did in their successful campaign for the abolition of the slave trade. The Evangelical emphasis on conversion also had an international dimension, underpinning the significant development of the missionary movement in the period (see extract 4.1).

Religion is central to the literary output of the period, providing the direct subject for a number of major texts, from the poetical enquiries of Coleridge's 'Religious Musings' and Wordsworth's *The Excursion*, through the sensational anti-Catholic horrors of Matthew Lewis's Gothic novel *The Monk* and precise dissections of the Anglican clergy in Jane Austen's social novels, to Mary Shelley's reinterpretation of *Frankenstein* in her 1831 'Author's Introduction' as a text about 'the effect of any human endeavour to mock the stupendous mechanism of the Creator of the World!'[3] Many of the works of the period conducted a dialogue with religious texts, especially the Bible and John Milton's *Paradise Lost*, turning to them for authority, rewriting them, or subjecting them to a radical critique (see, for example, Blake's *The Marriage of Heaven and Hell* and Byron's *Cain*). Critical accounts of Romanticism (such as those of M. H. Abrams discussed in the 'Introduction') have viewed it as a secularization of religious structures, achieving revelation through the imagination rather than through

---

3 Mary Shelley, *Frankenstein: 1818 text*, ed. Marilyn Butler (Oxford: Oxford World's Classics, 1994), p. 196.

contact with God, while more recent scholarship has sought to illustrate the part played by literary writers in the religious disputes enacted in the documents below.[4]

4.1   William Carey, *An Enquiry into the Obligations of Christians, to use means for the Conversion of the Heathens* (1792)

Often referred to as the 'Father of Modern Missions', William Carey (1761–1834) was a shoemaker and teacher who became a Baptist at the age of 18. Inspired by the work of early missionaries and by the lives of explorers like Captain Cook (see extracts 9.2 and 9.3), Carey developed an Evangelical passion on a global scale. His Enquiry, *which gives a history, justification, and practical programme for missionary activity, was published in 1792. Together with a sermon of the same year, it was influential in the formation of the 'Particular Baptist Society for the Propagation of the Gospel Amongst the Heathen' (renamed the Baptist Missionary Society), which began the modern Evangelical missionary movement. Carey himself went to India as a missionary in 1793, and translated the Bible into several different languages.*

Our Lord Jesus Christ, a little before his departure, commissioned his apostles to *Go*, and *teach all nations*; or, as another evangelist expresses it, *Go into all the world, and preach the gospel to every creature.* This commission was as extensive as possible, and laid them under obligation to disperse themselves into every country of the habitable globe, and preach to all the inhabitants, without exception, or limitation. They accordingly went forth in obedience to the command, and the power of God evidently wrought with them. Many attempts of the same kind have been made since their day, and which have been attended with various success; but the work has not been taken up, or prosecuted of late years (except by a few individuals) with that zeal and perseverance with which the primitive Christians went about it. . . .

Alas! the far greater part of the world, as we shall see presently, are still covered with heathen darkness! . . . It has been said that we ought not to force our way, but to wait for the openings, and leadings of Providence; but it might with equal propriety be answered in this case, neither ought we to neglect embracing those openings in providence which daily present themselves to us. What openings of providence do we wait for? We can neither expect to be transported into the heathen world without ordinary means, nor to be endowed with the gift of tongues, &c. when we arrive there. These would not be providential interpositions,

---

4   See, for example, Ryan, *The Romantic Reformation*, and Martin Priestman, *Romantic Atheism: Poetry and Freethought, 1780–1830* (Cambridge: Cambridge University Press, 2000).

but miraculous ones. Where a command exists nothing can be necessary to render it binding but a removal of those obstacles which render obedience impossible, and these are removed already. Natural impossibility can never be pleaded so long as facts exist to prove the contrary. Have not the popish missionaries surmounted all those difficulties which we have generally thought to be insuperable? Have not the missionaries of the *Unitas Fratrum*, or Moravian Brethren,[5] encountered the scorching heat of Abyssinia, and the frozen climes of Greenland, and Labrador, their difficult languages, and savage manners? Or have not English traders, for the sake of gain, surmounted all those things which have generally been counted insurmountable obstacles in the way of preaching the gospel? Witness the trade to Persia, the East-Indies, China, and Greenland, yea even the accursed Slave-Trade on the coasts of Africa. Men can insinuate themselves into the favour of the most barbarous clans, and uncultivated tribes, for the sake of gain; and how different soever the circumstances of trading and preaching are, yet this will prove the possibility of ministers being introduced there; and if this is but thought a sufficient reason to make the experiment, my point is gained. . . .

The inhabitants of the world according to this calculation, amount to about seven hundred and thirty-one millions; four hundred and twenty millions of whom are still in pagan darkness; an hundred and thirty millions the followers of Mahomet; an hundred millions catholics; forty-four millions protestants; thirty millions of the greek and armenian churches, and perhaps seven millions of jews. It must undoubtedly strike every considerate mind, what a vast proportion of the sons of Adam there are, who yet remain in the most deplorable state of heathen darkness, without any means of knowing the true God, except what are afforded them by the works of nature; and utterly destitute of the knowledge of the gospel of Christ, or of any means of obtaining it. In many of these countries they have no written language, consequently no Bible, and are only led by the most childish customs and traditions. . . . In many of these parts also they are cannibals, feeding upon the flesh of their slain enemies, with the greatest brutality and eagerness. The truth of this was ascertained, beyond a doubt, by the late eminent navigator, Cooke, of the New Zealanders, and some of the inhabitants of the western coast of America. Human sacrifices are also very frequently offered, so that scarce a week elapses without instances of this kind. They are in general poor, barbarous, naked pagans, as destitute of civilization, as they are of true religion. . . .

Barbarous as these poor heathens are, they appear to be as capable of knowledge as we are; and in many places, at least, have discovered uncommon genius and tractableness; and I greatly question whether most of the barbarities practiced by

---

5 An evangelical Christian group who undertook considerable missionary work during the eighteenth century.

them, have not originated in some real or supposed affront, and are therefore, more properly, acts of self-defence, than proofs of inhuman and blood-thirsty dispositions. . . .

The Missionaries must be men of great piety, prudence, courage, and forbearance; of undoubted orthodoxy in their sentiments, and must enter with all their hearts into the spirit of their mission; they must be willing to leave all the comforts of life behind them, and to encounter all the hardships of a torrid, or a frigid climate, an uncomfortable manner of living, and every other inconvenience that can attend this undertaking. . . . [T]heir first business must be to gain some acquaintance with the language of the natives, (for which purpose two would be better than one,) and by all lawful means to endeavour to cultivate a friendship with them, and as soon as possible let them know the errand for which they were sent. They must endeavour to convince them that it was their good alone, which induced them to forsake their friends, and all the comforts of their native country. They must be very careful not to resent injuries which may be offered to them, nor to think highly of themselves, so as to despise the poor heathens, and by those means lay a foundation for their resentment, or rejection of the gospel. They must take every opportunity of doing them good, and labouring, and travelling, night and day, they must instruct, exhort, and rebuke, with all long suffering, and anxious desire for them, and, above all, must be instant in prayer for the effusion of the Holy Spirit upon the people of their charge. Let but missionaries of the above description engage in the work, and we shall see that it is not impracticable. . . .

We are exhorted *to lay up treasure in heaven, where neither moth nor rust doth corrupt, nor thieves break through and steal.*[6] . . . What a heaven will it be to see the many myriads of poor heathens, of Britons amongst the rest, who by their labours have been brought to the knowledge of God. Surely a *crown of rejoicing* like this is worth aspiring to. Surely it is worth while to lay ourselves out with all our might, in promoting the cause, and kingdom of Christ.

4.2   William Godwin, *An Enquiry Concerning Political Justice, and its Influence on General Virtue and Happiness* (1793)

Despite his reputation for being an atheist (Burke called Political Justice *'Pure defecated Atheism, the brood of that putrid carcase [sic] the French Revolution'[7]), it was only in his essay of 1818 'On Religion' (unpublished until after his death) that Godwin presented himself as such, claiming to be 'thoroughly satisfied that no book in existence*

---

6 Matthew, 6:19–21.
7 Quoted in Ford K. Brown, *The Life of William Godwin* (London, 1926), p. 155.

contains a record and history of the revelation of the will of an invisible being, the master of us all, to his creatures'.[8] *In the influential* Political Justice, *however, Godwin criticized the Christian doctrine of reward or punishment in the afterlife and the enforcement of conformity inherent within organized religion.*

It has been held by some divines and some politicians, that the doctrine which teaches that men will be eternally tormented in another world for their errors and misconduct in this, is 'in its own nature unreasonable and absurd, but that it is nevertheless necessary, to keep mankind in awe. Do we not see,' say they, 'that notwithstanding this terrible denunciation the world is overrun with vice? What then would be the case, if the irregular passions of mankind were set free from their present restraint, and they had not the fear of this retribution before their eyes?' . . .

Nothing can be more contrary to a just observation of the nature of the human mind, than to suppose that these speculative tenets have much influence in making mankind more virtuous than they would otherwise be found. Human beings are placed in the midst of a system of things, all the parts of which are strictly connected with each other, and exhibit a sympathy and unison by means of which the whole is rendered intelligible and as it were palpable to the mind. The respect I shall obtain and the happiness I shall enjoy for the remainder of my life are topics of which my mind has a complete comprehension. I understand the value of plenty, liberty and truth to myself and my fellow men. I perceive that these things and a certain conduct intending them are connected, in the visible system of the world, and not by the supernatural interposition of an invisible director. But all that can be told me of a future world, a world of spirits or of glorified bodies, where the employments are spiritual and the first cause is to be rendered a subject of immediate perception, or of a scene of retribution, where the mind, doomed to everlasting inactivity, shall be wholly a prey to the upbraidings of remorse and the sarcasms of devils, is so foreign to the system of things with which I am acquainted, that my mind in vain endeavours to believe or to understand it. If doctrines like these occupy the habitual reflections of any, it is not of the lawless, the violent and ungovernable, but of the sober and conscientious, persuading them passively to submit to despotism and injustice, that they may receive the recompense of their patience hereafter. This objection is equally applicable to every species of deception. Fables may amuse the imagination; but can never stand in the place of reason and judgment as the principles of human conduct. . . .

---

8 *Political and Philosophical Writings of William Godwin*, ed. Mark Philp (London: William Pickering, 1993), vol. 7, p. 63.

One of the most striking instances of the injurious effects of the political patronage of opinion, as it at present exists in the world, is to be found in the system of religious conformity. Let us take our example from the church of England, by the constitution of which subscription is required from its clergy to thirty-nine articles of precise and dogmatical assertion upon almost every subject of moral and metaphysical enquiry. Here then we have to consider the whole honours and revenues of the church, from the archbishop who takes precedence next after the princes of the blood royal to the meanest curate in the nation, as employed in support of a system of blind submission and abject hypocrisy. Is there one man through this numerous hierarchy that is at liberty to think for himself? Is there one man among them that can lay his hand upon his heart, and declare, upon his honour and conscience, that his emoluments have no effect in influencing his judgment? The declaration is literally impossible. The most that an honest man under such circumstances can say is, 'I hope not; I endeavour to be impartial.'

First, the system of religious conformity is a system of blind submission. In every country possessing a religious establishment, the state, from a benevolent care it may be for the manners and opinions of its subjects, publicly encourages a numerous class of men to the study of morality and virtue. What institution, we might naturally be led to enquire, can be more favourable to public happiness? Morality and virtue are the most interesting topics of human speculation; and the best effects might be expected to result from the circumstance of many persons perpetually receiving the most liberal education, and setting themselves apart for the express cultivation of these topics. But unfortunately these very men are fettered in the outset by having a code of propositions put into their hands, in a conformity to which all their enquiries must terminate. The natural tendency of science is to increase from age to age, and proceed from the slenderest beginnings to the most admirable conclusions. But care is taken in the present case to anticipate these conclusions, and to bind men by promises and penalties not to improve upon the science of their ancestors. The plan is to guard against degeneracy and decline, but never to advance. It is founded in the most sovereign ignorance of the nature of mind, which never fails to do either the one or the other.

Secondly, the tendency of a code of religious conformity is to make men hypocrites. . . . [A] whole body of men, set apart as the instructors of mankind . . . are held up to their contemporaries as the votaries of truth, and political institution tyrannically commands them, in all their varieties of understanding and succession of ages, to model themselves to one invariable standard.

Such are the effects that a code of religious conformity produces upon the clergy themselves; let us consider the effects that are produced upon their countrymen. They are bid to look for instruction and morality to a denomination of men, formal, embarrassed and hypocritical, in whom the main spring of intellect is unbent and incapable of action. If the people be not blinded with religious zeal, they will discover and despise the imperfections of their spiritual guides. If they be so blinded, they will not the less transplant into their own characters the imbecil and unworthy spirit they are not able to detect. Is virtue so deficient in attractions as to be incapable of gaining adherents to her standard? Far otherwise. Nothing can bring the wisdom of a just and pure conduct into question, but the circumstance of its being recommended to us from an equivocal quarter. The most malicious enemy of mankind could not have invented a scheme more destructive of their true happiness, than that of hiring at the expense of the state a body of men, whose business it should seem to be to dupe their contemporaries into the practice of virtue.

4.3   Joseph Priestley, *The Present State of Europe Compared with Antient Prophecies; A Sermon, Preached at The Gravel Pit Meeting in Hackney, February 28, 1794, Being the Day appointed for a General Fast* (1794)

Joseph Priestley (1733–1804) was a Dissenting minister and enlightenment philosopher, active as a scientist, grammarian, political thinker, and teacher (see also extract 10.1). His support for the French Revolution gave him a notoriety which led to the burning of his house and library during anti-revolutionary riots in Birmingham in 1791. His sermon is one of the period's most famous examples of the renewed interest in 'millenarianism' stimulated by the events in France (see also Price, extract 1.2, Brothers, extract 4.4, and Southcott, extract 4.7). Though it took different forms, millenarianism was essentially the belief in the biblical prophecy of a second coming of Christ and in a thousand-year period of peace and happiness culminating in the Last Judgement (the order of these events was much disputed). As Priestley's sermon illustrates, millenarian thinkers used the Bible, and especially the Book of Revelation, to interpret and comprehend world events, in Priestley's case the violence of the French Revolution. Not long after delivering his sermon, Priestley left England for the United States.

REPENT YE, FOR THE KINGDOM OF HEAVEN IS AT HAND!   MATT. iii. 2

[B]eing a second time called upon by our rulers to humble ourselves before God, on account of the calamities we already feel, and those that we have reason to fear, and repentance being the only means of averting his anger, and procuring a cessation, or mitigation, of his heavy judgments, I shall take this opportunity of urging it, from that very critical and truly alarming situation, in which almost the whole of Europe now finds itself, and this country of ours, as having most at stake, perhaps more than any other.

If we can learn anything concerning what is before us, from the language of prophecy, great calamities, such as the world has never yet experienced, will precede that happy state of things, in which 'the kingdoms of this world will become the kingdom of our Lord Jesus Christ;'[9] and these calamities will chiefly affect those nations which have been the seat of great antichristian power; or, as all Protestants, and I believe justly, suppose, have been subject to the see of Rome. And it appears to me highly probable, as I hinted in my last discourse on this occasion, that the present disturbances in Europe are the beginning of those very calamitous times. . . . Let us look back to the antient prophecies, and compare them with the present state of things around us, and let us then look to ourselves, to our own sentiments and conduct, that we may feel and act as our peculiar circumstances require. . . .

This great event of the late revolution in France appears to me, and many others, to be not improbably the accomplishment of the following part of the Revelation, chap. xi. 3. 'And the same hour there was a great earthquake, and the tenth part of the city fell, and in the earthquake were slain of men (or literally, *names of men*) seven thousand, and the remnant were affrighted, and gave glory to God.'

An earthquake, as I have observed, may signify a great convulsion, and revolution, in states; and as the Papal dominions were divided into ten parts, one of which, and one of the principal of them, was France, it is properly called *a tenth part of the city*, or of the mystical *Babylon*. And if by *names of men*, we understand their *titles*, such as those of the nobility, and other hereditary distinctions, all of which are now abolished, the accomplishment of the prediction will appear to be wonderfully exact. It is farther remarkable, that this passage immediately precedes what I have quoted before concerning the *nations being angry*, and the wrath of God being come, for the *destruction of those who have destroyed the earth*. . . .

The aspect of things, it cannot be denied, is, in the highest degree, alarming, making life, and everything in it, peculiarly uncertain. What could have been more unexpected than the events of any one of the last four years, at the beginning of it? What a total revolution in the ideas, and conduct of a whole nation! What a total subversion of principles, what reverses of fortune, and what a waste of life! In how bloody and eventful a war are we engaged, how inconsiderable in its beginning, how rapid and wide in its progress, and how dark with respect to its termination! At first it resembled Elijah's cloud, appearing no bigger than a *man's hand*; but now it covers, and darkens, the whole European hemisphere!

Now, whatever we may think, as politicians (and with us every man will have his own opinion, on a subject so interesting to us all) I would, in this place, admonish you not to overlook the hand of God in the great scene that is now opening upon us. Nothing can ever come to pass without his appointment, or permission; and then, whatever be the views of men, we cannot doubt, but that his are always wise, righteous, and good. Let us, therefore, exercise faith in him,

9 Revelation, 11:15.

believing that though 'clouds and darkness are round about him, righteousness and judgment are for ever the habitation of his throne'.[10] All those who appear on the theatre of public affairs, in the field, or the cabinet, both those whom we praise, and those whom we blame, are equally instruments in his hands, and execute all his pleasure. Let this reflection, then, in our cooler moments, (and I hope we shall endeavour, in all the tumult of affairs, to make these as many as possible) lead us to look more to God, and less to man; and consequently, in all the troubles in which we may be involved, repose the most unshaken confidence in him, and thence 'in patience possess our own souls,'[11] especially when it is evident that it is wholly out of our power to alter the course of events. If we be careful so to live as to be at all times prepared to die, what have we to fear, even though, as the Psalmist says, the 'earth be removed, and the mountains be carried into the midst of the sea?'[12] Whatever turn the course of things may take, it cannot then be to our disadvantage. What, then, should hinder our contemplating the great scene, that seems now to be opening upon us, awful as it is, with tranquillity, and even with satisfaction, from our firm persuasion, that its termination will be glorious and happy?

4.4   Richard Brothers, *A Revealed Knowledge of the Prophecies and Times: Book the First. Wrote under the Direction of the Lord God and Published by His Sacred Command, It Being the First Sign of Warning for the Benefit of all Nations; containing, with other Great and Remarkable Things, Not Revealed to any other Person on Earth, The Restoration of the Hebrews to Jerusalem, by the year 1798, under their Revealed Prince and Prophet* (1794)

Richard Brothers (1757–1824) had been a lieutenant in the Royal Navy until he left for theological reasons in 1789. He gained a following as a millenarian prophet with the two volumes of A Revealed Knowledge, *both published in 1794. These volumes drew on Brothers's own visions and on biblical prophecy (especially that of Revelation) to comment on contemporary events and to predict, as his title emphasizes, the 'restoration of the Hebrews to Jerusalem'. His radical interpretations of current events resulted in his arrest and imprisonment for treason in 1795 following which he was transferred to an asylum, where he continued to produce prophetic writings. Brothers was a major figure in the millenarianism of the 1790s and his work (along with that of Joanna Southcott – extract 4.7) has been seen to have important parallels with the prophetic visions of William Blake.*

---

10 Psalms, 97:2.
11 Luke, 21:19.
12 Psalms, 46:2.

When I was commanded to write the Chronology of [t]he World, I was immediately after instructed by Revelation How; without which, I could not, nor could any other Man on the Face of the Earth, with certainty, however eminent for Wisdom and Learning he might be. After it was done, the LORD GOD said to me, in a Vision at night, – 'That is the True Age of the World, and the general computed One is erroneous'. . . .

Although I am enabled, from Revealed Knowledge, to write considerably more than what this Book contains, and which, in justice to the Divine Spirit of Truth from whom it flows, ought to be believed: yet GOD who instructs me in all things, that I may shew an Example of Precision to the Learned, and be admired for it by the Wise; – that I may give instruction to the Poor, and demonstrate the certainty of what I do write to every Man that has the least Knowledge of his CREATOR, commands me to additionally seal its truth by that great Testimony of Scriptural Evidence, *which no Nation can deny, and which no human arguments can oppose. . . .*

The new Heavens and the new Earth mean an entire regeneration of man through the power and knowledge from the Spirit of God. At present, all nations oppose the Gospel of the Kingdom of Heaven in the two most essential commands for them to obey, which are, War – and Swearing. Remember that form of praying, called the Lord's prayer; which says, Thy Will be done on Earth, as it is in Heaven. There is no War in Heaven, neither is there any Swearing: how is it then that the people of Europe, the most numerous professing Christianity, and certainly the most enlightened with knowledge of any in the world, can seriously say to God, Thy Will be done on earth, when they are instructed in their Public Laws and forms of Worship to oppose it?

Although national Laws are undesignedly made to oppose Christ, it is a duty incumbent on the People to take care that none of their prayers are; but that every supplication, and all their forms of Worship are, as they should be, – in strict obedience to his blessed Gospel of peace. . . .

To the KING and PARLIAMENT of GREAT BRITAIN

Hear what the Lord God additionally says to me by Revelation, and commands me to write. *France* seeing England left alone, deserted by her allies will require, as the condition of peace – an acknowledgement of the Republic, a restoration of the Colonies and the ships taken away from Toulon. For a short time the Lord God will permit *England*, as he will *Russia* and *Germany*, to succeed in the acquisition of delusive conquest but it is the better – the more effectual, and the more imperceptible to human foresight, to accomplish his judgment on her, according to the prophecy of Daniel and Revelation of St. John, after that short time is expired, which is nearly so now, new enemies will rise up, some warring against her openly, others privately; all will prevail, until she that now sits as a *Queen among the Nations*, is, according to the vision of God in my first book, without a covering on her head, worn thread-bare – and rent in many places.

Will England continue this war any longer against a people that has the judgment of God in their favour? Will she by the continuance of the present war against France, enter into another for the safety of Hanover against the Emperor of Germany, who will be rendered invincible for a time, as a scourge to fulfil the recorded judgments of God? Will she continue this war any longer for her destruction, that she may enter into a fresh one with America to hasten it? Is the King of England so regardless of his own life and the preservation of his family, as to involve them with himself in certain misery and death, by a longer continuance of this war? Is the Government, the Parliament, the Clergy and People, so insensible to the blessings of Peace and the happiness of Fortune, as to prefer the absolute certainty of losing all they possess, and being destroyed themselves, to support a war which in its consequences, to fulfil the judgment of God, is designed shall throw down for ever the English Monarchy; and from the confusion it will make throughout the country, involve almost every family of wealth in beggary and death!

Are you, William Pitt, to whom I wrote in May and June, 1792, informing you of the consequences of this war to your country when the war was not intended, so insensible to your own preservation and the benefit of your Brother, as to continue any longer a war, that will involve both you and him in certain death. What I acquainted you with in 1792, and often since, was made known to me by visions and revelations from the Lord God. The *death* of *Louis XVI* and removal of the English crown from the King's head to a level with the ground, according to the seventh chapter of Daniel; the fall of the Queen's palace, and the destruction of the Tower; your own removal from Administration, and afterwards Death, were among the things which I informed you of would most certainly come to pass as the evil consequence of this delusive war. My account to you then of futurity concluded with these words – 'The visions are established, and the things mentioned most certain and true.'. . .

My knowledge of future things is given me from God, therefore what I wrote is true: A little time longer and England will be so much entangled as not to be able to go forward without feeling the pains of that *Colonial Conquest* which is to be the cause of her death; nor to retire without falling under that foreign blow, which will break the Empire in pieces, and throw herself down on the ground; from whence she is never to rise up any more.

Neither evil can be prevented, and both will take place to fulfil the *Judgment of God*, according to the prophecy of Daniel and Revelation of St. John, unless what I write is believed to be true, and the advice I give is strictly followed. Fleets and Armies are great things to talk of, because terrible to destroy mankind, but when opposed by the power of Heaven they become weak, they loose their force and terror: for most of those in Europe are destined for the Rocks and the Flames. They are permitted to conquer a little for a short time now, but it is, like Russia and Germany, to hasten the dreadful fall of Human government which will soon take place in the world, for they ever have been in the hand of God the very instruments to effect what Princes designed them to prevent.

4.5   Thomas Paine, *The Age of Reason; Being an Investigation of True and Fabulous Theology* (1794–5)

The Age of Reason *was the major Deist text of the period. Paine himself declared it to be a 'bold investigation [which] will alarm many'. Deism involves the belief in a supreme being, deducible through reason and the evidence of the natural world, but the rejection of supernatural occurrences (such as miracles or the resurrection of Christ, see below), divine revelation, and often, as in the case of Paine, organized religion of any sort. Paine presents his critique of Christianity and the Bible as necessary in an era of growing scepticism: 'The suspicion that the theory of what is called the Christian church is fabulous, is becoming very extensive in all countries; and it will be a consolation to men staggering under that suspicion, and doubting what to believe and what to disbelieve, to see the subject freely investigated.' The first part of* The Age of Reason *was published in 1794 to considerable controversy, with the book seen by many to be politically as well as religiously subversive.*

It has been my intention, for several years past, to publish my thoughts upon religion. I am well aware of the difficulties that attend the subject; and from that consideration, had reserved it to a more advanced period of life. I intended it to be the last offering I should make to my fellow-citizens of all nations: and that at a time, when the purity of the motive that induced me to it, could not admit of a question, even by those who might disapprove the work.

The circumstance that has now taken place in France, of the total abolition of the whole national order of priesthood, and of everything appertaining to compulsive systems of religion, and compulsive articles of faith, has not only precipitated my intention, but rendered a work of this kind exceedingly necessary; lest, in the general wreck of superstition, of false systems of government, and false theology, we lose sight of morality, of humanity, and of the theology that is true.

As several of my colleagues, and others of my fellow-citizens of France, have given me the example of making their voluntary and individual profession of faith, I also will make mine; and I do this with all that sincerity and frankness with which the mind of man communicates with itself.

I believe in one God, and no more; and I hope for happiness beyond this life.

I believe the equality of man, and I believe that religious duties consist in doing justice, loving mercy, and endeavouring to make our fellow-creatures happy.

But lest it should be supposed that I believe many other things in addition to these, I shall, in the progress of this work, declare the things I do not believe, and my reasons for not believing them.

I do not believe in the creed professed by the Jewish church, by the Roman church, by the Greek church, by the Turkish church, by the Protestant church, nor by any church that I know of. My own mind is my own church.

All national institutions of churches, whether Jewish, Christian, or Turkish, appear to me no other than human inventions set up to terrify and enslave mankind, and monopolize power and profit.

I do not mean by this declaration to condemn those who believe otherwise. They have the same right to their belief as I have to mine. But it is necessary to the happiness of man, that he be mentally faithful to himself. Infidelity does not consist in believing, or in disbelieving; it consists in professing to believe what he does not believe. . . .

Jesus Christ . . . was a virtuous and an amiable man. The morality that he preached and practiced was of the most benevolent kind; and though similar systems of morality had been preached by Confucius, and by some of the Greek philosophers, many years before; by the quakers since; and by many good men in all ages; it has not been exceeded by any. . . . His historians, having brought him into the world in a supernatural manner, were obliged to take him out again in the same manner, or the first part of the story must have fallen to the ground. . . . But the resurrection of a dead person from the grave, and his ascension through the air, is a thing very different as to the evidence it admits of, to the invisible conception of a child in the womb. The resurrection and ascension, supposing them to have taken place, admitted of public and occular demonstration, like that of the ascension of a balloon, or the sun at noon day, to all Jerusalem at least. A thing which everybody is required to believe, requires that the proof and evidence of it should be equal to all and universal; and as the public visibility of this last related act was the only evidence that could give sanction to the former part, the whole of it falls to the ground, because that evidence never was given. Instead of this, a small number of persons, not more than eight or nine, are introduced as proxies for the whole world, to say, they *saw it*, and all the rest of the world are called upon to believe it. But it appears that Thomas did not believe the resurrection; and, as they say, would not believe, without having occular and manual demonstration himself. *So neither will I*; and the reason is equally as good for me, and for every other person, as for Thomas.

It is in vain to attempt to palliate or disguise this matter. The story, so far as relates to the supernatural part has every mark of fraud and imposition stamped upon the face of it. . . .

Having now extended the subject to a greater length than I first intended, I shall bring it to a close by abstracting a summary from the whole.

First, That the idea or belief of a word of God existing in print, or in writing, or in speech, is inconsistent in itself for the reasons already assigned. These reasons, among many others, are the want of an universal language; the mutability of language; the errors to which translations are subject; the possibility of totally suppressing such a word; the probability of altering it, or of fabricating the whole, and imposing it upon the world.

Secondly, That the Creation we behold is the real and ever-existing word of God, in which we cannot be deceived. It proclaimeth his power, it demonstrates his wisdom, it manifests his goodness and beneficence.

Thirdly, That the moral duty of man consists in imitating the moral goodness and beneficence of God manifested in the creation towards all his creatures. That seeing as we daily do, the goodness of God to all men, it is an example calling upon all men to practise the same towards each other, and consequently that every thing of persecution and revenge between man and man, and every thing of cruelty to animals is a violation of moral duty.

I trouble not myself about the manner of future existence. I content myself with believing, even to positive conviction, that the power that gave me existence is able to continue it, in any form and manner he pleases, either with or without this body; and it appears more probable to me that I shall continue to exist hereafter, than that I should have had existence, as I now have, before that existence began.

It is certain that, in one point, all nations of the earth and all religions agree. All believe in a God. The things in which they disgrace, are the redundancies annexed to that belief; and therefore, if ever an universal religion should prevail, it will not be believing any thing new, but in getting rid of redundancies, and believing as man believed at first. Adam, if ever there was such a man, was created a Deist; – but in the mean time let every man follow, as he has a right to do, the religion and worship he prefers.

4.6 William Wilberforce, *A Practical View of the Prevailing Religious System of Professed Christians, in the Higher and Middle Classes in this Country, contrasted with Real Christianity* (1797)

William Wilberforce (1759–1833), best known for his role in the abolition of slavery and the slave trade (see Section 9), was a major figure in the Evangelical revival that was partly inspired by the Methodism of John and Charles Wesley in the eighteenth century. The Evangelical revival was perhaps the most significant religious feature of the Romantic period. Wilberforce was the leader of the 'Clapham Sect', an important group of predominantly Tory Evangelicals who worked for social reform but did not seek to fundamentally change the structure of society. A Practical View *has been described as 'after Burke's* Reflections, *the most influential book of the decade among the upper classes'.[13] Critical of the 'nominal Christianity' practised in England at a time of national crisis, Wilberforce's description of 'real Christianity' illustrates many of the central beliefs of the Evangelicals, including: the importance of the Gospels (or 'Holy Scriptures'); the belief in the fallen nature of man; the centrality of the crucifixion of Christ as the means of salvation; the guiding role of the Holy Spirit; and the overwhelming need for faith and grace.*

---

13 Ryan, *The Romantic Reformation*, p. 17.

It is indeed a most lamentable consequence of the practice of regarding Religion as a compilation of statutes, and not as an internal principle, that it soon comes to be considered as being conversant about *external actions* rather than about *habits of mind*. This sentiment sometimes has even the hardiness to insinuate and maintain itself under the guise of extraordinary concern for *practical Religion*; but it soon discovers the falsehood of this pretension, and betrays its real nature. The expedient indeed of attaining to superiority in practice, by not wasting any of the attention on the internal principles from which alone practice can flow, is about as reasonable, and will answer about as well, as the œconomy of the architect, who should account it mere prodigality to expend any of his materials in laying foundations, from an idea that they might be more usefully applied to the raising of the superstructure. We know what would be the fate of such an edifice.

It is indeed true, and a truth never to be forgotten, that all pretensions to internal principles of holiness are vain when they are contradicted by the conduct; but it is no less true, that the only effectual way of improving the latter, is by a vigilant attention to the former. It was therefore our blessed Saviour's injunction, 'Make the tree good'[14] as the necessary means of obtaining good fruit; and the holy scriptures abound in admonitions, to make it our chief business to cultivate our hearts with all diligence, to examine into their state with impartiality, and watch over them with continual care. Indeed it is the *Heart* which constitutes the *Man*; and external actions derive their whole character and meaning from the motives and dispositions of which they are the indications. . . .

[I]t is the comprehensive compendium of the character of true Christians, that 'they are walking by faith, and not by sight.' By this description is meant, not merely that they so firmly believe in the doctrine of future rewards and punishments, as to be influenced by that persuasion to adhere in the main to the path of duty, though tempted to forsake it by present interest, and present gratification; but farther, that the great truths revealed in Scripture concerning the unseen world, are the thoughts for the most part uppermost in their thoughts, and about which habitually their hearts are most interested. This state of mind contributes, if the expression may be allowed, to rectify the illusions of vision, to bring forward into nearer view those eternal things which from their remoteness are apt to be either wholly overlooked, or to appear but faintly in the utmost bounds of the horizon; and to remove backward, and reduce to their true comparative dimensions, the objects of the present life, which are apt to fill the human eye, assuming a false magnitude from their vicinity. . . . Thus this just impression of the relative value of temporal and eternal things, maintains in the soul a dignified composure through all the vicissitudes of life. It quickens our diligence, yet moderates our ardour; urges us to just pursuits, yet checks any

---

14 Matthew, 12:33.

undue solicitude about the success of them, and thereby enables us in the language of Scripture, 'to use this world as not abusing it,'[15] rendering us at once beneficial to others and comfortable to ourselves.

But this is not all – besides the distinction between the nominal and the real Christian, which results from the impressions produced on them respectively by the *eternal duration* of heavenly things, there is another grounded on their *nature*, no less marked, nor less important. They are stated in Scripture, not only as entitling themselves to the notice of the true Christian from considerations of interest, but as approving themselves to his judgement from a conviction of their excellence, and yet further, as recommending themselves to his feelings by their being suited to the renewed dispositions of his heart. Indeed were the case otherwise, did not their qualities correspond with his inclinations; however he might endure them on principles of duty, and be coldly conscious of their superior worth, he could not lend himself to them with cordial complacency, much less look to them as the surest source of pleasure. But this is the light in which they are habitually regarded by the true Christian. He walks in the ways of Religion, not by constraint, but willingly; they are to him not only safe, but comfortable; 'ways of pleasantness as well as of peace.'[16] Not but that here also he is from experience aware of the necessity of constant support, and continual watchfulness; without these, his old estimate of things is apt to return on him, and the former objects of his affections to resume their influence. With earnest prayers, therefore, for the Divine Help, with jealous circumspection, and resolute self-denial, he guards against whatever might be likely again to darken his *enlightened judgement*, or to vitiate his reformed taste; thus making it his unwearied endeavour to grow in the knowledge and love of heavenly things, and to obtain a warmer admiration, and a more cordial relish of their excellence. . . .

[T]he grand radical defect in the practical system of these nominal Christians, is their forgetfulness of all the peculiar doctrines of the Religion which they profess –the corruption of human nature – the atonement of the Saviour – and the sanctifying influence of the Holy Spirit.

Here then we come again to the grand distinction, between the Religion of Christ and that of the bulk of nominal Christians in the present day. The point is of the utmost *practical importance*, and we would therefore trace it into its actual effects. . . .

[T]he Holy Scriptures, and with them the Church of England, call upon those who [wish to reform], to *lay afresh the whole foundation of their Religion*. In concurrence with the Scripture, that Church call upon them, in the first place, gratefully to adore that undeserved goodness which has awakened them from the sleep of death; to prostrate themselves before the Cross of Christ with humble

---

15 1 Corinthians, 7:31.
16 Proverbs, 3:17.

penitence and deep self-abhorrence, solemnly resolving to forsake all their sins, but relying on the Grace of God alone for power to keep their resolution. Thus, and thus only, she assures them that all their crimes will be blotted out, and that they will receive from above a new living principle of holiness. . . .

[A]ll men of enlightened understandings, who acknowledge the moral government of God, must also acknowledge, that vice must offend and virtue delight him. In short they must, more or less, assent to the Scripture declaration, 'without holiness no man shall see the Lord'.[17] But the grand distinction which subsists between the true Christian and all other Religionists, (the class of persons, in particular, whom it is our object to address) is concerning the *nature* of this holiness, and *the way in which it is to be obtained*. The views entertained by the latter, of the *nature* of holiness, are of all degrees of inadequateness; and they conceive it is to be *obtained* by their own natural, unassisted efforts; or if they admit some vague, indistinct notion of the assistance of the Holy Spirit, it is unquestionably obvious, on conversing with them, that this does not constitute the *main practical* ground of their dependence. *But the nature of the holiness, to which the desires of the true Christian are directed, is no other than the restoration of the image of God; and as to the manner of acquiring it, disclaiming with indignation every idea of attaining it by his own strength, all his hopes of possessing it rest altogether on the divine assurances of the operation of the Holy Spirit, in those who cordially embrace the Gospel of Christ. He knows therefore that this holiness is not to PRECEDE his reconciliation to God, and be its CAUSE; but to FOLLOW it, and be its EFFECT. That in short it is by FAITH IN CHRIST only that he is to be justified in the sight of God; to be delivered from the condition of a child of wrath, and a slave of Satan; to be adopted into the family of God; to become an heir of God and a joint heir with Christ, entitled to all the privileges which belong to this high relation: here, to the Spirit of Grace, and a partial renewal after the image of his Creator; hereafter, to the more perfect possession of the Divine likeness, and an inheritance of eternal glory.*

4.7   Joanna Southcott, *The Strange Effects of Faith; With Remarkable Prophecies (Made in 1792, &c.) Of Things which are to Come: Also, some Account of my Life* (1801–2)

The prophetess Joanna Southcott (1750–1814) was brought up as a Methodist. In 1792 (by her own account) voices started to inform her of Christ's second coming and instructed her to note down their prophecies. She gained a large following after publishing The Strange Effects of Faith *in 1801–2, the first of over fifty prophetic texts. She is thought to have had 100,000 followers in London when she died in 1814.*

---

17 Hebrews, 12:14.

Now, I must be candid with my Readers, and tell you plain, I have not been one of them that build their faith on a sandy foundation. I have been powerfully led by a Spirit invisible for 8 years past; and though I was strongly influenced to write by it, as a Spirit invisible, and convinced in my own mind it was from God; yet knowing Satan might come as an angel of light, made me earnest in prayer, that the Lord would be my Director, my Guide, and my Keeper; that I might not be permitted to say, 'The Lord saith,' if he had not spoken. In answer to my prayers, I had signs set before me of what was to happen, to assure me it was of God; that, was I to pen them all, it would fill a volume, and how true they all came. Therefore, I have not imposed upon the world with prophecies, till I was clearly convinced they was of God, and not from the Devil. The truths of the harvests I put in the hands of Ministers, for them to be judges, if it came true. The war continued, as I was told it would, in 1794, continue till we were in war with the Turks, and then our arms would be victorious, as you will see in what was answered me in prayer; that as a God, the Lord would begin like man, and make the same promise to me that Herod did to the Damsel. My petition and request was, if I had found favour in the sight of the Lord, that he would defend us from the foreign enemy, that the heathen nations might not say, 'Where is now the God in whom they trusted?' that Satan might be cut off from the earth, as John the Baptist was. I shall not mention all I asked in prayer; but you will see the answer of the Spirit to it: But there are storms arising; and those that clearly discern the days that are to come will shelter themselves against the storm, and screen themselves when it comes; but thousands will perish through unbelief, and many will perish through want of knowledge; but every wise man will be like Solomon, search out the mystery, to judge for themselves; but fools will judge of things they know nothing about, and stop their ears, like the deaf adder, that will not listen to the voice of the charmer, charm he never so wisely. By such I am sure to be cursed; but thus it must be to fulfil the Revelation. The Dragon was wroth with the woman and cast out floods against her; and this he will do in the hearts of men: So I may say, with David, 'If Shimei curse, let him curse; for the Lord hath bidden him.' – and as our Saviour said to Judas, 'What thou dost, do quickly.' As to my friends, I love and esteem them; and my daily prayers shall be for them. As to my enemies, I forgive and pity, knowing this must be, to fulfil the Scripture: but they cannot hurt me; for I am dead to the world, and the world to me. By my own Master, I must stand or fall. Deep is the mystery of my writing eight years, and keeping it sealed up, and putting it in print the new century. This is a deep type to the land, that I shall explain in my other writings. Deep is the mystery of the tree of knowledge being good and evil – I am Alpha and Omega, the beginning and the ending – the first shall be last, and the last shall be first; so the knowledge of the evil fruit came the first, the knowledge of the good fruit must come last. . . .

I shall now add the copy of a letter that I sent to a Minister in 1796, after he had disputed with me, that the marriage of the lamb was to take place in heaven. I said, 'No; the marriage of the Lamb meaneth when he cometh to unite all

nations, to be as one sheep under one shepherd, and Christ to be the shepherd
of the whole. The Lamb's wife meant a woman. That all these things should be
revealed; and readiness was perfect obedience to all the commands of the Lord.'
He seemed at a loss to believe it. I was ordered to send him the following letter:

> 'Now, this to him I bid thee write:
>   If thou art not the bride,
> Tell him to bring one that is right,
>   My Gospel's so applied.
> For to the fullness it cannot come,
>   Until the bride be found
> Out of her closet she must go,
>   With jewels deck'd around.
> For here's the pearl of great price,
>   And unto thee 'tis given;
> And in their jewels of no use;
>   Then she shall enter heaven,
> In white appear before me there,
>   While you in grief will mourn;
> And all shall know her words are true,
>   For vengeance fast shall come.
> In heaven the wonder first was seen,
>   And you may wonder here.
> The woman clothed with the sun
>   Shall make all nations fear
> Then let the stars begin to shine,
>   And publish my decree.' . . .

This publication that I have made to the world, is to convince mankind the Bible
is fulfilling and near to the end; and I must bring you to the Apostle's words:
*When the fullness of the time is come, God sent his Son, made of a woman, made under
the law, a mystery no man can explain.* But the reader will be ready to say, 'What
makest thou thyself.' I answer, 'I make nothing of myself. I give myself up to the
judgment of men, for so it must be, to fulfil the Scripture. In ages past, men were
tried and condemned for prophecies, until our Saviour and his Disciples put an
end to that persecution with man; for prophecies have ceased in so strong a
manner ever since with man, as not to bring persecution on them. Again, but be
it known unto all men, if it began with the woman at first, it must end with her
at last; and now I must stand the trial of what I say, as I am ordered to put in
print. The woman in the 12th chap. of Revelation is myself, the 19th and last.
Therefore, it was written by Isaiah, *Rejoice, thou Barren, that does not bear*; and it
is written, *All her children shall be taught of the Lord, and great shall be the peace
upon the earth*. This chapter is hid from man's understanding, as well as all the
others I have mentioned, now all men must know, the man cast the blame on

the Lord for the fall; and the Lord of life and glory beared it on the cross for man and by man. The woman cast the blame on the serpent, and in the end the woman must cast the blame on him; and he must bear it, as the Lord of life and glory did for men. Here I must appeal to men's conscience, if the sentence is not just. When the Lord cometh to reason with man, and it is written, *I will gather them together at the valley of Jehoshaphat, and plead with them there*; that meaneth, that he will bring all nations low together, as a valley is low, and plead with them by his Spirit; and by his Spirit he will reason with men, and make plain all his Bible to their view; but although I say, it is explained to me by the Spirit, it must be judged by man, and by the truth it must be judged from whence it came; but all these truths cannot be put in print for the present. Little do men know what is hasting on.

4.8 William Paley, *Natural Theology: or, Evidences of the Existence and Attributes of the Deity, Collected from the Appearances of Nature* (1802)

In Natural Theology, *the philosopher and divine William Paley (1743–1805) gave the period's most famous statement of the 'argument from design' for the existence of God, opening with the analogy of the watch and watchmaker that had been used previously by Voltaire, Rousseau, and Boyle. The 'argument from design' proposed that the existence of God can be deduced from the orderliness and complexity of the natural world. Paley writes: 'The marks of* design *are too strong to be got over. Design must have had a designer. That designer must have been a person. That person is God.' Paley's God is 'a perceiving, intelligent, designing Being; at the head of Creation, and from whose will it proceeded'. Paley illustrates his argument through detailed examination of animals and plants, for example analysing the barb on the tongue of the woodpecker, which he sees as 'decisive proof of mechanical contrivance'. Such minutiae are also proof of God's beneficence for the optimistic Paley, revealing the immense care with which the Deity presides over a created world in which pleasure outweighs pain.*

In crossing a heath, suppose I pitched my foot against a *stone*, and were asked how the stone came to be there, I might possibly answer, that, for any thing I knew to the contrary, it had lain there for ever: nor would it perhaps be very easy to show the absurdity of this answer. But suppose I had found a *watch* upon the ground, and it should be enquired how the watch happened to be in that place, I should hardly think of the answer which I had before given, that, for any thing I knew, the watch might have always been there. Yet why should not this answer serve for the watch, as well as for the stone? Why is it not as admissible in the second case, as in the first? For this reason, and for no other, viz. that, when we come to inspect the watch, we perceive (what we could not discover in the stone) that its several parts are framed and put together for a purpose, e.g. that

they are so formed and adjusted as to produce motion, and that motion so regulated as to point out the hour of the day; that, if the several parts had been differently shaped from what they are, of a different size from what they are, or placed
after any other manner, or in any other order, than that in which they are
placed, either no motion at all would have been carried on in the machine, or
none which would have answered the use, that is now served by it. To reckon
up a few of the plainest of these parts, and of their offices, all tending to one
result: – We see a cylindrical box containing a coiled elastic spring, which, by its
endeavour to relax itself, turns round the box. We next observe a flexible chain
(artificially wrought for the sake of flexure) communicating the action of the
spring from the box to the fusee. We then find a series of wheels, the teeth of
which catch in, and apply to, each other, conducting the motion from the fusee
to the balance, and from the balance to the pointer; and at the same time, by the
size and shape of those wheels, so regulating that motion, as to terminate in
causing an index, by an equable and measured progression, to pass over a given
space in a given time. We take notice that the wheels are made of brass, in order
to keep them from rust; the springs of steel, no other metal being so elastic; that
over the face of the watch there is placed a glass, a material employed in no other
part of the work, but, in the room of which, if there had been any other than a
transparent substance, the hour could not be seen without opening the case.
This mechanism being observed (it requires indeed an examination of the instrument, and perhaps some previous knowledge of the subject, to perceive and
understand it; but being once, as we have said, observed and understood), the
inference, we think, is inevitable; that the watch must have had a maker: that
there must have existed, at some time and at some place or other, an artificer or
artificers who formed it for the purpose which we find it actually to answer; who
comprehended its construction, and designed its use. . . .

There cannot be design without a designer; contrivance without a contriver;
order without choice; arrangement, without any thing capable of arranging;
subserviency and relation to a purpose, without that which could intend a
purpose; means suitable to an end, and executing their office in accomplishing
that end, without the end ever having been contemplated, or the means accommodated to it. Arrangement, disposition of parts, subserviency of means to an
end, relation of instruments to an use, imply the presence of intelligence and
mind. . . .

One question may possibly have dwelt in the reader's mind during the perusal
of these observations [of various forms of the 'mechanism' of the eye in humans,
birds and fish], namely, Why should not the Deity have given to the animal the
faculty of vision *at once*? Why this circuitous perception; the ministry of so many
means; an element provided for the purpose; reflected from opaque substances,
refracted through transparent ones; and both according to precise laws; then, a
complex organ, an intricate and artificial apparatus, in order, by the operation
of this element, and in conformity with the restrictions of these laws, to produce

an image upon a membrane communicating with the brain? Wherefore all this? Why make the difficulty in order only to surmount it? If to perceive objects by some other mode than that of touch, or objects which lay out of the reach of that sense, were the thing purposed, could not a simple volition of the Creator have communicated the capacity? Why resort to contrivance, where power is omnipotent? Contrivance, by its very definition and nature, is the refuge of imperfection. To have recourse to expedients, implies difficulty, impediment, restraint, defect of power. This question belongs to the other senses, as well as to sight; to the general functions of animal life, as nutrition, secretion, respiration; to the œconomy of vegetables; and indeed to almost all the operations of nature. The question therefore is of very wide extent; and, amongst other answers, which may be given to it, beside reasons of which probably we are ignorant, one answer is this. It is only by the display of contrivance, that the existence, the agency, the wisdom of the Deity, *could* be testified to his rational creatures. This is the scale by which we ascend to all the knowledge of our Creator which we possess, so far as it depends upon the phænomena, or the works of nature. Take away this, and you take away from us every subject of observation, and ground of reasoning; I mean as our rational faculties are formed at present. Whatever is done, God could have done, without the intervention of instruments or means: but it is in the construction of instruments, in the choice and adaptation of means, that a creative intelligence is seen. It is this which constitutes the order and beauty of the universe. God, therefore, has been pleased to prescribe limits to his own power, and to work his ends within those limits.

4.9   Leigh Hunt, 'An Attempt to Shew the Folly and Danger of Methodism. In a series of Essays. Essay 1 – On the Ignorance and Vulgarity of the Methodists', *The Examiner* (1808)

James Henry Leigh Hunt (1784–1859) was the central figure of the so-called 'Cockney School', which also included John Keats and William Hazlitt (see extract 8.8). In 1808, he published a series of essays in the newspaper he edited, The Examiner, *critical of the nature and growing public influence of the various forms of Methodism, which for him were linked with the reactionary politics of the Tory party. The 'lamentable follies' of Methodism, Hunt argues, are principally the result of 'a want of sense', and he was particularly concerned by 'the ignorance of the Methodists', who, he felt, privileged feeling over reason, passion over learning.*

I do not oppose the Methodists from an intolerant spirit, but simply from a love of toleration. This is no solecism. My country, my reason, my veneration for the doctrines of JESUS CHRIST, have all taught me the beauty and reason of a tolerant spirit; and it is merely because this spirit is threatened with annihilation by one of intolerance and gloom, by a phantom raised out of the vapours of spleen and

Figure 7 Anon., 'The Established Church and The True Doctrine', 1818; © Copyright the Trustees of the British Museum.

This cartoon captures the contrasting styles of worship of the Church of England ('Dearly beloved Brethren . . .') and Dissent ('You'll all be D[amne]d'). In his essay on Methodism (extract 4.9), Leigh Hunt described the 'violent Methodist' as 'delighting to terrify the feeble and foolish with the thunders of everlasting damnation'.

the fumes of vanity, that I have ventured to encounter the supernaturals of Methodism. I do not attack, I merely defend: not a day passes, but the Methodists are endeavouring to overthrow the Episcopal Church by a thousand weapons open and secret; by railing against the regular Clergy, by the distribution of thousands of tracts, by their hosts of Missions abroad and at home, by tampering with the consciences of the gloomy and inflaming the fancies of the impassioned. . . . They come forward in all places, they thunder out their anathemas in the midst of the sunshine and the bountiful fields, they cry out that they are the only wise, and that every immortal soul who presumes to think otherwise is a present from the all-merciful God to his adversary the Devil.

By the followers of this sect I understand not only the immediate followers of WHITFIELD[18] and WESLEY,[19] but all that enthusiastic multitude who in the spirit of Christian modesty call themselves the *Godly*, whether Arminians, who are always preaching instantaneous perfection by faith, salvation by faith, and the utter inefficacy of good works; or Calvinists, who in addition to the doctrine of salvation by faith alone are always insisting that GOD of his infinite goodness has predestinated from all eternity the everlasting happiness of some and the everlasting misery of others; or the innumerable divisions of these sects, who all claim the miracles of the Apostolic age, the immediate interference of the Deity, and the holy ecstacies of the blessed. . . .

I.   The most striking difference between the Methodists and the other sects is their universal passion for preaching. In the churches of England, of France and Rome, the unlearned have been content to receive the mysteries of their faith from those men, whose education has enabled them to search into the original languages of the scriptures and the antiquities of the church, and who are, therefore, the only men competent to search into the truth of what they teach: but among the Methodists every body teaches, men and boys, learned and unlearned: the great disproportion of the gentry to the vulgar in their persuasion, produces a great overbalance of ignorant professors of divinity, and a melancholy barber has nothing to do but to receive the *new light*, and he instantly begins to 'shine before men.' The worst of it is, that these preachers neglect the morality of the scriptures, which is the only part they are likely to comprehend, and addict themselves to mysteries, which have called forth all the learning and ingenuity of the Christians since the days of their origin. . . . The Methodists are peculiarly attached to mysteries, and, in these rejected gospels and epistles they have lost a vast quantity of wonders that would have done honour to the most capacious faith. But how are their ignorant preachers to know what to reject and what to retain? Not only is their want of education a satire upon almost every word they utter, but their superiors, who have really had an education, confirm them in all their ignorance by teaching them to

---

18 George Whitfield (1714–70).
19 John Wesley (1703–91).

despise scholastic learning, which they entitle *worldly wisdom, carnal knowledge,* and the *learning of this world.* As to reason, it is altogether useless and abominable: the world indeed have generally imagined, that it was a most excellent gift of GOD and assisted us considerably in discerning truth from falsehood, but the Methodists will have nothing to do with it; if you dispute the subject they tell you it is *carnal reason,* the *blind guide,* the *old Adam;* that faith has nothing to do with common sense; that you must not pretend to be wise before GOD; in short, that you must be excessively stupid and have a perfect comprehension of mysteries. Thus they utterly reject reason, and then proceed to give you the reason why. . . .

II.   . . . Ignorance produces vulgarity; a want of rational conviction produces vehemence; and accordingly our Methodist preachers are vulgar and vehement. Those who have contrived to enter the Established Church sometimes restrain their ardour and manage to be on friendly terms with their cushions, but many of the others take the Saint's advice literally, and 'fight the good fight of faith' with so alarming a determination of fist; that it seems as if they wished to convert the pulpit as well as the sinner. I am surprised that the opponents of Methodism do not particularly object to this mode of preaching as altogether unworthy a Christian Minister and indicative of an Anti-Christian spirit. Meekness of behaviour is the most affecting trait in the manners of JESUS; St. PAUL, though a determined was not a boisterous character, he was remarkable for the dignity both of his eloquence and manners; and the rest of the Apostles, though men of low origin, appear to have learnt refinement from their intercourse with the great author of Christianity. Let us figure to ourselves CHRIST preaching his sublime code of morality on the Mount with the mildness of Heaven beaming on his countenance and breathing through his words, and then let us hear the violent Methodist, who arrogates to himself the Supreme title of the Beloved of CHRIST, crying out against the preachers of morality, contradicting the doctrine and behaviour of his Master, and delighting to terrify the feeble and the foolish with the thunders of everlasting damnation.

4.10   Leigh Hunt, 'On the Rejection of the Catholic Petition', *The Examiner* (1808)

During the eighteenth century, the political and public roles of Roman Catholics were restricted under various pieces of legislation such as the Acts of Uniformity and the Test and Corporation Acts. Catholics could not hold public office, join the armed forces, stand for election to Parliament, or vote. The movement for Catholic Emancipation produced some limited reforms towards the end of the century, with the Relief Acts of 1778 and 1791 lifting the ban on Catholic worship, making it possible for Catholics to serve in the armed forces, and introducing an oath of allegiance in place of one that required a rejection of transubstantiation (the transformation of the bread and wine into the body and blood of Christ, central to the Catholic faith). As Hunt's essay shows,

anxiety about Catholicism was linked to political concern about Ireland. Though the
Irish Catholic Relief Act of 1793 had given some political representation to Irish
Catholics, George III remained hostile to further developments, despite the Act of Union
of 1800 and William Pitt's advocacy (both Pitt and William Grenville resigned as
Prime Ministers over the emancipation issue, in 1801 and 1807 respectively). It was
not until 1829 that many of the restrictions on Catholics were removed by the Catholic
Relief Act of 1829.

If posterity were to judge the present times by their general character, they
would be somewhat amazed at our late rejection of the Catholic Petition. The
age is more generally refined than any preceding era in modern history, knowledge is every where diffused, continental superstition is daily decreasing, and
men are more inclined to judge of each other not by what they think but by
what they do. The Roman Catholics, whose political errors have almost always
originated in the influence of the POPE, have become moderate since the utter
extinction of that influence;[20] and they themselves in fact have given an additional blow to the papal authority by rejecting it's infallibility; not only in the
United Kingdom, but in all the first Universities on the Continent. Thus at
length the Catholics and Protestants differ very little from each other except in
the use of religious symbols; the very name of Papist, once so expressive of every
thing fiery and intolerant, has scarcely a jot of it's former meaning; and the great
odium of bigotry and superstition has passed from the Catholic body to that
body of modern Jesuits without Jesuitical learning, the violent Methodists.

The Ministry acknowledge that the Catholics are no longer dangerous to a
state with regard to their papal credulities; they acknowledge that the opinions
and statements of their Petition are not objectionable; but they reject it entirely
because it is not the proper time for indulgence to the Irish. This is a little singular. The Irish are very poor and oppressed, but they have lost their bigotry and
have a great deal of courage: the English have united them to the nation, and
they want their hearty assistance. The Irish on the other hand want the assistance of the English, and are ready, upon reasonable terms, not only to fight in
union with them, but what is a great deal more, to fight heartily for them: the
English are very ready to receive this assistance and they require it in a very
peremptory manner, but though the mutual enemy is watching for their
disunion, they refuse to grant a petition acknowledged to be just. In short, the
Irish must do every thing for the English, but the English will do nothing for
them.

Let us look at the three particular classes of men who refuse the petition. The
first are those who oppose it partly upon a political and partly on a religious
account; the second are those whose opposition arises from the very bigotry they

---

20 Napoleon's interventions in Rome weakened the influence of the Pope.

condemn; the third, and most violent, are the ministers who wish to keep their places by flattering the royal scruples. It must be evident that none of these persons, whatever they may say to the contrary, actually believe the protestations of the petitioners to be true. Perhaps Mr. PERCEVAL,[21] whom at the same time I believe to be a man of amiable private life, belongs in some degree to all the three classes, and it is a stain on the general character of this gentleman that he has raised such an outcry against the whole body of Catholics.

Now it is a little extraordinary that the Government should at the same time oppose the Catholics, who declare they will not meddle with the Church, and allow every privilege to the Calvinist and other violent Dissenters, who openly accuse and threaten the Church. I do not wish to defend the religious peculiarities of the Catholics, which in general are quite as absurd and hideous as those of Methodism; but let us always recollect that there is at this minute a considerable body of Methodists in the state, and that it is much more likely we may have a Methodist King than a Catholic one. Nothing but an alteration or violation of the royal oath, or the general consent of the state, a circumstance the most improbable in the world, can give us a Popish Monarch; but the Methodists, while they are plotting the downfal of the Church, call themselves the real members of it; and if ever an ill-spent youth, or a weak mind, or a set of Methodist Ministers, should give us a bigoted Methodist King, the bench of Bishops might be altered in a minute; the darkest mysteries would again take the place of intelligible and useful preaching; opinions would not be tolerated, so easily as at present, by men who thought themselves infallible; and thus we should have all the superstition and intolerance of a temporal Romish Church under the name of our own moderate Establishment. Let those therefore who looked to the Catholics, look to the Methodists also. I do not contend that the Catholics should be admitted to the highest offices of state, but I contend at the same time that known Methodists should not be admitted to them either. Liberty of conscience ought to be the most sacred of rights in every well ordered state; but liberty of religion and a power to impose new religions upon the state are very different things. The Church should at least have its own liberty when it does not interfere with that of others.

If the first offices of state however be utterly denied to the sectarians, I cannot see why the second, which have very little comparative influence, should be refused to any of them. Let the Catholics and the Methodists enjoy every privilege in the world except that of dictating to our consciences.

---

21 Spencer Perceval (1762–1812), who would become Prime Minister in 1809, was a vehement opponent of Catholic Emancipation and had opposed the attempts of Grenville's government to remove some of the limits on Catholics in Ireland.

4.11   Percy Shelley, *The Necessity of Atheism* (1811)

The poet Percy Shelley (1792–1822) was sent down from Oxford University in 1811 following the publication of the boldly titled pamphlet The Necessity of Atheism, *which was probably jointly written with his friend Thomas Jefferson Hogg. In 1813, Shelley appended an extended and revised version as a note to the line 'There is no God' in his poem* Queen Mab, *though he qualified his argument by beginning the note: 'This negation must be understood solely to affect a creative Deity. The hypothesis of a pervading Spirit co-eternal with the universe remains unshaken.' Though Shelley was drawing on ideas from Locke, Hume and Holbach, his pamphlet has gained an important status as 'almost the first known open avowal of atheism in print in England'.[22]*

[W]e are naturally led to consider what arguments we receive . . . to convince us of the existence of a Deity.

1ST. The evidence of the senses. – If the Deity should appear to us, if he should convince our senses of his existence; this revelation would necessarily command belief; – Those to whom the Deity has thus, appeared have the strongest possible conviction of his existence.

Reason claims the 2nd, it is urged that man knows that whatever is, must either have had a beginning or have existed from all eternity, he also knows that whatever is not eternal must have had a cause. – Where this is applied to the existence of the universe, it is necessary to prove that it was created, until that is clearly demonstrated, we may reasonably suppose that it has endured from all eternity. – In a case where two propositions are diametrically opposite, the mind believes that which is less incomprehensible, it is easier to suppose that the Universe has existed from all eternity, than to conceive a being capable of creating it, if the mind sinks beneath the weight of one, is it an alleviation to increase the intolerability of the burden? –

The other argument which is founded on a man's knowledge of his own existence, stands thus. – A man knows not only he now is, but that there was a time when he did not exist; consequently there must have been a cause. – But what does this prove? we can only infer from effects causes exactly adequate to those effects; – But there certainly is a generative power which is effected by certain instruments: we cannot prove that it is inherent in these instruments, nor is the contrary hypothesis capable of demonstration; we admit that the generative power is incomprehensible; but to suppose that the same effect is produced by an eternal, omniscient, Almighty Being, leaves the cause in the same obscurity, but renders it more incomprehensible.

The 3rd. and last degree of assent is claimed by Testimony – it is required that it should not be contrary to reason. – The testimony that the Deity convinces

---

22 Richard Holmes, *Shelley: The Pursuit* (London: Quartet, 1976), p. 50.

the senses of men of his existence can only be admitted by us, if our mind considers it less probable that these men should have been deceived, than that the Deity should have appeared to them – our reason can never admit the testimony of men, who not only declare that they were eye-witnesses of miracles but that the Deity was irrational, for he commanded that he should be believed, he proposed the highest rewards for faith, eternal punishments for disbelief – we can only command voluntary actions, belief is not an act of volition, the mind is even passive, from this it is evident that we have not sufficient testimony, or rather that testimony is insufficient to prove the being of a God, we have before shown that it cannot be deduced from reason, – they who have been convinced by the evidence of the senses, they only can believe it.

From this it is evident that having no proofs from any of the three sources of conviction: the mind *cannot* believe the existence of a creative God, it is also evident that as belief is a passion of the mind, no degree of criminality is attached to disbelief, they only are reprehensible who willingly neglect to remove the false medium thro' which their mind views the subject.

It is almost unnecessary to observe, that the general knowledge of the deficiency of such proof, cannot be prejudicial to society: Truth has always been found to promote the best interests of mankind. – Every reflecting mind must allow that there is no proof of the existence of a Deity. Q.E.D.[23]

4.12 Richard Carlile, *An Address to Men of Science; Calling upon them to Stand Forward and Vindicate the Truth from the Foul Grasp and Persecution of Superstition; and Obtain for the Island of Great Britain the Noble Appellation of The Focus of Truth; whence Mankind shall be Illuminated, and the Black and Pestiferous Clouds of Persecution and Superstition be Banished from the Face of the Earth; as the only sure Prelude to Universal Peace and Harmony among the Human Race. In which a Sketch of a Proper System for the Education of Youth is Submitted to their Judgment* (1821)

Richard Carlile (1790–1843; see also extract 1.14) wrote his Address to Men of Science *in Dorchester Gaol where he had been sentenced to three years' imprisonment for blasphemy and seditious libel for republishing various controversial and banned texts, including Paine's* The Age of Reason *(see extract 4.5 and Figure 8). The powerful call of Carlile, an avowed atheist, to Men of Science to confront 'Kingcraft and Priestcraft' illustrates the increasing challenge science posed to theological and religious orthodoxy.*

---

23 '*Quod Erat Demonstrandum*', which was to be proved.

Instead of viewing ourselves as the particular and partial objects of the care of a great Deity, or of receiving those dogmas of the priest which teach us that every thing has been made for the convenience and use of man, and that man has been made in the express image of the Deity, we should consider ourselves but as atoms of organized matter, whose pleasure or whose pain, whose existence in a state of organization, or whose non-existence in that state, is a matter of no importance in the laws and operations of Nature; we should view ourselves with the same feelings, as we view the leaf which rises in the spring, and falls in the autumn, and then serves no further purpose but to fertilize the earth for a fresh production; we should view ourselves but as the blossoms of May, which exhibit but a momentary splendour and beauty, and often within that moment are cut off prematurely by a blast. We are of no more importance in the scale of Nature than those myriads of animalcules whose natural life is but for the space of an hour, or but a moment. We come and pass like a cloud – like a shower – those of us who possess a brilliancy superior to others, are but as the rainbow, the objects of a momentary admiration, and a momentary recollection. Man has been most aptly compared to the seasons of the year, in our own climate, the spring, is his infancy; the summer, the time of his ardent manhood; the autumn, his decline of life; and the winter, his old age and death – he passes, and another series comes. He is produced by, and produces his like, and so passes away one generation after another, from, and to all eternity. How ridiculous then is the idea about divine revelations, about prophesies, and about miracles, to procure proselytes to such notions! To what generation do they apply, or if they apply to all future generations, why were not the same revelations, prophesies, and miracles, necessary to all the past generations? What avail the dogmas of the priest about an end to the world, about a resurrection, about a day of judgment, about a Heaven and Hell, or about rewards and punishments after this life, when we assert that matter is imperishable and indestructible – that it always was what it now is, and that it will always continue the same. Answer this, ye Priests. Come forward, ye Men of Science, and support these plain truths, which are as familiar to your minds as the simplest demonstration in mathematics is to the experienced and accomplished mathematician. Future rewards and punishments are cried up as a necessary doctrine wherewith to impress the minds of men, and to restrain them from vice: but how much more impressive and comprehensible would be the plain and simple truth, that, in this life, virtue produces happiness, and vice nothing but certain misery.

Away then with the ridiculous idea, and the priestly dogma of immortality. Away with the contemptible notion that our bones, our muscles, and our flesh shall be gathered together after they are rotted and evaporated for a resurrection to eternal life. Away with the idea that we have a sensible soul which lives distinct from and after the dissolution of the body. It is all a bugbear, all a priestly imposture. The Chemist can analyse the body of man, and send it into its primitive gaseous state in a few minutes. His crucible and fire, or his galvanic battery, will cause it to evaporate so as not to leave a particle of substance or

Figure 8 George Cruikshank, 'The Age of Reason or the World turned Topsy turvy exemplified by Tom Paines Works!! Dedicated to the Archbishop of Carlile – !!!', 16 October 1819; © Copyright the Trustees of the British Museum.

Richard Carlile (see extracts 1.14 and 4.12) republished Thomas Paine's works, including *The Age of Reason* (see extract 4.5). His subsequent prosecution in 1818 for blasphemous libel further raised the profile of Paine's deist text. Note the association between atheism and Jacobinism and the presentation of representatives of other faiths (lower left-hand corner).

solid matter, and this chemical process is but an anticipation, or a hastening, of the workings of Nature; for the whole universe might be aptly termed a great chemical apparatus, in which a chemical analysis, and a chemical composition is continually and constantly going on. The same might be said of every organized body, however large, or however minute; its motions produce a constant chemical analysis and composition, a continual change; so that the smallest particle of matter is guided by the same laws, and performs the same duties, as the great whole. Here is an harmony indeed! Man alone seems to form an exception by his vicious conduct and demoralizing character. By assuming to himself a character or a consequence to which he is not entitled, and by making a pretension to the possession of supernatural powers, he plays such fantastic tricks as to disturb every thing within his influence, and carries on a perpetual war with Nature and her laws.

After those few observations upon the properties of matter either organized or inert, (to which I know every Chemist in the country, whose science has conquered the bigotry of his education, will give his assent) I would call upon them all and every one to stand forward and teach mankind those important, those plain truths, which are so clear and so familiar to their own minds. It is the Man of Science who is alone capable of making war upon the Priest, so as to silence him effectually. It is the duty of the Man of Science to make war upon all error and imposture, or why does he study? Why does he analyze the habits, the customs, the manners, and the ideas of mankind, but to separate truth from falsehood, but to give force to the former, and to extinguish the latter? Why does he search into Nature and her laws, but to benefit himself and his fellow man by his discoveries, by the explosion of erroneous ideas, and by the establishment of correct principles? Science must be no longer studied altogether as an amusement or a pastime, which has been too much the case hitherto; it must be brought forward to combat the superstitions, the vices, and the too long established depravities among mankind, whence all their present and past miseries have emanated, and unless the former can be destroyed, the latter will still ensue, as a regular cause and effect.

5
Philosophy

Introduction

The extracts in this section engage with some of the fundamental philosophical issues of the Romantic period, especially the question of the relation of the self to the world. John Locke's *An Essay Concerning Human Understanding* (1690, extract 5.1) remained a key text in this respect and underpinned Enlightenment theories of knowledge. Locke argues that the mind has no innate ideas or principles but is like a *tabula rasa* – a blank slate – which is written upon by experience. All ideas are the product of experience, though the mind does play a role in the transformation of sensation and perception into sophisticated ideas and abstract concepts. Locke's account of this process was developed by David Hartley in his *Observations on Man, His Frame, His Duty, and His Expectations* (1749; extract 5.2), in which he analysed in detail how primary sensations become associated together to produced all ideas and emotions.

The empiricism of Locke and Hartley – their emphasis on experience as the basis of knowledge and identity – had important implications for political, social and ethical thinking in the eighteenth and early nineteenth centuries. Locke's distinction between ideas of sensation and of reflection and Hartley's account of the association of ideas feed into many forms of writing. Underpinning the political programme of William Godwin's *Political Justice* (extract 5.8), for example, is his belief that 'the actions and dispositions of men . . . flow entirely from the operations of circumstances and events acting upon a faculty of receiving sensible impressions'. For him, both individuals and society are 'perfectible', or always capable of further improvement.

The theory that individuals are shaped by experience, particularly early experience, was linked to an increasing philosophical interest in education and childhood, key themes in Romantic-period writing. Locke's 'blank slate' theory of the mind implicitly questioned influential and often Calvinistic accounts of mankind which saw it as inherently evil as a result of Original Sin. This idea of humans as fallen remained strongly held by some throughout the period. For example, in 1799 the Evangelical educator Hannah More commented that it is 'a fundamental error to consider children as innocent beings, whose little weaknesses may perhaps want some correction, rather than as beings who bring into the world a corrupt nature and evil disposition, which it should be the great end of education to rectify'.[1] The innocent child is a key theme in the period, of course, most obviously in Blake's *Songs of Innocence*, and More's vehement reaction to it reminds us of the extent to which such writings changed our understanding of childhood. The innocence of the new-born child was an idea particularly associated with the Swiss-born philosopher Jean-Jacques Rousseau, who opens *Émile* – his novelistic programme for 'natural education' – with the forceful statement that 'All things are good as their Creator made them, but every thing degenerates in the hands of man' (extract 5.5). Rousseau's argument about the innocent individual corrupted by society has its historical corollary in his account of human 'progress' – for him largely a process of degeneration after a brief 'golden age' – in *A Discourse Upon the Origin and Foundation of the Inequality among Mankind* (extract 5.3). In this work, he juxtaposes the debased state of the 'civilised Man' of his own age with the simplicity of the primitive 'savage man', an argument that contributed strongly to the eighteenth-century interest in the 'noble savage'. The third extract included here from Rousseau is taken from his *Confessions* (extract 5.6), illustrating his importance as a pioneer of what would become a major romantic genre, the autobiography. With his interest in child development, his advocacy of the natural over the civilized, and his readiness to scrutinize his own life in his writing, Rousseau both anticipates and influences much of the writing of the Romantic period, perhaps most clearly that of Wordsworth, whose *Prelude* gives an autobiographical account of the poet's development in the natural setting of the Lake District. As William Hazlitt commented in his 'On the Character of Rousseau', 'The writer who most resembles [him] in our times is the author of *Lyrical Ballads*. We see no other difference between them, than that the one wrote in prose and the other in poetry.'[2]

Allied to these developments in ideas about the self was the growth of the so-called 'cult of sensibility', which exerted a powerful influence on the literature and culture of the Romantic period. A complex term, 'sensibility' refers to the capacity to feel pleasure or pain, especially emotionally, and particularly the ability to experience the pain of others as if it were one's own. Locke's emphasis on sensation provided one philosophical justification for the eighteenth century's growing interest in feeling and emotion, well represented by David Hume's reversal of the standard Enlightenment hierarchy of reason and passion in his *A Treatise of Human Nature* (1739–40) where he comments, 'Reason is, and ought only to be the slave of the passions, and can never pretend to any other office than to serve and obey them.' The most important philosophic account of sensibility was Adam Smith's exploration of the role of sympathy in his *The Theory of Moral Sentiments* (1759, extract 5.4). During the eighteenth century, a refined sensibility became increasingly prized and was often associated with

---

1 Quoted in Zachary Leader, *Reading Blake's 'Songs'* (London: Routledge and Kegan Paul, 1981), p. 9.
2 William Hazlitt, *The Complete Works of William* Hazlitt, 21 vols, ed. P. P. Howe (London: J. M. Dent, 1930–4), vol. IV, p. 92.

femininity and women's writing (see, for example, the novels and poems of Charlotte Smith). It played an important political role, reinforcing the case for humanitarian concerns such as the abolition of slavery, though by the end of the century there was increasing cultural anxiety about the dangers of excessive emotion and the potential links of the cult of feeling with Jacobinism.

While Locke provided the philosophical basis for the interest in the self, a number of writers and thinkers including Wordsworth and Coleridge came to see empiricism as too mechanical and as failing to account for the creative power of the artist and the imagination. Against Locke's emphasis on the mind as a passive receiver of sensation, Wordsworth developed a poetics of the mind as actively involved in the creation of the world around it. In his description of child development in *The Prelude*, he describes how a baby's mind, 'Even as an agent of the one great mind, / Creates, creator and receiver both, / Working but in alliance with the works / Which it beholds' (II.272–5). Coleridge, in his thinking about the creative power of the mind, was strongly influenced by developments in German philosophy and particularly the work of Immanuel Kant, who argued that categories inherent within the mind shape the external world as it is perceived. Coleridge's image of the mind as a plant in *The Statesman's Manual* (extract 5.9), absorbing oxygen and light while emitting vapour and fragrance, beautifully illustrates his sense of the mind as vital, active and growing through a reciprocal relationship with the world around it. Coleridge also adds a theological dimension to Kant's account of the active mind, famously presenting the Imagination as a 'repetition in the finite mind of the eternal act of creation in the infinite I AM' (extract 5.9). The important role given to the Imagination and the creative powers of the artist has generally been seen as one of the most significant developments in philosophical and aesthetic theory in a period when writers frequently presented their literary output not as reflections of an external reality but as natural and organic expressions of their own personalities (for example, Wordsworth's claim that 'Poetry is the spontaneous overflow of powerful feelings', Byron's description of poetry as the 'lava of the imagination', and Keats's comment that 'if Poetry come not as naturally as the leaves of a tree it had better not come at all').[3]

5.1   John Locke, *An Essay Concerning Human Understanding* (1690)

John Locke's (1632–1704) Essay provided one of the most important theories of the mind and of human understanding for the eighteenth century. Locke rejected the previously dominant view that the mind has innate ideas, and argued instead that the mind, at birth, is like a blank piece of paper, which then gains its 'Ideas' through the two

---

3 For a detailed account of this development, see M. H. Abrams's *The Mirror and the Lamp: Romantic Theory and the Critical Tradition* (Oxford: Oxford University Press, 1953).

processes of experience and reflection. This emphasis on the role of experience is termed 'empiricism'. With its stress on the shaping role of experience, Locke's theory was central to many of the debates of the Romantic period, especially those on character formation and education (Locke himself wrote significantly in this area in his Thoughts Concerning Education, *1693). In* Frankenstein, *Mary Shelley uses a specifically Lockean model of human development in the creature's account of its early life. For other writers and philosophers of the period, however, Locke's empirical philosophy was in opposition to their own belief in the mind's creative ability.*

Of Ideas in general, and their Original

–1.   Every Man being conscious to himself, That he thinks, and that which his Mind is employ'd about whilst thinking, being the *Ideas*, that are there, 'tis past doubt, that Men have in their minds several *Ideas*, such as are those expressed by the words, *Whiteness, Hardness, Sweetness, Thinking, Motion, Man, Elephant, Army, Drunkenness*, and others: It is in the first place then to be enquired, How he comes by them? . . .

–2.   Let us then suppose the Mind to be, as we say, white Paper, void of all Characters, without any *Ideas*; How comes it to be furnished? Whence comes it by that vast store, which the busy and boundless Fancy of Man has painted on it, with an almost endless variety? Whence has it all the materials of Reason and Knowledge? To this I answer, in one word, From *Experience*: In that, all our Knowledge is founded; and from that it ultimately derives it self. Our Observation employ'd either about *external, sensible Objects; or about the internal Operations of our Minds, perceived and reflected on by our selves, is that, which supplies our Understandings with all the materials of thinking.* These two are the Fountains of Knowledge, from whence all the *Ideas* we have, or can naturally have, do spring.

–3.   First, *Our Senses*, conversant about particular, sensible Objects, do *convey into the Mind*, several distinct *Perceptions* of things, according to those various ways, wherein those Objects do affect them: And thus we come by those *Ideas*, we have of *Yellow, White, Heat, Cold, Soft, Hard, Bitter, Sweet*, and all those which we call sensible qualities. This great Source, of most of the *Ideas* we have, depending wholly upon our Senses, and derived by them to our Understanding, I call *SENSATION*.

–4.   Secondly, the other Fountain, from which Experience furnisheth the Understanding with *Ideas*, is the *Perception of the Operations of our own Mind* within us, as it is employ'd about the *Idea's* it has got; which Operations, when the Soul comes to reflect on, and consider, do furnish the Understanding with another sett of *Ideas*, which could not be had from things without; and such are, *Perception, Thinking, Doubting, Believing, Reasoning, Knowing, Willing*, and all the different actings of our own Minds; which we being conscious of, and observing in our selves, do from these receive into our Understanding, as distinct *Ideas*, as we do from Bodies affecting our Senses. This Source of *Ideas*, every Man has wholly in himself: And though it be not Sense, as having nothing to do with external Objects; yet it is very like it, and might properly enough be call'd internal Sense. But as I call the other *Sensation*, so I Call this *REFLECTION*, the *Ideas* it affords being such only, as the Mind gets by reflecting on its own Operations within it self. . . . These two, I say, *viz.* External, Material things, as the Objects of *SENSATION*; and the Operations of our own Minds within, as the Objects of *REFLECTION*, are, to me, the only Originals, from whence all our *Idea's* take their beginnings. The term *Operations* here, I use in a large sense, as comprehending not barely the Actions of the Mind about its Ideas, but some sort of Passions arising sometimes from them, such as is the satisfaction or uneasiness arising from any thought. . . .

–6.   He that attentively considers the state of a *Child*, at his first coming into the World, will have little reason to think him stored with plenty of *Ideas*, that are to be the matter of his future Knowledge. 'Tis by degrees he comes to be furnished with them: And though the *Ideas* of obvious and familiar qualities, imprint themselves, before the Memory begins to keep a Register of Time and Order, yet 'tis often so late before some unusual qualities come in the way, that there are few Men that cannot recollect the beginning of their acquaintance with them. . . .

–7.   Men then come to be furnished, with fewer or more simple *Ideas* from without, according as the Objects they converse with afford greater or less variety; and from the Operations of their Minds within, according as they more or less *reflect* on them.

5.2   David Hartley, *Observations on Man, His Frame, His Duty, and His Expectations* (1749)

David Hartley (1705–57) developed John Locke's empiricist theory of human understanding (extract 5.1) by emphasizing the 'association of ideas' (Locke's phrase), the process whereby the pleasurable and painful physical reactions of the nerves and brain to sensation became associated with other sensations, which also have an empirical origin. Working through memory, these increasingly complex networks of association are responsible for all thought and emotion – 'all reasoning, as well as affection, is the mere result of association'. Coleridge (who called his son Hartley) and Wordsworth were both heavily influenced by Hartley's account for a period, though they increasingly found his passive model of the mind problematic. Coleridge's 'The Æolian Harp' and Wordsworth's 'There was a Boy' both offer poetic examinations of the theory of association, and Wordsworth draws on Hartleyan ideas and terminology in his 'Preface' to Lyrical Ballads.

Now it will be a sufficient Proof, that all the intellectual Pleasures and Pains are deducible ultimately from the sensible ones, if we can shew of each intellectual

Pleasure and Pain in particular, that it takes its Rise from other Pleasures and Pains, either sensible or intellectual. For thus none of the intellectual Pleasures and Pains can be original. But the sensible Pleasures and Pains are evidently Originals. They are therefore the only ones, *i.e.* they are the common Source from whence all the intellectual Pleasures and Pains are ultimately derived. . . .

If we admit the Power of Association, and can also shew, that Associations, sufficient in Kind and Degree, concur, in fact, in the several Instances of our intellectual Pleasures and Pains, this will, of itself, exclude all other Causes for these Pleasures and Pains, such as Instinct for Instance. . . .

The Pleasures arising from the Contemplation of the Beauties of the natural World seem to admit of the following Analysis.

The pleasant Tastes, and Smells, and the fine Colours of Fruits and Flowers, the Melody of Birds, and the grateful Warmth or Coolness of the Air, in the proper Seasons, transfer Miniatures of these Pleasures upon rural Scenes, which start up instantaneously so mixed with each other, and with such as will be immediately enumerated, as to be separately indiscernible.

If there be a Precipice, a Cataract, a Mountain of Snow, &c. in one Part of the Scene, the nascent Ideas of Fear and Horror magnify and enliven all the other Ideas, and by degrees pass into Pleasures, by suggesting the Security from Pain.

In like manner the Grandeur of some Scenes, and the Novelty of others, by exciting Surprize and Wonder, *i.e.* by making a great Difference in the preceding and subsequent States of Mind, so as to border upon, or even enter the Limits of Pain, may greatly enhance the Pleasure.

Uniformity and Variety in Conjunction are also principal Sources of the Pleasures of Beauty, being made so partly by their Association with the Beauties of Nature; partly by that with the Works of Art; and with the many Conveniences which we receive from the Uniformity and Variety of the Works of Art. They must therefore transfer part of the Lustre borrowed from the Works of Art, and from the Head of Convenience, upon the Works of Nature.

Poetry and Painting are much employed in setting forth the Beauties of the natural World, at the same time that they afford us a high Degree of Pleasure from many other Sources. Hence the Beauties of Nature delight Poets and Painters, and such as are addicted to the Study of their Works, more than others. Part of this Effect is indeed owing to the greater Attention of such Persons to the other Sources; but this comes to the same thing, as far as the general Theory of the factitious, associated Nature of these Pleasures is concerned.

The many Sports and Pastimes, which are peculiar to the Country, and whose Ideas and Pleasures are revived by the View of rural Scenes, in an evanescent State, and so mixed together as to be separately indiscernible, do farther augment the Pleasures suggested by the Beauties of Nature.

To these we may add, the Opposition between the Offensiveness, Dangers, and Corruption of populous Cities, and the Health, Tranquillity, and Innocence, which the actual View, or the mental Contemplation, of rural Scenes introduces;

also the Pleasures of Sociality and Mirth, which are often found in the greatest Perfection in Country Retirements, the amorous Pleasures, which have many Connexions with rural Scenes, and those which the Opinions and Encomiums of others beget in us, in this, as in other Cases, by means of the Contagiousness observable in mental Dispositions, as well as bodily ones.

Those Persons who have already formed high Ideas of the Power, Knowledge, and Goodness, of the Author of Nature, with suitable Affections, generally feel the exalted Pleasures of Devotion upon every View and Contemplation of his Works, either in an explicit and distinct Manner, or in a more secret and implicit one. . . .

When a beautiful Scene is first presented, there is generally great Pleasure from Surprize, from being struck with Objects and Circumstances which we did not expect. This presently declines; but is abundantly compensated afterwards by the gradual alternate Exaltation of the several constituent Parts of the complex Pleasures, which also do probably enhance one another. And thus we may take several Reviews of the same Scene, before the Pleasure, which it affords, comes to its *Maximum*. After this the Pleasure must decline, if we review it often: But if at considerable Intervals, so as that many foreign States of Mind intervene, also so as that new Sources of the Pleasures of this Kind be broken up, the Pleasure may recur for many Successions of nearly the same Magnitude.

5.3   Jean-Jacques Rousseau, *A Discourse upon the Origin and Foundation of the Inequality among Mankind* (1754, translation 1761)

The Enlightenment philosopher Jean-Jacques Rousseau (1712–78) was highly influential for writers and thinkers of the Romantic period in a range of fields, particularly politics, education, and aesthetics. In his Discourse upon the Origin and Foundation of the Inequality among Mankind, *he argues that inequality did not exist when men lived independently of each other in a state of nature but is a result of individuals joining together in civil society and acquiring private property. As Rousseau also argues influentially elsewhere (extract 5.5), for him man is by nature good and becomes corrupt through living in society. As this would suggest, Rousseau's writing was particularly valuable for those who wished to challenge theological arguments in support of 'original sin'. His writings contributed considerably to the eighteenth-century cult of primitivism with its interest in the figure of the 'noble savage' (see extract 9.2), though this was not a term he himself ever used.*

By thus discovering and following the lost and forgotten Tracks, by which Man from the natural must have arrived at the civil State; by restoring, with the intermediate Positions which I have been just indicating, those which want of Leisure obliges me to suppress, or which my Imagination has not suggested, every attentive Reader must unavoidably be struck at the immense Space which separates

these two States. . . . In a word, he will find himself in a Condition to understand how the Soul and the Passions of Men by insensible Alterations change as
it were their Nature; how it comes to pass, that at the long run our Wants and
our Pleasures change Objects; that, original Man vanishing by degrees, Society
no longer offers to our Inspection but an assemblage of artificial Men and factitious Passions, which are the Work of all these new Relations, and have no
Foundation in Nature. Reflection teaches us nothing on that Head, but what
Experience perfectly confirms. Savage Man and civilised Man differ so much at
bottom in point of Inclinations and Passions, that what constitutes the supreme
Happiness of the one would reduce the other to despair. The first sighs for nothing but Repose and Liberty; he desires only to live, and to be exempt from
Labour. . . . On the contrary, the Citizen always in Motion, is perpetually sweat-
ing and toiling, and racking his Brains to find out Occupations still more laborious: He continues a Drudge to his last Minute; nay, he courts Death to be able
to live, or renounces Life to acquire Immortality. He cringes to Men in Power
whom he hates, and to rich Men whom he despises; he sticks at nothing to have
the Honour of serving them; he is not ashamed to value himself on his own
Weakness and the Protection they afford him; and proud of his Chains, he
speaks with Disdain of those who have not the Honour of being the Partner of
his Bondage. What a Spectacle must the painful and envied Labours of an
European Minister of State form in the Eyes of a *Carribean*! How many cruel
Deaths would not this indolent Savage prefer to such a horrid Life, which very
often is not even sweetened by the Pleasure of doing good? But to see the drift
of so many Cares, his Mind should first have affixed some Meaning to these
Words *Power* and *Reputation*; he should be apprised that there are Men who
consider as something the looks of the rest of Mankind, who know how to be
happy and satisfied with themselves on the Testimony of others sooner than
upon their own. In fact, the real Source of all those Differences, is that the Savage
lives within himself, whereas the Citizen, constantly beside himself, knows only
how to live in the Opinion of others; insomuch that it is, if I may say so, merely
from their Judgement that he derives the Consciousness of his own Existence. It
is foreign to my subject to show how this Disposition engenders so much
Indifference for good and evil, notwithstanding so many and such fine
Discourses of Morality; how every thing, being reduced to Appearances, becomes
mere Art and Mummery; Honour, Friendship, Virtue, and often Vice itself,
which we at last learn the secret to boast of; how, in short, ever inquiring of
others what we are, and never daring to question ourselves on so delicate a
point, in the midst of so much Philosophy[,] Humanity and Politeness, and so
many sublime Maxims, we have nothing to shew for ourselves but a deceitful
and frivolous Exterior, Honour without Virtue, Reason without Wisdom, and
Pleasure without Happiness. It is sufficient that I have proved that this is not the
original Condition of Man, and that it is merely the Spirit of Society, and the
Inequality which Society engenders, that thus change and transform all our
natural Inclinations.

I have endeavoured to exhibit the Origin and Progress of Inequality, the Institution and Abuse of Political Societies, as far as these things are capable of being deduced from the Nature of Man by the mere light of Reason, and independently of those sacred Maxims which give to the Sovereign Authority the Sanction of Divine Right. It follows from this Picture, that as there is scarce any Inequality among Men in a State of Nature, all that which we now behold owes its force and its growth to the Development of our Faculties and the Improvement of our Understanding, and at last becomes permanent and lawful by the Establishment of Property and of Laws. It likewise follows that moral Inequality, authorised by any Right that is merely positive, clashes with natural Right, as often as it does not combine in the same Proportion with Physical Inequality; a Distinction which sufficiently determines, what we are able to think in that respect of that Kind of Inequality which obtains in all civilised Nations, since it is evidently against the Law of Nature that Infancy should command old Age, Folly conduct Wisdom, and a handful of Men should be ready to choak with Superfluities, while the famished Multitude want the commonest Necessaries of Life.

5.4   Adam Smith, *The Theory of Moral Sentiments* (1759)

Adam Smith (1723–90) was Professor of Moral Philosophy at the University of Glasgow and became best know for his The Wealth of Nations *(1776; extract 2.2). Underpinning that economic text, however, was Smith's more fundamental account of human nature, social relationships, and ethical and moral values presented in* The Theory of Moral Sentiments. *In this text Smith provided the period's most important account of the role played by sympathy between individuals and within society, and offered a heavyweight, philosophical foundation for the burgeoning cult of sensibility.*

How selfish soever man may be supposed, there are evidently some principles in his nature, which interest him in the fortune of others, and render their happiness necessary to him, though he derives nothing from it except the pleasure of seeing it. Of this kind is pity or compassion, the emotion which we feel for the misery of others, when we either see it, or are made to conceive it in a very lively manner. That we often derive sorrow from the sorrow of others is too obvious to require any instances to prove it; for this sentiment, like all the other original passions of human nature, is by no means confined to the virtuous and humane, though they perhaps may feel it with the most exquisite sensibility. The greatest ruffian, the most hardened violator of the laws of society, is not altogether without it.

As we have no immediate experience of what other men feel, we can form no idea of the manner in which they are affected, but by conceiving what we ourselves should feel in the like situation. Though our brother is upon the rack, as long as we are at our ease, our senses will never inform us of what he suffers. They never did and never can carry us beyond our own persons, and it is by the imagination only that we can form any conception of what are his sensations. Neither can that faculty help us to this any other way, than by representing to us what would be our own if we were in his case. It is the impressions of our own senses only, not those of his, which our imaginations copy. By the imagination we place ourselves in his situation, we conceive ourselves enduring all the same torments, we enter as it were into his body, and become in some measure him, and thence form some idea of his sensations, and even feel something which, though weaker in degree, is not altogether unlike them. His agonies, when they are thus brought home to ourselves, when we have thus adopted and made them our own, begin at last to affect us, and we then tremble and shudder at the thought of what he feels. For as to be in pain or distress of any kind excites the most excessive sorrow, so to conceive or to imagine that we are in it, excites some degree of the same emotion, in proportion to the vivacity or dulness of the conception.

That this is the source of our fellow-feeling for the misery of others, that it is by changing places in fancy with the sufferer, that we come either to conceive or to be affected by what he feels, may be demonstrated by many obvious observations, if it should not be thought sufficiently evident of itself. When we see a stroke aimed and just ready to fall upon the leg or arm of another person, we naturally shrink and draw back our own leg or our own arm; and when it does fall, we feel it in some measure, and are hurt by it as well as the sufferer. The mob, when they are gazing at a dancer on the slack rope, naturally writhe and twist and balance their own bodies, as they see him do, and as they feel that they themselves must do in his situation. Persons of delicate fibres and a weak constitution of body, complain that in looking on the sores and ulcers that are exposed by beggars in the streets, they are apt to feel an itching or uneasy sensation in the correspondent part of their own bodies. The horror which they conceive at the misery of those wretches affects that particular part in themselves more than any other; because that horror arises from conceiving what they themselves would suffer, if they really were the wretches whom they are looking upon, and if that particular part in themselves was actually affected in the same miserable manner. The very force of this conception is sufficient, in their feeble frames, to produce that itching or uneasy sensation complained of. Men of the most robust make, observe that in looking upon sore eyes they often feel a very sensible soreness in their own, which proceeds from the same reason; that organ being in the strongest man more delicate than any other part of the body is in the weakest.

Neither is it those circumstances only, which create pain or sorrow, that call forth our fellow-feeling. Whatever is the passion which arises from any object in the person principally concerned, an analogous emotion springs up, at the thought of his situation, in the breast of every attentive spectator. Our joy for the deliverance of those heroes of tragedy or romance who interest us, is as sincere as our grief for their distress, and our fellow-feeling with their misery is not more real than that with their happiness. We enter into their gratitude towards those faithful friends who did not desert them in their difficulties; and we heartily go along with their resentment against those perfidious traitors who injured, abandoned, or deceived them. In every passion of which the mind of man is susceptible, the emotions of the by-stander always correspond to what, by bringing the case home to himself, he imagines, should be the sentiments of the sufferer.

Pity and compassion are words appropriated to signify our fellow-feeling with the sorrow of others. Sympathy, though its meaning was, perhaps, originally the same, may now, however, without much impropriety, be made use of to denote our fellow-feeling with any passion whatever. . . .

Sympathy, therefore, does not arise so much from the view of the passion, as from that of the situation which excites it. We sometimes feel for another, a passion of which he himself seems to be altogether incapable; because when we put ourselves in his case, that passion arises in our breast from the imagination, though it does not in his from the reality. We blush for the impudence and rudeness of another, though he himself appears to have no sense of the impropriety of his own behaviour; because we cannot help feeling with what confusion we ourselves should be covered, had we behaved in so absurd a manner.

5.5   Jean-Jacques Rousseau, *Emilius and Sophia: or, A New System of Education* (1762)

Rousseau's Émile, ou De l'éducation was published in 1762 and quickly translated into English. In it, Rousseau uses the novel form to give a detailed account of his programme of 'natural education' for the fictional figure Émile. The book was highly influential on educational thinking and on conceptions of childhood in the Romantic period, presenting the child as inherently good and innocent and corrupted only by society. Though Rousseau's educational programme was widely admired by many liberals, a number of women writers (most notably Mary Wollstonecraft) were highly critical of his proposals in Book Five for the education of Sophie, which is designed to make her subservient to her husband.

All things are good as their Creator made them, but every thing degenerates in the hands of man. By human art is our native soil compelled to nourish exotic plants, and one tree to bear the fruits of another. Improving man makes a general confusion of elements, climates, and seasons: he mutilates his dogs, his horses, and his slaves: he defaces, he confounds every thing, as if he delighted in nothing but monsters and deformity. He is not content with any thing in its natural state, not even with his own species. His very offspring must be trained up for him, like a horse in the menage, and be taught to grow, after his own fancy, like a tree in his garden. . . .

Plants are formed by culture, and men by education. If a man should come into the world in full growth and vigour, his bulk and strength would be useless, till he should have learnt how to exert them: they would be even prejudicial to him, as they would prevent others from thinking it needful to lend him any assistance; and thus, left to himself, he would perish before he had discovered the objects of his wants. We lament the state of infancy, without reflecting that the human race must have been extinct, had not man been first a child.

We are born weak, we have need of help; we are born destitute of every thing, we stand in need of assistance; we are born stupid, we have need of understanding. All that we are not possessed of at our birth, and which we require when grown up, is bestowed on us by education.

This education we receive from nature, from men, or from circumstances. The constitutional exertion of our organs and faculties is the education of nature: the uses we are taught to make of that exertion, constitute the education given us by men; and in the acquisitions made by our own experience, on the objects that surround us, consists our education from circumstances.

We are formed, therefore, by three kinds of masters. The pupil, in whom the effects of their different lessons are contradictory, is badly educated, and can never be consistent with himself. He, in whom they are perfectly consonant, and always tend to the same point, hath only attained the end of a complete education. His life and actions demonstrate this, and that he alone is well brought up.

Of these three different kinds of education, that of nature depends not on ourselves; and but in a certain degree that of circumstances: the third, which belongs to men, is that only we have in our power: and even of this we are masters only in imagination; for who can flatter himself he will be able entirely to govern the discourse and actions of those who are about a child?

No sooner, then, doth education become an art, or profession, than it is almost impossible it should succeed, as the concurrent circumstances necessary to its success are not to be depended on. All that can be done, with our utmost solicitude, is to approach as near as possible the end we aim at, attributing it to good fortune if it be attained.

If it be asked, what is this end? it may be answered, that of nature, which has been already proved. For, since the concurrence of three kinds of education is necessary to its perfection, it is by that one, which is entirely independent of us, we must regulate the two others. . . .

We are born capable of sensibility, and from our birth are variously affected by the different objects that surround us. We no sooner acquire, if I may so express myself, a consciousness of our sensations, than we are disposed to avoid or pursue, the objects producing them, in proportion as they are at first sight agreeable or displeasing: We next learn to approve or dislike them, according to the convenient or inconvenient relation that subsists between ourselves and such objects; and lastly, according to the judgment we form of their consistency with those ideas, which reason gives us of happiness or perfection. These dispositions extend and confirm themselves, in proportion as we become more susceptible and enlightened: but, subject to the restraint of custom, they are more or less diversified by our opinions. Before they have taken this tincture of habit, they are what I call the dispositions of our nature.

It is to these original dispositions, therefore, we should on every occasion recur. . . . According to the order of nature, all men being equal, their common vocation is the profession of humanity; and whoever is well educated to discharge the duties of a man, cannot be badly prepared to fill up any of those offices that have a relation to him.

5.6   Jean-Jacques Rousseau, *The Confessions of Jean-Jacques Rousseau, Citizen of Geneva* (1782 and 1789, translation 1796)

Rousseau's Confessions *have a crucial place in the development of what would become one of the major genres of the Romantic period, the autobiography. Though there was a tradition of Christian spiritual narratives of self-development (most importantly St Augustine's), Rousseau's* Confessions *were the first major secular literary work in which the author took himself as the main subject. The controversial nature of this undertaking was heightened for Rousseau's readers by his willingness to reveal the less admirable elements of his character and his behaviour. Rousseau's writing of the self can be seen as directly influencing works such as William Hazlitt's* Liber Amoris *and De Quincey's* Confessions of an English Opium-Eater. *It is testimony to both the bravery of Rousseau's autobiographical undertaking and the hostile reaction it provoked that Wordsworth never published his poetic account of his own life,* The Prelude, *while Byron presented his own life only in fictionalized form in* Childe Harold's Pilgrimage *and* Don Juan.

I have entered on a performance which is without example, whose accomplishment will have no imitator. I mean to present my fellow-mortals with a man in all the integrity of nature; and this man shall be myself!

I know my heart, and have studied mankind: I am not made like any one I have been acquainted with, perhaps like no one in existence; if not better, I at least claim originality, and whether Nature did wisely in breaking the mould with which she formed me, can only be determined after having read this Work.

Whenever the last trumpet shall sound, I will present myself before the sovereign Judge with this Book in my hand, and loudly proclaim, thus have I acted; these were my thoughts; such was I. With equal freedom and veracity have I related what was laudable or wicked, I have concealed no crimes, added no virtues; and if I have sometimes introduced superfluous ornament, it was merely to occupy a void occasioned by defect of memory: I may have supposed that certain which I only knew to be probable, but have never asserted, as truth, a conscious falsehood. Such as I was, I have declared myself; sometimes vile and despicable, at others, virtuous, generous, and sublime; even as thou hast read my inmost soul: Power eternal! assemble round thy throne the innumerable throng of my fellow-mortals, let them listen to my Confessions, let them blush at my depravity, let them tremble at my sufferings; let each in his turn expose with equal sincerity the failings, the wanderings of his heart, and, if he dare, aver, *I was better than that man. . . .*

We suffer before we think; it is the common lot of humanity: I experienced more than my proportion of it. I have no knowledge of what passed prior to my fifth or sixth year; I recollect nothing of learning to read, I only remember what effect the first considerable exercise of it produced on my mind; and from that moment I date an uninterrupted knowledge of myself.

Every night, after supper, we read some part of a small collection of romances which had been my mother's. My father's design was only to improve me in reading, and he thought these entertaining works were calculated to give me a fondness for it; but we soon found ourselves so interested in the adventures they contained, that we alternately read whole nights together, and could not bear to give over until at the conclusion of a volume. . . .

I soon acquired, by this dangerous custom, not only an extreme facility in reading and comprehending, but, for my age, a too intimate acquaintance with the passions. An infinity of sensations were familiar to me, without possessing any precise idea of the objects to which they related – I had conceived nothing – I had felt the whole. This confused succession of emotions did not retard the future efforts of my reason, though they added an extravagant, romantic notion of human life, which experience and reflection have never been able to eradicate.

5.7   Constantin François de Chasseboeuf, comte de Volney, *The Ruins, or a Survey of the Revolutions of Empires* (1791)

Constantin François de Chasseboeuf, comte de Volney (1757–1820), was a French philosopher and travel writer. Les Ruines, published in 1791 and translated into English the following year, became a crucial text for readers interested in questioning political and religious power. In The Ruins, *Volney uses the genre of dream vision to present human history as a series of tyrannical regimes and religion as an ideological force; Marilyn Butler has commented that 'In today's terms Volney was not so much the Marx as the Foucault of his day, a man who taught a totalizing theory which showed a generation how to overestimate the efficacy of Power.'[4] In*

---

4 Marilyn Butler, 'Orientalism', in *The Romantic Period: The Penguin History of Literature*, ed. David B. Pirie (London: Penguin Books, 1994), p. 407.

Frankenstein, *Mary Shelley give* The Ruins *a crucial role when the monster over-*
hears Felix reading it to Safie, while Volney's radicalism and his imagery of ruins
were particularly important for Percy Shelley, informing poems such as Queen Mab
and 'Ozymandias'.

Solitary Ruins, sacred Tombs, ye mouldering and silent Walls, all hail! To you I
address my INVOCATION. While the vulgar shrink from your aspect with secret
terror, my heart finds in the contemplation a thousand delicious sentiments, a
thousand admirable recollections. Pregnant, I may truly call you, with useful
lessons, with pathetic and irresistible advice to the man who knows how to
consult you. A while ago the whole world bowed the neck in silence before the
tyrants that oppressed it; and yet in that hopeless moment you already
proclaimed the truths that tyrants hold in abhorrence: mixing the dust of the
proudest kings with that of the meanest slaves, you called upon us to contemplate this example of EQUALITY. From your caverns, whither the musing and
anxious love of LIBERTY led me, I saw escape its venerable shade, and with unexpected felicity direct its flight and marshal my steps the way to renovated
France.

    Tombs what virtues and potency do you exhibit! Tyrants tremble at your
aspect; you poison with secret alarm their impious pleasures; they turn from
you with impatience, and, coward like, endeavor to forget you amid the sump-
tuousness of their palaces. It is you that bring home the rod of justice to the
powerful oppressor; it is you that wrest the ill gotten gold from the merciless
extortioner, and avenge the cause of him that has none to help; you compen-
sate the narrow enjoyments of the poor, by dashing with care the goblet of the
rich; to the unfortunate you offer a last and inviolable asylum; in fine, you
give to the soul that just equilibrium of strength and tenderness which constitutes the wisdom of the sage and the science of life. The wise man looks
towards you, and scorns to amass vain grandeur and useless riches with which
he must soon part: you check his lawless flights, without disarming his adventure and courage; he feels the necessity of passing through the period assigned
him, and he gives employment to his hours, and makes use of the goods that
fortune has assigned him. Thus do you reign in the wild sallies of cupidity,
calm the fever of tumultuous enjoyment, free the mind from the anarchy of
the passions, and raise it above those little interests which torments the mass
of mankind. We ascend the eminence you afford us, and, viewing with one
glance the limits of nations and the succession of ages, are incapable of any
affections but such as are sublime, and entertain no ideas but those of virtue
and glory. Alas! when this uncertain dream of life shall be over, what then will
avail all our busy passions, unless they have left behind them the footsteps of
utility[.] . . .

In the eleventh year of the reign of Abd-ul-Hamid, son of Ahmed, emperor of the

Turks[5] . . . I journeyed in the empire of the Ottomans, and traversed the provinces which formerly were kingdoms of Egypt and of Syria.

Directing all my attention to what concerns the happiness of mankind in a state of society, I entered cities, and studied the manners of inhabitants; I gained admission into palaces, and observed the conduct of those who govern; I wandered over the country, and examined the condition of the peasants: and no where perceiving ought but robbery and devastation, tyranny and wretchedness, my heart was oppressed with sorrow and indignation.

Every day I found in my route fields abandoned by the plough, villages deserted, and cities in ruins. Frequently I met with antique monuments; wrecks of temples, palaces, and fortifications; pillars, aqueducts, sepulchres. By these objects my thoughts were directed to past ages, and my mind absorbed in serious and profound meditation.

Arrived at Hamsa on the borders of the Orontes, and being at no great distance from the city of Palmyra, situated in the desert, I resolved to examine for myself its boasted monuments. After three days of travel in barren solitude, and having passed through a valley filled with grottos and tombs, my eyes were suddenly struck, on leaving this valley and entering a plain, with a most astonishing scene of ruins. It consisted of a countless multitude of superb columns standing erect, and which, like the avenues of our parks, extended in regular files farther than the eye could reach. Among these columns magnificent edifices were observable, some entire, others in a state half demolished. The ground was covered on all sides with fragments of similar buildings, cornices, capitals, shafts, entablatures, and pilasters, all constructed of a marble of admirable whiteness and exquisite workmanship. . . .

Every day I visited some of the monuments which covered the plain; and one evening . . . I fell into a profound reverie.

Here, said I to myself, an opulent city once flourished; this was the seat of a powerful empire. Yes, these places, now so desert, a living multitude formerly animated, and an active crowd circulated in the streets which at present are so solitary. . . .

And now a mournful skeleton is all that subsists of this opulent city, and nothing remains of its powerful government but a vain and obscure remembrance! To the tumultuous throng which crowded under these porticos, the solitude of death has succeeded. The silence of the tomb is substituted for the hum of public places. The opulence of a commercial city is changed into hideous poverty. The palaces of kings are become the receptacle of deer, and unclean reptiles inhabit the sanctuary of the Gods. . . . What glory is here eclipsed, and how many labours are annihilated! . . . Thus perish the works of men, and thus do nations and empires vanish away! . . .

---

5 1784.

Figure 9 Henry Fuseli, 'The Artist Moved by the Grandeur of Antique Fragments', 1778–80; © 2008. Kunsthaus, Zürich. All rights reserved.

Fuseli's drawing of the colossal right hand and left foot of a statue of Constantine the Great powerfully captures the period's engagement with the grandeur and fragmentation of the past and the challenge posed by antiquity to the modern artist, themes seen in works such as Volney's *Ruins* (extract 5.7) and Percy Shelley's 'Ozymandias' with its 'vast and trunk-less legs of stone'.

Reflecting that if the places before me had once exhibited this animated picture; who, said I to myself, can assure me that their present desolation will not one day be the lot of our own country? who knows but that hereafter some traveller like myself will sit down upon the banks of the Seine, the Thames, or the Zuyder sea, where now, in the tumult of enjoyment, the heart and the eyes are too slow to take in the multitude of sensations; who knows but he will sit down solitary amid silent ruins, and weep a people inurned, and their greatness changed into an empty name?

5.8   William Godwin, *Enquiry Concerning Political Justice, and Its Influence on Morals and Happiness* (1793)

Godwin's influential and controversial political and social thinking (extracts 1.8, 4.2) is underpinned by a number of philosophic assumptions. Following Locke (see extracts 5.1), Godwin believed that ideas come from experience (note the reference to 'sensible impressions' below) and that individuals are formed by their environment rather than by any innate qualities or characteristics; as a result, both individuals and the society of which they are a part are capable of progress. Godwin argues that 'sound reasoning and truth' can overcome the 'vices and moral weakness' of mankind and that man is perfectible, by which he means not that individuals are capable of reaching perfection but that they, like everything else, are capable of constant improvement: 'There is no science that is not capable of additions; there is no art that may not be carried to a still higher perfection.'

The actions and dispositions of men are not the offspring of any original bias that they bring into the world in favour of one sentiment or character rather than another, but flow entirely from the operation of circumstances and events acting upon a faculty of receiving sensible impressions. . . .

Education will proceed with a firm step and with genuine lustre, when those who conduct it shall know what a vast field it embraces; when they shall be aware, that the effect, the question whether the pupil shall be a man of perseverance and enterprise or a stupid and inanimate dolt, depends upon the powers of those under whose direction he is placed, and the skill with which those powers shall be applied. Industry will be exerted with tenfold alacrity, when it shall be generally confessed that there are no obstacles to our improvement, which do not yield to the powers of industry. Multitudes will never exert the energy necessary to extraordinary success, till they shall dismiss the prejudices that fetter them, get rid of the chilling system of occult and inexplicable causes, and consider the human mind as an intelligent agent, guided by motives and prospects presented to the understanding, and not by causes of which we have no proper cognisance and can form no calculation. . . .

It has appeared that the characters of men are determined in all their most essential circumstances by education. By education in this place I would be understood to convey the most comprehensive sense that can possibly be annexed to that word, including every incident that produces an idea in the mind, and can give birth to a train of reflexions. . . .

The corollaries respecting political truth, deducible from the simple proposition, which seems clearly established by the reasonings of the present chapter, that the voluntary actions of men are in all instances conformable to the deductions of their understanding, are of the highest importance. Hence we may infer what are the hopes and prospects of human improvement. The doctrine which may be founded upon these principles, may perhaps best be expressed in the five following propositions: Sound reasoning and truth, when adequately communicated, must always be victorious over error: Sound reasoning and truth are capable of being so communicated: Truth is omnipotent: The vices and moral weakness of man are not invincible: Man is perfectible, or in other words susceptible of perpetual improvement. . . .

By perfectible it is not meant that he is capable of being brought to perfection. But the word seems sufficiently adapted to express the faculty of being continually made better and receiving perpetual improvement; and in this sense it is here to be understood. The term perfectible, thus explained, not only does not imply the capacity of being brought to perfection, but stands in express opposition to it. If we could arrive at perfection, there would be an end to our improvement. There is however one thing of great importance that it does imply: every perfection or excellence that human beings are competent to conceive, human beings, unless in cases that are palpably and unequivocally excluded by the structure of their frame, are competent to attain.

5.9   Samuel Taylor Coleridge, *The Statesman's Manual, or The Bible the Best Guide to Political Skill and Foresight: A Lay Sermon* and *Biographia Literaria* (1816 and 1817)

In addition to being a poet, Samuel Taylor Coleridge (1772–1834) was a philosopher and theologian whose writings on symbol and the imagination have been particularly influential. In The Statesman's Manual, *in which (as its title suggests) Coleridge sought to show how the Bible could be used as a political guide, he gives a famous definition of what he means by 'symbol', distinguishing it from allegory and presenting it as a part of the whole that it represents and as providing the link between the human imagination and the divine. Coleridge's representation of the mind as a living plant in this volume provides a central example of the organicism often associated with Romanticism, illustrating his sense, influenced by Immanuel Kant, that the mind is not passive or mechanical but vital, creative, and contributing to the world of which it is a part. Coleridge gave his most famous definition of the Imagination in* Biographia Literaria, *linking the creative power of the artist with that of God.*

From *The Statesman's Manual*

It is among the miseries of the present age that it recognizes no medium between *Literal* and *Metaphorical*. Faith is either to be buried in the dead letter, or its name and honors usurped by a counterfeit product of the mechanical understanding, which in the blindness of self-complacency confounds SYMBOLS with ALLEGORIES. Now an Allegory is but a translation of abstract notions into a picture-language which is itself nothing but an abstraction from objects of the senses; the principal being more worthless even than its phantom proxy, both alike unsubstantial, and the former shapeless to boot. On the other hand a Symbol . . . is characterized by a translucence of the Special in the Individual or of the General in the Especial or of the Universal in the General. Above all by the translucence of the Eternal through and in the Temporal. It always partakes of the Reality which it renders intelligible; and while it enunciates the whole, abides itself as a living part in that Unity, of which it is the representative. The other are but empty echoes which the fancy arbitrarily associates with apparitions of matter, less beautiful but not less shadowy than the sloping orchard or hill-side pasture-field seen in the transparent lake below. . . .

[W]ith particular reference to that undivided Reason, neither merely speculative or merely practical, but both in one, which I have in this annotation endeavoured to contra-distinguish from the Understanding, I seem to myself to behold in the quiet objects, on which I am gazing, more than an arbitrary illustration, more than a mere *simile*, the work of my own Fancy! I feel an awe, as if there were before my eyes the same Power, as that of the REASON – the same Power in a lower dignity, and therefore a symbol established in the truth of things. I feel it alike, whether I contemplate a single tree or flower, or meditate on vegetation throughout the world, as one of the great organs of the life of nature. Lo! – with the rising sun it commences its outward life and enters into open communion with all the elements, at once assimilating them to itself and to each other. At the same moment it strikes its roots and unfolds its leaves, absorbs and respires, steams forth its cooling vapour and finer fragrance, and breathes a repairing spirit, at once the food and tone of the atmosphere, into the atmosphere that feeds *it*. Lo! – at the touch of light how it returns an air akin to light, and yet with the same pulse effectuates its own secret growth, still contracting to fix what expanding it had refined. Lo!– how upholding the ceaseless plastic motion of the parts in the profoundest rest of the whole it becomes the visible organismus of the whole *silent* or *elementary* life of nature and, therefore, in incorporating the one extreme becomes the symbol of the other; the natural symbol of that higher life of reason, in which the whole series (known to us in our present state of being) is perfected, in which, therefore, all the subordinate gradations recur, and are re-ordained '*in more abundant honor.*'[6] We had seen each in its own cast, and we now recognize them all as co-existing in the unity of a higher form, the Crown and Completion of the Earthly, and the Mediator of a new and heavenly series. Thus finally, the vegetable creation, in the simplicity and uniformity of its *internal* structure symbolizing the unity of nature, while it represents the omniformity of her delegated functions in its *external* variety and manifoldness, becomes the record and chronicle of her ministerial acts, and inchases the vast unfolded volume of the earth with the hieroglyphics of her history. . . .

True natural philosophy is comprized in the study of the science and language of *symbols*. The power delegated to nature is all in every part: and by a symbol I mean, not a metaphor or allegory or any other figure of speech or form of fancy, but an actual and essential part of that, the whole of which it represents. Thus our Lord speaks symbolically when he says that 'the eye is the light of the body.'[7] The genuine naturalist is a dramatic poet in his own line: and such as our myriad-minded Shakespear is, compared with the Racines and Metastasios,[8] such and by a similar process of self- transformation would the man be, compared with the Doctors of the mechanic school, who should construct his physiology on the heaven-descended, Know Thyself.[9]

From Biographia Literaria

The IMAGINATION then I consider either as primary, or secondary. The primary IMAGINATION I hold to be the living Power and prime Agent of all human Perception, and as a repetition in the finite mind of the eternal act of creation in the infinite I AM. The secondary I consider as an echo of the former, co-existing with the conscious will, yet still as identical with the primary in the *kind* of its agency, and differing only in *degree*, and in the *mode* of its operation. It dissolves, diffuses, dissipates, in order to re-create; or where this process is rendered impossible, yet still at all events it struggles to idealize and to unify. It is essentially *vital*, even as all objects (*as* objects) are essentially fixed and dead.

FANCY, on the contrary, has no other counters to play with, but fixities and definites. The Fancy is indeed no other than a mode of Memory emancipated from the order of time and space; and blended with, and modified by that empirical phenomenon of the will, which we express by the word CHOICE. But equally with the ordinary memory the Fancy must receive all its materials ready made from the law of association.

---

6 1 Corinthians, 12:24.
7 Matthew, 6:22.
8 Jean Racine (1639–99), French playwright, and Pietro Metastio (1698–1782), Italian poet.
9 Juvenal, *Satires*, 11, 27.

5.10   John Stuart Mill, 'The Spirit of the Age', *Political Examiner* (1831)

John Stuart Mill's four-essay series 'The Spirit of the Age' is often cited as an example of the unprecedented historical self-consciousness of the intellectual climate in Britain during the Romantic period (Mill argues that the phrase was not used before 1780). As James Chandler has shown, Mill's comparison of the present moment with earlier periods is illustrative of the emergence of 'historicism' and was published at a time when there was a 'a kind of journalistic obsession' in the characteristics of the current era, seen in William Hazlitt's The Spirit of the Age *(1825) and Thomas Carlyle's 'Signs of the Times' (1829).*[10]

The 'spirit of the age' is in some measure a novel expression. I do not believe that it is to be met with in any work exceeding fifty years in antiquity. The idea of comparing one's own age with former ages, or with our notion of those which are yet to come, had occurred to philosophers; but it never before was itself the dominant idea of any age.

It is an idea essentially belonging to an age of change. Before men begin to think much and long on the peculiarities of their own times, they must have begun to think that those times are, or are destined to be, distinguished in a very remarkable manner from the times which preceded them. Mankind are then divided, into those who are still what they were, and those who have changed: into the men of the present age, and the men of the past. To the former, the spirit of the age is a subject of exultation; to the latter, of terror; to both, of eager and anxious interest. The wisdom of ancestors, and the march of intellect, are bandied from mouth to mouth; each phrase originally an expression of respect and homage, each ultimately usurped by the partisans of the opposite catch-word, and in the bitterness of their spirit, turned into the sarcastic jibe of hatred and insult.

The present times possess this character. A change has taken place in the human mind; a change which, being effected by insensible gradations, and without noise, had already proceeded far before it was generally perceived. When the fact disclosed itself, thousands awoke as from a dream. They knew not what processes had been going on in the minds of others, or even in their own, until the change began to invade outward objects; and it became clear that those were indeed new men, who insisted upon being governed in a new way.

But mankind are now conscious of their new position. The conviction is already not far from being universal, that the times are pregnant with change; and that the nineteenth century will be known to posterity as the era of one of the greatest revolutions of which history has preserved the remembrance, in the

---

10 James Chandler, 'History', in Iain McCalman et al. (ed.), *An Oxford Companion to the Romantic Age* (Oxford: Oxford University Press, 1999), p. 355.

human mind, and in the whole constitution of human society. Even the religious world teems with new interpretations of the Prophecies, foreboding mighty changes near at hand. It is felt that men are henceforth to be held together by new ties, and separated by new barriers; for the ancient bonds will now no longer unite, nor the ancient boundaries confine. Those men who carry their eyes in the back of their heads and can see no other portion of the destined track of humanity than that which it has already travelled, imagine that because the old ties are severed mankind henceforth are not to be connected by any ties at all; and hence their affliction, and their awful warnings. . . .

The first of the leading peculiarities of the present age is, that it is an age of transition. Mankind have outgrown old institutions and old doctrines, and have not yet acquired new ones. When we say outgrown, we intend to prejudge nothing. A man may not be either better or happier at six-and-twenty, than he was at six years of age: but the same jacket which fitted him then, will not fit him now.

The prominent trait just indicated in the character of the present age, was obvious a few years ago only to the more discerning: at present it forces itself upon the most inobservant. Much might be said, and shall be said on a fitting occasion, of the mode in which the old order of things has become unsuited to the state of society and of the human mind. But when almost every nation on the continent of Europe has achieved, or is in the course of rapidly achieving, a change in its form of government; when our own country, at all former times the most attached in Europe to its old institutions, proclaims almost with one voice that they are vicious both in the outline and in the details, and that they *shall* be renovated, and purified, and made fit for civilized man, we may assume that a part of the effects of the cause just now pointed out, speak sufficiently loudly for themselves. To him who can reflect, even these are but indications which tell of a more vital and radical change. Not only, in the conviction of almost all men, things as they are, are wrong – but, according to that same conviction, it is not by remaining in the old ways that they can be set right. Society demands, and anticipates, not merely a new machine, but a machine constructed in another manner. Mankind will not be led by their old maxims, nor by their old guides; and they will not choose either their opinions or their guides as they have done heretofore.

6
Aesthetics

Introduction

Though the word 'aesthetics' was not widely used in Britain during the Romantic age, gaining its current meaning later in the nineteenth century, the issues of judgement and taste with which aesthetics is concerned were much debated and a knowledge of the key concepts is essential to an understanding of the literary and cultural output of the period. Many of the extracts in this section offer definitions of the three major aesthetic categories of the eighteenth and early nineteenth centuries – the sublime, the beautiful, and the picturesque – which provided frameworks for the creation and reception of artistic and literary works while also shaping the way in which individuals responded to the world around them. While there are clear links between the aesthetic theories of this section and the philosophical debates of the previous one, it is important to recognize that these aesthetic theories are also inseparable from the social and political concerns focused on in other sections. For example, Edmund Burke would exploit the full force of his own conceptualizing of the sublime when presenting the horrors of the French Revolution in *Reflections* (see extract 1.4), while his opposed categories of the sublime and the beautiful are constructed in terms of a gendered hierarchy (sublime as masculine, beautiful as feminine) which they consolidate.

The most important aesthetic development for an understanding of the literary and cultural output of the Romantic period was the increasing significance attached to the idea of the sublime. Theories of the sublime date back to the first-century Greek writer Longinus, whose 'On the Sublime' was translated into English in the middle of the seventeenth century. Longinus was concerned with the rhetorical sublime, with the uplifting effect of elevated language, which can fill listeners with exaltation and joy and potentially overwhelm them. This rhetorical sublime was still current in the mid-eighteenth century – Dr. Johnson defines it as 'the grand and lofty style' in his *Dictionary* of 1755 – but the effects of the sublime were becoming increasingly associated with the natural world. A number of philosophers of the late seventeenth and early eighteenth centuries experienced what would become known as the sublime when visiting the Alps as part of the Grand Tour. As early as 1688, for example, when describing his ascent of an Alpine mountain, John Dennis commented that the experience 'produced different emotions in me, *viz.* a delightful Horrour, a terrible Joy, and at the same time, that I was infinitely pleas'd, I trembled'.[1] Joseph Addison, in his 'Essay on the Pleasures of the Imagination' of 1712, wrote of the effect of the 'Greatness' 'of huge Heaps of Mountains, high Rocks and precipices', commenting that: 'Our Imagination loves to be filled with an Object, or to grasp at anything that is too big for its capacity. We are flung into a pleasing Astonishment at such unbounded Views, and feel a delightful Stillness and Amazement in the Soul at the Apprehension of them.'[2]

In his *A Philosophical Enquiry into the Origin of our Ideas of the Sublime and Beautiful* (1757, extract 6.2), Edmund Burke clarified previous accounts of the sublime by defining it against the beautiful. His association of the sublime with terror and danger (albeit experienced from a position of safety) was highly influential, and the mingled pain and delight that the sublime produced was sought in a variety of ways, from visits to the mountain scenery of the Alps or Lake District to the reading of contemporary Gothic novels (see Figure 15) or the great sublime writers of the past, Milton and Shakespeare. Running parallel to the philosophical developments of the period and its preoccupation with the creative power of the artist or writer, engagement with the sublime came increasingly to question whether it was produced by an external object or by the mind itself. For example, in one of the most important episodes of *The Prelude*, it is Wordsworth's failure to experience the sublime when crossing the Alps which causes him fully to appreciate the power of the imagination, while Coleridge redefined Burke's duality in terms of subject–object relations, writing 'I meet, I *find* the Beautiful – but I give, contribute, or rather attribute the Sublime.'[3] In this shift of emphasis to the sublime creative powers of the mind, Wordsworth and Coleridge were anticipated by (and in the latter's case, influenced by) the work of the German philosopher Immanuel Kant, whose *Critique of Judgement* of 1790 is often used to provide a valuable theoretical framework for thinking about the Romantic sublime, though Kant's work was little known in Britain until later in the nineteenth century. Increasingly associated with the creative power of the artist and with the importance of strong emotion, the sublime provided a powerful counter-aesthetic to the Neoclassical insistence on rules seen in Reynolds's *Discourses* (extract 6.3), though even Reynolds began to conceive of the genius as one who may move beyond such rules.

The other significant aesthetic development focused on in this section is the rise of the picturesque, a concept which shaped ideas about landscape (real, represented or imagined) in the period. In 1768, William Gilpin had defined the picturesque as 'a term expressive of that particular kind of beauty, which is agreeable in a picture', and picturesque theorists often turned to the landscapes

---

1 Printed in Clarence D. Thorpe, 'Two Augustans Crossing the Alps', *Studies in Philology*, 32 (1935), pp. 463–82.
2 'Essay on the Pleasures of the Imagination', *The Spectator*, 412 (1712), p. 540.
3 Quoted in *An Oxford Companion to the Romantic Age*, ed. Iain McCalman et al. (Oxford: Oxford University Press, 1999), p. 723.

of Claude Lorraine and Salvator Rosa for their models. According to Gilpin, what distinguished such paintings and landscapes was the quality of 'roughness', which defined them against the regularity, smoothness, and neatness of non-picturesque beauty (extract 6.5). For him, roughness produced the key picturesque qualities of irregularity, ruggedness, variety, and contrast, particularly of light and shade. The nature of the picturesque was the subject of a keenly argued debate during the 1790s, to which the other main contributors were Richard Payne Knight and Uvedale Price (extract 6.6), but it provided an aesthetic for appreciating the British landscape at a time of significant increase in domestic tourism, illustrated by the popularity of West's *Guide to the Lakes* (extract 6.4). West's *Guide*, along with the picturesque writings of Gilpin and Price, illustrates the re-evaluation of landscape and the countryside, which in much of the literature of the period gained a spiritual or restorative power. There is a political dimension to much picturesque writing, in its wartime celebration of a British landscape at a time when political commentators were exposing rural poverty and hardship. Though the picturesque is often criticized for being formulaic, it should be recognized that it gives a considerable role to the viewer, who frames the scene with a Claude Glass (a darkened mirror used to view the landscape), re-creates it through sketching or memory, or even creates it in ideal form through the imagination. One indication of the popularity of the picturesque is the way in which it became a subject for satire; William Combe published a satirical poem entitled *The Tour of Doctor Syntax in Search of the Picturesque* in 1809, while Jane Austen frequently mocks the taste for the picturesque in her novels.

While the picturesque might be seen as a particularly British aesthetic, this section also includes two extracts (6.1 and 6.8) illustrating the impact of classical Greek culture on ideas of art. The writing of Johann Joachim Winckelmann (extract 6.1), the excavations of Pompeii and Herculaneum, the acquisition of the Elgin Marbles by the British Museum (extract 6.7), and political sympathy for Greece under the domination of the Ottoman Empire, all stimulated what is known as 'Romantic Hellenism'. This interest in Greek culture is illustrated by the poetry of Shelley (*Prometheus Unbound*, *Hellas*), Keats ('Ode on a Grecian Urn', 'On First Looking into Chapman's Homer', *Hyperion*), Felicia Hemans (*Modern Greece*) and Byron (*Childe Harold's Pilgrimage*, *The Giaour*), the last of whom died in Missolonghi in 1824 assisting the Greeks in their fight for independence from Turkey.

6.1   Johann Joachim Winckelmann, *Reflections on the Painting and Sculpture of the Greeks: With Instructions for the Connoisseur, and An Essay on Grace in Works of Art* (1755, translation by Henry Fuseli, 1765)

The German art historian and archaeologist Johann Joachim Winckelmann (1717–68) was a major influence on aesthetic theory and taste in the Romantic period, stimulating

interest in Hellenism and Neoclassicism. In the extract below, he gives his famous defi-
nition of the essence of Greek art as being a 'noble simplicity and sedate grandeur'. He
illustrates this with an account of a first-century Greek sculpture that had been exca-
vated in Rome in 1506 depicting the Trojan priest Laocoön and his sons being attacked
by a sea serpent (see William Blake's drawing reproduced in Figure 10).

The last and most eminent characteristic of the Greek works is a noble simplicity and sedate grandeur in Gesture and Expression. As the bottom of the sea lies
peaceful beneath a foaming surface, a great soul lies sedate beneath the strife of
passions in Greek figures.

'Tis in the face of Laocoon this soul shines with full lustre, not confined
however to the face, amidst the most violent sufferings. Pangs piercing every
muscle, every labouring nerve; pangs which we almost feel ourselves, while we
consider – not the face, nor the most expressive parts – only the belly contracted
by excruciating pains: these however, I say, exert not themselves with violence,
either in the face or gesture. He pierces not heaven, like the Laocoon of *Virgil*;
his mouth is rather opened to discharge an anxious overloaded groan, as *Sadolet*[4]
says; the struggling body and the supporting mind exert themselves with equal
strength, nay balance all the frame.

Laocoon suffers, but suffers like the Philoctetes of *Sophocles*:[5] we weeping feel
his pains, but wish for the hero's strength to support his misery.

The Expression of so great a soul is beyond the force of mere nature. It was in
his own mind the artist was to search for the strength of spirit with which he
marked his marble. Greece enjoyed artists and philosophers in the same persons;
and the wisdom of more than one Metrodorus[6] directed art, and inspired its
figures with more than common souls.

Had Laocoon been covered with a garb becoming an ancient sacrificer, his
sufferings would have lost one half of their Expression. *Bernini* pretended to
perceive the first effects of the operating venom in the numbness of one of the
thighs.

Every action or gesture in Greek figures, not stamped with this character of
sage dignity, but too violent, too passionate, was called 'Parenthyrsos.'

For, the more tranquillity reigns in a body, the fitter it is to draw the true
character of the soul; which, in every excessive gesture, seems to rush from her
proper centre, and being hurried away by extremes becomes unnatural. Wound
up to the highest pitch of passion, she may force herself upon the duller eye;
but the true sphere of her action is simplicity and calmness. In Laocoon sufferings alone had been Parenthyrsos; the artist therefore, in order to reconcile the

4　The Italian poet Jacopo Sadoleto (1477–1547), one of whose best known works was on Laocoön.
5　Philoctetes was a Greek hero of the Trojan Wars and subject of a play by Sophocles.
6　Greek Philosopher of the fourth century BC.

Figure 10 William Blake, copy of the Laocoon, for Rees's *Cyclopedia*, 1815; ® Yale Center for British Art, Paul Mellon Fund, USA/Bridgeman Art Library.

Johann Joachim Winckelmann gave a detailed description of the statue of Laocoön to illustrate his theory that Greek art was characterized by 'noble simplicity and sedate grandeur' (extract 6.1). William Blake was strongly influenced by Winckelmann's *Reflections*, which were translated into English by Blake's friend Henry Fuseli.

significative and ennobling qualities of his soul, put him into a posture, allowing for the sufferings that were necessary, the next to a state of tranquillity: a
tranquillity however that is characteristical: the soul will be herself – this individual – not the soul of mankind; sedate, but active; calm, but not indifferent or
drowsy.

6.2   Edmund Burke, *A Philosophical Enquiry into the Origin of our Ideas of the Sublime and Beautiful* (1757)

In his Philosophical Enquiry, *Edmund Burke (1729–97) gave an account of the difference between the sublime and the beautiful that would prove highly influential, examining both the nature of the objects that could be placed in either category and the
psychological effects they produced. The beautiful, he argued, was defined by qualities
of smallness, smoothness, roundness and delicacy, with gentle variations of shape and
muted colour, and it produced a feeling of love. The sublime was defined by vastness,
obscurity and infinity, and produced feelings of admiration, astonishment, and, most
crucially, terror. As Burke writes (in the second edition), 'terror is in all cases whatsoever, either more openly or latently the ruling principle of the sublime'. Burke's account
of the sublime provides a crucial framework for thinking about many of the literary,
cultural and philosophical aspects of the Romantic period, aiding an understanding of
developments such as the popularity of John Martin's apocalyptic paintings, the growing interest in sublime landscapes (such as the mountain scenery of Wordsworth's* The
Prelude *and Shelley's 'Mont Blanc'), and the emergence of the Gothic novel (or 'terrorist writing', as it was called in the 1790s; see extracts 8.4 and 8.9).*

PART I
SECTION VI.   Of the passions which belong to SELF-PRESERVATION

Most of the ideas which are capable of making a powerful impression on the
mind, whether simply of Pain or Pleasure, or of the modifications of those, may
be reduced very nearly to these two heads, *self-preservation* and *society*; to the
ends of one or the other of which all our passions are calculated to answer. The
passions which concern self-preservation, turn mostly on *pain* or *danger*. The
ideas of *pain*, *sickness*, and *death*, fill the mind with strong emotions of horror;
but *life* and *health*, though they put us in a capacity of being affected with pleasure, they make no such impression by the simple enjoyment. The passions
therefore which are conversant about the preservation of the individual, turn
chiefly on *pain* and *danger*, and they are the most powerful of all the passions.

SECTION VII.   Of the SUBLIME

Whatever is fitted in any sort to excite the ideas of pain, and danger, that is to say, whatever is in any sort terrible, or is conversant about terrible objects, or operates in a manner analogous to terror, is a source of the *sublime*; that is, it is productive of the strongest emotion which the mind is capable of feeling. When danger or pain press too nearly, they are incapable of giving any delight, and are simply terrible; but at certain distances, and with certain modifications, they may be, and they are delightful, as we every day experience. . . .

PART II
SECTION I.   Of the passion caused by the SUBLIME

The passion caused by the great and sublime in *nature*, when those causes operate most powerfully, is Astonishment; and astonishment is that state of the soul, in which all its motions are suspended, with some degree of horror. In this case the mind is so entirely filled with its object, that it cannot entertain any other, nor by consequence reason on that object which employs it. Hence arises the great power of the sublime, that far from being produced by them, it anticipates our reasonings, and hurries us on by an irresistible force. Astonishment, as I have said, is the effect of the sublime in its highest degree; the inferior effects are admiration, reverence and respect.

SECTION II. TERROR

No passion so effectually robs the mind of all its powers of acting and reasoning as fear. For fear being an apprehension of pain or death, it operates in a manner that resembles actual pain. Whatever therefore is terrible, with regard to sight, is sublime too, whether this cause of terror, be endued with greatness of dimensions or not; for it is impossible to look on anything as trifling, or contemptible, that may be dangerous. There are many animals, who though far from being large, are yet capable of raising ideas of the sublime, because they are considered as objects of terror. As serpents and poisonous animals of almost all kinds. Even to things of great dimensions, if we annex any adventitious idea of terror, they become without comparison greater. An even plain of a vast extent on land, is certainly no mean idea; the prospect of such a plain may be as extensive as a prospect of the ocean; but can it ever fill the mind with any thing so great as the ocean itself? this is owing to several causes, but it is owing to none more than to this, that the ocean is an object of no small terror.

SECTION III.   OBSCURITY

To make anything very terrible, obscurity seems in general to be necessary. When we know the full extent of any danger, when we can accustom our eyes to it, a great deal of the apprehension vanishes. Every one will be sensible of this, who considers how greatly night adds to our dread, in all cases of danger, and how much the notions of ghosts and goblins, of which none can form clear ideas, affect minds, which give credit to the popular tales concerning such sorts of beings. Those despotic governments, which are founded on the passions of men, and principally upon the passion of fear, keep their chief as much as may be from the public eye. The policy has been the same in many cases of religion. Almost all the heathen temples were dark. Even in the barbarous temples of the Americans at this day, they keep their idol in a dark part of the hut, which is consecrated to his worship. For this purpose too the druids performed all their ceremonies in the bosom of the darkest woods, and in the shade of the oldest and most spreading oaks. No person seems better to have understood the secret of heightening, or of setting terrible things, if I may use the expression, in their strongest light by the force of a judicious obscurity, than Milton. His description of Death in the second book is admirably studied; it is astonishing with what a gloomy pomp, with what a significant and expressive uncertainty of strokes and colouring he has finished the portrait of the king of terrors.

> The other shape,
> If shape it might be called that shape had none
> Distinguishable, in member, joint, or limb;
> Or substance might be called that shadow seemed,
> For each seemed either; black he stood as night;
> Fierce as ten furies; terrible as hell;
> And shook a deadly dart. What seemed his head
> The likeness of a kingly crown had on. [7]

In this description all is dark, uncertain, confused, terrible, and sublime to the last degree. . . .

SECTION VII.   VASTNESS

Greatness of dimension, is a powerful cause of the sublime. This is too evident, and the observation too common, to need any illustration; but it is not so common, to consider in what ways greatness of dimension, vastness of extent, or quantity, has the most striking effect. For certainly, there are ways, and modes, wherein the same quantity of extension shall produce greater effects than it is found to do in others. Extension is either in length, height, or depth. Of these the length strikes least; an hundred yards of even ground will never work such an effect as a tower an hundred yards high, or a rock or mountain of that altitude. I am apt to imagine likewise, that height is less grand than depth; and that we are more struck at looking down from a precipice, than at looking up at an object of equal height; but of that I am not very positive. A perpendicular has more force in forming the sublime, than an inclined plane; and the

---

7 *Paradise Lost*, II. 666–73.

effects of a rugged and broken surface seem stronger than where it is smooth and polished. . . .

SECTION VIII. INFINITY

Another source of the sublime, is *infinity*; if it does not rather in some sort belong to the last. Infinity has a tendency to fill the mind with that sort of delightful horror, which is the most genuine effect, and truest test of the sublime. There are scarce any things which can become the objects of our senses that are really, and in their own nature infinite. But the eye not being able to perceive the bounds of many things, they seem to be infinite, and they produce the same effects as if they were really so. We are deceived in the like manner, if the parts of some large object, are so continued to any indefinite number, that the imagination meets no check which may hinder its extending them at pleasure. . . .

SECTION XVIII. RECAPITULATION [On Beauty]

On the whole, the qualities of beauty, as they are merely sensible qualities, are the following. First, to be comparatively small. Secondly, to be smooth. Thirdly, to have a variety in the direction of the parts; but fourthly, to have those parts not angular, but melted as it were into each other. Fifthly, to be of a delicate frame, without any remarkable appearance of strength. Sixthly, to have its colours clear and bright; but not very strong and glaring. Seventhly, or if it should have any glaring colour, to have it diversified with others. These are, I believe, the properties on which beauty depends; properties that operate by nature, and are less liable to be altered by caprice, or confounded by a diversity of tastes, than any others.

6.3   Joshua Reynolds, *Discourses on Art* (1769–70)

Sir Joshua Reynolds (1723–92) was a major eighteenth-century portrait painter and the first president of the Royal Academy, which he had helped found. His Discourses, *initially delivered as lectures at the Royal Academy, give a key statement of Neoclassical ideas, offering a hierarchy of artistic genres (with history painting at the top, followed by portraits, then landscapes, and finally still-life), emphasizing the importance of the rules of art derived from the great works of the past, valuing instruction and observation above spontaneity, and arguing that the best art should represent the general and the ideal rather than the individual or the particular.*

I would chiefly recommend, that an implicit obedience to the *Rules of Art*, as established by the practice of the great MASTERS, should be exacted from the *young* Students. That those models, which have passed through the approbation

of ages, should be considered by them as perfect and infallible guides; as subjects
for their imitation, not their criticism.

I AM confident, that this is the only efficacious method of making a progress
in the Arts; and that he who sets out with doubting, will find life finished before
he becomes master of the rudiments. For it may be laid down as a maxim, that
he who begins by presuming on his own sense, has ended his studies as soon as
he has commenced them. Every opportunity, therefore, should be taken to
discountenance that false and vulgar opinion, that rules are the fetters of genius.
They are fetters only to men of no genius; as that armour, which upon the strong
is an ornament and a defence, upon the weak and mis-shapen becomes a load,
and cripples the body which it was made to protect.

How much liberty may be taken to break through those rules, and, as the Poet
expresses it,

> *To snatch a grace beyond the reach of art,*[8]

may be a subsequent consideration, when the pupils become masters themselves. It is then, when their genius has received its utmost improvement, that
rules may possibly be dispensed with. But let us not destroy the scaffold, until
we have raised the building. . . .

All the objects which are exhibited to our view by nature, upon close examination will be found to have their blemishes and defects. The most beautiful forms
have something about them like weakness, minuteness, or imperfection. But it
is not every eye that perceives these blemishes. It must be an eye long used to
the contemplation and comparison of these forms; and which, by a long habit
of observing what any set of objects of the same kind have in common, has
acquired the power of discerning what each wants in particular. This long laborious comparison should be the first study of the painter, who aims at the greatest style. By this means, he acquires a just idea of beautiful forms; he corrects
nature by herself, her imperfect state by her more perfect. His eye being enabled
to distinguish the accidental deficiencies, excrescences, and deformities of
things, from their general figures, he makes out an abstract idea of their forms
more perfect than any one original; and what may seem a paradox, he learns to
design naturally by drawing his figures unlike to any one object. This idea of the
perfect state of nature, which the artist calls the Ideal Beauty, is the great leading principle by which works of genius are conducted. . . .

This is the idea which has acquired, and which seems to have a right to the
epithet of *divine*; as it may be said to preside, like a supreme judge, over all the
productions of nature; appearing to be possessed of the will and intention of the
Creator, as far as they regard the external form of living beings. When a man

---

8 Alexander Pope, *An Essay on Criticism*, l. 152.

once possesses this idea in its perfection, there is no danger but that he will be sufficiently warmed by it himself, and be able to warm and ravish every one else.

Thus it is from a reiterated experience, and a close comparison of the objects in nature, that an artist becomes possessed of the idea of that central form, if I may so express it, from which every deviation is deformity.

6.4 Thomas West, *A Guide to the Lakes: Dedicated to the Lovers of Landscape Studies, and to all who have visited, or intend to visit the Lakes in Cumberland, Westmorland, and Lancashire* (1778)

Thomas West's (1720–79) Guide to the Lakes *illustrates the growing fashion for travel within Britain and the developing interest in the British landscape, particularly that of the Lake District, which was seen as both sublime and picturesque and which has become a key location of Romanticism as the birthplace, home and subject matter of the poet William Wordsworth. The extract below, from the opening of the* Guide, *provides a valuable account of the motivations for travel in the period and of the perceived powers of the rural environment (particularly for those who were city dwellers). West's* Guide *was frequently reprinted, often accompanied by a map which showed the various 'stations' recommended for viewing the landscape.*

Since persons of genius, taste, and observation, began to make the tour of their own country, and give such pleasing accounts of the natural history, and improving state, of the northern parts of the BRITISH Empire, the curious of all ranks have caught the spirit of visiting the same.

The taste for landscape, as well as for the other objects of the noble art (cherished under the protection of the greatest of kings, and best of men), in which the genius of BRITAIN rivals ancient GREECE and ROME, induce many to visit the lakes of CUMBERLAND, WESTMORLAND, and LANCASHIRE, there to contemplate, in Alpine scenery, finished in nature's highest tints, what refined art labours to imitate; the pastoral and rural landscape, varied in all the stiles, the soft, the rude, the romantic, and sublime. Combinations not found elsewhere assembled within so small a tract of country. Another inducement to making the tour of the lakes, is the goodness of the roads; . . .

The design of the following sheets, is to encourage the taste of visiting the lakes, by furnishing the traveller with a Guide; and for that purpose are here collected and laid before him, all the select stations,[9] and points of view, noticed by those who have made the tour of the lakes, verified by repeated observations, with remarks on the principal objects as they appear viewed from different

---

9 West's 'stations', for which his guide became particularly famous, were particular recommended viewpoints from which to appreciate the scenery.

stations; with such incidents as will greatly facilitate, and much heighten the pleasure of the tour, and relieve the traveller from the burthen of dull and tedious information on the road, or at the inn, that frequently embarasses, and often misguides.

The local knowledge here communicated, will not affect, much less prevent, the agreeable surprise that attends the first sight of scenes that surpass all description, and of objects which affect the mind of the spectator only in the highest degree.

Such as wish to unbend the mind from anxious cares, or fatiguing studies, will meet with agreeable dissipation and useful relaxation, in making the tour of the lakes. Something new will open itself at the turn of every mountain, and a succession of ideas will be supported by a perpetual change of objects, and display of scenes behind scenes, in a succession of perpetual variety, and endless perspective. In the depth of solitude may be reviewed, in figure, the hurry and bustle of busy life, in all its gradations, in the variety of unshaded rills that hang on the mountains sides, or hasty brooks that warble through the dell, or mighty torrents precipitating themselves at once with thundering noise from tremendous rocky heights; all pursuing one general end, their increase in the vale, and their union in the ocean. The contemplative traveller will be charmed with the sight of the sweet retreats, that he will observe in these enchanting regions of calm repose.

Such as spend their lives in cities, and their time in crowds, will here meet with contrasts that enlarge the mind, by contemplation of sublime objects, and raise it from nature, to nature's first cause. Whoever takes a walk into these scenes, will return penetrated with a sense of the creator's power and unsearchable wisdom, in heaping mountains upon mountains, and enthroning rocks upon rocks. Such exhibitions of sublime and beautiful objects surprise and please, exciting at once rapture and reverence.

When change of air is recommended, and exercise for health; the convalescent will find the former here in the purest state, and the latter will be the concomitant of the tour. The many hills and mountains of various heights, separated by narrow vales, through which the air is agitated, and hurried on, by a multiplicity of brooks, and mountain torrents, keep up a constant circulation. The vales and dales being heated by the reverberated solar rays, the air thereby rarified, is refreshed from the tops of the mountains. The water is pure as the air, and on that account recommends itself to the valetudinarian.[10]

There is no person but may find a motive for visiting this extraordinary region; especially those who intend to make the continental tour, should begin here; as it will give, in miniature, an idea of what they are to meet with there, in traversing the ALPS and APENNINES; to which our northern mountains are not inferior in beauty of line, or variety of summit; not in number of lakes, diversity of

10 A sickly or weak person.

fish, and transparency of water; not in colouring of rock, or softness of turf; but in height and extent only. The mountains here are all accessible to the summit, and furnish prospects no less surprising, and with more variety th[a]n the ALPS themselves. . . .

Those who have traversed the ALPS, who have visited the lake of GENEVA, and viewed Mount BLANC, the highest of the GLACIERS, from the valley of CHAMOUNI, in SAVOY, may still find entertainment in this home tour; where nature, on a reduced scale, has performed wonders in the epitome of her greater works: The analogy of mountainous countries, and their difference, furnishes the observant traveller with amusement; and the travelled visitor of the CUMBRIAN lakes and mountains, will not be disappointed in this particular.

6.5 William Gilpin, *Three Essays: On Picturesque Beauty; On Picturesque Travel; and on Sketching Landscape* (1792)

The clergyman and teacher William Gilpin (1724–1804) was a leading theorist of the picturesque, the characteristics of which he outlined most fully in his Three Essays. *Developed during his sketching tours of Britain (particularly the Lake District), Gilpin's theory of the picturesque differentiated it from the beautiful by emphasizing the desirability of 'roughness' and 'ruggedness' in landscapes, qualities which produced the effects of chiaroscuro (mixed light and shade), richness, and variety. Gilpin's* Three Essays *proved extremely popular, providing guidelines for the appreciation of landscapes and works of art at a time when there was a significant growth in domestic tourism (a year after the publication of the volume, the outbreak of war with France closed the continent to most travellers). Importantly, Gilpin's picturesque traveller is no passive recorder of landscapes, and Gilpin's emphasis on memory and imagination in response to landscape has significant parallels with much poetry of the period.*

Disputes about beauty might perhaps be involved in less confusion, if a distinction were established, which certainly exists, between such objects as are *beautiful*, and such as are *picturesque* – between those, which please the eye in their *natural state*; and those, which please from some quality, capable of being *illustrated in painting*.

Ideas of beauty vary with the object, and with the eyes of the spectator. Those artificial forms appear generally the most beautiful, with which we have been the most conversant. Thus . . . the painter, who compares his object with the rules of his art, sees it in a different light from the man of general taste, who surveys it only as simply beautiful.

As this difference therefore between the *beautiful*, and the *picturesque* appears really to exist, and must depend on some peculiar construction of the object; it may be worth while to examine, what that peculiar construction is. . . . The question simply is, *What is that quality in objects, which particularly marks them as picturesque?*

Figure 11 William Gilpin, 'Picturesque Beauty', 1794. Courtesy of the Rare Books Archive, Lancaster University Library.

Used as an illustration to his *Three Essays* (extract 6.5), Gilpin's painting aims to display many of the key features of the picturesque, including roughness, irregularity, ruggedness, variety and contrast of light and shade.

In examining the *real object*, we shall find, one source of beauty arises from that species of elegance, which we call *smoothness*, or *neatness*; for the terms are nearly synonymous. The higher the marble is polished, the brighter the silver is rubbed, and the more the mahogany shines, the more each is considered as an object of beauty: as if the eye delighted in gliding smoothly over a surface.

In the class of larger objects the same idea prevails. In a pile of building we wish to see neatness in every part added to the elegance of the architecture. And if we examine a piece of improved pleasure-ground, every thing rough, and slovenly offends. . . .

Thus then, we suppose, the matter stands with regard to *beautiful objects in general*. But in *picturesque representation* it seems somewhat odd, yet perhaps we shall find it equally true, that the reverse of this is the case; and that the ideas of *neat* and *smooth*, instead of being picturesque, in fact disqualify the object, in which they reside, of all pretensions to *picturesque beauty*. – Nay farther, we do not scruple to assert, that *roughness* forms the most essential point of difference between the *beautiful*, and the *picturesque*; as it seems to be that particular quality, which makes objects chiefly pleasing in painting. – I use the general term *roughness*; but properly speaking roughness relates only to the surfaces of bodies: when we speak of their delineation, we use the word *ruggedness*. Both ideas however equally enter into the picturesque; and both are observable in the smaller, as well as in the larger parts of nature – in the outline, and bark of a tree, as in the rude summit, and craggy sides of a mountain. . . .

Variety too is equally necessary in composition: so is *contrast*. Both these [the artist] finds in rough objects; and neither of them in smooth. Variety indeed, in some degree, he may find in the outline of a smooth object: but by no means enough to satisfy the eye, without including the surface also.

From *rough* objects also he seeks the *effect of light and shade*, which they are as well disposed to produce, as they are the beauty of composition. One uniform light, or one uniform shade produces no effect. It is the various surfaces of the objects, sometimes turning to the light in one way, and sometimes in another, that give the painter his choice of opportunities in massing, and graduating both his lights, and shades. – The *richness* also of the light depends on the breaks, and little recesses, which it finds on the surfaces of bodies. What the painter calls *richness* on a surface, is only a variety of little parts; on which the light shining, shews all it's small inequalities, and roughnesses; and in the painter's language, *inriches* it. . . .

In treating of picturesque travel, we may consider first it's *object*; and secondly it's sources of *amusement*.

It's *object* is beauty of every kind, which either art, or nature can produce: but it is chiefly that species of *picturesque beauty*, which we have endeavoured to characterize in the preceding essay. This great object we pursue through the scenery of nature; and examine it by the rules of painting. We seek it among all the ingredients of landscape – trees – rocks – broken-grounds – woods – rivers –

lakes – plains – vallies – mountains – and distances. These objects *in themselves* produce infinite variety. No two rocks, or trees are exactly the same. They are varied, a second time, by *combination*; and almost as much, a third time, by different *lights, and shades*, and other aerial effects. Sometimes we find among them the exhibition of *a whole*; but oftener we find only beautiful *parts*. . . .

But the picturesque eye is not merely restricted to nature. It ranges through the limits of art. The picture, the statue, and the garden are all the objects of it's attention. . . .

The first source of amusement to the picturesque traveller, is the *pursuit* of his object – the expectation of new scenes continually opening, and arising to his view. . . . After the pursuit we are gratified with the *attainment* of the object. Our amusement, on this head, arises from the employment of the mind in examining the beautiful scenes we have found. . . . We are most delighted, when some grand scene, tho perhaps of incorrect composition, rising before the eye, strikes us beyond the power of thought . . . and every mental operation is suspended. . . . The general idea of the scene makes an impression, before any appeal is made to the judgment. We rather *feel*, than *survey* it. . . .

From this correct knowledge of objects arises another amusement; that of representing, by a few strokes in a sketch, those ideas, which have made the most impression upon us. A few scratches, like a short-hand scrawl of our own, legible at least to ourselves, will serve to raise in our minds the remembrance of the beauties they humbly represent; and recal to our memory even the splendid colouring, and force of light, which existed in the real scene. . . . There may be more pleasure in recollecting, and recording, from a few transient lines, the scenes we have admired, than in the present enjoyment of them. If the scenes indeed have *peculiar greatness*, this secondary pleasure cannot be attended with those enthusiastic feelings, which accompanied the real exhibition. But, in general, tho it may be a calmer species of pleasure, it is more uniform, and uninterrupted. It flatters us too with the idea of a sort of creation of our own; and it is unallayed with that fatigue, which is often a considerable abatement to the pleasures of traversing the wild, and savage parts of nature. – After we have amused *ourselves* with our sketches, if we can, in any degree, contribute to the amusement of others also, the pleasure is surely so much inhanced.

There is still another amusement arising from the correct knowledge of objects; and that is the power of creating, and representing *scenes of fancy*; which is still more a work of creation, than copying from nature. The imagination becomes a camera obscura,[11] only with this difference, that the camera represents objects as they really are; while the imagination, impressed with the most beautiful scenes, and chastened by rules of art, forms it's pictures, not only from the most admirable parts of nature; but in the best taste.

––––––––––––––––––––

11 Literally a *dark chamber*, or early form of camera, used to project an image.

6.6   Uvedale Price, *An Essay on the Picturesque, as compared with the Sublime and the Beautiful; and, on the Use of Studying Pictures, for the Purpose of Improving Real Landscape* (1794)

Sir Uvedale Price (1747–1829) contributed significantly to the debate over the picturesque with his Essay *(published in two volumes in 1794 and 1796–8), a work which was particularly influential on fashions in landscape gardening (Price remodelled his own estate at Foxley along the principles he outlined in the* Essay*). Following Gilpin, he identified 'roughness', 'sudden variation' and 'irregularity' as essential to the picturesque, but, developing his argument in relation to Burke's aesthetic theory, he conceived the picturesque as occupying 'a station between beauty and sublimity' and as modifying the effects of both, correcting the languor of beauty and the horror of sublimity. Price's championing of Gothic architecture and landscaping as picturesque – in opposition to the Neoclassical or Grecian style – was influential on literary taste and can be read in relation to developments such as the increasing popularity of the Gothic novel.*

I am . . . persuaded, that the two opposite qualities of roughness, and of sudden variation, joined to that of irregularity, are the most efficient causes of the picturesque.

This, I think, will appear very clearly, if we take a view of those objects, both natural and artificial, that are allowed to be picturesque, and compare them with those which are as generally allowed to be beautiful.

A temple or palace of Grecian architecture in its perfect entire state, and its surface and colour smooth and even, either in painting or reality, is beautiful; in ruin it is picturesque. Observe the process by which time (the great author of such changes) converts a beautiful object into a picturesque one. First, by means of weather stains, partial incrustations, mosses, &c. it at the same time takes off from the uniformity of its surface and of its colour; that is, gives it a degree of roughness, and variety of tint. Next, the various accidents of weather loosen the stones themselves; they tumble in irregular masses upon what was perhaps smooth turf or pavement, or nicely trimmed walks and shrubberies, now mixed and overgrown with wild plants and creepers, that crawl over and shoot among the fallen ruins. Sedums, wall-flowers, and other vegetables that bear drought, find nourishment in the decayed cement from which the stones have been detached: Birds convey their foods into the chinks, and yew, elder, and other berried plants project from the sides, while the ivy mantles over other parts, and crowns the top. The even regular lines of the doors and windows are broken. . . .

Gothic architecture is generally considered as more picturesque, though less beautiful, than Grecian; and, upon the same principle that a ruin is more so than a new edifice. The first thing that strikes the eye in approaching any building is the general outline against the sky (or whatever it may be opposed to) and the effect of the openings: in Grecian buildings the general lines of the roof are

strait, and even when varied and adorned by a dome or a pediment, the whole
has a character of symmetry and regularity.

In Gothic buildings, the outline of the summit presents such a variety of
forms, of turrets and pinnacles, some open, some fretted and variously enriched,
that even where there is an exact correspondence of parts, it is often disguised
by an appearance of splendid confusion and irregularity. In the doors and
windows of Gothic churches, the pointed arch has as much variety as any regular figure can well have, the eye too is not so strongly conducted from the top of
the one to that of the other, as by the parallel lines of the Grecian; and every
person must be struck with the extreme richness and intricacy of some of the
principal windows of our cathedrals and ruined abbeys. In these last is displayed
the triumph of the picturesque; and its charms to a painter's eye are often so
great as to rival those of beauty itself. . . .

Picturesqueness, therefore, appears to hold a station between beauty and sublimity; and on that account, perhaps, is more frequently and more happily blended
with them both than they are with each other. It is, however, perfectly distinct
from either; and first, with respect to beauty, it is evident, from all that has been
said, that they are founded on very opposite qualities; the one on smoothness,
the other on roughness; – the one on gradual, the other on sudden variation; –
the one on ideas of youth and freshness, the other on those of age, and even of
decay. . . .

According to Mr. Burke, the passion caused by the great and sublime in *nature*,
when those causes operate most powerfully, is astonishment; and astonishment
is that state of the soul in which all its motions are suspended with some degree
of horror: the sublime also, being founded on ideas of pain and terror, like them
operates by stretching the fibres beyond their natural tone. The passion excited
by beauty is love and complacency; it acts by relaxing the fibres somewhat below
their natural tone,[12] and this is accompanied by an inward sense of melting and
languor.

Whether this account of the effects of sublimity and beauty be strictly philosophical, has, I believe, been questioned, but whether the fibres, in such cases,

---

12 Price's note: 'I have heard this part of Mr. Burke's book criticised, on a supposition that pleasure is
more generally produced from the fibres being stimulated than from their being relaxed. To me it
appears that Mr. Burke is right with respect to that pleasure which is the effect of beauty, or whatever has an analogy to beauty, according to the principles he has laid down. . . .

If we examine our feelings on a warm genial day, in a spot full of the softest beauties of nature,
the fragrance of spring breathing around us, pleasure then seems to be our natural state; to be
received, not sought after; it is the happiness of existing to sensations of delight only; we are unwilling to move, almost to think, and desire only to feel, to enjoy.

How different is that active pursuit of pleasure when the fibres are braced by a keen air in a wild
romantic sensation; when the activity of the body almost keeps pace with that of the mind, and
eagerly scales every rocky promontory, explores every new recess. Such is the difference between the
beautiful and the picturesque.'

are really stretched or relaxed, it presents a lively image of the sensations often produced by love and astonishment. To pursue the same train of ideas, I may add, that the effect of the picturesque is curiosity; an effect which, though less splendid and powerful, has a more general influence; it neither relaxes nor violently stretches the fibres, but by its active agency keeps them to their full tone, and thus, when mixed with either of the other characters, corrects the languor of beauty, or the horror of sublimity. But as the nature of every corrective must be to take off from the peculiar effect of what it is to correct, so does the picturesque when united to either of the others. It is the coquetry of nature; it makes beauty more amusing, more varied, more playful . . . by its variety, its intricacy, its partial concealments, it excites that active curiosity which gives play to the mind, loosening those iron bonds with which astonishment chains up its faculties.

6.7 Benjamin Robert Haydon, *Life of Benjamin Robert Haydon, Historical Painter, from his Autobiography and Journals,* ed. Tom Taylor (1853)

The Elgin Marbles are the sculptures that were removed from the Parthenon in Athens, Greece, and brought to Britain in the early years of the nineteenth century by Thomas Bruce, seventh Earl of Elgin. They were bought by the government in 1816, when they were housed in the British Museum. Though controversial (Byron objected to the snatching of the 'shrinking gods to northern climes abhorred!' in Childe Harold's Pilgrimage*), the presence of the Marbles in Britain was a major stimulant to Romantic Hellenism. For example, John Keats wrote two sonnets on the statues and they have been seen to have influenced his adoption of a 'Grecian' style in his poetry (illustrated by the opening of* Hyperion *with its statuesque descriptions of the fallen Titans). In the extract below, the history painter Benjamin Robert Haydon, with whom Keats went to see the Marbles in 1817, describes his visit to the statues in 1808 when they were housed privately (see Figure 12).*

To Park Lane then we went, and after passing through the hall, and thence into an open yard, entered a damp, dirty pent-house, where lay the marbles, ranged within sight and reach. The first thing I fixed my eyes on, was the wrist of a figure in one of the female groups, in which were visible, though in a feminine form, the radius and ulna. I was astonished, for I had never seen them hinted at in any female wrist in the antique. I darted my eye to the elbow, and saw the outer condyle visibly affecting the shape as in nature. I saw that the arm was in repose and the soft parts in relaxation. That combination of nature and idea which I had felt was so much wanting for high art was here displayed to midday conviction. My heart beat! If I had seen nothing else, I had beheld sufficient to keep me to nature for the rest of my life. But when I turned to the Theseus

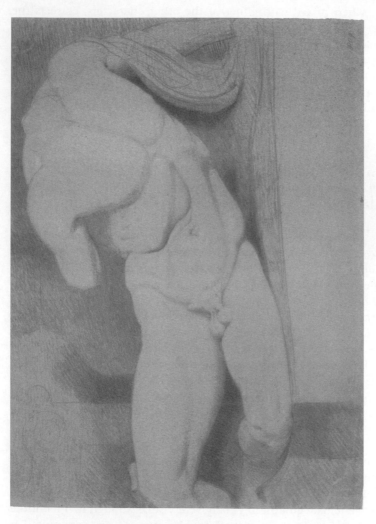

Figure 12 Benjamin Robert Haydon, sketch of Illissus, 1809; © Copyright the Trustees of the British Museum.

This is one of innumerable sketches by Haydon of the Elgin Marbles, the Greek sculptures which for him combined 'the most heroic style of art' with 'all the essential detail of actual life' and showed the future direction for all great art (extract 6.7). In 1817, Haydon took John Keats to see the Marbles at the British Museum, a visit which inspired the poet to write two sonnets on the subject ('On seeing the Elgin Marbles' and 'To B. R. Haydon, with a Sonnet Written on Seeing the Elgin Marbles').

and saw that every form was altered by action or repose – when I saw that the two sides of his back varied, one side stretched from the shoulder blade being pulled forward, and the other side compressed from the shoulder blade being pushed close to the spine, as he rested on his elbow, with the belly flat because the bowels fell into the pelvis as he sat, – and when, turning to the Ilyssus, I saw the belly protruded, from the figure lying on its side, – and again, when in the figure of the fighting metope I saw the muscle shown under the one arm-pit in that instantaneous action of darting out, and left out in the other arm-pits because not wanted – when I saw, in fact, the most heroic style of art, combined with all the essential detail of actual life, the thing was done at once and for ever.

Here were principles which the common sense of the English people would understand; here were principles which I had struggled for in my first picture, with timidity and apprehension; here were the principles which the great Greeks in their finest time established, and here was I, the most prominent historical student, perfectly qualified to appreciate all this by my own determined mode of study under the influence of my old friend the watchmaker,[13] – here was the hint at the skin perfectly comprehended by knowing well what was underneath it!

Oh, how I inwardly thanked God that I was prepared to understand all this! Now I was rewarded for all the petty harassings I had suffered. Now was I mad for buying Albinus without a penny to pay for it? Now was I mad for lying on the floor hours together, copying its figures? I felt the future, I foretold that they would prove themselves the finest things on earth, that they would overturn the false beau-ideal, where nature was nothing, and would establish the true beau-ideal, of which nature alone is the basis.

I shall never forget the horses' heads – the feet in the metopes! I felt as if a divine truth had blazed inwardly upon my mind and I knew that they would at last rouse the art of Europe from its slumber in the darkness.

I do not say this *now*, when all the world acknowledges it, but I said it then, *when no one would believe me.*

---

13 Taylor's note: 'Reynolds of Plymouth'.

7

Popular Culture, Leisure and Entertainment

Introduction

The documents in this section illustrate the extent and diversity of the cultural activities and leisure pursuits undertaken during the Romantic age, ranging from rural communities' fireside narratives of supernatural beings to visits to see the solar microscope in London, from the travelling puppet shows exhibited at fairs to the grand tragic performances of Sarah Siddons at Drury Lane, and from broadside confessions of murder to the illuminations of Vauxhall pleasure gardens. The Romantic age has also been identified by a number of historians as the period which sees the beginning of the study of popular culture, with John Brand's *Observations on Popular Antiquities* (1777, extract 7.1) and Joseph Strutt's *Sports and Pastimes of the People of England* (1801, extract 7.2) occupying important positions as early and influential examples of this work. In the case of Pierce Egan's *Life in London* (1821, extract 7.4), we have a work purporting to undertake a study of contemporary cultural pursuits in the Metropolis – 'the grand object of this work is an attempt to portray what is termed "SEEING LIFE" in all its various bearings upon society' – which itself proved enormously popular, becoming a publishing phenomenon of the nineteenth century and generating a series of further versions in broadsheet and dramatic forms.

As Henry Bourne and John Brand show, storytelling was an important cultural activity for a large part of the population, and the subject matter and form of such stories powerfully influenced much literature of the Romantic period. Walter Scott began his literary career as a collector of the oral ballads of the Scottish Borders, James Hogg drew on the supernatural tales told by his mother in his masterpiece *Confessions of a Justified Sinner*, William Wordsworth argued in his 'Preface' to *Lyrical Ballads* that the language of poetry should be, 'as far as is possible, a selection of the language really spoken by men',[1] and Coleridge's 'Rime of the Ancient Mariner' gained much of its force from its textual re-creation of the Mariner's spellbinding telling of his tale of adventure,

---

1 William Wordsworth, *The Major Works*, ed. Stephen Gill (Oxford: Oxford University Press, 1984), p. 602.

crime and the supernatural. There is a clear cross-over, too, between the oral culture of the period and the growing forms of street literature, a range of cheap, ephemeral texts that included chapbooks, broadsides, broadsheets, and almanacs. These publications often printed versions of oral tales or ballads, with the most popular subjects being the supernatural (including fairy tales), legends, and crime. The vast range of material on the latter is sometimes grouped together as 'Newgate literature' in reference to the accounts of criminals given in the *Newgate Calendar*. The popular interest in crime and criminality contributed to the success of *Life in London*, whose author, Pierce Egan, had been London's leading crime journalist.

Recent work by critics such as Gillian Russell, Judith Pascoe and Jane Moody has shown that the Romantic period was an age obsessed by drama and performance, from the staging of Shakespeare at the patent theatres to the puppet-shows of the fairs. Covent Garden and Drury Lane were the two London patent theatres, licensed by the 1737 Licensing Act to perform 'legitimate' theatrical productions (though also subject to censorship from the Lord Chancellor). These theatres provided the opulent, capacious, and sometimes rowdy environment to which theatre-goers would flock to see stage celebrities in their great roles: John Philip Kemble as Coriolanus, Sarah Siddons as Lady Macbeth, and Edmund Kean as Shylock and Richard III (see extract 7.3). Beyond the patent theatres were a range of so-called 'illegitimate theatres' offering a variety of types of performance, including the dramas of the 'minor' theatres, the pantomime, with its spectacular sets and comic action, and the circus, pioneered at Astley's Amphitheatre (extracts 7.2 and 7.6). Freed from the censorship that restricted the patent theatres, these 'illegitimate' theatres were able to incorporate material on contemporary political and social themes, such as the war with France or the state of the royal family. The ambivalent relationship of many of the period's literary writers with theatrical culture has been the subject of much recent critical discussion. While often scornful of the crudeness and vulgarity of stage performance, they also participated in production; Coleridge's play *Remorse* was staged at Drury Lane in 1813, and Byron was on the management committee of this theatre. Dramatic developments certainly had a strong impact on literature beyond the theatre; for example, Joanna Baillie's 'Introductory Discourse' to her *Plays on the Passions* (1798) anticipated by two years Wordsworth's 'Preface' to *Lyrical Ballads* of 1800 in its arguments about language.

As Prince Pückler-Muskau's account of his time in London illustrates (extract 7.6), the visual and spectacular were major sources of entertainment in the early nineteenth century, particularly but not exclusively in the metropolis. For example, on 2nd August 1828, the German nobleman was able to visit three different examples of the panorama, an encircling painting on the walls of a large round room, which the spectator viewed from a central platform. The panorama had been introduced to London in 1793 by Robert Baker and often presented exotic or sublime landscapes (as in the examples Pückler-Muskau saw), depictions of battles (such as Waterloo), and views of London. Pückler-Muskau also visited one of the major developments of the panorama, the diorama, which used optical effects to create the illusion of a changing scene. The panorama and diorama were only two of the many forms of visual and spectacular entertainment available in London, which also included scientific and zoological exhibits (such as the solar microscope and giraffe seen by Pückler-Muskau) and the art galleries (Egan presents 'a *lounge* at the Royal Academy' as among the attractions of life in London).

A further aspect of the popular culture of the Romantic period illustrated by these extracts is the watching of, and participation in, sports of various kinds, ranging from the pastimes of 'lower-class' Londoners and the games undertaken by men and women at the rural fairs described by Strutt (extract 7.2), to the regency and late-Romantic popularity of horseracing and boxing (or 'The Fancy', as it was known), described by Egan and Pückler-Muskau (extracts 7.4 and 7.6).

The relationship of these various forms of entertainment and popular culture to the literary output of the Romantic period has only recently begun to be addressed, and it can be argued, of course, that a work like Egan's *Life in London* is as much a part of the literature of the age as Wordsworth's *The Prelude* or Byron's *Don Juan*. Indeed, in many ways Byron inhabited the same world as Egan's fictional creations. He was taught to box by 'Gentleman' John Jackson, whose gym is visited by Egan's Corinthian Tom and Jerry Hawthorn (see Figure 14), and the adventures of his epic hero have much in common with the sprees of Egan's protagonists, as John Clare noted, while also drawing on other popular forms. As Byron says of Don Juan in the poem's opening stanza, 'We all have seen him in the pantomime / Sent to the devil, somewhat ere his time'). One critical approach has been to argue that the period saw an increasing division between popular and high forms of culture, exemplified by Coleridge's and the painter John Constable's critiques of delusive simulations such as the panorama and by Wordsworth's description of Bartholomew's Fair as a 'Parliament of Monsters' (*The Prelude*, VII. 692). Such attacks can be seen as part of the middle- and upper-class anxiety about plebeian pursuits, which contributed to the desire for their reformation or abolition. In such accounts, the visionary powers of high Romanticism are achieved through definition against the cruder visual displays of popular culture. However, it is notable that it is not only William Hazlitt (the author of 'The Fight', an essay on boxing in the style of Egan) who appears among the attractions of *Life in London*, but also 'Coleridge, Fuseli, Flaxman, and Soane', lecturers on literature and the fine arts. Such an elevated roll-call suggests that while some figures may have sought to create a distinction between high art and low entertainment, to others such a distinction was meaningless and obscured the creative interchange between different cultural forms.

7.1 John Brand, *Observations on Popular Antiquities: Including the whole of Mr Bourne's Antiquitates Vulgares* (1777)

The historian David Vincent has commented that 'the study of popular culture in Britain begins with the publication in 1777 of John Brand's Observations on Popular Antiquities'.[2] *John Brand (1744–1806) was a clergyman (and from 1784 secretary to the Society of Antiquaries), whose* Observations *operated by alternating chapters of an earlier study – Henry Bourne's* Antiquitates Vulgares, or the Antiquities of the Common People *of 1725 – followed by his own comments (a structure reproduced in the following extract). In the section below, Bourne and Brand document the oral culture of the rural society of the eighteenth century and illustrate the importance of ideas of the supernatural in the popular consciousness. Oral culture and the supernatural were important influences on Romantic writing and the fireside story-telling sessions described can be compared with the childhood experience of James Hogg, the Scottish author of one of the great supernatural works of the period,* Confessions of a Justified Sinner, *whose brother commented: 'Our mother's mind was well stored with tales of spectres, ghosts, fairies, brownies, voices, &c. . . . These tales arrested our attention, and filled our minds with the most dreadful apprehensions.'[3]*

Chapter X.   Of the Country Conversation in a Winter's Evening: Their Opinions of Spirits and Apparitions; of the Devil's appearing with a cloven Foot; of Fairies and Hobgoblins; of the walking Places of Spirits; and of haunted Houses.

Nothing is commoner in *Country Places*, than for a whole family in a *Winter's Evening*, to sit round the Fire, and tell Stories of Apparitions and Ghosts. And no Question of it, but this adds to the natural Fearfulness of Men, and makes them many Times imagine they see Things, which really are nothing but their own Fancy. From this, and seldom any other Cause, it is, that *Herds* and *Shepherds* have all of them seen *frequent Apparitions*, and are generally so well stock'd with Stories of their own Knowledge. Some of them have seen *Fairies*, some *Spirits* in the Shapes of *Cows* and *Dogs* and *Horses*; and some have seen even the *Devil* himself, with a *cloven Foot*. All which, is either *Hearsay* or a *strong Imagination*. Not that there have not been, or may not be Apparitions; we know that there have undoubtedly been such Things, and that there still are, upon particular Occasions; but that almost all the Stories of Ghosts and Spirits, are grounded on no other Bottom, than the Fears and Fancies, and weak Brains of Men.

In their Account of the Apparition of the Devil, they always describe him with a *cloven Foot*: That is always his distinguishing Badge, whatever Shape he appears

---

2 'The Decline of the Oral Tradition in Popular Culture', in *Popular Culture and Custom in Nineteenth-Century England* (London and New York: Croom Helm and St Martin's, 1982), pp. 20–47, p. 22.

3 Ibid., p. 31.

in; whether it be in Beauty or Deformity, he never appears without it. Such is the old Tradition they have received of his appearing, and such is their Belief of it. . . .

Another part of this Conversation generally turns upon *Fairies*. These, they tell you, have frequently been heard and seen, nay that there are some still living who were stolen away by them, and confined seven Years. According to the Description they give of them, who pretend to have seen them, they are in the Shape of Men, exceeding little: They are always clad in Green, and frequent the Woods and Fields; when they make Cakes (which is a Work they have often been heard at) they are very noisy; and when they have done, they are full of Mirth and Pastime. But generally they dance in *Moon-Light* when Mortals are asleep, and not capable of seeing them, as may be observed on the following Morn; their dancing Places being very distinguishable. For as they dance Hand in Hand, and so make a *Circle* in their Dance, so next Day there will be seen *Rings* and *Circles* on the Grass.

Now in all this there is really nothing, but an old fabulous Story, which has been handed down even to our Days from the Times of *Heathenism*, of a certain Sort of Beings called *Lamiæ*, which were esteemed so mischievous and cruel, as to take away young Children and slay them. These, together with the *Fauns*, the *Gods of the Woods*, seem to have formed the Notion of Fairies. . . .

Another Tradition they hold, and which is often talk'd of, is, that there are particular Places allotted to Spirits to walk in. Thence it was that formerly, such frequent Reports were abroad of this and that particular Place being haunted by a Spirit, and that the common People say now and then, such a Place is danger-ous to be pass'd through at Night, because a Spirit walks there. . . .

The last Topick of this Conversation I shall take Notice of, shall be the Tales of *haunted* Houses. And indeed it is not to be wonder'd at, that this is never omit-ted. For formerly almost every Place had a House of this Kind. If a House was seated on some melancholy Place, or built in some old romantic Manner; or if any particular Accident had happen'd in it, such as Murder, sudden Death, or the like, to be sure that House had a Mark set on it, and was afterwards esteemed the Habitation of a Ghost. In talking upon this Point, they generally show the Occasion of the House's being *haunted*, the merry Pranks of the Spirit, and how it was laid. Stories of this Kind are infinite, and there are few *Villages* which have not either had such an House in it, or near it.

OBSERVATIONS ON CHAPTER X

. . . To the Account of the *Fairies* may be added that of the *Brownies*, a kind of Ghosts, of whom, says the Author of the Glossary to Douglas' Virgil, the igno-rant common People and old Wives in Scotland tell many ridiculous Stories, and represent to have been not only *harmless*, but *useful* – *Spirits* possest of a Servility of Temper that made them, provided they were civilly used, submit to do the meanest Offices of Drudgery. They are now extinct as well as the *Fairies*. – It was supposed that from their hard Labour and mean Employment they became of a swarthy or tawny Colour; whence their name of *Brownies*, as the other, who moved in a higher Sphere, are called *Fairies*, from their *Fairness*.

7.2 Joseph Strutt, *The Sports and Pastimes of the People of England; including the Rural and Domestic Recreations, May Games, Mummeries, Shows, Processions, Pageants, and Pompous Spectacles, from the Earliest Period to the Present Time* (1801, new edition 1830)

The Sports and Pastimes of the People of England *by the antiquary Joseph Strutt (1749–1802) was first published in 1801 and issued in a new indexed edition by William Hone in 1830 (the source for the current text). Strutt produced a number of studies of British society, including* The Regal and Ecclesiastical Antiquities of England *(1773),* Manners, Customs, Arms, Habits, etc. of the People of England *(1774–6) and* Dresses and Habits of the English People *(1796–9). Sports and Pastimes gives detailed accounts of a range of the popular entertainments of the Romantic period.*

MODERN PASTIMES OF THE LONDONERS

A general view of the pastimes practised by the Londoners soon after the commencement of the [eighteenth] century occurs in Strype's edition of Stow's Survey of London, published in 1720. 'The modern sports of the citizens,' says the editor, 'besides drinking, are cock-fighting, bowling upon greens, playing at tables, or backgammon, cards, dice, and billiards; also musical entertainments, dancing, masks, balls, stage-plays, and club-meetings, in the evenings; they sometimes ride out on horseback, and hunt with the lord-mayor's pack of dogs when the common hunt goes out. The lower classes divert themselves at football, wrestling, cudgels, ninepins, shovelboard, cricket, stowball, ringing of bells, quoits, pitching the bar, bull and bear baitings, throwing at cocks,' and, what is worst of all, 'lying at ale-houses.' To these are added, by an author of later date, Maitland, in his History of London, published in 1739, 'Sailing, rowing, swimming and fishing, in the river Thames, horse and foot races, leaping, archery, bowling in allies, and skittles, tennice, chess, and draughts; and in the winter skating, sliding, and shooting.' Duck-hunting was also a favourite amusement, but generally practised in the summer. The pastimes here enumerated were by no means confined to the city of London, or its environs: the larger part of them were in general practice throughout the kingdom. . . .

NATURE OF PERFORMANCES BY PUPPETS

The puppet-shows usually made their appearance at great fairs, and especially at those in the vicinity of the metropolis; they still[4] continue to be exhibited in

---

4 1830 footnote: 'In 1801'.

Figure 13   James Gillray, 'Very Slippy Weather', 10 February 1808; © Copyright
the Trustees of the British Museum.

In part a retrospective celebration of his own work, Gillray's cartoon shows Hannah
Humphrey's print shop in London with several of the artist's own caricatures in the
window. The image illustrates the wide popularity enjoyed by caricatures in the period.

Smithfield at Bartholomew-tide, though with very little traces of their former greatness; indeed, of late years, they have become unpopular, and are frequented only by children. It is, however, certain, that the puppet-shows attracted the notice of the public at the commencement of the last century, and rivalled in some degree the more pompous exhibitions of the larger theatres. . . .

GIANTS AND OTHER PUPPET CHARACTERS

The subjects of the puppet-dramas were formerly taken from some well known and popular stories, with the introduction of knights and giants; hence the following speech in the Humorous Lovers, a comedy, printed in 1617: 'They had like to have frighted me with a man dressed up like a gyant in a puppet-show.' In my memory, these shows consisted of a wretched display of wooden figures, barbarously formed and decorated, without the least degree of taste or propriety; the wires that communicated the motion to them appeared at the tops of their heads, and the manner in which they were made to move, evinced the ignorance and inattention of the managers; the dialogues were mere jumbles of absurdity and nonsense, intermixed with low immoral discourses passing between Punch and the fiddler, for the orchestra rarely admitted of more than one minstrel; and these flashes of merriment were made offensive to decency by the actions of the puppet. . . .

PUPPET-PLAYS SUPERSEDED BY PANTOMIMES

The introduction, or rather the revival of pantomimes, which indeed have long disgraced the superior theatres, proved the utter undoing of the puppet-show men; in fact, all the absurdities of the puppet-show, except the discourses, are retained in the pantomimes, the difference consisting principally in the substitution of living puppets for wooden ones; but it must be confessed, though nothing be added to the rationality of the performances, great pains is taken to supply the defect, by fascinating the eyes and the ears; and certainly the brilliancy of the dresses and scenery, the skilful management of the machinery, and the excellence of the music, in the pantomimes, are great improvements upon the humble attempts of the vagrant motion-master.

THE MODERN PUPPET-SHOW MAN

In the present day, the puppet-show man travels about the streets when the weather will permit, and carries his motions, with the theatre itself, upon his back! The exhibition takes place in the open air; and the precarious income of the miserable itinerant depends entirely on the voluntary contributions of the spectators, which, as far as one may judge from the square appearance he usually makes, is very trifling. . . .

FAIRS

The church-ales have long been discontinued; the wakes are still kept up in the northern parts of the kingdom; but neither they nor the fairs maintain their former importance; many of both, and most of the latter, have dwindled into mere markets for petty traffic, or else they are confined to the purposes of drinking, or the displayment of vulgar pastimes.

7.3   William Hazlitt, On Sarah Siddons and Edmund Kean (1818 and 1820)

The essayist William Hazlitt (1778–1830) worked for several years as a theatre critic, collecting together many of his reviews in A View of the English Stage. *In the following two extracts, he provides valuable accounts of two of the leading performers of the Romantic age, Sarah Siddons and Edmund Kean. As Hazlitt shows, Sarah Siddons (1755–1831) gained a high public profile as a result of her passionate, forceful, and stately acting style, qualities which she brought together most famously in the character of Lady Macbeth. Edmund Kean (c.1797–1833) made his name as Shylock in Shakespeare's* The Merchant of Venice *at Drury Lane in 1814 and went on to embody a Romantic acting style, more emotionally charged and less stately and classical than Siddons or John Kemble. Coleridge famously wrote that to see Kean act 'was to read Shakespeare by flashes of lightning'.*

The homage [Sarah Siddons] has received is greater than that which is paid to Queens. The enthusiasm she excited had something idolatrous about it; she was regarded less with admiration than with wonder, as if a being of a superior order had dropped from another sphere to awe the world with the majesty of her appearance. She raised Tragedy to the skies, or brought it down from thence. It was something above nature. We can conceive of nothing grander. She embodied to our imagination the fables of mythology, of the heroic and deified mortals of elder time. She was not less than a goddess, or than a prophetess inspired by the gods. Power was seated on her brow, passion emanated from her breast as from a shrine. She was Tragedy personified. She was the stateliest ornament of the public mind. She was not only the idol of the people, she not only hushed the tumultuous shouts of the pit in breathless expectation, and quenched the blaze of surrounding beauty in silent tears, but to the retired and lonely student, through long years of solitude, her face has shone as if an eye had appeared from heaven; her name has been as if a voice had opened the chambers of the human heart, or as if a trumpet had awakened the sleeping and the dead. To have seen Mrs. SIDDONS, was an event in every one's life. . . .

The first of [the present day actors] in tragedy is Mr. Kean. To show that we do not conceive that tragedy regularly declines in every successive generation, we shall say, that we do not think there has been in our remembrance any tragic performer (with the exception of Mrs. Siddons) equal to Mr. Kean. Nor, except in voice and person, and the conscious ease and dignity naturally resulting from those advantages, do we know that even Mrs. Siddons was greater. In truth of nature and force of passion, in discrimination and originality, we see no inferiority to any one on the part of Mr. Kean: but there is an insignificance of figure, and a hoarseness of voice, that necessarily *vulgarize*, or diminish our idea of the characters he plays: and perhaps to this may be added, a want of a certain correspondent elevation and magnitude of thought, of which Mrs. Siddons's noble form seemed to be only the natural mould and receptacle. Her nature seemed always above the circumstances with which she had to struggle: her soul to be greater than the passion labouring in her breast. Grandeur was the cradle in which her genius was rocked: for *her* to be, was to be sublime! She did the greatest things with child-like ease: her powers seemed never tasked to the utmost, and always as if she had inexhaustible resources still in reserve. The least word she uttered seemed to float to the end of the stage: the least motion of her hand seemed to command awe and obedience. Mr. Kean is all effort, all violence, all extreme passion: he is possessed with a fury, a demon that leaves him no repose, no time for thought, or room for imagination. He perhaps screws himself up to as intense a degree of feeling as Mrs. Siddons, strikes home with as sure and as hard a blow as she did, but he does this by straining every nerve, and winding up every faculty to this single point alone: and as he does it by an effort himself, the spectator follows him by an effort also. Our sympathy in a manner ceases with the actual impression, and does not leave the same grand and permanent image of itself behind. His Othello furnishes almost the only exception to these remarks. The solemn and beautiful manner in which he pronounces the farewell soliloquy, is worth all gladiatorship and pantomime in the world. . . . Neither can we think Mr. Kemble equal to him, with all his study, his grace, and classic dignity of form. He was the statue of perfect tragedy, not the living soul. Mrs. Siddons combined the advantage of form and other organic requisites with nature and passion: Mr. Kemble has the external requisites (at least of face and figure), without the internal workings of the soul: Mr. Kean has the last without the first, and, if we must make our election between the two, we think the *vis tragica*[5] must take precedence of every thing else. Mr. Kean, in a word, appears to us a test, an *experimentum crucis*,[6] to shew the triumph of genius over physical defects, of nature over art, of passion over affectation, and of originality over common-place monotony.

7.4   Pierce Egan, *Life in London; or, the Day and Night Scenes of Jerry Hawthorn, esq. and his Elegant Friend Corinthian Tom, Accompanied by Bob Logic, The Oxonian, in their Rambles and Sprees through the Metropolis* (1821)

Pierce Egan (c.1774–1849) was a sports writer and crime reporter whose works were

---

5 Tragic power.
6 Crucial experiment.

extremely popular. Much of his writing on boxing, which he christened 'the sweet science', was collected together as Boxiana. *In 1820, he began publishing* Life in London *in weekly parts, and it was phenomenally successful, republished innumerable times in complete editions, adapted into other forms (such as broadsides and stage plays), widely copied, and influential on later writers such as Dickens and Thackeray. Making extensive use of slang,* Life in London *depicts the exploits and scrapes of Corinthian Tom and Jerry Hawthorne (the original Tom and Jerry), often describing scenes that were illustrated by Isaac Robert and George Cruikshank (see Figure 14). The extract below, from the introduction, gives a characteristically lively outline of the various attractions of the metropolis (as well as of* Life in London *itself).*

The *Camera Obscura*[7] is now at work; the table is covered with objects for the amusement of my readers; and whenever it is necessary to change the scene it is only requisite to pull the string, *i.e.* to turn over leaf after leaf, and LIFE IN LONDON will be seen without any fear or apprehension of danger from *fire* or *water*; avoiding also breaking a limb, receiving a *black* eye, losing a pocket-book, and getting into a watch-house, or picking up a *Cyprian*[8] and being exposed the next morning before a magistrate for being found *disorderly*; likewise in steering clear of all those innumerable rows and troubles incident or allied to 'keeping it up, and the loving of fun.' It would have been fortunate indeed for poor JERRY and CORINTHIAN TOM if they had possessed such advantages. But 'experience makes fools wise;' and as good-natured HAWTHORN and laughing TOM are now about to relate their *adventures* for the benefit of *fire-side* heroes and sprightly maidens, who may feel a wish to 'see Life' without receiving a *scratch*, it must be considered that the Metropolis is now before them. . . .

[T]he Metropolis is a complete CYCLOPÆDIA,[9] where every man of the most religious or moral habits, attached to any sect, may find something to please his palate, regulate his taste, suit his pocket, enlarge his mind, and make himself happy and comfortable. If places of worship give any sort of character to the *goodness* of the Metropolis, between four and five hundred are opened for religious purposes on Sundays. In fact, every SQUARE in the Metropolis is a sort of *map* well worthy of exploring, if riches and titles operate as a source of curiosity to the visitor. There is not a *street* in London but what may be compared to a large or small volume of intelligence, abounding with anecdote, incident, and peculiarities. A *court* or *alley* must be obscure indeed, if it does not afford some remarks; and even the *poorest* cellar contains some *trait* or other, in unison with

---

7 'Dark Chamber', a prototype camera which worked through projecting an image onto the side of a box or screen.
8 Prostitute.
9 Containing all branches of learning.

the manners and feelings of this great city, that may be put down in the note-book, and reviewed, at an after period, with much pleasure and satisfaction.

Then, the grand object of this work is an attempt to portray what is termed 'SEEING LIFE,' in all its various bearings upon society, from the *high-mettled* CORINTHIAN[10] of St. James's, *swaddled* in luxury, down to the *needy* FLUEFAKER of Wapping, *born without a shirt*, and not *a bit of scran*[11] in his cup to allay his piteous cravings.

'LIFE IN LONDON' is the sport in view, and, provided the *chase* is turned to good account, '*seeing Life*' will be found to have its advantages. Upon this calculation, whether an evening is spent over a bottle of champagne at *Long's*, or in taking a '*third of a daffy*'[12] at Tom Belcher's, if the MIND does not decide it *barren*, then the purposes are gained. Equally so, in *waltzing* with the *angelics* at my Lady FUBB's assembly, at Almacks,[13] or *sporting a toe* at Mrs. SNOOKS's *hop* at St. Kit's, among the pretty *straw* damsels and *dashing* chippers, if a *knowledge* of 'Life,' an acquaintance with *character*, and the importance of *comparisons*, are the ultimate results . . .

A *blow out* may likewise be found as *savoury* and as *high scented* at Mother O'Shaughnessy's, in the *back settlements* of the *Holy Land*, by the hungry *cut-away* Paddy Mulroony, as the *Mulligatawny soup* may be swallowed with peculiar *goût* by one of the fastidious, squeamish, screwed-up descendants of the OGELBY train at Grillion's hotel. A morning at TATTERSALS,[14] among the *top-of-the-tree* heroes in society, *legs* and *levanters*; or an hour *en passant* at Smithfield,[15] on a Friday after-noon, among 'I's Yorkshire' and the *copers*, may also have its effect.

Rubbing against the CORINTHIANS in the circle of Hyde Park on Sundays, and breathing the air of nobilty, contrasted with the aping, behind-the-counter, *soi-disant*[16] gentry, supported by their *helegant*, tender creatures, deck out in all the made-up paraphenalia of Cranbourne-Alley; and, carrying the contrast still further, of the various modes of disposing of time, practised by the rude unso-phisticated residents in the purlieus of St. Giles, down to the vulgar inmates of St. Catherines, Wapping, – if duly appreciated, the *tout ensemble* is one of the finest pictures of 'LIFE IN LONDON!' . . .

Paying a visit to the *Fives-court*, to view the NONPAREIL and Turner exhibit, or in taking a turn in the evening to listen to Coleridge, Fuseli, Flaxman, and Soane,[17] if the MIND make a *hit*, and some *striking* impressions are implanted upon the memory, then the advantages resulting from the *varieties* of 'LIFE' must here again be acknowledged.

---

10 One devoted to pleasure, or a frequenter of brothels.
11 Egan's note: 'Food'.
12 Egan's note: 'Third part of a quartern of gin'.
13 Almack's Assembly Rooms.
14 Bloodstock auctioneers.
15 Meat market.
16 So-called.
17 S. T. Coleridge, Henry Fuseli, John Flaxman, and Sir John Soane, all of whom gave public lectures.

The ITALIAN OPERA (this luxurious wardrobe of the great, this jeweller's shop of the nation, this *scent* and *perfume* repository of the world, and Arabian Nights' spectacle of Fortunatus's cap) is one of the most *brilliant* collections of portraits in LIFE IN LONDON. It possesses such fascinations, and the *spell* is so powerful, that to be *'seen there'* is quite enough, the performances being mere *dumb show* to most of its visiters; . . . yet, how strange it is, that the *Italian Opera*, to the great majority of JOHN BULL's descendants, is positively worse than *physic*. They who prefer being almost squeezed to suffocation, amidst clouds of tobacco, the fumes of porter, and the strong spell of *Deady's Fluid*, at a Free and Easy Club, to hear TOM OWEN's *'Rum Ould Mog,'* and, from the richness of its slang, pronounce it 'fine!' Such is the diversity of LIFE IN LONDON . . .

Again, while many prefer attending to hear the elevated judgements delivered by the LORD CHANCELLOR; others listening to the wit and elegance of CANNING,[18] and to the solid oratory and comprehensive mind of BROUGHAM;[19] thousands in the Metropolis are to be seen setting at defiance wind, weather, and even property, enjoying beyond description the humour and antics of CALEB BALDWIN's *bull* upon Tothill-Downs.

It should seem, then, that TASTE is every thing in *'this* here LIFE!' but it is also observed to be of so meretricious a nature to its admirers, that it is as perplexing to fix a decisive hold upon 'good taste' as to take into custody the 'will-o'-the-wisp' that plays such whimsical tricks with the benighted traveller: and, perhaps, after all our researches and anxiety to obtain the desideratum of character, it matters but little to the mass of society in London, whether the *relish* for this chameleon sort of article is obtained over a quartern of *three outs* of Hodges's *full proof*, to complete a bargain of 'lively soals' at Billingsgate,[20] before peep of day, by *Poll Fry*, so that happiness is the result; or whether it is realized with all the qualities of a barometer by Mr. HAZLITT,[21] in the evening lolling at his ease upon one of *Ben Medley's*[22] elegant couches, enjoying the reviving comforts of a good *tinney*,[23] smacking his *chaffer*[24] over a glass of old hock, and topping his *glim*[25]

---

18 George Canning (1770–1827), a statesman famous for his oratory.

19 Henry Brougham (1778–1868), politician renowned for speechmaking.

20 Fishmarket.

21 The writer and critic William Hazlitt, author of a number of Egan-style essays, including 'The Fight'.

22 Egan's note: 'A well-known hero in the Sporting World, from his determined contest with the late pugilistic phenomenon, *Dutch Sam*. Distinguished also as a *good judge* in trotting matches, and, at one period of his life, for having one of the *fastest* trotting horses in the kingdom; likewise in making *stylish couches* for the *easy* moments of the FANCY [boxing]; this part of society always making it a decided point, that when any opportunity offers in trade, to give each other a *turn*, - i.e. anxious to promote the interest of each other. However, if Mr. Hazlitt is not viewed as an admirer of "The Fancy," it will not be denied that few gentlemen have had more to do with the "*imagination*" than Mr. H.'

23 Egan's note: 'Fire.'

24 Egan's note: 'The tongue.'

25 Egan's note: 'A candle.'

ART OF SELF DEFENCE. *Tom and Jerry receiving Instructions from Mr Jackson, at his Rooms in Bond Street?*

Drawn & Engd. by I.R. & G. Cruikshank.

Figure 14 I. R. and G. Cruikshank, 'Art of Self Defence. Tom and Jerry receiving Instructions from Mr. Jackson at his Rooms in Bond Street', from Pierce Egan's *Life in London*, 1823; © The British Library. All rights reserved. Shelfmark 838.i.1 (opposite 217).

Taken from Pierce Egan's enormously popular *Life in London* (extract 7.4), the Cruikshanks' engraving shows the gym of 'Gentleman' John Jackson, who was Lord Byron's boxing instructor. Egan had come to prominence with his history of pugilism, *Boxiana*, and the subject inspired a number of other works, most famously William Hazlitt's essay 'The Fight' (1822).

to a *classic* nicety, in order to throw a *new light* upon the elegant leaves of Roscoe's Life of Lorenzo de' Medici, as a *composition* for a New Lecture at the Surrey Institution. This is also Life in London.

A *peep* at Bow-Street-Office; a *stroll* through Westminster-Abbey; a *lounge* at the Royal Academy; an hour passed with the Eccentrics; a *strut* through the lobbies of the Theatres; and *trot* on Sundays on Rotten-row, in calculation, have all turned to good account. Even, if out of wind, and compelled to make a *stand-still* over the Elgin marbles at the British Museum, it will be found the time has not been misapplied. Washing the *ivory* with a prime *screw*[26] under the *spikes* in Saint George's Fields, or in tossing off, on the shy, some *tape*[27] with a *pal* undergoing a *three month's preparation*[28] to come out as a new member of society, is a scene that developes a great deal of the human heart.

7.5   James Catnach (publisher), 'Confession and Execution of William Corder, The Murderer of Maria Marten' (1828)

James Catnach (1792–1842) was a highly successful publisher of popular literature who claimed (to the writer Henry Mayhew) that his broadside 'Confession and Execution of William Corder, The Murderer of Maria Marten' had sold over one and a half million copies. Such extraordinary sales make the broadsheet one of the best-selling examples of the street literature of the age, a form of publication that included chapbooks and almanacs and that grew significantly during the Romantic period. Like many of the most popular examples of these ephemeral texts, 'William Corder' was concerned with crime, though supernatural subjects were also prevalent, illustrating the link between street literature and oral culture (extract 7.1). Broadsides, like broadsheets (which were printed on both sides), were sold cheaply, usually by travelling hawkers or pedlars.

Since the tragical affair between Thurtell and Weare,[29] no event has occurred connected with the criminal annals of our country which has excited so much interest as the trial of Corder, who was justly convicted of the murder of Maria Marten on Friday last.

---

26 Egan's note: 'A turnkey.'
27 Egan's note: 'Gin. But spirituous liquor not being admitted into any prison they are disguised under various appellations.'
28 Egan's note: '*Whitewashing*; but this old phrase is now nearly obsolete.'
29 The so-called 'Radlett Murder' of 1823 when William Weare was killed by John Thurtell over a gambling debt.

THE CONFESSION

Bury Gaol, August 10th, 1828. – Condemned cell. Sunday evening, half-past Eleven.

'I acknowledge being guilty of the death of poor Maria Marten, by shooting her with a pistol. The particulars are as follows: – When we left her father's house, we began quarrelling about the burial of the child: she apprehended the place wherein it was deposited would be found out. The quarrel continued about three quarters of an hour upon this sad and about other subjects. A scuffle ensued, and during the scuffle, and at the time I think that she had hold of me, I took the pistol from the side pocket of my velveteen jacket and fired. She fell, and died in an instant. I never saw her even struggle. I was overwhelmed with agitation and dismay: – the body fell near the front doors on the floor of the barn. A vast quantity of blood issued from the wound, and ran on to the floor and through the crevices. Having determined to bury the body in the barn (about two hours after she was dead. I went and borrowed a spade of Mrs Stow, but before I went there I dragged the body from the barn into the chaff-house, and locked the barn. I returned again to the barn, and began to dig a hole, but the spade being a bad one, and the earth firm and hard, I was obliged to go home for a pickaxe and a better spade, with which I dug the hole, and then buried the body. I think I dragged the body by the handkerchief that was tied round her neck. It was dark when I finished covering up the body. I went the next day, and washed the blood from off the barn-floor. I declare to Almighty God I had no sharp instrument about me, and no other wound but the one made by the pistol was inflicted by me. I have been guilty of great idleness, and at times led a dissolute life, but I hope through the mercy of God to be forgiven. WILLIAM CORDER.'

Witness to the signing by the said William Corder,

JOHN ORRIDGE.

Condemned cell, Eleven o'clock, Monday morning,

August 11th, 1828.

The above confession was read over carefully to the prisoner in our presence, who stated most solemnly it was true, and that he had nothing to add to or retract from it. W. STOCKING, chaplain; TIMOTHY R. HOLMES, Under-Sheriff.

THE EXECUTION

At ten minutes before twelve o'clock the prisoner was brought from his cell and pinioned by the hangman, who was brought from London for the purpose. He appeared resigned, but was so weak as to be unable to stand without support; when his cravat was removed he groaned heavily, and appeared to be labouring under great mental agony. When his wrists and arms were made fast, he was led round towards the scaffold, and as he passed the different yards in which the prisoners were confined, he shook hands with them, and speaking to two of them by name, he said, 'Good bye, God bless you.' They appeared considerably affected by the wretched appearance which he made, and 'God bless you!' 'May God receive your soul!' were frequently uttered as he passed along. The chaplain walked before the prisoner, reading the usual Burial Service, and the Governor and Officers walking immediately after him. The prisoner was supported to the steps which led to the scaffold; he looked somewhat wildly around, and a constable was obliged to support him while the hangman was adjusting the fatal cord. There was a barrier to keep off the crowd, amounting to upwards of 7,000 persons, who at this time had stationed themselves in the adjoining fields, on the hedges, the tops of houses, and at every point from which a view of the execution could be best obtained. The prisoner, a few moments before the drop fell, groaned heavily, and would have fallen, had not a second constable caught hold of him. Everything having been made ready, the signal was given, the fatal drop fell, and the unfortunate man was launched into eternity. Just before he was turned off, he said in a feeble tone, 'I am justly sentenced, and may God forgive me.'

The Murder of Maria Marten.
BY W. CORDER.

Come all you thoughtless young men, a warning take by me,
And think upon my unhappy fate to be hanged upon a tree;
My name is William Corder, to you I do declare,
I courted Maria Marten, most beautiful and fair.

I promised I would marry her upon a certain day,
Instead of that, I was resolved to take her life away.
I went into her father's house the 18th day of May,
Saying, my dear Maria, we will fix the wedding day.

If you will meet me at the Red-barn, as sure as I have life,
I will take you to Ipswich town, and there make you my wife;
I then went home and fetched my gun, my pickaxe and my spade,
I went into the Red-Barn, and there I dug her grave.

With her heart so light, she thought no harm, to meet him she did go.
He murdered her all in the barn, and laid her body low:
After the horrible deed was done, she lay weltering in her gore,
Her bleeding mangled body he buried beneath the Red-barn floor.

Now all things being silent, her spirit could not rest,
She appeared unto her mother, who suckled her at her breast;
For many a long months or more, her mind being sore oppress'd,
Neither night or day she could not take any rest.

Her mother's mind being so disturbed, she dreamt three nights o'er,
Her daughter she lay murdered beneath the Red-barn floor;
She sent the father to the barn, where he the ground did thrust,
And there he found his daughter mingling with the dust.

My trial is hard, I could not stand, most woeful was the sight,
When her jaw-bone was brought to prove, which pierced my heart quite;
Her aged father standing by, likewise his loving wife,
And in her grief her hair she tore, she scarcely could keep life.

Adieu, adieu, my loving friends, my glass is almost run,
On Monday next will be my last, when I am to be hang'd;
So you, young men, who do pass by, with pity look on me,
For murdering Maria Marten, I was hang'd upon the tree.

7.6   Prince Hermann von Pückler-Muskau, *Tour in Germany, Holland and England, in the Years 1826, 1827, and 1828, with remarks on the Manners and Customs of the Inhabitants, and Anecdotes of Distinguished Public Characters. In a Series of Letters, by a German Prince* (1832)

Prince Hermann von Pückler-Muskau (1785–1871) was a German nobleman best known as a writer on, and practitioner of, landscape gardening. His four-volume account of his travels through Europe provides a detailed description of each of the countries he visited and the English volumes (3 and 4) are particularly informative on the leisure activities and environments of the late-Romantic age, including those described below: the opera, the theatre, the race course, the London pleasure gardens, the diorama, the pantomime, the circus, a gallery of embroidery, the solar microscope, the panorama, and the stables Pückler-Muskau visited to see a giraffe.

October 13 [1826]
In the evening I visited the English Opera. The house is neither large nor elegant, but the actors very good. There was no opera, however, but hideous melodrames; first, Frankenstein, where a human being is made by magic, – a manufacture which answers very ill; and then the Vampire, after the well-known tale falsely attributed to Lord Byron.[30] The principal part in both was acted by Mr. Cooke, who is distinguished for a very handsome person, skilful acting, and a remarkably dignified, noble deportment. The acting was, indeed, admirable through-

---

30 Stage adaptations of Mary Shelley's novel *Frankenstein* and John Polidori's short story 'The Vampyre'.

out, but the pieces so stupid and monstrous that it was impossible to sit out the performance. The heat, the exhalations, and the audience were not the most agreeable. Besides all this, the performance lasted from seven to half-past twelve, – too long for the best.

Newmarket, October 19th [Newmarket races]
At a certain distance from the goal,[31] about a hundred paces to the side, stands another white post called the betting-post. Here the bettors assemble, after they have seen the horses saddled in the stables at the beginning of the course, thoroughly examined into all the circumstances of the impending race, or perhaps given a wink to some devoted jockey. The scene which ensues would to many appear the most strange that ever was exhibited. In noise, uproar, and clamour, it resembles a Jews' synagogue, with a greater display of passion. The persons of the drama are the first peers of England, livery-servants, the lowest 'sharpers' and 'black-legs'; – in short, all who have money to bet here claim equal rights; nor is there any marked difference in their external appearance. Most of them have pocket-books in their hands, each calls aloud his bet, and when it is taken, each party immediately notes it in his book. Dukes, lords, grooms, and rogues, shout, scream and halloo together, and bet together, with a volubility and in a technical language out of which a foreigner is puzzled to make anything; till suddenly the cry is heard, 'The horses have started!' In a minute the crowd disperses; but the bettors soon meet again at the ropes which inclose the course. You see a multitude of telescopes, opera-glasses and eye-glasses, levelled from the carriages and by the horsemen, in the direction whence the jockeys are coming. With the speed of the wind they are seen approaching; and for a few moments a deep and anxious silence pervades the motley crowd; while a manager on horseback keeps the course clear, and applies his whip without ceremony to the shoulders of any intruder. The calm endures but a moment; – then once more arises the wildest uproar; shouts and lamentations, curses and cheers re-echo on every side, from Lords and Ladies, far and wide. 'Ten to four upon the Admiral!' 'A hundred to one upon Madame Vestris!' 'Small Beer against the field!' &c. are heard from the almost frantic bettors: and scarcely do you hear a 'Done!' uttered here and there, when the noble animals are before you – past you – in the twinkling of an eye; the next moment at the goal, and luck, or skill, or knavery have decided the victory. The great losers look blank for a moment; the winners triumph aloud; many make 'bonne mine à mauvais jeu', and dart to the spot, where the horses are unsaddled and the jockeys weighed, to see if some irregularity may not yet give them a chance. In a quarter of an hour the same scene begins anew with other horses, and is repeated six or seven times. 'Voilà les courses de Newmarket!'

---

31 Winning post.

November 23rd

The most striking thing to a foreigner in English theatres is the unheard-of coarseness and brutality of the audiences. The consequence of this is that the higher and more civilized classes go only to the Italian Opera, and very rarely visit their national theatre. Whether this be unfavourable or otherwise to the stage, I leave others to determine.

English freedom here degenerates into the rudest licence, and it is not uncommon in the midst of the most affecting part of a tragedy, or the most charming 'cadenza' of a singer, to hear some coarse expression shouted from the galleries in stentor voice. This is followed, according to the taste of the bystanders, either by loud laughter and approbation, or by the castigation and expulsion of the offender.

Whichever turn the thing takes, you can hear no more of what is passing on the stage, where actors and singers, according to ancient usage, do not suffer themselves to be interrupted by such occurrences, but declaim or warble away, 'comme si rien n'était'. And such things happen not once, but sometimes twenty times, in the course of a performance, and amuse many of the audience more than that does. It is also no rarity for some one to throw the fragments of his 'gouté', which do not always consist of orange-peels alone, without the smallest ceremony on the heads of the people in the pit, or to shail them with singular dexterity into the boxes; while others hang their coats and waistcoats over the railing of the gallery, and sit in shirt-sleeves; in short, all that could be devised for the better excitement of a phlegmatic *Harmonie* Society of the workmen in Berlin, under the renowned Wisotsky, is to be found in the national theatre of Britain.

Another cause for the absence of respectable families is the resort of hundreds of those unhappy women with whom London swarms. They are to be seen of every degree, from the lady who spends a splendid income, and has her own box, to the wretched beings who wander houseless in the streets. Between the acts they fill the large and handsome 'foyers', and exhibit their boundless effrontery in the most revolting manner.

It is most strange that in no country on earth is this afflicting and humiliating spectacle so openly exhibited as in the religious and decorous England. The evil goes to such an extent, that in the theatres it is often difficult to keep off these repulsive beings, especially when they are drunk, which is not seldom the case. They beg in the most shameless manner, and a pretty, elegantly dressed girl does not disdain to take a shilling or a sixpence, which she instantly spends in a glass of rum, like the meanest beggar. And these are the scenes, I repeat, which are exhibited in the national theatre of England, where the highest dramatic talent of the country should be developed; where immortal artists like Garrick, Mrs. Siddons, Miss O'Neil, have enraptured the public by their genius, and where such actors as Kean, Kemble, and Young still adorn the stage.

December 23rd

Yesterday we visited, 'en attendant', the parks in town, – Kensington Gardens; –

Regent's Park, 'en détail', &c., on which occasion we did not omit to look in at the Diorama[32] exhibited there. This far surpassed my expectations, and all that I had formerly seen of the same kind. It is certainly impossible to deceive the senses more effectally; even with the certitude of illusion one can hardly persuade oneself it exists. The picture represented the interior of a large abbey-church, appearing perfectly in its real dimensions. A side door is open, ivy climbs through the windows, and the sun occasionally shines through the door, and lightens with a cheering beam the remains of coloured windows, glittering through cobwebs. Through the opposite window at the end you see the neglected garden of the monastery, and above it, single clouds in the sky, which, flitting stormily across, occasionally obscure the sunlight, and throw deep shadows over the church – tranquil as death; where the crumbled but magnificent monument of an ancient knight reposes in gloomy majesty.

London, January 13th [1827]
By bright gas-light, which is always like a festal illumination here, we drove into town, and as I wished to have an instant contrast with my park-and-garden life, I alighted at Covent Garden to see my first Christmas pantomime. This is a very favourite spectacle in England, particularly with children; so that I was quite in my place. Playwrights and scene-painters take great pains to make every year's wonders exceed the last. . . . The web of story is then spun on through a thousand transformations and extravagances, without any particular connexion, but with occasional good hits at the incidents of the day; and above all, with admirable decorations, and great wit on the part of the machinist. One of the best scenes was the witch's kitchen. A rock cleaves open and displays a large cave, in the midst of which more than a cart-load of wood forms the fire, before which a whole stag with its antlers, a whole ox, and a pig, are turning rapidly on the spit. On a hearth on the right side is baking a pie as big as a waggon, and on the left a plum-pudding of equal calibre is boiling. The 'chef de cuisine' appears with a dozen or two assistants in a grotesque white uniform, with long tails, and each armed with a gigantic knife and fork. The commandant makes them go through a ludicrous exercise, present arms, &c. He then draws them up, 'en péloton' to baste the roast, which is performed with ladles of the same huge proportions as the other utensils, while they industriously fan the fire with their tails.

The scene next represents a high castle, to which this colossal 'batterie de cuisine' is conveyed like a park of artillery. It appears smaller and smaller along the winding path, till at length the pie disappears in the horizon like the setting moon. . . . In the last act, Tivoli at Paris is well given. A balloon ascends with a pretty child. While he floats from the stage over the heads of the audience the earthly scene gradually sinks, and as the balloon reaches the lofty roof, where it

---

32 A version of the panorama (see below) which used optical effects to produce an illusion of a changing scene.

makes a circuit round the chandelier, the stage is filled with rolling clouds through which a thousand stars shine and produce a very pretty illusion.

As the balloon sinks, town and gardens gradually rise again. A rope is next stretched, on which a lady drives a wheelbarrow to the summit of a gothic tower, in the midst of fire-works; while other 'equilibristes' perform their break-neck feats on level ground.

At the conclusion, the stage is transformed, amid thunder and lightning, into a magnificent Chinese hall with a thousand gay paper lanterns; where all spells are dissolved, the witch banished to the centre of the earth by a beneficent enchanter, and Harlequin, recognised as legitimate prince, marries his Columbine.

July 12th
Yesterday evening I went for the first time to Vauxhall, a public garden, in the style of Tivoli at Paris, but on a far grander and more brilliant scale. The illumination with thousands of lamps of the most dazzling colours is uncommonly splendid. Especially beautiful were large bouquets of flowers hung in the trees, formed of red, blue, yellow, and violet lamps, and the leaves and stalks of green; there were also chandeliers of a gay Turkish sort of pattern of various hues, and a temple for the music, surmounted with the royal arms and crest. Several triumphal arches were not of wood, but of cast-iron, of light transparent patterns, infinitely more elegant, and quite as rich as the former. Beyond this the gardens extended with all their variety and their exhibitions, the most remarkable of which was the battle of Waterloo. . . .

July 19th
From hence I went to Astley's theatre, the Franconi's of London,[33] and superior to its rival. A horse called Pegasus, with wings attached to his shoulders, performs wonderful feats; and the drunken Russian courier, who rides six or eight horses at once, cannot be surpassed for dexterity and daring. The dramatic part of the exhibition consisted of a most ludicrous parody of the Freischütz.[34] Instead of the casting of the bullets, we had Pierrot and Pantaloon making a cake, to which Weber's music formed a strangely ludicrous accompaniment. The spirits which appear are all kitchen spirits, and Satan himself a 'chef de cuisine.' As the closing horror, the ghost of a pair of bellows blows out all the lights, except one great taper, which continually takes fire again. A giant fist seizes poor Pierrot; and a cook almost as tall as the theatre, in red and black devilish costume, covers both with an 'extinguisher' as big as a house. . . .

33 Two early forms of the circus. Franconi's was established in Paris in 1793 by Antonio Franconi.
34 The story of a marksman ('free-shooter') that was the subject of an opera by Carl Maria von Weber.

August 2nd

To-day I saw an exhibition of an entire gallery of pictures embroidered with the needle, and the work of one person: their excellence is really surprising. The name of the artist, the most patient of women, is Miss Linwood. At a little distance the copies are very like the originals, and the enormous prices she gets for them shows that their merit is recognised. I heard that one such piece of tapestry, after Carlo Dolce, sold for three thousand guineas. There was a portrait of Napoleon during the Consulate, which must have been very like him at that time, and was regarded by some Frenchmen present with great admiration.

I next went to see the solar microscope, the magnifying power of which is a million. What it shows is really enough to drive a man of lively imagination mad. Nothing can be more horrible, – no more frightful devilish figures could possibly be invented, – than the hideous, disgusting water animalculae (invisible to the naked eye, or even to glasses of an inferior power,) which we daily swallow. They looked like damned souls darting about their filthy pool with the rapidity of lightning, while every motion and gesture seemed to bespeak deadly hate, horrid torture, warfare, and death.

As I was seized with a sight-seeing fit, and wished to efface the shocking impressions of that infernal world by something more agreeable, I visited three panoramas,[35] – Rio Janeiro, Madrid, and Geneva.

The first is a singular and paradisaically luxuriant country, differing completely from the forms and appearance of that which surround us. The second, in its treeless sandy plain, looks the picture of blank stationariness and of the Inquisition: burning heat broods over the whole scene like an 'auto da fè.'[36] The third appeared to me like an old acquaintance; and with a full heart I looked long at the immoveable and unchangeable fatherlandish friend, – the majestic Mont Blanc.

August 28th

We hastened accordingly to secure a sight of the giraffe,[37] which was led out before us by two Moors who had accompanied her from Africa. A wonderful creature indeed! You know her form; but nothing can give an idea of the beauty of her eyes. Imagine something midway between the eye of the finest Arab horse, and the loveliest Southern girl, with long and coal-black lashes, and the most exquisite beaming expression of tenderness and softness, united to volcanic fire.

---

35 Panoramas were a popular entertainment in London from the 1790s onwards. Spectators stood in the centre of a large cylindrical room, encircled by a depiction of a particular scene. The optical effects were heightened by lighting and props.

36 The public burnings at the stake of the Spanish Inquisition.

37 The giraffe had been presented to George IV by Mohammed Ali, Pasha of Egypt, and was kept at Windsor from 1827 until its death in 1829.

8

Literary Production and Reception

Introduction

In 1791, the successful London publisher James Lackington observed in his *Memoirs* that 'the sale of books in general has increased prodigiously within the last twenty years', estimating a four-fold growth since 1771 (extract 8.2). The expansion of the publishing industry and the growth of what Coleridge christened the 'Reading Public' were significant developments in the Romantic period. Lackington himself pointed to a number of changes in the demographics of reading and in the structures of publishing that stimulated these changes. Famously commenting that 'all ranks and degrees now READ', he argued that the rise in literacy was encouraging a shift among the lower classes from an oral culture of storytelling and the supernatural (of the sort described by Bourne and Brand in the previous section, see extract 7.1) to a literate culture of the printed book and the novels of Henry Fielding, Tobias Smollett and Samuel Richardson. Simultaneously, he suggested, the development of book-clubs and the growth of circulating libraries made books available to a much greater readership among the middle classes, especially women: 'Circulating libraries have also greatly contributed towards the amusement and cultivation of the other sex; by far the greatest part of ladies have now a taste for books.' Not all commentators were as positive about these developments as Lackington, many reviewers complaining of the sheer number of publications that were now produced. In 1788, for example, the *Critical Review* referred to a novel as 'One of the buzzing insects which has received a temporary life from the warmth of a circulating library'.[1]

As we have seen in earlier sections, in the highly charged atmosphere of the 1790s the issue of who was writing and reading was political. The ideological power of the written word was forcefully captured by the conservative satirist T. J. Mathias when he commented that 'Literature, *well or ill conducted*, is the great engine *by which*, I am fully persuaded, all civilized States *must ultimately be supported or overthrown*.'[2] Like Lackington, Mathias identified an increased participation in print culture by members of the lower class ('Our peasantry now read

---

1 *Critical Review*, 65 (June 1788), p. 486.
2 T. J. Mathias, *The Pursuits of Literature: A Satirical Poem in Dialogue. Part the Fourth*, 2nd edition (London, 1797), p. i.

the *Rights of Man* on mountains and moors and by the way side') and by women ('Our *unsexed* female writers now instruct or confuse us and themselves in the labyrinth of politics, or turn us wild with Gallic Frenzy').[3] For Mathias, the involvement of these groups undermined the hierarchies of literature and culture, threatening a collapse of both. Mathias was joined in his satirical attempts to restore these hierarchies by *The Anti-Jacobin* newspaper (see extract 8.3), which ridiculed Southey's use of classical forms in his poetry about social outcasts, and Richard Polwhele (extract 8.5), who developed Mathias's term 'unsexed female' into an entire poem.

Many of the anxieties about developments in literary culture in the Romantic period became focused on the emergent genre of the novel. Often linked to, or synonymous with, romance in the early part of the period (as in Barbauld's account of the popularity of the form, in which she describes the romance as representing 'common life', see extract 8.1), the novel became increasingly differentiated from the genre of the marvellous and supernatural out of which it had developed. Clara Reeves, for example, defined the form as follows in *The Progress of Romance* (1785):

> The Novel gives a familiar relation of such things, as pass every day before our eyes, such as may happen to our friend, or to ourselves; and the perfection of it, is to represent every scene, in so easy and natural a manner, and to make them appear so probable, as to deceive us into a persuasion (at least while we are reading) that all is real, until we are affected by the joys or distresses, of the persons in the story, as if they were our own.[4]

Anna Barbauld gave an indication of the status of the novel in the period when she commented in her essay 'On the Origin and Progress of Novel-Writing', which prefaced her multi-volume edition of *The British Novelists*, that 'A collection of Novels has a better chance of giving pleasure than of commanding respect.'[5] As her comic essay 'On Romances' illustrates (extract 8.1), the novel was always vulnerable to detrimental juxtaposition with supposedly higher forms of literature or knowledge ('the investigation of truth'), though she argues that the basis of the novel in sensibility served an educative purpose: 'They teach us to think, by inuring us to feel.' In appealing to sensibility in this defence of the novel, however, Barbauld illustrates another of the grounds on which it was attacked, its feminization and association with women readers. For example, in his essay 'On Reading New Books' (1827), William Hazlitt commented that 'Only young ladies from boarding-school, or milliners' girls read all the new novels

3 Ibid., p. ii.
4 Clara Reeve, *The Progress of Romance* (Colchester: W. Keymer, 1785), I, 111.
5 Anna Barbauld, *The British Novelists, with an Essay, and Prefaces Biographical and Critical*, 50 vols (London: Rivington et al., 1810) I, i.

that come out'[6] (though Hazlitt's term 'new novels' implies a distinction from the 'old novels' by Smollett and Fielding, of which he was fond and which, as a result of changes in copyright law, were increasingly available in a variety of editions). However, as recent research on the novel has shown, it was with some justification that Anna Barbauld was able to make a strident defence of the form in her essay, placing it on a level with what was conventionally seen as the most elevated literary genre when she argued that a 'good novel is an epic in prose' and pointing to the work of 'D'Arblay [Frances Burney], Edgeworth, Inchbald, Radcliffe, and a number more' as proof that 'it will not be said that either taste or morals have been the losers by [ladies] taking the pen in hand'.[7]

There were a number of sub-genres of the novel in the period (including the Jacobin and anti-Jacobin novel, the regional novel, the comic novel, the society novel or novel of manners, and the historical novel) but the most controversial form was the Gothic novel, criticized as absurd, excessive, and formulaic as well as symbolic of the worst corruption of modern literature and society (extract 8.4).

Moving from novels to poetry, as extracts 8.6, 8.7 and 8.8 illustrate, the writers of the period were never thought of in terms of any coherent movement but rather as a number of disparate groups – or schools – of poets, such as the 'Lake School' (Wordsworth, Coleridge, and Southey), the 'Cockney School' (Leigh Hunt, Keats, sometimes Shelley and Byron), and the 'Satanic School' (Byron and Shelley). However, an emphasis on these schools fails to acknowledge the popular writers who were not assigned to them (such as Walter Scott, by far the most popular poet prior to the dramatic arrival of Byron in 1812), those whose work was not widely known (such as William Blake), or the many women poets of the period, be they those prominent in the 1790s vilified or celebrated by Polwhele in 'The Unsex'd Females' or the next generation of 'poetesses' such as Felicia Hemans and Letitia Elizabeth Landon (extract 8.10). Influential in the reception of these writers and in the creation of these schools were the literary reviews and magazines, which themselves were subject to a significant development in 1802 with the launch of the *Edinburgh Review*, the first of the new quarterly periodicals whose format facilitated extended essays on particular writers or literary trends. Established by Francis Jeffrey and others in the Scottish capital, the *Edinburgh* illustrates Scotland's influence in British literary culture (something to which Byron alludes in the title of his poem *English Bards and Scotch Reviewers*). The *Edinburgh's* Whig politics prompted the establishment of Tory rivals, the *Quarterly Review* in 1809 and *Blackwood's Edinburgh Magazine* in 1817. *Blackwood's*, like the *New Monthly Magazine* (established 1814) and the *London Magazine* (established 1820), provided significant outlets for the emerging form

---

6 'On Reading New Books', *The Mirror of Literature, Amusement and Instruction*, vol. 10, issue 267 (4 August 1827).

7 Barbauld, *The British Novelists*, I, 3, 58.

of the essay as practised by writers like William Hazlitt, Thomas De Quincey and Charles Lamb. While the myth encouraged by Byron and Shelley that John Keats was killed by a review overstates the power of the periodicals, they could never-theless have real impact on the literary scene, as is illustrated by the reviews of Anna Barbauld's *Eighteen Hundred and Eleven*, which were so harsh that they ended her poetic career.

8.1   Anna Barbauld, 'On Romances, An Imitation' (1773)

The Dissenter Anna Laetitia Barbauld (née Aikin, 1743–1825) wrote across a range of fields, including poetry, children's literature, and literary criticism, addressing many of the major political and social issues of the day (including the war with France, slavery, and the rights of women). Her early essay 'On Romances', published in a collection of prose pieces with others written by her brother John Aikin, examines the reasons for the rising popularity of the novel (or romance), stressing its accessibility when compared with other forms of knowledge and literature. With its emphasis on 'feeling' and the 'passions', the essay is notable for the links it makes between the novel form and the culture of sensibility. The text is taken from Miscellaneous Pieces, in Prose *by J. and A. L. Aikin (1773).*

Of all the multifarious productions which the efforts of superior genius, or the labours of scholastic industry, have crowded upon the world, none are perused with more insatiable avidity, or disseminated with more universal applause, than the narrations of feigned events, descriptions of imaginary scenes, and delineations of ideal characters. . . .

It is however easy to account for this enchantment. To follow the chain of perplexed ratiocination, to view with critical skill the airy architecture of systems, to unravel the web of sophistry, or weigh the merits of opposite hypotheses, requires perspicacity, and presupposes learning. Works of this kind, therefore, are not so well adapted to the generality of readers as familiar and colloquial composition; for few can reason, but all can feel; and many who cannot enter into an argument, may yet listen to a tale. The writer of Romance has even an advantage over those who endeavour to amuse by the play of fancy; who from the fortuitous collision of dissimilar ideas produce the scintillations of wit; or by the vivid glow of poetical imagery delight the imagination with colours of ideal radiance. The attraction of the magnet is only exerted upon simi-lar particles; and to taste the beauties of Homer it is requisite to partake his fire: but every one can relish the author who represents common life, because every one can refer to the originals from whence his ideas were taken. He relates events to which all are liable, and applies to passions which all have felt. The gloom of solitude, the languor of inaction, the corrosions of disappointment, and the toil of thought, induce men to step aside from the rugged road of life, and wander in the fairy land of fiction; where every bank is sprinkled with flowers, and every gale loaded with perfume; where every event introduces a hero, and every cottage is inhabited by a Grace. Invited by these flattering scenes, the student quits the investigation of truth, in which he perhaps meets with no less fallacy, to exhilarate his mind with new ideas, more agreeable, and more easily attained: the busy relax their attention by desultory reading, and smooth the agitation of a ruffled mind with images of peace, tranquillity, and pleasure: the idle and the gay relieve the listlessness of leisure, and diversify the round of life by a rapid series of events pregnant with rapture and astonishment; and the pensive solitary fills up the vacuities of his heart by interesting himself in the fortunes of imaginary beings, and forming connections with ideal excellence.

It is, indeed, no ways extraordinary that the mind should be charmed by fancy, and attracted by pleasure; but that we should listen to the groans of misery, and delight to view the exacerbations of complicated anguish, that we should chuse to chill the bosom with imaginary fears, and dim the eyes with fictitious sorrow, seems a kind of paradox of the heart, and only to be credited because it is universally felt. Various are the hypotheses which have been formed to account for the disposition of the mind to riot in this species of intellectual luxury. Some have imagined that we are induced to acquiesce with greater patience in our own lot, by beholding pictures of life tinged with deeper horrors, and loaded with more excruciating calamities; as, to a person suddenly emerging out of a dark room, the faintest glimmering of twilight assumes a lustre from the contrasted gloom. Others, with yet deeper refinement, suppose that we take upon ourselves this burden of adscititious[8] sorrows in order to feast upon the consciousness of our own virtue. We commiserate others (say they) that we may applaud ourselves; and the sigh of compassionate sympathy is always followed by the gratulations of self-complacent esteem. But surely they who would thus reduce the sympathetic emotions of pity to a system of refined selfishness, have but ill attended to the genuine feelings of humanity. It would however exceed the limits of this paper, should I attempt an accurate investigation of these sentiments. But let it be remembered, that we are more attracted by those scenes which interest our passions, or gratify our curiosity, than those which delight our fancy: and so far from being indifferent to the miseries of others, we are, at the time, totally regardless of our own. And let not those, on whom the hand of time has impressed the characters of oracular wisdom, censure with too much acrimony productions which are thus calculated to please the imagination, and interest the heart. They teach us to think, by inuring us to feel: they ventilate the mind by sudden gusts of passion; and prevent the stagnation of thought, by a fresh infusion of dissimilar ideas.

-----

8 Taken from outside; unnecessary.

8.2   James Lackington, *Memoirs of the Forty-Five First Years of The Life of James Lackington* (1794)

James Lackington (1746–1815) was a London bookseller with a strong understanding of the literary marketplace. He published his Memoirs *in 1791, expanding them in a new edition of 1794 (from which the text below is taken). These* Memoirs *give a valuable first-hand account of the trends and fashions of publishing in the period, addressing issues such as the overall rise of sales, the growth of circulating libraries and book-clubs, the influence of Sunday schools, and the changing demographics of reading in relation to class and gender.*

I formed my judgment by observing what kind of stock in trade I had in hand, and by considering how that stock was adapted to the different tastes and pursuits of the times; in doing this I was obliged to be pretty well informed of the state of politics in Europe, as I have always found that *bookselling* is much affected by the political state of affairs. For as mankind are in search of amusement, they often embrace the first that offers; so that if there is any thing in the news-papers of consequence, that draws many to the coffee-house, where they chat away the evenings, instead of visiting the shops of booksellers (*as they ought to do, no doubt*) or *reading* at home. The best time for bookselling, is when there is no kind of news stirring; then many of those who for months would have done nothing but talk of war or peace, revolutions, and counter revolutions, &c. &c. for want of other amusements, will have recourse to books; so that I have often experienced that the report of a war, or the trial of a great man, or indeed any subject that attracts the public attention, has been some hundreds of pounds out of my pocket in a few weeks. . . .

I cannot help observing, that the sale of books in general has increased prodigiously within the last twenty years. According to the best estimation I have been able to make, I suppose that more than four times the number of books are sold now than were sold twenty years since. The poorer sort of farmers, and even the poor country people in general, who before that period spent their winter evenings in relating stories of witches, ghosts, hobgoblins, &c. now shorten the winter nights by hearing their sons and daughters read tales, romances, &c. and on entering their houses, you may see Tom Jones, Roderick Random,[9] and other entertaining books, stuck up on their bacon racks, &c. If *John* goes to town with a load of hay, he is charged to be sure not to forget to bring home 'Peregrine Pickle's Adventures;' and when *Dolly* is sent to market to sell her eggs, she is commissioned to purchase 'The History of Pamela Andrews.'[10] In short, all ranks

---

9 Novels by Henry Fielding and Tobias Smollett.
10 Novels by Smollett and Samuel Richardson.

and degrees now READ. But the most rapid increase of the sale of books has been since the termination of the late war.[11]

A number of book-clubs are also formed in every part of England, where each member subscribes a certain sum quarterly to purchase books; in some of these clubs the books after they have been read by all the subscribers, are sold among them to the highest bidders, and the money produced by such sale, is expended in fresh purchases, by which prudent and judicious mode, each member has it in his power to become possessed of the work of any particular author he may judge deserving a superior degree of attention; and the members at large enjoy the advantage of a continual succession of different publications, instead of being restricted to a repeated perusal of the same authors; which must have been the case with many, if so rational a plan had not been adopted.

I have been informed, that when circulating libraries were first opened, the booksellers were much alarmed, and their rapid increase added to their fears, and led them to think that the sale of books would be much diminished by such libraries. But experience has proved that the sale of books, so far from being diminished by them, has been greatly promoted, as from those repositories, many thousand families have been cheaply supplied with books, by which the taste for reading has become much more general, and thousands of books are purchased every year, by such as have first borrowed them at those libraries, and after reading, approving of them, become purchasers.

Circulating libraries have also greatly contributed towards the amusement and cultivation of the other sex; by far the greatest part of ladies have now a taste for books.

' – Learning, once the man's exclusive pride,
Seems verging fast towards the female side.'[12]

It is true, that I do not, with Miss Mary Wolstonecraft, 'earnestly wish to see the distinction of sex confounded in society,' not even with her exception, 'unless where love animates the behaviour.'[13] And yet I differ widely from those gentlemen, who would prevent the ladies from acquiring a taste for books; and as yet I have never seen any solid reason advanced, why ladies should not polish their understandings, and render themselves fit companions for men of sense. And I have often thought that one great reason, why some gentlemen spend all their leisure hours abroad, is for want of rational companions at home; for if a gentleman happens to marry a fine lady, as justly painted by Miss Wolstonecraft, or the square elbow family drudge, as drawn to the life by the same hand, I must confess that I see no great inducement that he has to desire the company of his

---

11 I.e. the end of the American War of Independence in 1783.
12 William Cowper, *The Progress of Error*, ll. 429–30.
13 Mary Wollstonecraft, *A Vindication of the Rights of Woman*, Chapter 4.

wife, as she scarce can be called a rational companion, or one fit to be entrusted with the education of her children; and even Rousseau is obliged to acknowledge that it 'is a melancholy thing for a father of a family, who is fond of home, to be obliged to be always wrapped up in himself, and to have nobody about him to whom he can impart his sentiments.'[14] Lord Lyttleton advises well in the two following lines:

> 'Do you, my fair, endeavour to possess
> An elegance of mind, as well as dress.'[15]

I cannot help thinking, that the reason why some of the eastern nations treat the ladies with such contempt, and look upon them in such a degrading point of view, is owing to their marrying them when mere children both as to age and understanding; which last being intirely neglected, they seldom are capable of rational conversation, and of course are neglected and despised. But this is not the case with English ladies; they now in general read, not only novels, although many of that class are excellent productions, and tend to polish both the heart and head; but they also read the best books in the English language, and many read the best works in various languages; and there are some thousands of ladies, which come to my shop, that know as well what books to choose, and are as well acquainted with works of taste and genius, as any gentlemen in the kingdom, notwithstanding the snear against novel readers, &c. . . .

The *Sunday-Schools* are spreading very fast in most parts of England, which will accelerate the diffusion of knowledge among the lower classes of the community, and in a very few years exceedingly increase the sale of books.

8.3 George Canning and John Hookham Frere, On Jacobin Poetry and 'The Friend of Humanity and the Knife-Grinder', *The Anti-Jacobin* (1797)

The Anti-Jacobin *was a weekly newspaper established by future Prime Minister George Canning in 1797 to combat Jacobinism in all its forms, including literary ones. It was edited by William Gifford and published from 20 November 1797 to 7 July 1798 when it was superseded by* The Anti-Jacobin Review. *Canning's 'Introduction to the Poetry of the Anti-Jacobin' of the first issue provides an interesting portrait of the poetic scene, presenting the anti-war and pro-Gallic verses of the 'Jacobin Poet' as dominant. For Canning, Robert Southey was the major example of this literary figure, and in 'The Friend of Humanity and the Knife-Grinder' (of the second issue, of 27 November 1797) he and John Hookham Frere parodied Southey's 'The Widow', particularly its use of a*

---

14 Jean-Jacques Rousseau, *Emile*.
15 George Lyttelton, *Advice to a Lady*, ll. 27–8.

classical stanza form, Sapphics. Their satire also ridicules the major tropes of human-
itarian verse (such as that written by Wordsworth), including the poet's encounter with
an impoverished individual who tells his or her story of suffering and social injustice.
The parody was also issued as a broadside, accompanied by a caricature by James
Gillray.

'Introduction to the Poetry of the *Anti-Jacobin*'

It might not be unamusing to trace the springs and principles of this species of
[Jacobin] Poetry, which are to be found, some in the exaggeration, and others in
the direct inversion of the sentiments and passions which have in all ages
animated the breast of the favourite of the Muses, and distinguished him from
the 'vulgar throng.'[16]

The poet in all ages has despised riches and grandeur.

The *Jacobin* Poet improves this sentiment into a hatred of the rich and the
great.

The Poet of other times has been an enthusiast in the love of his native soil.

The *Jacobin* Poet rejects all restriction in his feelings. *His* love is enlarged and
expanded so as to comprehend all human kind. The love of all human kind is
without doubt a noble passion: it can hardly be necessary to mention, that its
operation extends to *Freemen,* and them only, all over the world.

The Old Poet was a Warrior, at least in imagination; and sung the actions of
the Heroes of his Country, in strains which 'made Ambition Virtue,'[17] and which
overwhelmed the horrors of War in its glory.

The *Jacobin* Poet would have no objection to sing battles too – but *he* would
take a distinction. The prowess of BUONAPARTE indeed he might chant in his loftiest strain of exultation. *There* we should find nothing but trophies, and
triumphs, and branches of laurel and olive, phalanxes of Republicans shouting
victory, satellites of Despotism biting the ground, and geniusses of Liberty plant-
ing standards on mountain-tops.

But let his own Country triumph, or her Allies obtain an advantage; – straight-
away the 'beauteous face of War' is changed; the 'pride, pomp, and circumstance,'[18] of Victory are kept carefully out of sight – and we are presented with
nothing but contusions and amputations, plundered peasants and deserted looms.
Our Poet points the thunder of his blank verse at the head of the Recruiting
Serjeant, or roars in dithyrambics against the Lieutenants of Pressgangs. . . .

---

16 Horace, *Odes*, 3.1.1.
17 Shakespeare, *Othello*, III.iii.350.
18 Ibid., 354.

(Imitation.) Sapphics. The Friend of Humanity and the Knife-Grinder.

FRIEND OF HUMANITY

'Needy Knife-grinder! whither are you going?
Rough is the road, your Wheel is out of order –
Bleak blows the blast; – your hat has got a hole in't,
                    So have your breeches!

'Weary Knife-grinder! little think the proud ones,
Who in their coaches roll along the turnpike-
road, what hard work 'tis crying all day "Knives and
                    Scissars to grind O!"

'Tell me, Knife-grinder, how you came to grind knives?
Did some rich man tyrannically use you?
Was it the 'Squire? or Parson of the Parish?
                    Or the Attorney?

'Was it the 'Squire, for killing of his Game? or
Covetous Parson, for his Tythes distraining?
Or roguish Lawyer made you lose your little
                    All in a law-suit?

'(Have you not read the Rights of Man, by TOM PAINE?)
Drops of compassion tremble on my eye-lids,
Ready to fall, as soon as you have told your
                    Pitiful story.'

KNIFE-GRINDER

'Story! God bless you! I have none to tell, Sir,
Only last night a-drinking at the Chequers,
This poor old hat and breeches, as you see, were
                    Torn in a scuffle.

'Constables came up for to take me into
Custody; they took me before the Justice;
Justice OLDMIXON put me in the Parish-
                    Stocks for a Vagrant.

'I should be glad to drink your Honour's health in
A Pot of Beer, if you will give me Sixpence;
But for my part, I never love to meddle
                    With Politics, Sir.'

FRIEND OF HUMANITY
'*I* give thee Sixpence! I will see thee damn'd first –
Wretch! whom no sense of wrongs can rouse to vengeance;
Sordid, unfeeling, reprobate, degraded,
                                        Spiritless outcast!'

(*Kicks the Knife-grinder, overturns his Wheel, and exits in a transport of republican enthusiasm and universal philanthropy.*)

8.4 Anon., 'Terrorist Novel Writing', *The Spirit of the Public Journals for 1797* (1798)

This anonymous letter addresses the genre now known as the 'Gothic novel', here referred to as the 'terrorist novel', a term that emphasizes the link with Edmund Burke's theory of the sublime (extract 6.2). As a footnote in the original text makes clear, the particular target of this satire is Ann Radcliffe, whose novels, it suggests, like other examples of the genre, are formulaic and unrealistic and lack any moral or ethical purpose.

Sir,

I never complain of fashion, when it is confined to externals – to the form of a cap, or the cut of a lapelle; to the colour of a wig, or the tune of a ballad; but when I perceive that there is such a thing as fashion even in composing books, it is, perhaps, full time that some attempt should be made to recall writers to the old boundaries of common sense.

I allude, Sir, principally to the great quantity of novels with which our circulating libraries are filled, and our parlour tables covered, in which it has been the fashion to make *terror* the *order of the day*, by confining the heroes and heroines in old gloomy castles, full of spectres, apparitions, ghosts, and dead men's bones. This is now so common, that a Novelist blushes to bring about a marriage by ordinary means, but conducts the happy pair through long and dangerous galleries, where the light burns blue, the thunder rattles, and the great window at the end presents the hideous visage of a *murdered* man, *uttering* piercing groans, and developing shocking mysteries. If a curtain is withdrawn, there is a bleeding body behind it; if a chest is opened, it contains a skeleton; if a noise is heard, somebody is receiving a deadly blow; and if a candle goes out, its place is sure to be supplied by a flash of lightening. Cold hands grasp us in the dark, statues are seen to move, and suits of armour walk off their pegs, while the wind whistles louder than one of Handel's chorusses, and the still air is more melancholy than the dead march in Saul.

Such are the dresses and decorations of a modern novel, which, as Bayes says, is calculated to 'elevate and surprise;' but in doing so, carries the young reader's

Figure 15   James Gillray, 'Tales of Wonder!', 1 February 1802; © Copyright the
Trustees of the British Museum.

Some versions of this satire on the fashion for the Gothic novel carry the inscription 'This
attempt to describe the effects of the Sublime and Wonderful is dedicated to M. G. Lewis
Esq. M.P.', illustrating the link between aesthetic theory (see extract 6.2) and literary taste.
It is Lewis's novel *The Monk* that is being read aloud to a fascinated and horrified audience
of women in this nocturnal scene.

imagination into such a confusion of terrors, as must be hurtful. It is to great
purpose, indeed, that we have forbidden our servants from telling the children
stories of ghosts and hobgoblins, if we cannot put a novel into their hands
which is not filled with monsters of the imagination, more frightful than are to
be found in Glanvil,[19] the famous *bug-a-boo* of our forefathers.

A novel, if at all useful, ought to be a representation of human life and
manners, with a view to direct the conduct in the most important duties of life,
and to correct its follies. But what instruction is to be reaped from the distorted
ideas of lunatics, I am at a loss to conceive. Are we come to such a pass, that the
only commandment necessary to be repeated is, 'Thou shalt do no murder?' Are

19 Joseph Glanvill's book on witchcraft, *Sadducismus Triumphatus* (1681).

the duties of life so changed, that all the instructions necessary for a young person is to learn to walk at night upon the battlements of an old castle, to creep hands and feet along a narrow passage, and meet the devil at the end of it? Is the corporeal frame of the female sex so masculine and hardy, that it must be softened down by the touch of dead bodies, clay-cold hands, and damp sweats? Can a young lady be taught nothing more necessary in life, than to sleep in a dungeon with venomous reptiles, walk through a ward[20] with assassins, and carry bloody daggers in their pockets, instead of pin-cushions and needle-books?

Every absurdity has an end, and as I observe that almost all novels are of the terrific cast, I hope the insipid repetition of the same bugbears will at length work a cure. In the mean time, should any of your female readers be desirous of catching the season of terrors, she may compose two or three very pretty volumes from the following recipe:

Take –   An old castle, half of it ruinous.
A long gallery, with a great many doors, some secret ones.
Three murdered bodies, quite fresh.
As many skeletons, in chests and presses.
An old woman hanging by the neck; with her throat cut.
Assassins and desperadoes, *'quant. suff.'*[21]
Noises, whispers, and groans, threescore at least.

Mix them together, in the form of three volumes, to be taken at any of the watering places, before going to bed.

PROBATUM EST. [22]

8.5   Richard Polwhele, *The Unsex'd Females: A Poem, Addressed to the Author of The Pursuits of Literature* (1798)

The cleric and antiquarian Richard Polwhele (1760–1838) is best known for his satire on many women writers of the period in his poem The Unsex'd Females, *inspired by and dedicated to Thomas Mathias. As the extract below illustrates, Polwhele's primary object of ridicule is Mary Wollstonecraft, though he groups together disparate women writers as her followers. Against this 'female band despising Nature's law' (l. 2), he sets another grouping of more conservative writers, headed by Hannah More.*

See Wollstonecraft,[23] whom no decorum checks,
Arise, the intrepid champion of her sex;

---

20 Wood.
21 Quantity sufficient to produce desired result.
22 It is proved.
23 Mary Wollstonecraft.

O'er humbled man assert the sovereign claim,
And slight the timid blush of virgin fame.
'Go, go' (she cries) 'ye tribes of melting maids,
Go, screen your softness in sequester'd shades;
With plaintive whispers woo the unconscious grove,
And feebly perish, as despis'd ye love.
What tho' the fine Romances of Rousseau
Bid the frame flutter, and the bosom glow;
Tho' the rapt Bard, your empire fond to own,
Fall prostrate and adore your living throne,
The living throne his hands presum'd to rear,
Its seat a simper, and its base a tear;
Soon shall the sex disdain the illusive sway,
And wield the sceptre in your blaze of day;
Ere long, each little artifice discard,
No more by weakness winning fond regard;
Nor eyes, that sparkle from their blushes, roll,
Nor catch the languors of the sick'ning soul,
Nor the quick flutter, nor the coy reserve,
But nobly boast the firm gymnastic nerve;
Nor more affect with Delicacy's fan
To hide the emotion from congenial man;
To the bold heights where glory beams, aspire,
Blend mental energy with Passion's fire,
Surpass their rivals in the powers of mind
And vindicate *the Rights of womankind*.'

She spoke: and veteran BARBAULD[24] caught the strain,
And deem'd her songs of Love, her Lyrics vain;
And ROBINSON[25] to Gaul her Fancy gave,
And trac'd the picture of a Deist's grave!
And charming SMITH[26] resign'd her power to please,
Poetic feeling and poetic ease;
And HELEN,[27] fir'd by Freedom, bade adieu
To all the broken visions of Peru;
And YEARSELEY,[28] who had warbled, Nature's child,
Midst twilight dews, her minstrel ditties wild,
(Tho' soon a wanderer from her meads and milk,
She long'd to rustle, like her sex, in silk)

---

24 Anna Laetitia Barbauld.
25 Mary Robinson.
26 Charlotte Smith.
27 Helen Maria Williams.
28 Ann Yearsley.

Now stole the modish grin, the sapient sneer,
And flippant HAYS[29] assum'd a cynic leer;
While classic KAUFFMAN[30] her Priapus drew,
And linger'd a sweet blush with EMMA CREWE. . . .

'O come' (a voice seraphic seems to say)
'Fly that pale form – come sisters! come away.
Come, from those livid limbs withdraw your gaze,
Those limbs which virtue views in mute amaze;
Nor deem, that Genius lends a veil, to hide
The dire apostate, the fell suicide. –
Come, join, with wonted smiles, a kindred train,
Who court, like you, the Muse; nor court in vain.
Mark, where the sex have oft, in ancient days,
To modest Virtue, claim'd a nation's praise;
Chas'd from the public scene the fiend of strife,
And shed a radiance o'er luxurious life;
In silken fetters bound the obedient throng,
And soften'd despots by the power of song.
Yet woman owns a more extensive sway
Where Heaven's own graces pour the living ray:
And vast its influence o'er the social ties,
By Heaven inform'd, if female genius rise –
Its power how vast, in critic wisdom sage,
If MONTAGUE[31] refine a letter'd age;
And CARTER,[32] with a milder air, diffuse
The moral precepts of the Grecian Muse;
And listening girls perceive a charm unknown
In grave advice, as utter'd by CHAPONE;[33]
If SEWARD[34] sting with rapture every vein,
Or gay PIOZZI[35] sport in lighter strain;
If BURNEY[36] mix with sparkling humour chaste
Delicious feelings and the purest taste,
Or RADCLIFFE[37] wrap in necromantic gloom
The impervious forest and the mystic dome;

---

29 Mary Hays.
30 Angelica Kauffman.
31 Elizabeth Montague.
32 Elizabeth Carter.
33 Hester Chapone
34 Anna Seward.
35 Hester Thrale Piozzi.
36 Frances Burney.
37 Ann Radcliffe.

If BEAUCLERK[38] paint Lenora's spectre-horse,
The uplifted lance of death, the grisly corse;
And e'en a Princess[39] lend poetic grace
The pencil's charm, and breathe in every trace.'
She ceas'd and round their MORE[40] the sisters sigh'd!
Soft on each tongue repentant murmurs died;
And sweetly scatter'd (as they glanc'd away)
Their conscious 'blushes spoke a brighter day.'

8.6   Francis Jeffrey, On the Lake School of Poetry, *Edinburgh Review* (1802)

Francis Jeffrey (1773–1850) was one of the leading reviewers of the Romantic period while also working as a Scottish advocate and Judge (playing a significant role in the Scottish Reform Bill of 1832). He helped establish the first of the new type of periodicals, the Edinburgh Review, *in 1802, and he edited it from 1803 to 1829. In the first issue of the* Edinburgh *(1 October 1802), Jeffrey used a review of Robert Southey's* Thalaba The Destroyer *to began his campaign against the 'Lake School' of poets (Wordsworth, Coleridge and Southey), a term used because of their association with the isolated region of the Lake District in the north-west of England. Renowned for his hostility towards Wordsworth (he began his review of* The Excursion *'This will never do.'), Jeffrey did recognize the talents of these writers but saw them as being misapplied. Ironically, though presenting them critically, Jeffrey's reviews highlight what have come to be seen as the distinctive (and even revolutionary) elements of Wordsworth's and his fellow Lakers' poetry, especially their use of simple and familiar language and their choice of low subject matter.*

Poetry has this much, at least, in common with religion, that its standards were fixed long ago, by certain inspired writers, whose authority it is no longer lawful to call in question; and that many profess to be entirely devoted to it, who have no *good works* to produce in support of their pretensions. . . .

The author [Southey] who is now before us, belongs to a *sect* of poets, that has established itself in this country within these ten or twelve years, and is looked upon, we believe, as one of its chief champions and apostles. The peculiar doctrines of this sect, it would not, perhaps, be very easy to explain; but, that they are *dissenters* from the established systems in poetry and criticism, is admitted, and proved indeed, by the whole tenor of their compositions. Though they lay claim, we believe, to a creed and a revelation of their own, there can be little doubt, that their doctrines are of *German* origin, and have been derived from

---

38 Diana Beauclerk.
39 Princess Elizabeth.
40 Hannah More.

some of the great modern reformers in that country. Some of their leading principles, indeed, are probably of an earlier date, and seem to have been borrowed from the great apostle of Geneva.[41] . . .

The disciples of this school boast much of its originality, and seem to value themselves very highly, for having broken loose from the bondage of ancient authority, and re-asserted the independence of genius. Originality, however, we are persuaded, is rarer than mere alteration; and a man may change a good master for a bad one, without finding himself at all nearer to independence. That our new poets have abandoned the old models, may certainly be admitted; but we have not been able to discover that they have yet created any models of their own; and are very much inclined to call in question the worthiness of those to which they have transferred their admiration. The productions of this school, we conceive, are so far from being entitled to the praise of originality, that they cannot be better characterised, than by an enumeration of the sources from which their materials have been derived. The greater part of them, we apprehend, will be found to be composed of the following elements: 1. The antisocial principles, and distempered sensibility of Rousseau – his discontent with the present constitution of society – his paradoxical morality, and his perpetual hankerings after some unattainable state of voluptuous virtue and perfection. 2. The simplicity and energy (*horresco referens*[42]) of Kotzebue and Schiller.[43] 3. The homeliness and harshness of some of Cowper's language and versification, interchanged occasionally with the *innocence* of Ambrose Philips, or the quaintness of Quarles and Dr. Donne.[44] From the diligent study of these few originals, we have no doubt that an entire art of poetry may be collected, by the assistance of which, the very *gentlest* of our readers may soon be qualified to compose a poem as correctly versified as Thalaba, and to deal out sentiment and description, with all the sweetness of Lambe, and all the magnificence of Coleridge.

The authors, of whom we are now speaking, have, among them, unquestionably, a very considerable portion of poetical talent, and have, consequently, been enabled to seduce many into an admiration of the false taste (as it appears to us) in which most of their productions are composed. They constitute, at present, the most formidable conspiracy that has lately been formed against sound judgement in matters poetical; and are entitled to a larger share of our censorial notice, than could be spared for an individual delinquent. . . .

Their most distinguishing symbol, is undoubtedly an affectation of great simplicity and familiarity of language. They disdain to make use of the common poetical phraseology, or to ennoble their diction by a selection of fine or dignified expressions. . . .

---

41 Jean-Jacques Rousseau.
42 'To tell it makes me shudder', Virgil, *Aeneid*, II.204.
43 August von Kotzebue (1761–1819) and Johan Schiller (1759–1805), two German dramatists.
44 The English poets William Cowper (1731–1800), Ambrose Philips (1674–1749), Francis Quarles (1592–1644) and John Donne (1572–1631).

But the mischief of this new system is not confined to the deprivations of language only; it extends to the sentiments and emotions, and leads to the debasement of all those feelings which poetry is designed to communicate. . . . The poor and vulgar may interest us, in poetry, by the *situation*; but never, we apprehend, by any sentiments that are peculiar to their condition, and still less by any language that is characteristic of it. The truth is, that it is impossible to copy their diction or their sentiments correctly, in a serious composition; and this, not merely because poverty makes men ridiculous, but because just taste and refined sentiment are rarely to be met with among the uncultivated part of mankind; and a language, fitted for their expression, can still more rarely form any part of their 'ordinary conversation.'

8.7   Walter Scott, On Lord Byron (1818)

In 1812 Lord Byron published the first two cantos of his poem Childe Harold's Pilgrimage *and, as he himself put it, 'awoke to find myself famous', initiating a period of 'Byromania' among the British reading public. With a series of tales describing the adventures and passions of a variety of Byronic heroes – a brooding but sensitive outsider with a secret past, associated by many readers with the author himself – Byron became the period's best-selling poet and the leading celebrity of London until his self-imposed exile in 1816 amidst rumours of mistreatment of his wife and an incestuous affair with his half-sister. Byron published the fourth and final canto of* Childe Harold *in 1818 and Walter Scott (1771–1832), previously the period's most popular poet, used the opportunity to reflect in the* Quarterly Review *on the reasons for Byron's unprecedented success.*

In applying these general remarks to Lord Byron's gravest and most serious performance, we must recal to the reader's recollection that since the time of Cowper[45] he has been the first poet who, either in his own person, or covered by no very thick disguise, has directly appeared before the public, an actual living man expressing his own sentiments, thoughts, hopes and fears. Almost all the poets of our day, who have possessed a considerable portion of public attention, are personally little known to the reader, and can only be judged from the passions and feelings assigned by them to persons totally fictitious. Childe Harold appeared – we must not say in the character of *the* author – but certainly in that of a real existing person, with whose feelings as such the public were disposed to associate those of Lord Byron. Whether the reader acted right or otherwise in persisting to neglect the shades of distinction

---

45 William Cowper (1731–1800), English poet.

which the author endeavoured to point out betwixt his pilgrim and himself, it is certain that no little power over the public attention was gained from their being identified. Childe Harold may not be, nor do we believe he is, Lord Byron's very self, but he is Lord Byron's picture, sketched by Lord Byron himself, arrayed in a fancy dress, and disguised perhaps by some extrinsic attributes, but still bearing a sufficient resemblance to the original to warrant the conclusion that we have drawn. . . .

But besides the pleasing novelty of a traveller and a poet, throwing before the reader his reflections and opinions, his loves and his hates, his raptures and his sorrows; besides the novelty and pride which the public felt, upon being called as it were into familiarity with a mind so powerful, and invited to witness and partake of its deep emotions; the feelings themselves were of a character which struck with awe those to whom the noble pilgrim thus exposed the sanctuary of his bosom. . . . The banquet had ceased, and it was the pleasure of its melancholy lord that his guests should witness that gloominess, which seems most dismal when it succeeds to exuberant and unrestrained gaiety. The emptied wine-cup lay on the ground, the withered garland was flung aside and trodden under foot, the instruments of music were silent, or waked but those few and emphatic chords which express sorrow; while, amid the ruins of what had once been the palace of pleasure, the stern pilgrim stalked from desolation to desolation, spurning from him the implements of former luxury, and repelling with equal scorn the more valuable substitutes which wisdom and philosophy offered to supply their place. The reader felt as it were in the presence of a superior being, when, instead of his judgment being consulted, his imagination excited or soothed, his taste flattered or conciliated in order to bespeak his applause, he was told, in strains of the most sublime poetry, that neither he, the courteous reader, nor aught the earth had to shew, was worthy the attention of the noble traveller.– All countries he traversed with a heart for entertaining the beauties of nature, and an eye for observing the crimes and follies of mankind; and from all he drew subjects of sorrow, of indignation, of contempt. . . . A mind like that of Harold, apparently indifferent to the usual enjoyments of life, and which entertains, or at least exhibits, such contempt for its usual pursuits, has the same ready road to the respect of the mass of mankind, who judge that to be superior to humanity which can look down upon its common habits, tastes, and pleasures.

This fashion of thinking and writing of course had its imitators, and those right many. But the humorous sadness which sat so gracefully on the original made but a poor and awkward appearance on those who

> – wrapp'd themselves in Harold's inky cloak,
> To show the world how 'Byron' did *not* 'write.'

Their affected melancholy shewed like the cynicism of Apemantus contrasted with the real misanthropy of Timon.[46] And, to say the truth, we are not sorry that the fashion has latterly lost ground. . . .

But it was not merely to the novelty of an author speaking in his own person, and in a tone which arrogated a contempt of all the ordinary pursuits of life, that 'Childe Harold' owed its extensive popularity: these formed but the point or sharp edge of the wedge by which the work was enabled to insinuate its way into that venerable block, the British public. The high claims inferred at once in the direct appeal to general attention, and scorn of general feeling, were supported by powers equal to such pretensions. He who despised the world intimated that he had the talents and genius necessary to win it if he had thought it worth while. There was a strain of poetry in which the sense predominated over the sound; there was the eye keen to behold nature, and the pen powerful to trace her varied graces of beauty or terror; there was the heart ardent at the call of freedom or of generous feeling, and belying every moment the frozen shrine in which false philosophy had incased it, glowing like the intense and concentrated alcohol, which remains one single but burning drop in the centre of the ice which its more watery particles have formed. In despite of the character which he had assumed, it was impossible not to see in the Pilgrim what nature designed him to be, and what, in spite of bad metaphysics and worse politics, he may yet be, a person whose high talents the wise and virtuous may enjoy without a qualifying sigh or frown. Should that day arrive, and if time be granted, it will arrive, we who have ventured upon the precarious task of prophecy – we who have been censured for not mingling the faults of genius with its talents – we shall claim our hour of heartfelt exultation.

8.8 'Z' (John Gibson Lockhart), 'The Cockney School of Poetry', *Blackwood's Edinburgh Magazine* (1818)

In October 1817, the critic and editor John Gibson Lockhart (1794–1854), writing as 'Z', launched the first of a series of attacks on what he termed 'The Cockney School of Poetry' in Blackwood's Edinburgh Magazine. *A Cockney is a Londoner (supposedly born within the sound of Bow Bells, a reference to the bells of St. Mary-le-Bow in what was the predominantly working-class area of Cheapside in the City of London) and Lockhart's phrase suggested that the members of the 'School' were of low origin and lacked the classical education and gentlemanly credentials necessary to be a true poet. The central figure of the 'School' was Leigh Hunt, who with his brother James had established the radical newspaper* The Examiner *in 1808. Lockhart's other main targets were John Keats and William Hazlitt, though the grouping has also been seen to include Charles Lamb, Percy and Mary Shelley, Benjamin Robert Haydon and a number of other less well known figures. The term 'Cockney School' was also used by*

---

46 Characters in Shakespeare's *Timon of Athens*.

John Wilson Croker in the Quarterly Review. *After Keats's death in 1821, Percy Shelley and Byron encouraged the myth that his demise had been hastened by Lockhart's and Croker's harsh reviews.*

Of all the manias of this mad age, the most incurable, as well as the most common, seems to be no other than the *Metromanie*.[47] The just celebrity of Robert Burns and Miss Baillie has had the melancholy effect of turning the heads of we know not how many farm-servants and unmarried ladies; our very foot-men compose tragedies, and there is scarcely a superannuated governess in the island that does not leave a roll of lyrics behind her in her band-box. To witness the disease of any human understanding, however feeble, is distressing; but the spectacle of an able mind reduced to a state of insanity is of course ten times more afflicting. It is with such sorrow as this that we have contemplated the case of Mr John Keats. This young man appears to have received from nature talents of an excellent, perhaps even of a superior order – talents which, devoted to the purposes of any useful profession, must have rendered him a respectable, if not an eminent citizen. His friends, we understand, destined him to the career of medicine, and he was bound apprentice some years ago to a worthy apothecary in town. But all has been undone by a sudden attack of the malady to which we have alluded. Whether Mr John had been sent home with a diuretic or compos-ing draught to some patient far gone in the poetical mania, we have not heard. This much is certain, that he has caught the infection, and that thoroughly. For some time we were in hopes, that he might get off with a violent fit or two; but of late the symptoms are terrible. The phrenzy of the 'Poems' was bad enough in its way; but it did not alarm us half so seriously as the calm, settled, imper-turbable drivelling idiocy of 'Endymion.' We hope, however, that in so young a person, and with a constitution originally so good, even now the disease is not utterly incurable. Time, firm treatment, and rational restraint, do much for many apparently hopeless invalids; and if Mr Keats should happen, at some interval of reason, to cast his eye upon our pages, he may perhaps be convinced of the existence of his malady, which, in such cases, is often all that is necessary to put the patient in a fair way of being cured.

The readers of the Examiner newspaper were informed, some time ago, by a solemn paragraph, in Mr Hunt's best style, of the appearance of two new stars of glorious magnitude and splendour in the poetical horizon of the land of Cockaigne.[48] One of these turned out, by and by, to be no other than Mr John Keats. This precocious adulation confirmed the wavering apprentice in his desire to quit the gallipots, and at the same time excited in his too susceptible mind a

---

47 A mania for writing poetry.
48 In an article entitled 'Young Poets' in *The Examiner* of December 1816, Leigh Hunt had declared that there was 'a new school of poetry rising of late' and pointed to the emergence of Percy Shelley, John Hamilton Reynolds, and John Keats.

fatal admiration for the character and talents of the most worthless and affected of all the versifiers of our time [Leigh Hunt]. . . . [In his sonnet addressed to Haydon] it will be observed, that Mr Keats classes together WORDSWORTH, HUNT, and HAYDON, as the three greatest spirits of the age, and that he alludes to himself, and some others of the rising brood of Cockneys, as likely to attain hereafter an equally honourable elevation. Wordsworth and Hunt! what a juxta-position! The purest, the loftiest, and, we do not fear to say it, the most classical of living English poets, joined together in the same compliment with the meanest, the filthiest, and the most vulgar of Cockney poetasters. No wonder that he who could be guilty of this should class Haydon with Raphael, and himself with Spencer. . . .

Having cooled a little from this 'fine passion,' our youthful poet passes very naturally into a long strain of foaming abuse against a certain class of English Poets, whom, with Pope at their head, it is much the fashion with the ignorant unsettled pretenders of the present time to undervalue. Begging these gentlemen's pardon, although Pope was not a poet of the same high order with some who are now living, yet, to deny his genius, is just about as absurd as to dispute that of Wordsworth, or to believe in that of Hunt. Above all things, it is most pitiably ridiculous to hear men, of whom their country will always have reason to be proud, reviled by uneducated and flimsy striplings, who are not capable of understanding either their merits, or those of any other *men of power* – fanciful dreaming tea-drinkers, who, without logic enough to analyse a single idea, or imagination enough to form one original image, or learning enough to distinguish between the written language of Englishmen and the spoken jargon of Cockneys, presume to talk with contempt of some of the most exquisite spirits the world ever produced, merely because they did not happen to exert their faculties in laborious affected descriptions of flowers seen in window-pots, or cascades heard at Vauxhall; in short, because they chose to be wits, philosophers, patriots, and poets, rather than to found the Cockney school of versification, morality, and politics, a century before its time. . . .

We had almost forgot to mention, that Keats belongs to the Cockney School of Politics, as well as the Cockney School of Poetry.

It is fit that he who holds Rimini to be the first poem, should believe the Examiner to be the first politician of the day.[49] We admire consistency, even in folly. Hear how their bantling has already learned to lisp sedition.

8.9   Ann Radcliffe, 'On the Supernatural in Poetry', *New Monthly Magazine* (1826)

The Gothic novelist Ann Radcliffe (1764–1823) was the author of The Romance of

---

49 *The Story of Rimini* was a poem by Leigh Hunt; *The Examiner* was the newspaper he edited.

the Forest *(1791)*, The Mysteries of Udolpho *(1794) and* The Italian *(1797). In 1826, two years after her death, the* New Monthly Magazine *published Radcliffe's essay in dialogue form that would become the prologue to her novel* Gaston de Blondeville. *The essay illustrates the influence on Gothic fiction of Burke's theory of the sublime (see extract 6.2) and makes a distinction between horror and terror that a number of critics have found useful in differentiating between the different forms of the Gothic as practised by Matthew Lewis and Radcliffe herself.*

'I perceive you are not one of those who contend that obscurity does not make any part of the sublime' [said Mr. S–]. 'They must be men of very cold imaginations,' said W–, 'with whom certainty is more terrible than surmise. Terror and horror are so far opposite, that the first expands the soul, and awakens the faculties to a high degree of life; the other contracts, freezes, and nearly annihilates them. I apprehend, that neither Shakspeare nor Milton by their fictions, nor Mr. Burke by his reasoning, anywhere looked to positive horror as a source of the sublime, though they all agree that terror is a very high one; and where lies the great difference between horror and terror, but in the uncertainty and obscurity, that accompany the first, respecting the dreaded evil?'

'But what say you to Milton's image –

"On his brow sat horror plumed."' [50]

'As an image, it certainly is sublime; it fills the mind with an idea of power, but it does not follow that Milton intended to declare the feeling of horror to be sublime; and after all, his image imparts more of terror than of horror; for it is not distinctly pictured forth, but is seen in glimpses through obscuring shades, the great outlines only appearing, which excite the imagination to complete the rest; he only says, "sat horror plumed;" you will observe, that the look of horror and the other characteristics are left to the imagination of the reader; and according to the strength of that, he will feel Milton's image to be either sublime or otherwise. Milton, when he sketched it, probably felt, that not even his art could fill up the outline, and present to other eyes the countenance which his "mind's eye" gave to him. Now, if obscurity has so much effect on fiction, what must it have in real life, when to ascertain the object of our terror, is frequently to acquire the means of escaping it. You will observe, that this image, though indistinct or obscure, is not confused.'

'How can any thing be indistinct and not confused?' said Mr. S–.

'Ay, that question is from the new school,' replied W–; 'but recollect, that obscurity, or indistinctness, is only a negative, which leaves the imagination to act upon the few hints that truth reveals to it; confusion is a thing as positive as

---

50 John Milton, *Paradise Lost*, 4. 988–9.

distinctness, though not necessarily so palpable; and it may, by mingling and confounding one image with another, absolutely counteract the imagination, instead of exciting it. Obscurity leaves something for the imagination to exaggerate; confusion, by blurring one image into another, leaves only a chaos in which the mind can find nothing to be magnificent, nothing to nourish its fears or doubts, or to act upon in any way; yet confusion and obscurity are terms used indiscriminately by those, who would prove, that Shakspeare and Milton were wrong when they employed obscurity as a cause of the sublime, that Mr. Burke was equally mistaken in his reasoning upon the subject, and that mankind have been equally in error, as to the nature of their own feelings, when they were acted upon by the illusions of those great masters of the imagination, at whose so potent bidding, the passions have been awakened from their sleep, and by whose magic a crowded Theatre has been changed to a lonely shore, to a witch's cave, to an enchanted island, to a murderer's castle, to the ramparts of an usurper, to the battle, to the midnight carousal of the camp or the tavern, to every various scene of the living world.' . . .

['The soul of poetry', continued Mr W–] 'includes an instantaneous perception, and an exquisite love of whatever is graceful, grand, and sublime, with the power of seizing and combining such circumstances of them, as to strike and interest a reader by the representation, even more than a general view of the real scene itself could do. Whatever this may be called, which crowns the mind of a poet, and distinguishes it from every other mind, our whole heart instantly acknowledges it in Shakspeare, Milton, Gray, Collins, Beattie,[51] and a very few others, not excepting Thomson,[52] to whose powers the sudden tear of delight and admiration bears at once both testimony and tribute. . . . Yet, when I recollect the "Alexander's Feast," I am astonished at the powers of Dryden . . . I cannot, however, allow it to be the finest ode in the English language, so long as I remember Gray's Bard, and Collins's Ode on the Passions.

8.10   Francis Jeffrey, On Felicia Hemans, *The Edinburgh Review* (1829)

Felicia Hemans (1793–1835) was a very popular poet of the late-Romantic period and became the best-selling English poet of the nineteenth century. Francis Jeffrey (see also extract 8.6) reviewed her Records of Women: with other Poems *and* The Forest Sanctuary; with other Poems *for the* Edinburgh Review *in October 1829, and his essay illustrates how far the image of the woman poet had changed from that of the 'unsex'd female' of Polwhele's satire (extract 8.5). Along with Letitia Elizabeth Landon,*

---

51 Thomas Gray (1716), William Collins (1721–59) and James Beattie (1735–1803), British poets often classed as 'pre-romantic'.

52 James Thomson, Scottish poet (1700–48).

Hemans was elevated to the newly created status of 'poetess', and her work equated with a particular model of middle-class domestic femininity (though a number of critics have argued that these writers expose the dangers of this ideology, even as they write out of it).

Women, we fear, cannot do everything; nor even every thing they attempt. But what they can do, they do, for the most part, excellently – and much more frequently with an absolute and perfect success, than the aspirants of our rougher and more ambitious sex. . . . Their proper and natural business is the practical regulation of private life, in all its bearings, affections, and concerns; and the questions with which they have to deal in that most important department, though often of the utmost difficulty and nicety, involve, for the most part, but few elements; and may generally be better described as delicate than intricate; – requiring for their solution rather a quick tact and fine perception, than a patient or laborious examination. For the same reason, they rarely succeed in long works, even on subjects the best suited to their genius; their natural training rendering them equally averse to long doubt and long labour. . . .

Their business being, as we have said, with actual or social life, and the colours it receives from the conduct and dispositions of individuals, they unconsciously acquire, at a very early age, the finest perception of character and manners, and are almost as soon instinctively schooled in the deep and more dangerous learning of feeling and emotion; while the very minuteness with which they make and meditate on these interesting observations, and the finer shades and variations of sentiment which are thus treasured and recorded, trains their whole faculties to a nicety and precision of operation, which often discloses itself to advantage in their application to studies of a different character. When women, accordingly, have turned their minds – as they have done but too seldom – to the exposition or arrangement of any branch of knowledge, they have commonly exhibited, we think, a more beautiful accuracy, and a more uniform and complete justness of thinking, than their less discriminating brethren. . . .

We think the poetry of Mrs. Hemans a fine exemplification of Female Poetry – and we think it has much of the perfection which we have ventured to ascribe to the happier productions of female genius.

It may not be the best imaginable poetry, and may not indicate the very highest or most commanding genius; but it embraces a great deal of that which gives the very best poetry its chief power of pleasing; and would strike us, perhaps, as more impassioned and exalted, if it were not regulated and harmonised by the most beautiful taste. It is singularly sweet, elegant, and tender – touching, perhaps, and contemplative, rather than vehement and overpowering; and not only finished throughout with an exquisite delicacy, and even severity of execution, but informed with a purity and loftiness of feel-

Figure 16   Alfred Crowquill (pseudonym for Alfred Forrester), 'Four Specimens of the Reading Public', 7 August 1826; © Copyright the Trustees of the British Museum.

Crowquill satirizes contemporary literary taste according to representative readers' gender and social status. The 'four specimens' are: Romancing Molly, who enquires after a five-volume romance; Sir Larry Luscious, who wants the latest volume of the courtesan Harriette Wilson's scandalous *Memoirs*, first published in 1825; the Political Dustman, who wants something by the radical journalist and essayist William Cobbett; and Frank à la Mode, who requests the latest work by the best-selling novelist Walter Scott.

ing, and a certain sober and humble tone of indulgence and piety, which must satisfy all judgments, and allay the apprehensions of those who are most afraid of the passionate exaggerations of poetry. The diction is always beautiful, harmonious, and free – and the themes, though of great variety, uniformly treated with a grace, originality, and judgment, which mark the same master hand. These themes she has occasionally borrowed, with the peculiar imagery that belongs to them, from the legends of different nations, and the most opposite states of society; and has contrived to retain much of what is interesting and peculiar in each of them, without adopting, along with it, any of the revolting or extravagant excesses which may characterise the taste or manners of the people or the age from which it has been derived. . . . The great merit, however, of her poetry, is undoubtedly in its tenderness and its beautiful imagery. . . .

If taste and elegance . . . be titles to enduring fame, we might venture securely to promise that rich boon to the authoress before us; who adds to those great merits a tenderness and loftiness of feeling, and an ethereal purity of sentiment, which could only emanate from the soul of a woman. . . . [W]e do not hesitate to say, that she is, beyond all comparison, the most touching writer of occasional verse that our literature has yet to boast of.

9

Empire, Slavery and Exploration

Introduction

The Romantic age witnessed a remarkable growth in Britain's imperial power and confidence. Despite the loss of the thirteen American colonies as a result of the War of Independence, Britain had strengthened its control of its other colonies in India, Canada, and the Caribbean, and the defeat prompted a restructuring of colonial policy. Britain's victory over its major colonial rival, France, in the Revolutionary and Napoleonic Wars resulted in further acquisitions in the Mediterranean, Australia and South Africa, and increased dominion in India and the Caribbean, confirming the nation's status as the world's major imperial power and reinforcing a growing sense of the country's divinely sanctioned right to shape global politics. By 1820, 200 million people, 26 per cent of the world's population, lived under British rule, and Britain no longer saw itself as simply a trading or colonial nation but as an Empire with a mission to spread its own political, religious and moral values across the globe.

The most fiercely debated aspect of Britain's imperial role during the Romantic period was its involvement in the slave trade (see extracts 9.4, 9.5 and 9.7), which was central to the nation's trading system. During the eighteenth century, Britain had increasingly exported manufactured goods and imported raw materials, such as sugar from the West Indian Sugar Islands of the Caribbean (which Coleridge classed along with rum among the 'imaginary wants' on which the slave trade was based, calling for a boycott of their use – extract 9.7). This trading system was underpinned by the slave trade, which involved the kidnapping and imprisonment of Africans and their transportation from Africa to the West Indies to work as slaves. The horrors of the process are described in this section by the freed slave Ottobah Cugoano (extract 9.4) and the slave ship captain John Newton (extract 9.5). It has been estimated that between 1660 and 1807, 3.5 million slaves were shipped by British merchants, with a mortality rate as high as 20 per cent.[1]

---

1 *Cassell's Companion to Eighteenth-Century Britain*, ed. Stephen Brumwell and W. A. Speck (London: Cassell, 2001), p. 352.

Map 2 The slave trade

The campaign for the abolition of the slave trade became a major movement in the 1780s and early 1790s, led in Parliament by William Wilberforce, who drew on the extensive research of another important abolitionist, Thomas Clarkson (a friend of Wordsworth and Coleridge). Wilberforce was a leading Evangelical (see extract 4.6) and Clarkson was associated with the Quakers, and as these religious affiliations suggest, Christian spirituality together with the empathetic imperative of the cult of sensibility gave considerable emotional power to the movement, as did the evidence of those with first-hand experience of slavery's horrors, including those who had been slaves themselves, such as Cugoano and Olaudah Equiano, who published his autobiography in 1789. Though the campaign was stalled by the French Revolution and the outbreak of war with France, the slave trade was abolished in 1807 and slaves emancipated in 1833–8.

The slave trade was a major literary topic of the period. In 1788, for example, Hannah More, Ann Yearsley, and Helen Maria Williams all produced abolitionist poems, as did Blake, Southey, and Coleridge at other points in the period. More complex in their relationship to the issue are works like Coleridge's 'The Ancient Mariner', the imagery and sense of guilt of which have been read by a number of critics in the context of slave narratives, and Jane Austen's *Mansfield Park*, in which Sir Thomas Bertram is forced to return to his sugar plantations in Antigua.

Another important element of the relationship between literature and empire in the period is the development of what is termed 'orientalism', the cultural and scholarly representation of the Middle East and Asia that became highly fashionable and that some critics, most notably Edward Said, have seen as an integral part of the imaginative and actual domination of the 'East' by the 'West'. In his essay 'On the Poetry of the Eastern Nations' (extract 9.1), the poet William Jones turned to 'the poets of *Asia*' as a means of revitalizing poetry, while Maria Edgeworth's account of the popularity of the literature of 'voyages and travels' places the story of Sinbad from the *Arabian Nights* alongside the novels *Robinson Crusoe* and *Gulliver's Travels* as the texts which exert the most powerful hold over the imagination of the young (extract 9.8). So popular were 'oriental' subjects, that in 1813 Byron advised his fellow poet Tom Moore to 'Stick to the East',[2] a policy which he himself exploited in many of his poems, including *Childe Harold's Pilgrimage* and his *Turkish Tales*. Other writers of 'orientalist' texts included William Beckford (*Vathek*, 1786), Samuel Taylor Coleridge ('Kubla Khan', 1798), Robert Southey (*Thalaba the Destroyer*, 1801, and *The Curse of Kehama*, 1810), Charlotte Dacre (*Zofloya, or the Moor*, 1806), Lady Morgan (*Woman: or Ida of Athens*, 1809, and *The Missionary*, 1811), Thomas Moore (*Lalla Rookh*, 1817), and Percy Shelley (*Alastor*, 1815, and *Prometheus Unbound*, 1820). The relationship of these very diverse texts to British policy in the 'Orient' continues to be debated, but the overall development away from the scholarly and sympathetic respect for Asian culture exemplified by Jones (which some commentators none the less see as implicated within the colonial project) towards a denigrating dismissal of it as savage and corrupt is indicated by James Mill's utilitarian *History of British India* of 1817 (extract 9.10), which provides an implicit justification for an increasingly interventionist role on Britain's part.

The Romantic period was also an age of discovery and exploration, exemplified by the three journeys to the South Seas undertaken by James Cook between 1768 and his death in 1779. As David Samwell's account shows (extract 9.3), Cook himself became an embodiment of the heroic, enlightened explorer, offering a model and sanction for future expeditions by the so-called 'Sons of Cook'

---

2 *Byron's Letters and Journals*, ed. Leslie Marchand, 13 vols (London: John Murray, 1973–94), III, 101.

in Africa, Australia, North America and Canada. Though often undertaken for purposes of scientific or cultural research and backed by organizations such as the African Association or the Admiralty, these expeditions also served colonial and imperial agendas (the maverick explorer James Bruce treats rather ambivalently the nationalistic dimensions of his supposed discovery of the source of the Nile – extract 9.6). Though certain areas such as Tahiti (extract 9.2) came to represent earthly paradises inhabited by noble savages, the accounts of indigenous peoples often implied the need for some external civilizing force. The literature of exploration and discovery was itself a significant and popular genre in the period, inspiring a number of literary travel narratives, including the Ancient Mariner's journey towards the South Pole in Coleridge's poem and Captain Walton's expedition to 'unvisited regions' in the framing narrative of Mary Shelley's *Frankenstein*. As is suggested by the fatal consequences of both of these failed voyages of discovery, despite Britain's growing sense of its own imperial ambitions, there was genuine concern about the motivations and effects of its global mission.

9.1   William Jones, 'On the Poetry of the Eastern Nations' from *Poems consisting chiefly of Translations from the Asiatick Languages* (1772)

A major orientalist scholar and author of a series of Hindu Hymns, *Sir William Jones (1746–94) became a Judge in the Bengal Supreme Court and in 1784 founded the Asiatic Society of Bengal. In the previous decade, Jones had published his important* Poems consisting chiefly of Translations from the Asiatick Languages, *to which he had attached his essay 'On the Poetry of the Eastern Nations'. Arguing that 'It is certain (to say no more) that the poets of Asia have as much genius as ourselves' and describing 'the manners of the* Arabs, Persians, Indians, *and* Turks, *the four principal nations, that profess the religion of Mahomet', this essay was influential on orientalist poetry in the Romantic period, particularly as practised by Robert Southey, Thomas Moore and Lord Byron. With its emphasis on spontaneity and the 'primitive', Jones's essay can also be seen as a programme for poetry that anticipates Wordsworth's 'Preface' to* Lyrical Ballads.

Arabia . . . seems to be the only country in the world, in which we can properly lay the scene of pastoral poetry; because no nation at this day can vie with the *Arabians* in the delightfulness of their climate, and the simplicity of their manners. There is a valley, indeed, to the north of *Indostan*, called *Cashmere*, which, according to an account written by a native of it, is a perfect garden, exceedingly fruitful, and watered by a thousand rivulets: but when its inhabitants were subdued by the stratagem of a *Mogul* prince, they lost their happiness with their liberty, and *Arabia* retained its old title without any rival to dispute it. These are not the fancies of a poet: the beauties of *Yemen* are proved by the concurrent testimony of all travellers, by the descriptions of it in all the writings of *Asia*, and by the nature and situation of the country itself, which lies between the eleventh and fifteenth degrees of northern latitude, under a serene sky, and exposed to the most favourable influence of the sun; it is enclosed on one side by vast rocks and deserts, and defended on the other by a tempestuous sea, so that it seems to have been designed by providence for the most secure, as well as the most beautiful, region of the East. . . . Now it is certain that all poetry receives a very considerable ornament from the beauty of natural images; as the roses of *Sharon*, the verdure of *Carmel*, the vines of *Engaddi*, and the dew of *Hermon*, are the sources of many pleasing metaphors and comparisons in the sacred poetry: thus the odours of *Yemen,* the musk of *Hadramut*, and the pearls of *Omman*, supply the *Arabian* poets with a great variety of allusions; and, if the remark of *Hermogenes*[3] be just, that whatever is *delightful to the senses* produces the *Beautiful* when it is described, where can we find so much beauty as in the *Eastern* poems, which turn chiefly upon the loveliest objects in nature? . . .

[T]he poets of the *East* may vie with those of *Europe* in *the graces of their diction*, as well as in the loveliness of their images: but we must not believe that the *Arabian* poetry can please only by its descriptions of *beauty*; since the gloomy and terrible objects, which produce the *sublime*, when they are aptly described, are no where more common than in the *Desert* and *Stony Arabia's*; and, indeed, we see nothing so frequently painted by the poets of those countries, as wolves and lions, precipices and forests, rocks and wildernesses.

If we allow the natural objects, with which the *Arabs* are perpetually conversant, to be *sublime*, and *beautiful*, our next step must be, to confess that their comparisons, metaphors, and allegories are so likewise; for an allegory is only a string of metaphors, a metaphor is a short simile, and the finest similes are drawn from natural objects. It is true that many of the *Eastern* figures are common to other nations, but some of them receive a propriety from the manners of the *Arabians*, who dwell in the plains and woods, which would be lost, if they came from the inhabitants of cities: thus *the dew of liberality*, and the *odour of reputation*, are metaphors used by most people; but they are wonderfully proper in the mouths of those, who have so much need of being refreshed by *the dews*, and who gratify their sense of smelling with the *sweetest odours* in the world: Again; it is very usual in all countries to make frequent allusions to the brightness of the celestial luminaries, which give their light to all; but the metaphors taken from them have an additional beauty, if we consider them as made by a nation, who pass most of their nights in the open air, or in tents, and consequently see the moon and stars in their greatest splendour. . . .

These are not the only advantages, which the natives of *Arabia* enjoy above the inhabitants of most other countries: they preserve to this day the manners and customs of their ancestors, who, by their own account, were settled in the

---

3 Hermogenes of Tarsus, Greek rhetorician, of second century AD.

province of *Yemen* above three thousand years ago . . . and, except when their tribes are engaged in war, spend their days in watching their flocks and camels, or in repeating their native songs, which they pour out almost extempore, professing a contempt for the stately pillars, and solemn buildings of the cities, compared with the natural charms of the country, and the coolness of their tents: thus they pass their lives in the highest pleasure, of which they have any conception, in the contemplation of the most delightful objects, and in the enjoyment of perpetual spring. . . .

The descendants of *Tamerlane*[4] carried into *India* the language, and poetry of the *Persians*; and the *Indian* poets to this day compose their verses in imitation of them. . . . The *Indians* are soft, and voluptuous, but artful and insincere, at least to the *Europeans*, whom, to say the truth, they have had no great reason of late years to admire for the opposite virtues: but they are fond of poetry, which they learned from the *Persians*, and may, perhaps, before the close of the century, be as fond of a more formidable art, which they will learn from the *English*.

I must once more request, that, in bestowing these praises on the writings of *Asia*, I may not be thought to derogate from the merit of the *Greek* and *Latin* poems, which have justly been admired in every age; yet I cannot but think that our *European* poetry has subsisted too long on the perpetual repetition of the same images, and incessant allusions to the same fables: and it has been my endeavour for several years to inculcate this truth, *That, if the principal writings of the Asiaticks, which are reposited in our publick libraries, were printed with the usual advantage of notes and illustrations, and if the languages of the Eastern nations were studied in our places of education, where every other branch of useful knowledge is taught to perfection, a new and ample field would be opened for speculation; we should have a more extensive insight into the history of the human mind, we should be furnished with a new set of images and similitudes, and a number of excellent compositions would be brought to light, which future scholars might explain, and future poets might imitate.*

9.2 John Hawkesworth, *An Account of the Voyages Undertaken by the Order of his Present Majesty for Making Discoveries in the Southern Hemisphere, And Successively Performed by Commodore Byron, Captain Carteret, Captain Wallis, and Captain Cook . . . Drawn up from the Journals which were kept by the several Commanders, and from the Papers of Joseph Banks, Esq.* (1773)

In 1768, Captain James Cook (1728–79) began the first of his three voyages to the South Seas, undertaken in the Endeavour *for the purposes of astronomical and*

---

4 Fourteenth-century military leader.

Figure 17   Sydney Parkinson, 'The Head of a Chief of New Zealand, the face curiously tatowd, or mark'd, according to their Manner', from Sydney Parkinson, *A Journal of a Voyage to the South Seas, in His majesty's ship, the Endeavour (under the command of Captain James Cook)*, 1773; © Copyright the British Library. All rights reserved. Shelfmark L.R.294.c.7 (plate XVI).

Sydney Parkinson was a botanical artist who worked for the scientist Joseph Banks and accompanied him on Captain Cook's first voyage of exploration on the *Endeavour* from 1768 to 1771. During the period in New Zealand, Parkinson undertook several studies of the Maori people, such as this one which illustrates his particular interest in tattooing.

geographical research (the party included the botanist Joseph Banks). The expedition arrived in Tahiti in 1769. John Hawkesworth (1715–73) was an editor who was hired by the Admiralty to edit the papers of Cook and others, producing the official account of Cook's first voyage (which he chose to do writing in the first person). Though Hawkesworth's three-volume account was criticized for misrepresentation, it influenced ideas about the environment and the inhabitants of the South Sea islands, and can be read in relation to the Rousseau-inspired interest in the earthly paradise and the noble savage (see extract 5.3).

The produce of this island [Otaheite] is bread-fruit, cocoa-nuts, bananas, of thirteen sorts, the best we had ever eaten; plantains; a fruit not unlike an apple, which, when ripe, is very pleasant; sweet potatoes, yams, cocoas, a kind of *Arum*; a fruit known here by the name of *Jambu*, and reckoned most delicious; sugar cane, which the inhabitants eat raw; a root of the salop kind, called by the inhabitants *Pea*; a plant called *Ethee*, of which the root only is eaten; a fruit that grows in a pod, like that of a large kidney-bean, which, when it is roasted, eats very much like a chesnut, by the natives called *Ahee*; a tree called *Wharra*, called in the East Indies *Pandanes*, which produces fruit, something like the pine-apple; a shrub called *Nono*; the *Morinda*, which also produces fruit; a species of fern, of which the root is eaten, and sometimes the leaves; and a plant called *Theve*, of which the root also is eaten: but the fruits of the *Nono*, the fern, and the *Theve*, are eaten only by the inferior people, and in times of scarcity. All these, which serve the inhabitants for food, the earth produces spontaneously, or with so little culture, that they seem to be exempted from the first general curse, that 'man should eat his bread in the sweat of his brow.' . . . [T]he sea supplies them with great variety of most excellent fish, to eat which is their chief luxury, and to catch it their principal labour.

As to the people they are of the largest size of Europeans. The men are tall, strong, well-limbed and finely shaped. The tallest that we saw was a man upon a neighbouring island, called HUAHEINE, who measured six feet three inches and an half. The women of the superior rank are also in general above our middle stature, but those of the inferior class are rather below it, and some of them are very small. This defect in size probably proceeds from their early commerce with men, the only thing in which they differ from their superiors, that could possibly affect their growth.

Their natural complexion is that kind of clear olive, or *Brunette*, which many people in Europe prefer to the finest white and red. In those that are exposed to the wind and sun, it is considerably deepened, but in others that live under shelter, especially the superior class of women, it continues of its native hue, and the skin is most delicately smooth and soft; they have no tint in their cheeks, which we distinguish by the name of colour. The shape of the face is comely, the cheek bones are not high, neither are the eyes hollow, nor the brow prominent: the only feature that does not correspond with our ideas of beauty is the nose, which, in general, is somewhat flat; but their eyes, especially those of the women, are full of expression, sometimes sparkling with fire, and sometimes melting with softness; their teeth also are, almost without exception, most beautifully even and white, and their breath perfectly without taint. . . .

In other countries, the girls and unmarried women are supposed to be wholly ignorant of what others upon some occasions may appear to know; and their conduct and conversation are consequently restrained within narrower bounds, and kept at a more remote distance from whatever relates to a connection with the other sex: but here, it is just contrary. Among other diversions, there is a dance, called *Timorodee*, which is performed by young girls, whenever eight or ten of them can be collected together, consisting of motions and gestures beyond imagination wanton, in the practice of which they are brought up from their earliest childhood, accompanied by words, which, if it were possible, would more explicitly convey the same ideas. In these dances they keep time with an exactness which is scarcely excelled by the best performers upon the stages of Europe. But the practice which is allowed to the virgin, is prohibited to the woman from the moment that she has put these hopeful lessons in practice, and realized the symbols of the dance.

It cannot be supposed that, among these people, chastity is held in much estimation. It might be expected that sisters and daughters would be offered to strangers, either as a courtesy, or for reward; and that breaches of conjugal fidelity, even in the wife, should not be otherwise punished than by a few hard words, or perhaps a slight beating, as indeed is the case: but there is a scale in dissolute sensuality, which these people have ascended, wholly unknown to every other nation whose manners have been recorded from the beginning of the world to the present hour, and which no imagination could possibly conceive.

A very considerable number of the principal people of Otaheite, of both sexes, have formed themselves into a society, in which every woman is common to every man; thus securing a perpetual variety as often as their inclination prompts them to seek it, which is so frequent, that the same man and woman seldom cohabit together more than two or three days.

9.3 David Samwell, *A Narrative of the Death of Captain James Cook, to which are added some Particulars concerning his Life and Character* (1786)

David Samwell (1751–98) was a surgeon on Captain Cook's third voyage (1776–80), during which Cook was killed in Hawaii in 1779. Samwell's Narrative *culminated with an assessment of Cook's character and career which presented him as a humane, heroic figure and contributed to the growing cult of the explorer in the period (see also extracts 9.6 and 9.9).*

The character of Captain Cook will be best exemplified by the services he has performed, which are universally known, and have ranked his name above that of any navigator of ancient or of modern times. Nature had endowed him with a mind vigorous and comprehensive, which in his riper years he had cultivated with care and industry. His general knowledge was extensive and various: in that of his own profession he was unequalled. With a clear judgment, strong masculine sense, and the most determined resolution; with a genius peculiarly turned for enterprize, he pursued his object with unshaken perseverance: – vigilant and active in an eminent degree: – cool and intrepid among dangers; patient and firm under difficulties and distress; fertile in expedients; great and original in all his designs; active and resolved in carrying them into execution. These qualities rendered him the animating spirit of the expedition: in every situation, he stood unrivalled and alone; on him all eyes were turned; he was our leading-star, which at its setting, left us involved in darkness and despair.

His constitution was strong, his mode of living temperate. . . . He had no repugnance to good living; he always kept a good table, though he could bear the reverse without murmuring. He was a modest man, and rather bashful; of an agreeable lively conversation, sensible and intelligent. In his temper he was somewhat hasty, but of a disposition the most friendly, benevolent, and humane. His person was above six feet high, and though a good-looking man, he was plain both in address and appearance. His head was small, his hair, which was a dark brown, he wore tied behind. His face was full of expression, his nose exceedingly well-shaped, his eyes, which were small and of a brown cast, were quick and piercing: his eyebrows prominent, which gave his countenance altogether an air of austerity.

He was beloved by his people, who looked up to him as to a father, and obeyed his commands with alacrity. The confidence we placed in him was unremitting; our admiration of his great talents unbounded; our esteem for his good qualities affectionate and sincere.

In exploring unknown countries, the dangers he had to encounter were various and uncommon. On such occasions, he always displayed great presence of mind, and a steady perseverance in pursuit of his object. The acquisition he has made to our knowledge of the globe is immense, besides improving the art of navigation, and enriching the science of philosophy.

He was remarkably distinguished for the activity of his mind: it was that which enabled him to pay an unwearied attention to every object of the service. The strict œconomy he observed in the expenditure of the ship's stores, and the unremitting care he employed for the preservation of the health of his people, were the causes that enabled him to prosecute discoveries in remote parts of the globe, for such a length of time as had been deemed impracticable by former navigators. The method he discovered for preserving the health of seamen in long voyages, will transmit his name to posterity as the friend and benefactor of mankind: the success which attended it, afforded this truly great man more satisfaction, than the distinguished fame that attended his discoveries.

England has been unanimous in her tribute of applause to his virtues, and all Europe has borne testimony to his merit. There is hardly a corner of the earth, however remote and savage, that will not long remember his benevolence and humanity. The grateful Indian, in time to come, pointing to the herds grazing his fertile plains, will relate to his children how the first stock of them was introduced into the country; and the name of Cook will be remembered among those benign spirits, whom they worship as the source of every good, and the fountain of every blessing.

9.4   Ottobah Cugoano, *Thoughts and Sentiments on the Evil and Wicked Traffic of the Slavery and Commerce of the Human Species, humbly submitted to the Inhabitants of Great-Britain* (1787)

Quobna Ottobah Cugoano (1757–?) was born in what is now Ghana. As the following extract recounts, he was kidnapped at the age of 13 and sold to work as a slave on the Caribbean island of Grenada. Transported to England in 1772, he became a free man and leading figure in the black community of London, acquainted with other former slaves such as Olaudah Equiano and Ignatius Sancho. His Thoughts and Sentiments *was published in 1787, the first demand for the abolition of slavery and emancipation of slaves published by an African in English. There is no information about Cugoano's later life or his death.*

As several learned gentlemen of distinguished abilities, as well as eminent for their great humanity, liberality and candour, have written various essays against that infamous traffic of the African Slave Trade, carried on with the West-Indian planters and merchants, to the great shame and disgrace of all Christian nations wherever it is admitted in any of their territories, or in any place or situation amongst them; it cannot be amiss that I should thankfully acknowledge these truly worthy and humane gentlemen with the warmest sense of gratitude, for their beneficent and laudable endeavours towards a total suppression of that infamous and iniquitous traffic of stealing, kid-napping, buying, selling, and cruelly enslaving men! . . .

I was early snatched away from my native country, with about eighteen or twenty more boys and girls, as we were playing in a field . . . we went into the woods as usual; but we had not been above two hours before our troubles began, when several great ruffians came upon us suddenly, and said we had committed a fault against their lord, and we must go and answer for it ourselves before him.

Soon some of us attempted in vain to run away, but pistols and cutlasses were soon introduced, threatening, that if we offered to stir we should all lie dead on the spot. One of them pretended to be more friendly than the rest, and said, that he would speak to their lord to get us clear, and desired that we should follow him; we were then immediately divided into different parties, and drove after him. We were soon led out of the way which we knew, and towards the evening, as we came in sight of a town, they told us that this great man of theirs lived there, but pretended it was too late to go and see him that night. . . . [Cugoano describes being taken on a number of journeys and being separated from his companions.] Next day we travelled on, and in the evening came to a town, where I saw several white people, which made me afraid that they would eat me, according to our notion as children in the inland parts of the country. This made me rest very uneasy all the night, and next morning I had some victuals brought, desiring me to eat and make haste, as my guide and kid-napper told me that he had to go to the castle with some company that were going there, as he had told me before, to get some goods. After I was ordered out, the horrors I soon saw and felt, cannot be well described; I saw many of my miserable countrymen chained two and two, some hand-cuffed, and some with their hands tied behind. We were conducted along by a guard, and when we arrived at the castle, I asked my guide what I was brought there for, he told me to learn the ways of the *browsow*, that is the white faced people. I saw him take a gun, a piece of cloth, and some lead for me, and then he told me that he must now leave me there, and went off. This made me cry bitterly, but I was soon conducted to a prison, for three days, where I heard the groans and cries of many, and saw some of my fellow-captives. But when a vessel arrived to conduct us away to the ship, it was a most horrible scene; there was nothing to be heard but rattling of chains, smacking of whips, and the groans and cries of our fellow-men. Some would not stir from the ground, when they were lashed and beat in the most horrible manner. I have forgot the name of this infernal fort; but we were taken in the ship that came for us, to another that was ready to sail from Cape Coast. When we were put into the ship, we saw several black merchants coming on board, but we were all drove into our holes, and not suffered to speak to any of them. In this situation we continued several days in sight of our native land; but I could find no good person to give any information of my situation to Accasa at Agimaque. And when we found ourselves at last taken away, death was more preferable than life, and a plan was concerted amongst us, that we might burn and blow up the ship, and to perish all together in the flames; but we were betrayed by one of our own countrywomen, who slept with some of the head men of the ship, for it was common for the dirty filthy sailors to take African women and lie upon their bodies; but the men were chained and pent up in holes. It was the women and boys which were to burn the ship, with the approbation and groans of the rest; though that was prevented, the discovery was likewise a cruel bloody scene.

But it would be needless to give a description of all the horrible scenes which we saw, and the base treatment which we met with in this dreadful captive situation, as the similar cases of thousands, which suffer by this infernal traffic, are well known. Let it suffice to say, that I was thus lost to my dear indulgent parents and relations, and they to me. All my help was cries and tears, and these could not avail; nor suffered long, till one succeeding woe, and dread, swelled up another. Brought from a state of innocence and freedom, and, in a barbarous and cruel manner, conveyed to a state of horror and slavery: This abandoned

situation may be easier conceived than described. From the time that I was kidnapped and conducted to a factory, and from thence in the brutish, base, but
fashionable way of traffic, consigned to Grenada, the grievous thoughts which I
then felt, still pant in my heart; though my fears and tears have long since
subsided. And yet it is still grievous to think that thousands more have suffered
in similar and greater distress, under the hands of barbarous robbers, and merciless taskmasters; and that many even now are suffering in all the extreme bitterness of grief and woe, that no language can describe. The cries of some, and the
sight of their misery, may be seen and heard afar; but the deep sounding groans
of thousands, and the great sadness of their misery and woe, under the heavy
load of oppressions and calamities inflicted upon them, are such as can only be
distinctly known to the ears of Jehovah Sabaoth. . . .

Being in this dreadful captivity and horrible slavery, without any hope of
deliverance, for about eight or nine months, beholding the most dreadful scenes
of misery and cruelty, and seeing my miserable companions often cruelly lashed,
and as it were cut to pieces, for the most trifling faults; this made me often tremble and weep, but I escaped better than many of them. For eating a piece of
sugar-cane, some were cruelly lashed, or struck over the face to knock their teeth
out. Some of the stouter ones, I suppose often reproved, and grown hardened
and stupid with many cruel beatings and lashings, or perhaps faint and pressed
with hunger and hard labour, were often committing trespasses of this kind, and
when detected, they met with exemplary punishment. Some told me they had
their teeth pulled out to deter others, and to prevent them from eating cane in
future. Thus seeing my miserable companions and countrymen in this pitiful,
distressed and horrible situation, with all the brutish baseness and barbarity
attending it, could not but fill my little mind with horror and indignation. . . .

Thanks be to God, I was delivered from Grenada, and that horrid brutal slavery.
– A gentleman coming to England, took me for his servant, and brought me
away, where I soon found my situation become more agreeable.

9.5   John Newton, *Thoughts upon the African Slave Trade* (1788)

*John Newton (1725–1807) worked on slave ships during the 1740s and early 1750s before
becoming an Evangelical minister, abolitionist and writer of hymns (including 'Amazing
Grace' and the Olney Hymns with William Cowper). Norton was able to draw from his
own experience in his pamphlet,* Thoughts upon the African Slave Trade, *giving a
detailed account of the so-called 'Middle Passage', the journey of a minimum of six weeks
which saw the transportation of captured slaves from the coast of Africa to the Americas
and the Caribbean, where they were exchanged for products such as sugar and tobacco.*

With our ships, the great object is, to be full. When the ship is there, it is thought desirable, she should take as many as possible. The cargo of a vessel of a hundred tons, or little more, is calculated to purchase from two hundred and twenty to two hundred and fifty Slaves. Their lodging-rooms below the deck, which are three, (for the men, the boys, and the women,) besides a place for the sick, are sometimes more than five feet high, and sometimes less; and this height is divided towards the middle, for the Slaves lie in two rows, one above the other, on each side of the ship, close to each other, like books upon a shelf. I have known them so close, that the shelf would not, easily, contain one more.

And I have known a white man sent down, among the men, to lay them in these rows to the greatest advantage, so that as little space as possible might be lost. Let it be observed, that the poor creatures, thus cramped for want of room, are likewise in irons, for the most part both hands and feet, and two together, which makes it difficult for them to turn or move, to attempt either to rise or to lie down, without hurting themselves, or each other. Nor is the motion of the ship, especially her heeling, or stoop on one side, when under sail, to be omitted; for this, as they lie athwart, or across the ship, adds to the uncomfortableness of their lodging, especially to those who lie on the leeward, or leaning, side of the vessel. . . . The heat and smell of these rooms, when the weather will not admit of the Slaves being brought upon deck, and of having their rooms cleaned every day, would be, almost, insupportable, to a person not accustomed to them. If the Slaves and their rooms can be constantly aired, and they are not detained too long on board, perhaps there are not many die; but the contrary is often their lot. They are kept down, by the weather, to breathe a hot and corrupted air, sometimes for a week: this, added to the galling of their irons, and the despondency which seizes their spirits, when thus confined, soon becomes fatal. And every morning, perhaps, more instances than one are found, of the living and the dead, like the Captives of Mezentius,[5] fastened together.

Epidemical fevers and fluxes, which fill the ship with noisome and noxious effluvia, often break out, infect the Seamen likewise, and the Oppressors, and the Oppressed, fall by the same stroke. I believe, nearly one half of the Slaves on board, have, sometimes, died; and that the loss of a third part, in these circumstances, is not unusual. The ship, in which I was Mate, left the Coast with Two Hundred and Eighteen Slaves on board; and though we were not much affected by epidemical disorders, I find, by my journal of that voyage, (now before me,) that we buried Sixty-two on our passage to South-Carolina, exclusive of those which died before we left the Coast, of which I have no account.

I believe, upon an average between the more healthy, and the more sickly voyages, and including all contingencies, One Fourth of the whole purchase may be allotted to the article of Mortality. That is, if the English ships purchase *Sixty Thousand* Slaves annually, upon the whole extent of the Coast, the annual loss of lives cannot be much less than *Fifteen Thousand*.

---

5 Etruscan king, notorious for cruelty.

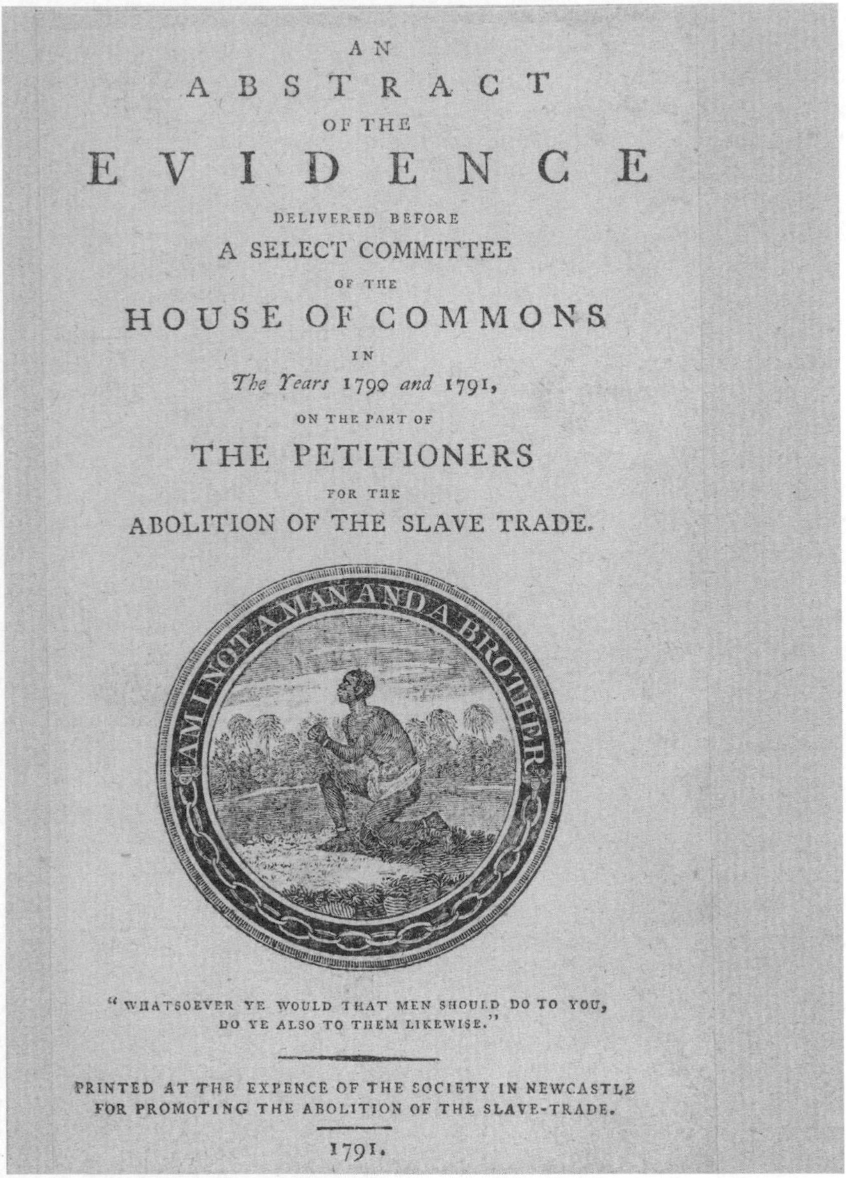

A N
A B S T R A C T
OF THE
E V I D E N C E
DELIVERED BEFORE
A SELECT COMMITTEE
OF THE
HOUSE OF COMMONS
IN
The Years 1790 *and* 1791,
ON THE PART OF
THE PETITIONERS
FOR THE
ABOLITION OF THE SLAVE TRADE.

" WHATSOEVER YE WOULD THAT MEN SHOULD DO TO YOU,
DO YE ALSO TO THEM LIKEWISE."

PRINTED AT THE EXPENCE OF THE SOCIETY IN NEWCASTLE
FOR PROMOTING THE ABOLITION OF THE SLAVE-TRADE.

1791.

Figure 18   Pamphlet on the abolition of the slave trade, 1791; © Copyright the Trustees of the British Museum.

This abolitionist pamphlet makes use of the period's most prominent anti-slavery image, the kneeling and enchained African encircled by the slogan 'Am I Not a Man and a Brother?' The design was first used in 1787 as the seal of the Society for Effecting the Abolition of the Slave Trade and was widely circulated in a number of forms, most notably the pottery medallion produced by Josiah Wedgwood in the same year.

I am now to speak of the survivors. – When the ships make the land, (usually the West-India islands,) and have their port in view, after having been four, five, six weeks, or a longer time, at sea, (which depends much upon the time that passes before they can get into the permanent Trade Winds, which blow from the North-East and East across the Atlantic,) then, and not before, they venture to release the Men Slaves from their irons. . . .

Yet, perhaps, they would wish to spend the remainder of their days on ship-board, could they know, before-hand, the nature of the servitude which awaits them, on shore; and that the dreadful hardships and sufferings they have already endured, would, to the most of them, only terminate in excessive toil, hunger, and the excruciating tortures of the cart-whip, inflicted at the caprice of an unfeeling Overseer, proud of the power allowed him of punishing whom, and when, and how he pleases.

9.6   James Bruce, *Travels to Discover the Source of the Nile, in the Years 1768, 1769, 1770, 1771, 1772, and 1773* (1790)

The Scottish scholar and traveller James Bruce (1730–94) set out in 1768 to discover the source of the Nile, which he believed could be found in Abyssinia (now called Ethiopia). In 1770, he discovered the source of the Blue Nile (as described here), not the larger White Nile, as he had hoped. Bruce's lively account of his travels was criticized for its self-glorification and its lack of scientific rigour, though it was widely read and, like the accounts of Cook (extracts 9.2 and 9.3), did much to glamorize the figure of the explorer. The Travels *have been seen as influential on a number of literary works of the period, including Coleridge's 'Kubla Khan' (the imagery of which has been seen as based on the passage below) and* The Prelude, *in which Wordsworth's initial despondency upon crossing the Alps in Book VI parallels Bruce's surprising melancholy on supposedly discovering the Nile's source.*

At three quarters after one we arrived at the top of the mountain, whence we had a distinct view of all the remaining territory of Sacala, the mountain Geesh, and the church of St Michael Geesh, about a mile and a half distant from St Michael Sacala, where we then were. We saw, immediately below us, the Nile itself, strangely diminished in size, and now only a brook that had scarcely water to turn a mill. I could not satiate myself with the sight, revolving in my mind all those classical prophecies that had given the Nile up to perpetual obscurity and concealment. . . . I enjoyed here, for the first time, the triumph which already, by the protection of Providence, and my own intrepidity, I had gained over all that were powerful, and all that were learned, since the remotest antiquity. . . .

'Come, come, said I [to the guide Woldo], we understand each other; no more words; it is now late, lose no more time, but carry me to Geesh, and the head of the Nile directly, without preamble, and shew me the hill that separates me from it. He then carried me round to the south side of the church, out of the grove of trees that surrounded it, 'This is the hill, says he, looking archly, that, when you was on the other side of it, was between you and the fountains of the Nile; there is no other; look at that hillock of green sod in the middle of that watery spot, it is in that the two fountains of the Nile are to be found: Geesh is on the face of the rock where yon green trees are: if you go the length of the fountains pull off your shoes as you did the other day, for these people are all Pagans, worse than those that were at the ford, and they believe in nothing that you believe, but only in this river, to which they pray every day as if it were God; but this perhaps you may do likewise.' Half undressed as I was by loss of my sash, and throwing my shoes off, I ran down the hill towards the little island of green sods, which was about two hundred yards distant; the whole side of the hill was thick grown over with flowers, the large bulbous roots of which appearing above the surface of the ground, and their skins coming off on treading upon them, occasioned two very severe falls before I reached the brink of the marsh; I after this came to the island of green turf, which was in the form of an altar, apparently the work of art, and I stood in rapture over the principal fountain which rises in the middle of it.

It is easier to guess than to describe the situation of my mind at that moment – standing in that spot which had baffled the genius, industry, and inquiry of both ancients and moderns, for the course of near three thousand years. Kings had attempted this discovery at the head of armies, and each expedition was distinguished from the last, only by the difference of the numbers which had perished, and agreed alone in the disappointment which had uniformly, and without exception, followed them all. Fame, riches, and honour, had been held out for a series of ages to every individual of those myriads these princes commanded, without having produced one man capable of gratifying the curiosity of his sovereign, or wiping off this stain upon the enterprise and abilities of mankind, or adding this desideratum for the encouragement of geography. Though a mere private Briton, I triumphed here, in my own mind, over kings and their armies; and every comparison was leading nearer and nearer to presumption, when the place itself where I stood, the object of my vain-glory, suggested what depressed my short-lived triumphs. I was but a few minutes arrived at the sources of the Nile, through numberless dangers and sufferings, the least of which would have overwhelmed me but for the continual goodness and protection of Providence; I was, however, but then half through my journey, and all those dangers which I had already passed, awaited me again on my return. I found a despondency gaining ground fast upon me, and blasting the crown of laurels I had too rashly woven for myself. I resolved therefore to divert, till I could on more solid reflection overcome its progress.

I saw Strates expecting me on the side of the hill. 'Strates, said I, faithful squire, come and triumph with your Don Quixote[6] at that island of Barataria

---

6 The eponymous hero of the seventeenth-century Spanish novel by Miguel de Cervantes Saavedra.

where we have wisely and fortunately brought ourselves; come and triumph with me over all the kings of the earth, all their armies, all their philosophers, and all their heroes. . . . Come, said I, take a draught of this excellent water, and drink with me a health to his majesty king George III. and a long line of princes.' I had in my hand a large cup made of cocoa-nut shell, which I procured in Arabia, and which was brim-full. He drank to the king speedily and cheerfully, with the addition of, 'Confusion to his enemies,' and tossed up his cap with a loud huzza.

9.7 Samuel Taylor Coleridge, 'On the Slave Trade', *The Watchman* (1796)

In June 1795, Samuel Taylor Coleridge (1772–1834) gave his powerful lecture 'On the Slave Trade' in the slave port of Bristol, publishing it the following March in his newspaper The Watchman. *Coleridge began the lecture with a critique of the role of 'imaginary wants' in the slave trade (citing the demand for unnecessary luxuries such as 'Sugars, Rum, Cotton, Logwood, Cocoa, Coffee, Pimento, Ginger, Indigo, Mahogany, and Conserves') and comparing the conditions of slaves to those of the 'Inhabitants of Hell' in Dante's* Inferno.

The Abbe Raynal[7] computes that at the time of his writing, nine millions of slaves had been consumed by the Europeans – add one million since, (for it is near thirty years since his book was first published) and recollect, that for one procured ten at least are slaughtered, that a fifth die in the passage, and a third in the seasoning; and the calculation will amount to ONE HUNDRED and EIGHTY MILLION! Ye who have joined in this confederacy, ask of yourselves this fearful question – 'if the God of Justice inflict on us that mass only of anguish which we have wantonly heaped on our brethren, what must a state of retribution be?' But who are they who have joined in this tartarean[8] confederacy? Who are these kidnappers, and assassins? In all reasonings neglecting the intermediate links we attribute the final effect to the first cause. And what is the first and constantly acting cause of the Slave-trade? That cause, by which it exists and deprived of which it would immediately cease? Is it not self-evidently the consumption of it's products? And does not then the guilt rest on the consumers? And is it not an allowed axiom in morality, that wickedness may be multiplied, but cannot be divided; and that the guilt of all, attaches to each one who is knowingly an accomplice? Think not of the slave-captains and slave-holders! these very men,

---

7 Guillaume Thomas François Raynal, *L'Histoire philosophique et politique des établissements et du commerce des Européens dans les deux Indes*, 1770.
8 Relating to Hades.

their darkened minds, and brutalized hearts, will prove one part of the dreadful charge against you. They are more to be pitied than the slaves; because more depraved. I address myself to you who independently of all political distinctions, profess yourself Christians! As you hope to live with Christ hereafter, you are commanded to do unto others as ye would that others should do unto you. Would you choose, that a slave merchant should incite an intoxicated Chieftain to make war on your Country, and murder your Wife and Children before your face, or drag them with yourself to the Market? Would you choose to be sold, to have the hot iron hiss upon your breasts, after having been crammed into the hold of a Ship with so many fellow-victims, that the heat and stench, arising from your diseased bodies, should rot the very planks? Would you that others should do this unto you? and if you shudder with selfish horror at the bare idea, do you yet dare be the occasion of it to others? – The application to the Legislature was altogether wrong. I am not convinced that on any occasion a Christian is justified in calling on the interference of secular power; but on the present occasion it was superfluous. If only one tenth part among you who profess yourselves Christians, if one half only of the Petitioners, instead of bustling about with ostentatious sensibility, were to leave off – not *all* the West-India commodities – but only Sugar and Rum, the one useless and the other pernicious – all this misery might be stopped. Gracious heaven! At your meals you rise up, and pressing you hands to your bosoms, you lift up your eyes to God, and say, 'O Lord! bless the food which thou hast given us!' A part of that food among most of you, is sweetened with Brother's Blood. 'Lord! bless the food which thou hast given us!' O Blasphemy! Did God give food mingled with the blood of the Murdered? Will God bless the food which is polluted with the Blood of his own innocent children? Surely if the inspired Philanthropist of Gallilee were to revisit Earth, and be among the Feasters as at Cana, he would not now change water into wine, but convert the produce into the things producing, the occasion into the things occasioned. Then with our fleshly eye should we behold what even now Imagination ought to paint to us; instead of conserves, tears and blood, and for music, groanings and the loud peals of the lash.

There is observable among the Many a false and bastard sensibility that prompts them to remove those evils and those evils alone, which by hideous spectacle or clamorous outcry are present to their senses, and disturb their selfish enjoyments. Other miseries, though equally certain and far more horrible, they not only do not endeavour to remedy – they support, they fatten on them. Provided the dunghill be not before their parlour window, they are well content to know that it exists, and that it is the hot-bed of their pestilent luxuries. – To this grievous failing we must attribute the frequency of wars, and the continuance of the Slave-trade. The merchant finds no argument against it in his ledger: the citizen at the crouded feast is not nauseated by the stench and filth of the slave-vessel – the fine lady's nerves are not shattered by the shrieks! She sips a beverage sweetened with human blood, even while she is weeping over the refined sorrows of Werter[9] or of Clementina![10] Sensibility is not Benevolence. Nay, by making us tremblingly alive to trifling misfortunes, it frequently prevents it, and induces effeminate and cowardly selfishness. Our own sorrows, like the Princes of Hell in Milton's Pandemonium, sit enthroned 'bulky and vast:'[11] while the miseries of our fellow-creatures dwindle into pigmy forms, and are crouded, an innumerable multitude, into some dark corner of the heart. There is one criterion by which we may always distinguish benevolence from mere sensibility – Benevolence impels to action, and is accompanied by self-denial.

9.8 Maria Edgeworth and Richard Lovell Edgeworth, *Practical Education* (1798)

In their manual Practical Education, *Maria Edgeworth (1767–1849) and her father Richard Lovell Edgeworth (1744–1817) give an interesting account of the popularity of the literature of 'voyages and travel', citing as examples two early novels of shipwreck and adventure – Daniel Defoe's* Robinson Crusoe *(1719) and Jonathan Swift's* Gulliver's Travels *(1726) – and the story of Sinbad the Sailor from the Arabian collection* The Book of One Thousand and One Nights.

There is a class of books which amuse the imagination of children without acting upon their feelings. We do not allude to fairy tales, for we apprehend that these are not now much read, but we mean voyages and travels; these interest young people universally. Robinson Crusoe, Gulliver, and the Three Russian Sailors, who were cast away upon the coast of Norway, are general favourites. No child ever read an account of a shipwreck, or even a storm, without pleasure. A desert island is a delightful place, to be equalled only by the skating land of the rein-deer, or by the valley of the diamonds in the Arabian tales. Savages, especially if they be cannibals, are sure to be admired, and the more hair breadth escapes the hero of the tale has survived, and the more marvellous his adventures, the more sympathy he excites.

Will it be thought to proceed from a spirit of contradiction if we remark, that this species of reading should not early be chosen for boys of an enterprising temper, unless they are intended for a seafaring life, or for the army. The taste for adventure is absolutely incompatible with the sober perseverance necessary to success in any other liberal professions. . . .

---

9 Hero of Goethe's novel of sensibility, *The Sorrows of Young Goethe* (1774).

10 Figure in Samuel Richardson's *The History of Sir Charles Grandison* (1754).

11 John Milton, *Paradise Lost*, I: 196–7.

When a young man deliberates upon what course of life he shall follow, the patient drudgery of a trade, the laborious mental exertions requisite to prepare him for a profession, must appear to him in a formidable light, compared with the alluring prospects presented by an adventuring imagination. At this time of life it will be too late suddenly to change the taste; it will be inconvenient, if not injurious, to restrain a young man's inclinations by force or authority; it will be imprudent, perhaps fatally imprudent, to leave them uncontrolled. Precautions should therefore be taken long before this period, and the earlier they are taken the better. It is not idle refinement to assert, that the first impressions which are made upon the imagination, though they may be changed by subsequent circumstances, yet are discernible in every change, and are seldom entirely effaced from the mind, though it may be difficult to trace them through all their various appearances. A boy, who at seven years old longs to be Robinson Crusoe, or Sinbad the sailor, may at seventeen retain the same taste for adventure and enterprise, though mixed so as to be less discernible, with the incipient passions of avarice and ambition; he has the same dispositions modified by a slight knowledge of real life, and guided by the manners and conversations of his friends and acquaintance. Robinson Crusoe and Sindbad will no longer be his favourite heroes; but he will now admire the soldier of fortune, the commercial adventurer, or the nabob, who has discovered in the east the secret of Aladdin's wonderful lamp; and who has realised the treasures of Aboulcasem.

9.9   Mungo Park, *Travels in the Interior Districts of Africa: Performed under the Direction and Patronage of the African Association, in the Years 1795, 1796, and 1797* (1799)

In 1795 the Scottish explorer Mungo Park (1771–1806) undertook an expedition to the west of Africa in search of the River Niger. As Park's title acknowledges, this expedition was sponsored by the African Association, an organization established by Sir Joseph Banks in 1788 which sought to gather information about the continent. In the opening of his very successful account of his quest, Travels in the Interior Districts of Africa, Park *describes his hopes of 'rendering the geography of Africa more familiar to my countrymen, and . . . opening to their ambition and industry new sources of wealth, and new channels of commerce', illustrating, as a number of critics have pointed out, the coming together of scientific and commercial ambitions within the nation's mission. In the following extract, perhaps the best known passage from the volume, Park describes how, after having been robbed, he finds comfort in the natural world (described in the language of the botanist) and religion, locating his own undertaking within a larger divine scheme.*

Aug. 25th.   I departed from Kooma, accompanied by two shepherds, who were going towards Sibidooloo. The road was very steep and rocky, and as my horse had hurt his feet much in coming from Bammakoo, he travelled slowly and with great difficulty; for in many places the ascent was so sharp, and the declivities so great, that if he had made one false step, he must inevitably have been dashed to pieces. The shepherds being anxious to proceed, gave themselves little trouble about me or my horse, and kept walking on at a considerable distance. It was about eleven o'clock, as I stopped to drink a little water at a rivulet (my companions being near a quarter of a mile before me), that I heard some people calling to each other, and presently a loud screaming, as from a person in great distress. I immediately conjectured that a lion had taken one of the shepherds, and mounted my horse to have a better view of what had happened. The noise, however, ceased; and I rode slowly towards the place from whence I thought it had proceeded, calling out; but without receiving any answer. In a little time, however, I perceived one of the shepherds lying among the long grass near the road; and though I could see no blood upon him, I concluded he was dead. But when I came close to him, he whispered to me to stop; telling me that a party of armed men had seized upon his companion, and shot two arrows at himself, as he was making his escape. I stopped to consider what course to take, and looking round, saw at a little distance a man sitting upon the stump of a tree: I distinguished also the heads of six or seven more, sitting among the grass, with muskets in their hands. I had now no hopes of escaping, and therefore determined to ride forward towards them. As I approached them, I was in hopes they were elephant hunters; and by way of opening the conversation, inquired if they had shot any thing; but without returning an answer, one of them ordered me to dismount; and then, as if recollecting himself, waved with his hand for me to proceed. I accordingly rode past, and had with some difficulty crossed a deep rivulet, when I heard somebody holloa; and looking behind, saw those I had taken for elephant hunters, running after me, and calling out to me to turn back. I stopped until they were all come up; when they informed me, that the King of the Foulahs had sent them on purpose to bring me, my horse, and every thing that belonged to me, to Fooladoo; and that therefore I must turn back, and go along with them. Without hesitating a moment, I turned round and followed them, and we travelled together near a quarter of a mile, without exchanging a word; when coming to a dark place in a wood, one of them said, in the Mandingo language, 'this place will do;' and immediately snatched my hat from my head. Though I was by no means free of apprehension, yet I resolved to show as few signs of fear as possible, and therefore told them, that unless my hat was returned to me, I should proceed no further. But before I had time to receive an answer, another drew his knife, and seizing upon a metal button which remained upon my waistcoat, cut it off, and put it into his pocket. Their intentions were now obvious; and I thought that the easier they were permitted to rob me of everything, the less I had to fear. I therefore allowed them to search my pockets without resistance, and examine every part of my apparel, which they did with the most scrupulous exactness. But observing that I had one waistcoat under another, they insisted that I should cast them both off; and at last, to make sure work, they stripped me quite naked. Even my half boots (though the sole of one of them was tied on to my foot with a broken bridle-rein), were minutely inspected. Whilst they were examining the plunder, I begged them, with great earnestness, to return my pocket compass; but when I pointed it out to them, as it was lying on the ground, one of the banditti, thinking I was about to take it up, cocked his musket and swore that he would lay me dead upon the spot, if I presumed to put my hand upon it. After this, some of them went away with my horse, and the remainder stood considering whether they should leave me quite naked, or allow me something to shelter me from the sun. Humanity at last prevailed: they returned me the worst of the two shirts, and a pair of trousers; and, as they went away, one of them threw back my hat, in the crown of which I kept my memorandums; and this was probably the reason they did not wish to keep it. After they were gone, I sat for some time, looking around me within amazement and terror. Which ever way I turned, nothing appeared but danger and difficulty. I saw myself in the midst of a vast wilderness, in the depth of the rainy season; naked and alone; surrounded by savage animals, and men still more savage. I was five hundred miles from the nearest European settlement. All these circumstances crowded at once on my recollection; and I confess that my spirits began to fail me. I considered my fate as certain, and that I had no alternative, but to lie down and perish. The influence of religion, however, aided and supported me. I reflected that no human prudence or foresight, could possibly have averted my present sufferings. I was indeed a stranger in a strange land, yet I was still under the protecting eye of that Providence who has condescended to call himself the stranger's friend. At this moment, painful as my reflections were, the extraordinary beauty of a small moss, in fructification, irresistibly caught my eye. I mention this to show from what trifling circumstances the mind will sometimes derive consolation; for though the whole plant was not larger than the top of one of my fingers, I could not contemplate the delicate conformation of its roots, leaves, and capsula, without admiration. Can that Being (thought I), who planted, watered, and brought to perfection, in this obscure part of the world, a thing which appears of so small importance, look within unconcern upon the situation and sufferings of creatures formed after his own image? – surely not! Reflections like these, would not allow me to despair. I started up, and disregarding both hunger and fatigue, travelled forwards, assured that relief was at hand; and I was not disappointed. In a short time I came to a small village, at the entrance of which I overtook the two shepherds who had come with me from Kooma. They were much surprised to see me; for they said, they never doubted that the Foulahs, when they had robbed, had murdered me. Departing from this village, we travelled over several rocky ridges, and at sunset, arrived at Sibidooloo; the frontier town of the kingdom of Manding.

9.10   James Mill, *The History of British India* (1817)

The Scottish philosopher James Mill (1773–1836) took eleven years to research and write his seven-volume History of British India, *in which he applies Utilitarian methods and principles (see extract 2.3). As the following extracts illustrate, Mill's attitude to India is very different from that of the orientalist scholar and poet William Jones (extract 9.1), drawing on a vast range of materials to present a vision of Hindu life and culture as immoral and barbaric and requiring the civilizing influence of Britain.*

In regard to the moral character of the Hindus, sources of information have recently been opened, to which more than usual attention is due.

In the year 1801, the Governor General in Council of Bengal addressed a number of interrogatories, to the judges of circuit, and the judges of districts, with a view to ascertain some of the more important circumstances in the situation of the people placed under the British authority. Of these interrogatories one related expressly to the moral character of the people. The answers returned by the judges to this interrogatory were printed by order of the House of Commons, in the year 1813; and compose a curious and authentic document. . . .

Of the answers returned by the judges to the interrogatory of government, two or three, on the excuse of ignorance, give no opinion; and one describes the morals of the people, in the district to which, it alludes, as far better than the morals of those in some other districts. In all the rest, without one exception, the report presented is exceedingly unfavourable. The judges of the Calcutta court of appeal and circuit declare, 'From the frequent instances that come before us, of duplicity, fraud, ingratitude and falsehood, we consider the moral character of the natives depraved to a degree.' The magistrates of the twenty-four pergunnahs say, 'We are sorry that we cannot make any favourable report respecting the moral character of the inhabitants of the districts subject to our jurisdiction. The lower classes are in general profligate and depraved: The moral duties are little attended to by the higher ones. All are litigious in the extreme; and the crime of perjury was never, we believe, more frequently practised amongst all ranks than at present.' The magistrate of the city of Dacca replies, 'The inhabitants of Bengal, in general, have that excessive feebleness of mind, which, far from resisting, appears to foster the baser passions, and in the criminal indulgence of which every moral principle seems to be forgotten.' The magistrate of Backergunge declares, 'The general moral character of the inhabitants of this district is at the lowest pitch of infamy; and very few exceptions, indeed, to this character are to be found. There is no species of fraud or villany the higher classes will not be guilty of; and to these crimes, in the lower classes, may be added murder, robbery, theft, wounding, &c., on the slightest occasion.' The judges of the Moorshedabad court of appeal and circuit affirm, 'The general moral character of the inhabitants of our division seems, in our opinion, much the same as we have always known the moral character of the natives in general. Ignorance; and its concomitant, gross superstition; an implicit faith in the efficacy of prayers, charms, and magic; selfishness, low cunning, litigiousness, avarice, revenge, disregard to truth, and indolence, are the principal features to be traced.' The magistrate of Juanpore says, 'I have observed, among the inhabitants of this country, some possessed of abilities qualified to rise to eminence in other countries; but a moral, virtuous man, I have never met with among them.' . . .

The missionary Mr. Ward, who has profited so greatly by the peculiar advantages which a missionary enjoys, has the following passage, corroborated by a variety of details.

'The Rev. Mr. Maurice seems astonished that a people, so mild, so benevolent, so benignant as the Hindoos . . . should have adopted so many bloody rites. But are these Hindoos indeed so humane? – these men, and women too, who drag their dying relations to the banks of the river at all seasons, day and night, and expose them to the heat and cold in the last agonies of death, without remorse; – who assist men to commit self-murder, encouraging them to swing with hooks in their backs, to pierce their tongues and sides, to cast themselves on naked knives, to bury themselves alive, throw themselves into rivers, from precipices, and under the cars of their idols; – who murder their own children, by burying them alive, throwing them to the alligators, or hanging them up alive in trees for the ants and crows before their own doors, or by sacrificing them to the Ganges; – who burn alive, amidst savage shouts, the heart-broken widow, by the hands of her own son, and with the corpse of a deceased father; – who every year butcher thousands of animals, at the call of superstition, covering themselves with their blood, consigning their carcases to the dogs, and carrying their heads in triumph through the streets? – Are these "the benignant Hindoos?" – a people who have never erected a charity school, an alms'-house, nor an hospital; who suffer their fellow creatures to perish for want before their very doors, refusing to administer to their wants while living, or to inter their bodies, to prevent their being devoured by vultures and jackals, when dead; who, when the power of the sword was in their hands, impaled alive, cut off the noses, the legs, and arms of culprits; and inflicted punishments exceeded only by those of the followers of the mild, amiable, and benevolent Boodhu, in the Burman empire! and who very often, in their acts of pillage, murder the plundered, cutting off their limbs with the most cold-blooded apathy, turning the house of the murdered into a disgusting shambles! – Some of these cruelties, no doubt, arise out of the religion of the Hindoos, and are the poisoned fruits of superstition, rather than the effects of natural disposition: but this is equally true respecting the virtues which have been so lavishly bestowed on this people. At the call of the shastru,[12] the Hindoo gives water to the weary traveller during the month Voishakhu; but he may perish at his door without pity or relief from the first of the following month, no reward being attached to such an act after these thirty days have expired. He will make roads, pools of water, and build lodging-houses for

---

12 Hindu sacred scripture.

pilgrims and travellers; but he considers himself as making a good bargain with the gods in all these transactions. It is a fact, that there is not a road in the country made by Hindoos except a few which lead to holy places; and had there been no future rewards held out for such acts of merit, even these would not have existed. Before the kulee-yoogu it was lawful to sacrifice cows; but the man who does it now, is guilty of a crime as heinous as that of killing a bramhun:[13] he may kill a buffalo, however, and Doorga[14] will reward him with heaven for it. A Hindoo, by any direct act, should not destroy an insect, for he is taught that God inhabits even a fly: but it is no great crime if he should permit even his cow to perish with hunger; and he beats it without mercy, though it be an incarnation of Bhuguvutee – it is enough, that he does not really deprive it of life; for the indwelling Brumhu feels no stroke but that of death. The Hindoo will utter falsehoods that would knock down an ox, and will commit perjuries so atrocious and disgusting, as to fill with horror those who visit the courts of justice; but he will not violate his shastru by swearing on the waters of the Ganges.'

---

13 Brahmin, member of the highest caste in Hindu society.
14 A Hindu god.

10
Science

Introduction

The word 'scientist' was first used in the 1830s, signalling a shift away from the integrated and comprehensive idea of 'natural philosophy' in which emerging disciplines such as astronomy, chemistry, geology, botany, biology, and electromagnetism were part of a more general 'enquiry into the phenomena and powers of nature', to use Richard Yeo's phrase.[1] Rather than being seen in a modern way as a number of rarefied and discrete fields that could be understood only by the specialist, natural philosophy was regarded as working alongside other forms of knowledge, including literature. Erasmus Darwin used verse to present scientific ideas to the public (extract 10.3), while in his poem 'Religious Musings', Samuel Taylor Coleridge presented 'Philosophers and Bards' as united in their endeavours (ll. 227–30). In the 1790s, when Coleridge wrote this poem, science was seen as fundamentally interlinked with ethical, religious, political, and literary debates. The anxiety expressed in a text like *Frankenstein*, written two decades later, was that science was beginning to cut itself free of its responsibilities to these wider concerns.

The relationship of scientific debates to political and theological issues can be illustrated with reference to two of the major controversies of the period, which are focused on in the following extracts, the geological disputes over the formation of the earth (extracts 10.2, 10.8, 10.9) and the medical disputes over vitalism (extracts 10.6 and 10.7). When James Hutton presented his theories of the gradual and cyclical formation of the earth (extract 10.2), his emphasis on the huge expanse of time such developments required (what is now known as 'deep time') implicitly undermined biblical narratives of the creation, in which the earth had been brought into being just 6,000 years ago. While he presents the process as evidence of a beneficent Nature that is 'wise and good', his later comment that 'we find no vestige of a beginning, no prospect of an end' exemplified for many the challenge his theory posed to conventional ideas of God's

---

1 'Natural Philosophy (Science)', *An Oxford Companion to the Romantic Age*, ed. Iain McCalman et al. (Oxford: Oxford University Press, 1999), p. 321. Yeo provides an excellent introduction to the subject, as does Tim Fulford in his essay 'Science' in *Romanticism: An Oxford Guide*, ed. Nicholas Roe (Oxford: Oxford University Press, 2005), pp. 90–101.

role. A possible solution for those who sought to reconcile science and theology was offered by the theories of the French scientist Georges Cuvier (extract 10.8), whose account of the earth's formation through a series of catastrophes seemed compatible with biblical accounts of Noah's flood, as the Oxford geologist William Buckland argued. It was one of Buckland's former pupils, Charles Lyell, who influentially challenged this linking of catastrophism and biblical narrative, emphasizing the need for empirical evidence rather than speculation, and establishing what has become known as 'uniformitarianism' (the uniform process of change through time) as the basis of modern geology.

The political as well as theological dimensions of scientific controversies in the period can be seen in the fierce debates over 'vitalism', the issue of whether life is a separate substance added to the body (a position often linked in discussions to belief in an immortal soul) or simply the product of the organization of matter (a materialist position). As Nicholas Roe has shown in a lively account, when the poet, orator and leader of the London Corresponding Society John Thelwall lectured on 'Animal Vitality' in 1793, his adoption of the materialist position highlighted the perceived link between atheism and radicalism.[2] In his lecture, Thelwall addressed the 'general question' of 'Whether life itself is to be considered as a distinct and positive essence, or, simply, as the result of a particular harmony and correspondence of the whole, or aggregate combination, preserved and acted upon by a particular stimulus?'[3] This was a highly divisive issue, raising the question of the role (or absence) of the divine in relation to human life. It divided thinkers into 'vitalists', who believed in this 'distinct and positive essence', such as the surgeon John Hunter, and materialists, who saw life as a product of the composition of the body, such as Thelwall himself. When the controversy was re-ignited two decades later in an exchange of lectures between the surgeons John Abernethy and William Lawrence (extracts 10.6 and 10.7), support tended to be polarized between Christian conservatives and freethinking liberals (or radicals). For example, when Lawrence was suspended by the Royal College of Surgeons and asked to suppress his lectures, he did so only for them to be serialized by the radical freethinker Richard Carlile, who denounced the treatment of Lawrence as an example of the continued ideological power of 'Priestcraft'.

Literary writers engaged closely with these scientific controversies. Byron drew on Cuvier's theories of catastrophe in a number of works, including *Cain*, *Heaven and Hell*, and *Don Juan*, and in *Beachy Head* Charlotte Smith examined the fossils found in the limestone at her feet – 'fantastic shapes / Of bivalves, and

---

2 Nicholas Roe, *Samuel Taylor Coleridge and the Sciences of Life* (Oxford: Oxford University Press, 2001), pp. 1–6. Roe reprints Thelwall's essay in his *Politics of Nature*, 2nd edn (Basingstoke: Palgrave Macmillan, 2002).

3 John Thelwall, *An Essay, Towards a Definition of Animal Vitality; read at the theatre, Guy's Hospital, January 26, 1793; in which several of the opinions of the celebrated John Hunter are examined and controverted* (London: T. Rickaby, 1793), p. 19.

inwreathed volutes' (ll. 379–80) – and joined in the contemporary geologic controversies: 'Or did this range of chalky mountains, once / Form a vast bason, where Ocean waves / Swell'd fathomless?' (ll. 382–4). Coleridge sided with Abernethy in the vitality debate, while the atheist Percy Shelley, who had known William Lawrence and had once planned to be a surgeon, wrote his own essay on the subject, 'On Life'. The most famous literary engagement with vitalism, of course, was Mary Shelley's *Frankenstein*, which also drew on the various experiments with electricity undertaken by Erasmus Darwin, Humphry Davy, Luigi Galvani, Alessandro Volta, and Giovanni Aldini (extract 10.5).

While Coleridge saw the potential in the 1790s for science and literature to unite in the pursuit of knowledge, a number of other writers questioned the nature of scientific pursuits, assessing them against what they conceived as more poetic ways of knowing the world. In 1780, Anna Barbauld wrote her poem 'The Mouse's Petition to Doctor Priestley Found in the Trap where he had been confined all Night', a witty retort to Priestley's accounts of his experiments (extract 10.1), which called for the modification of the scientific mind-set through the incorporation of compassion and pity, the central qualities of sentimental literature. In 1802, William Wordsworth expanded his 'Preface' to *Lyrical Ballads*, possibly in reponse to Davy's *Discourse* (extract 10.4), differentiating between the Poet and the 'Man of Science': 'The knowledge both of the Poet and the Man of Science is pleasure; but the knowledge of the one cleaves to us as a necessary part of our existence, our natural and unalienable inheritance; the other is a personal and individual acquisition, slow to come to us, and by no habitual and direct sympathy connecting us with our fellow-beings.'[4] And the best known Romantic scientist of all, Victor Frankenstein, is juxtaposed with the poetic figure of Henry Clerval, another kind of creator, who works not in the laboratory but in the imagination, as is emphasized by Victor's elegy for his friend:

> He was a being formed in the 'very poetry of nature'. His wild and enthusiastic imagination was chastened by the sensibility of his heart. . . . Has this mind so replete with ideas, imaginations fanciful and magnificent, which formed a world, whose existence depended on the life of its creator; has this mind perished?[5]

In this way, *Frankenstein* can be seen not simply as another Romantic text on science, but as a dramatization of the debates and tensions that characterize the period's ambivalent response to the scientific advancements of the age.

---

4 William Wordsworth, *The Major Works*, ed. Stephen Gill (Oxford: Oxford World's Classics, 2000), p. 606.
5 Mary Shelley, *Frankenstein: 1818 text*, ed. Marilyn Butler (Oxford: Oxford University Press, 1994), p. 130.

10.1   Joseph Priestley, *Experiments and Observations on Different Kinds of Air* (1775)

As well as being a Unitarian minister and political radical (extract 4.3), Joseph Priestley (1733–1804) was an experimental scientist, whose greatest discovery was oxygen, or what he termed 'dephlogisticated air'. In his account of the experiments which led to this breakthrough, he describes how he heated up red mercuric oxide in a 12-inch 'burning lens', producing the extraordinary gas whose properties he investigated in the manner outlined below. Priestley also carried out important research in a number of other scientific fields, most notably electricity and astronomy. In 1780 he settled in Birmingham, but his reputation as a radical (and specifically a reply to Burke) led to the destruction of his house, laboratory and library in a 'Church and King' riot in 1791.

On the 8th of this month [March 1775] I procured a mouse, and put it into a glass vessel, containing two ounce-measures of the air from mercurius calcinatus.[6] Had it been common air, a full-grown mouse, as this was, would have lived in it about a quarter of an hour. In this air, however, my mouse lived a full half hour; and though it was taken out seemingly dead, it appeared to have been only exceedingly chilled; for, upon being held to the fire, it presently revived, and appeared not to have received any harm from the experiment.

By this I was confirmed in my conclusion, that the air extracted from mercurius calcinatus, &c. was, *at least, as good* as common air; but I did not certainly conclude that it was any *better*; because, though one mouse would live only a quarter of an hour in a given quantity of air, I knew it was not impossible but that another mouse might have lived in it half an hour; so little accuracy is there in this method of ascertaining the goodness of air: and indeed I have never had recourse to it for my own satisfaction, since the discovery of that most ready, accurate, and elegant test that nitrous air furnishes. . . .

This experiment with the mouse, when I had reflected upon it some time, gave me so much suspicion that the air into which I had put it was better than common air, that I was induced, the day after, to apply the test of nitrous air to a small part of that very quantity of air which the mouse had breathed so long; so that, had it been common air, I was satisfied it must have been very nearly, if not altogether, as noxious as possible, so as not to be affected by nitrous air; when, to my surprize again, I found that though it had been breathed so long, it was still better than common air. For after mixing it with nitrous air, in the usual proportion of two to one, it was diminished in the proportion of $4\frac{1}{2}$ to $3\frac{1}{2}$; that is, the nitrous air had made it two ninths less than before, and this in a very short space of time; whereas I had never found that, in the longest time, any common air was reduced more than one fifth of its bulk by any proportion

---

6 Mercuric oxide.

of nitrous air, nor more than one fourth by any phlogistic process whatever. Thinking of this extraordinary fact upon my pillow, the next morning I put another measure of nitrous air to the same mixture, and, to my utter astonishment, found that it was farther diminished to almost one half of its original quantity. I then put a third measure to it; but this did not diminish it any farther: but, however, left it one measure less than it was even after the mouse had been taken out of it.

Being now fully satisfied that this air, even after the mouse had breathed it half an hour, was much better than common air; and having a quantity of it still left, sufficient for the experiment, viz. an ounce-measure and a half, I put the mouse into it; when I observed that it seemed to feel no shock upon being put into it, evident signs of which would have been visible, if the air had not been very wholesome; but that it remained perfectly at its ease another full half hour, when I took it out quite lively and vigorous. Measuring the air the next day, I found it to be reduced from 1½ to ⅔ of an ounce-measure. And after this, if I remember well (for in my *register* of the day I only find it noted, that it was *considerably diminished* by nitrous air) it was nearly as good as common air. It was evident, indeed, from the mouse having been taken out quite vigorous, that the air could not have been rendered very noxious.

For my farther satisfaction I procured another mouse, and putting it into less than two ounce-measures of air extracted from mercurius calcinatus and air from red precipitate (which, having found them to be of the same quality, I had mixed together) it lived three quarters of an hour. But not having had the precaution to set the vessel in a warm place, I suspect that the mouse died of cold. However, as it had lived three times as long as it could probably have lived in the same quantity of common air, and I did not expect much accuracy from this kind of test, I did not think it necessary to make any more experiments with mice.

10.2   James Hutton, *Abstract of a Dissertation read in the Royal Society of Edinburgh . . . Concerning the System of the Earth, its Duration, and Stability* (1785)

The pioneering Scottish geologist James Hutton (1726–97) challenged the dominant 'Neptunist' theories associated with Abraham Gottlob Werner that the earth had been created by a tremendous flood. He argued instead for a process in which 'the present land of the globe had been first formed at the bottom of the ocean, and then raised above the surface of the sea'. For Hutton this was a gradual and cyclical process as the heat of the earth forced compounded materials to the surface where they immediately began to decay, in turn providing the materials for the next cycle. Hutton's theory was termed 'Plutonist' (to define it against the 'Neptunist') and his emphasis on gradual change (as opposed to theories of catastrophic change, see extract 10.8) influenced the development of the geological concepts of 'deep time' and 'uniformitarianism'. In the

Abstract *of his theories delivered to the Royal Society of Edinburgh, Hutton emphasizes his methodology of close observation of the natural world and illustrates the ultimately providential nature of his vision of the earth's development.*

The purpose of this Dissertation is to form some estimate with regard to the time the globe of this Earth has existed, as a world maintaining plants and animals; to reason with regard to the changes which the earth has undergone; and to see how far an end or termination to this system of things may be perceived, from the consideration of that which has already come to pass.

As it is not in human record, but in natural history, that we are to look for the means of ascertaining what has already been, it is here proposed to examine the appearances of the earth, in order to be informed of operations which have been transacted in time past. It is thus that, from principles of natural philosophy, we may arrive at some knowledge of order and system in the oeconomy of this globe, and may form a rational opinion with regard to the course of nature, or to events which are in time to happen. . . .

A theory is thus formed, with regard to a mineral system. In this system, hard and solid bodies are to be formed from soft bodies, from loose or incoherent materials, collected together at the bottom of the sea; and the bottom of the ocean is to be made to change its place with relation to the centre of the earth, to be formed into land above the level of the sea, and to become a country fertile and inhabited.

That there is nothing visionary in this theory, appears from its having been rationally deduced from natural events, from things which have already happened; things which have left, in the particular constitution of bodies, proper traces of the manner of their production; and things which may be examined with all the accuracy, or reasoned upon with all the light, that science can afford. As it is only by employing science in this manner, that philosophy enlightens man with the knowledge of that wisdom or design which is to be found in nature, the system now proposed, from unquestionable principles, will claim the attention of scientific men, and may be admitted in our speculations with regard to the works of nature, notwithstanding many steps in the progress may remain unknown.

By thus proceeding upon investigated principles, we are led to conclude, that, if this part of the earth which we now inhabit had been produced, in the course of time, from the materials of a former earth, we should, in the examination of our land, find data from which to reason, with regard to the nature of that world, which had existed during the period of time in which the present earth was forming; and thus we might be brought to understand the nature of that earth which had preceded this; how far it had been similar to the present, in producing plants and nourishing animals. But this interesting point is perfectly ascertained, by finding abundance of every manner of vegetable production, as well as the several species of marine bodies, in the strata of our earth. . . .

[A]s there is not in human observation proper means for measuring the waste of land upon the globe, it is hence inferred, that we cannot estimate the duration of what we see at present, nor calculate the period at which it had begun; so that, with respect to human observation, this world has neither a beginning nor an end.

An endeavour is then made to support the theory by an argument of a moral nature, drawn from the consideration of a final cause. Here a comparison is formed between the present theory, and those by which there is necessarily implied either evil or disorder in natural things; and an argument is formed, upon the supported wisdom of nature, for the justness of a theory in which perfect order is perceived. For, [a]ccording to the theory, a soil, adapted to the growth of plants, is necessarily prepared, and carefully preserved; and, in the necessary waste of land which is inhabited, the foundation is laid for future continents, in order to support the system of this living world.

Thus, either in supposing Nature wise and good, an argument is formed in confirmation of the theory, or, in supposing the theory to be just, an argument may be established for wisdom and benevolence to be perceived in nature. In this manner, there is opened to our view a subject interesting to man who thinks; a subject on which to reason with relation to the system of nature; and one which may afford the human mind both information and entertainment.

10.3   Erasmus Darwin, 'The Loves of the Plants' and *The Temple of Nature* (1789 and 1803)

Erasmus Darwin (1731–1802) was a doctor and a member of the group of Enlightenment thinkers known as the Lunar Society (which also included James Watt, Matthew Boulton, Joseph Priestley and Josiah Wedgwood). A keen botanist, Darwin used poetry to present the classificatory system of the Swede Carolus Linnaeus (1707–78) to the wider public in his 'The Loves of the Plants' (1789), and included the poem in his very popular volume The Botanic Garden *(1791). In the 'Advertisement' for the volume, Darwin wrote that 'The general design of the following sheets is to inlist Imagination under the banner of Science, and to lead her votaries from the looser analogies, which dress out the imagery of poetry, to the stricter ones, which form the ratiocination of philosophy. While their particular design is to induce the ingenious to cultivate the knowledge of* BOTANY; *by introducing them to the vestibule of that delightful science, and recommending to their attention the immortal works of the Swedish Naturalist LINNEUS.' As the extract below illustrates, Darwin makes full use of the diction and techniques of late eighteenth-century sentimental verse in describing each species, presenting the Tremella fungus as the suffering victim of a clandestine marriage. Erasmus Darwin was the grandfather of the evolutionist Charles and anticipated some of the latter's theories, as is illustrated by the passage from the posthumously published* The Temple of Nature.

From 'The Loves of the Plants, A Poem', The Botanic Garden, 1791

In . . . LOVES OF THE PLANTS, which is here presented to the Reader, the Sexual System
of LINNEUS is explained, with the remarkable properties of many particular plants.

> BOTANIC MUSE! who in this latter age
> Led by your airy hand the Swedish sage,
> Bad his keen eye your secret haunts explore
> On dewy dell, high wood, and winding shore;
> Say on each leaf how tiny Graces dwell;
> How laugh the Pleasures in a blossom's bell;
> How insect-Loves arise on cob-web wings,
> Aim their light shafts, and point their little stings. . . .
>
> On DOVE's green brink the fair TREMELLA stood,[7]
> And view'd her playful image in the flood;
> To each rude rock, lone dell, and echoing grove
> Sung the sweet sorrows of her *secret* love.
> 'Oh, stay! – return!' – along the sounding shore
> Cry'd the sad Naiads, – she return'd no more! –
> Now girt with clouds the sullen Evening frown'd,
> And withering Eurus swept along the ground;
> The misty moon withdrew her horned light,
> And sunk with Hesper in the skirt of night;
> No dim electric streams, (the northern dawn,)
> With meek effulgence quiver'd o'er the lawn;
> No star benignant shot one transient ray
> To guide or light the wanderer on her way.
> Round the dark craggs the murmuring whirlwinds blow,
> Woods groan above, and waters roar below;
> As o'er the steeps with pausing foot she moves,
> The pitying Dryads shriek amid their groves;
> She flies,– she stops, – she pants – she looks behind,
> And hears a demon howl in every wind.
> – As the bleak blast unfurls her fluttering vest,
> Cold beats the snow upon her shuddering breast;
> Through her numb'd limbs the chill sensations dart,
> And the keen ice bolt trembles at her heart.
> 'I sink, I fall! oh, help me, help!' she cries,
> Her stiffening tongue the unfinish'd sound denies;
> Tear after tear adown her cheek succeeds,

---

7 Darwin's note: 'Clandestine marriage'.

And pearls of ice bestrew the glittering meads;
Congealing snows her lingering feet surround,
Arrest her flight, and root her to the ground;
With suppliant arms she pours the silent prayer;
Her suppliant arms hang crystal in the air;
Pellucid films her shivering neck o'erspread,
Seal her mute lips, and silver o'er her head,
Veil her pale bosom, glaze her lifted hands,
And shrined in ice the beauteous statue stands.
– DOVE's azure nymphs on each revolving year
For fair TREMELLA shed the tender tear;
With rush-wove crowns in sad procession move,
And sound the sorrowing shell to hapless love.

From The Temple of Nature, 1803

ORGANIC LIFE beneath the shoreless waves[8]
Was born and nurs'd in Ocean's pearly caves;
First forms minute, unseen by spheric glass,
Move on the mud, or pierce the watery mass;
These, as successive generations bloom,
New powers acquire, and larger limbs assume;
Whence countless groups of vegetation spring,
And breathing realms of fin, and feet, and wing.

Thus the tall Oak, the giant of the wood,
Which bears Britannia's thunders on the flood;
The Whale, unmeasured monster of the main,
The lordly Lion, monarch of the plain,
The Eagle soaring in the realms of air,
Whose eye undazzled drinks the solar glare,
Imperious man, who rules the bestial crowd,
Of language, reason, and reflection proud,
With brow erect who scorns this earthly sod,
And styles himself the image of his God;
Arose from rudiments of form and sense,
An embryon point[9], or microscopic ens!

---

8 Darwin's note: 'The earth was originally covered with water, as appears from some of its highest
mountains, consisting of shells cemented together by a solution of part of them, as the limestone
rocks of the Alps. . . . It must be therefore concluded, that animal life began beneath the sea.'
9 Darwin's note: 'The arguments showing that all vegetables and animals arose from such a small
beginning, as a living point or living fibre, are detailed in Zoonomia, Sect. XXXIX. 4.8. on
Generation.'

10.4 Humphry Davy, *A Discourse, Introductory to a Course of Lectures on Chemistry, delivered in the Theatre of the Royal Institution, on the 21st January* (1802)

The most famous scientist of the age, Humphry Davy (1778–1829) was a friend of Coleridge and Southey and helped Wordsworth with the proofs of the second edition of Lyrical Ballads. *Having begun as an assistant to Thomas Beddoes in Bristol, where he tested nitrous oxide (laughing gas) on his poetic friends, in 1802 Davy became professor of chemistry at the Royal Institution, delivering spectacular and popular lectures and working on electricity and Galvanism (see Figure 19 and also extract 10.5). His* Discourse *is a major statement of the role of the chemist and the value of science more generally. It has been seen as a text in dialogue with Wordsworth's 'Preface' to* Lyrical Ballads *and as the model for the self-aggrandizing rhetoric and ambitions of that most famous Romantic scientist, Victor Frankenstein.*

Chemistry is that part of Natural Philosophy which relates to those intimate actions of bodies upon each other, by which their appearances are altered, and their individuality destroyed.

This science has for its objects all the substances found upon our globe. It relates not only to the minute alterations in the external world, which are daily coming under the cognizance of our senses, and which, in consequence, are incapable of affecting the imagination; but likewise to the great changes and convulsions in nature, which, occurring but seldom, excite our curiosity, or awaken our astonishment.

The phenomena of combustion, of the solution of different substances in water, of the agencies of fire; the production of rain, hail, and snow, and the conversion of dead matter into living matter by vegetable organs, all belong to chemistry: and, in their various and apparently capricious appearances, can be accurately explained only by an acquaintance with the fundamental and general chemical principles. . . .

By means of this science man has employed almost all the substances in nature either for the satisfaction of his wants, or the gratification of his luxuries. Not contented with what is found upon the surface of the earth, he has penetrated into her bosom, and has even searched the bottom of the ocean, for the purpose of allaying the restlessness of his desires, or of extending and increasing his power. He is to a certain extent ruler of all the elements that surround him; and he is capable of using not only common matter according to his will and inclinations, but likewise of subjecting to his purposes the ethereal principles of heat and light. By his inventions they are elicited from the atmosphere; and under his control they become, according to circumstances, instruments of comfort and enjoyment, or of terror and destruction. . . .

Figure 19   James Gillray, 'Scientific Researches! – New Discoveries in Pneumaticks! – or – an Experimental Lecture on the Powers of Air', 23 May 1802; © Copyright the Trustees of the British Museum.

Gillray's caricature satirizes the recently founded Royal Institution and captures something of the sense of theatrical performance associated with its scientific demonstrations. The figure with the bellows is Humphry Davy, who had experimented with laughing gas on his friends the poets Samuel Taylor Coleridge and Robert Southey, and who would go on to become the Institution's star performer and professor of chemistry (see extract 10.4).

Man, in what is called a state of nature, is a creature of almost pure sensation. Called into activity only by positive wants, his life is passed either in satisfying the cravings of the common appetites, or in apathy, or in slumber. Living only in moments, he calculates but little on futurity. He has no vivid feelings of hope, or thoughts of permanent and powerful action. And, unable to discover causes, he is either harassed by superstitious dreams, or quietly and passively submitted to the mercy of nature and the elements. How different is man informed through the beneficence of the Deity, by science, and the arts! Knowing his wants, and being able to provide for them, he is capable of anticipating future enjoyments, and of connecting hope with an infinite variety of ideas. He is in some measure independent of chance or accident for his pleasures. Science has given to him an acquaintance with the different relations of the parts of the external world; and more than that, it has bestowed upon him powers which may be almost called creative; which have enabled him to modify and change the beings surrounding him, and by his experiments to interrogate nature with power, not simply as a scholar, passive and seeking only to understand her operations, but rather as a master, active with his own instruments.

But, though improved and instructed by the sciences, we must not rest contented with what has been done; it is necessary that we should likewise do. Our enjoyment of the fruits of the labours of former times should be rather an enjoyment of activity than of indolence; and, instead of passively admiring, we ought to admire with that feeling which leads to emulation.

Science has done much for man, but it is capable of doing still more; its sources of improvement are not yet exhausted; the benefits that it has conferred ought to excite our hopes of its capability of conferring new benefits; and, in considering the progressiveness of our nature, we may reasonably look forwards to a state of greater cultivation and happiness than that which we at present enjoy.

As a branch of sublime philosophy, chemistry is far from being perfect. It consists of a number of collections of facts, connected together by different relations; but as yet it is not furnished with a precise and beautiful theory. Though we can perceive, develope [sic], and even produce, by means of our instruments of experiment, an almost infinite variety of minute phenomena, yet we are incapable of determining the general laws by which they are governed; and, in attempting to define them, we are lost in obscure, though sublime imaginations concerning unknown agencies. That they may be discovered, however, there is every reason to believe. And who would not be ambitious of becoming acquainted with the most profound secrets of nature; of ascertaining her hidden operations; and of exhibiting to men that system of knowledge which relates so intimately to their own physical and moral constitution? . . .

At the beginning of the seventeenth century, very little was known concerning the philosophy of the intimate actions of bodies on each other: and before this time vague ideas, superstitious notions, and inaccurate practices, were the only effects of the first efforts of the mind to establish the foundations of chemistry. Men either were astonished and deluded by their first inventions, so as to become visionaries, and to institute researches after imaginary things, or they employed them as instruments for astonishing and deluding others, influenced by their dearest passions and interests, by ambition, or the love of money. Hence arose the dreams of Alchemy concerning the philosophers stone and the elixir of life. Hence for a long while the other metals were destroyed, or rendered useless, by experiments designed to transmute them into gold; and for a long while the means of obtaining earthly immortality were sought for amidst the unhealthy vapours of the laboratory. These views of things have passed away, and a new science has gradually arisen. The dim and uncertain twilight of discovery, which gave to objects false or indefinite appearances, has been succeeded by the steady light of truth, which has shown the external world in its distinct forms, and in its true relations to human powers. The composition of the atmosphere, and the properties of the gases, have been ascertained; the phenomena of electricity have been developed; the lightnings have been taken from the clouds; and, lastly, a new influence has been discovered, which has enabled man to produce from combinations of dead matter effects which were formerly occasioned only by animal organs. . . .

To the man of business, or of mechanical employment, the pursuit of experi-mental research may afford a simple pleasure, unconnected with the gratifica-tion of unnecessary wants, and leading to such an expansion of the faculties of the mind as must give to it dignity and power. To the refined and fashionable classes of society it may become a source of consolation and of happiness, in those moments of solitude when the common habits and passions of the world are considered with indifference. It may destroy diseases of the imagination, owing to too deep a sensibility; and it may attach the affections to objects, permanent, important, and intimately related to the interests of the human species. Even to persons of powerful minds, who are connected with society by literary, political, or moral relations, an acquaintance with the science that represents the operations of nature cannot be wholly useless. It must strengthen their habits of minute discrimination; and, by obliging them to use a language representing simple facts, may tend to destroy the influence of terms connected only with feeling. The man who has been accustomed to study natural objects philosophically, to be perpetually guarding against the delusions of the fancy, will not readily be induced to multiply words so as to forget things. From observ-ing in the relations of inanimate things fitness and utility, he will reason with deeper reverence concerning beings possessing life: and, perceiving in all the phenomena of the universe the designs of a perfect intelligence, he will be averse to the turbulence and passion of hasty innovations, and will uniformly appear as the friend of tranquillity and order.

10.5   Giovanni Aldini, *An Account of the Late Improvements in Galvanism, with a series of curious and interesting experiments performed before the commissioners of the French National Institute, and repeated lately in the anatomical theatres of London, by John Aldini. To which is added an Appendix, containing the Author's experiments on the body of a malefactor executed at Newgate* (1803)

The Italian physicist Giovanni Aldini (1762–1834) was the nephew of Luigi Galvani (1737–98). Galvani had experimented with electricity on the legs of frogs, making them jump even when detached from their bodies, leading to his conclusion that there was an 'animal electricity' carried by the nerves to the muscles which caused activity. One development of Galvani's work was the research of Alessandro Volta who developed the first battery, while Aldini carried out further experiments in Galvanism, as described in his popular Account of the Late Improvements. *According to Mary Shelley, hearing Byron and Shelley discuss these issues in the summer of 1816 was a direct inspiration for* Frankenstein: *'Perhaps a corpse would be reanimated; galvanism had given token of such things: perhaps the component parts of a creature might be manufactured, brought together, and endued with vital warmth.'*[10]

Experiments made on human bodies after death.

From the experiments already described [frog, ox, horses], one might by analogy conjecture what effect the action of Galvanism would produce on that noble being man, the sole object of my researches. But to enable philosophers to judge with more certainty respecting the effects of this wonderful agent, it was necessary to adhere to certain conditions, and to apply it immediately after death. The bodies of persons who had died of disease were not proper for my purpose; because it is to be presumed, that the development of the principle which occasions death destroys the elasticity of the fibres, and that the humours are changed from their natural to a corrupted state. It was therefore necessary to obtain the human body while it still retained, after death, the vital powers in the highest degree of preservation; and hence I was obliged, if I may be allowed the expression, to place myself under the scaffold, near the axe of justice, to receive the yet bleeding bodies of unfortunate criminals, the only subjects proper for my experiments. In consequence of an application made for that purpose, I obtained from Government the bodies of two brigands, who were decapitated at Bologna in the month of January 1802. As both these individuals had been very young, and of a robust constitution, and as the parts exhibited the utmost soundness, I entertained strong hopes of obtaining the happiest results from my proposed researches. Though accustomed to a more tranquil kind of operations in my closet, and little acquainted with anatomical dissections, the love of truth, and a desire to throw some light on the system of Galvanism, overcame all my repugnance, and I proceeded to the following experiments.

EXPERIMENT XXII

The first of these decapitated criminals being conveyed to the apartment provided for my experiments, in the neighbourhood of the place of execution, the head was first subjected to the Galvanic action. For this purpose I had constructed a pile consisting of a hundred pieces of silver and zinc. Having moistened the inside of the ears with salt water, I formed an arc with two metallic wires, which, proceeding from the two ears, were applied, one to the summit and the other to the bottom of the pile. When this communication was established, I observed strong contractions in all the muscles of the face, which were

---

10 Author's Introduction (1831), *Frankenstein: 1818 text*, pp. 195–6.

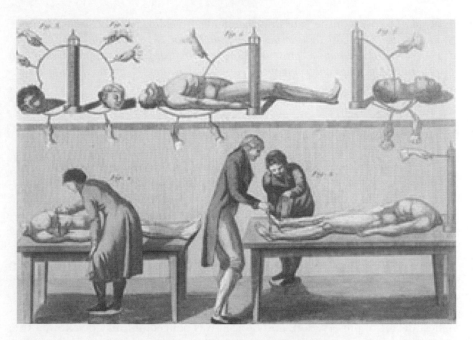

Figure 20 Giovanni Aldini, *Essai Théoretique et Expérimental sur le Galvanism*, 1804; courtesy of the Division of Rare and Manuscript Collections, Cornell University Library. Shelfmark: QC517.A36 E7 (plate 4).

This picture from Aldini's French account of his experiments in Galvanism shows the experiments on the heads and bodies of executed criminals that were an inspiration for Mary Shelley's *Frankenstein*.

contorted in so irregular a manner that they exhibited the appearance of the most horrid grimaces. The action of the eye-lids was exceedingly striking, though less sensible in the human head than in that of the ox.

EXPERIMENT XXIII

Having established an arc from the top of the left ear, and then from the bottom of that ear to the tongue, drawn about an inch without the mouth, contractions were observed in the face, and the tongue sensibly returned into the mouth. I then touched the upper or lower lips, and obtained contractions, which were remarkable chiefly in all the muscles of the left part of the face; so that the mouth appeared as if distorted by a partial kind of palsy. On the first application of the arc, a small quantity of saliva was discharged from the mouth. . . .

These researches are not an object of mere curiosity; they seem to open an extensive field for promoting the welfare of the human race, and may be of service in cases of apparent death, occasioned by an alteration of the brain, and sometimes in cases of asphyxia. Various learned academies are entitled to great praise for having turned their attention to this subject, and for having already recommended different stimulants as proper for being used on such occasions. But I must take the liberty of requesting that in similar cases the action of Galvanism may be tried, by employing the new method here proposed. It is of great importance that the means of affording relief to the sufferings of mankind should be multiplied, and especially in cases in which the old system of medicine presents to us so few resources. In the mean time I conceive it may be useful to make some trials on animals thrown into a state of asphyxia [in] different ways. These researches may lead to valuable discoveries, and produce some light to direct us in our attempts to save the lives of men. If the encouragement I have received from the medical and philosophical world, in general, induce others to pursue the same path, it will give me great satisfaction. Galvanism is yet in its infancy; and when we reflect on the slow progress which many other branches of science have made, and how long they remained almost stationary before the full importance of them was known, it would be presumption to set bounds to that which is the subject of the present work.

10.6 John Abernethy, *An Enquiry into the Probability and Rationality of Mr. Hunter's Theory of Life: Being the Subject of the First Two Anatomical Lectures Delivered before the Royal College of Surgeons, of London* (1814)

John Abernethy (1764–1831) was president of the Royal College of Surgeons in 1814 when he reignited the controversy over 'vitalism' that had surrounded John Thelwall's lecture at Guy's Hospital two decades earlier. Where Thelwall had set out to contest the anatomist John Hunter's proposition 'of the Vital Principle being resident in the blood', Abernethy supported it, arguing through analogy with electricity that life was 'a subtile invisible substance' which could be added to the body. In 1817, whilst involved in an increasingly acrimonious dispute with William Lawrence on the subject (see extract 10.7), Abernethy clarified the theological dimensions of his belief in 'vitalism', arguing that a belief in life as a substance separate from the physical body implied a belief in an immortal soul.

I proceed to enquire into Mr. Hunter's opinion, that irritability is the effect of some subtile, mobile, invisible substance, superadded to the evident structure of muscles, or other forms of vegetable and animal matter, as magnetism is to iron, and as electricity is to various substances with which it may be connected. Mr Hunter doubtless thought, and I believe most persons do think, that in magnetic and electric motions, a subtile invisible substance, of a very quickly and powerfully mobile nature, puts in motion other bodies which are evident to the senses, and are of a nature more gross and inert. . . .

There are some philosophers who think, that properties similar to those which in the aggregate mass become an object of our senses, likewise belong to every atom of which it is composed; whilst others, on the contrary, think, that the atoms have very different qualities, and that the vis inertiæ[11] is the property only of the aggregate mass. The matter of animals and vegetables is, however, an aggregate mass; it is as we express it, common matter, it is inert; so that the necessity of supposing the superaddition of some subtile and mobile substance is apparent.

Taking it for granted that the opinions generally entertained concerning the cause of electrical motions are true, analogy would induce us to suppose, that similar motions might be produced, by similar causes, in matter organized as it is found to be in the vegetable and animal systems.

The phænomena of electricity and of life correspond. Electricity may be attached to, or inhere, in a wire; it may be suddenly dissipated, or have its powers annulled, or it may be removed by degrees or in portions, and the wire may remain less and less strongly electrified, in proportion as it is abstracted. So life inheres in vegetables and animals; it may sometimes be suddenly dissipated, or have its powers abolished, though in general it is lost by degrees, without any apparent change taking place in the structure; and in either case putrefaction begins when life terminates.

The motions of electricity are characterized by their celerity and force; so are the motions of irritability. The motions of electricity are vibratory; so likewise are those of irritability. When by long continued exertion the power of muscles is fatigued, or when it is feeble, their vibratory or tremulous motions are manifest to common observation, but the same kind of motion may be perceived at all times by attention . . .

When hereafter I shall have to speak of other vital functions, I think it will appear that it is impossible to account for the phænomena in any other manner than that which Mr. Hunter has suggested. . . .

That electricity is something, I could never doubt, and therefore it follows as a consequence in my opinion, that it must be every where connected with those atoms of matter, which form the masses that are cognizable to our senses; and that it enters into the composition of every thing, inanimate or animate. If then it be electricity that produces all the chemical changes, we so constantly observe, in surrounding inanimate objects, analogy induces us to believe that it is electricity which also performs all the chemical operations in living bodies; that the universal chemist resides in them, and exercises in some degree peculiar powers because it possesses a peculiar apparatus. . . .

---

11 Abernethy had already defined this phrase in his lecture with reference to Sir Isaac Newton as meaning 'an indisposition to move unless compelled to motion, and a disposition to continue in motion unless retarded'.

It is not meant to be affirmed that electricity is life. There are strong analogies between electricity and magnetism, and yet I do not know that any one has been hardy enough to assert their absolute identity. I only mean to prove, that Mr. Hunter's Theory is verifiable, by shewing that a subtile substance of a quickly and powerfully mobile nature, seems to pervade every thing, and appears to be the life of the world; and therefore it is probable that a similar substance pervades organized bodies, and produces similar effects in them.

10.7   William Lawrence, *An Introduction to Comparative Anatomy and Physiology; Being the Two Introductory Lectures Delivered at The Royal College of Surgeons, on the 21st and 25th of March, 1816* (1816)

William Lawrence (1783–1865) was a former pupil of John Abernethy (see extract 10. 6), whose vitalist beliefs Lawrence chose to attack in 1816 in his inaugural lectures as Professor at the Royal College of Surgeons. Against Abernethy (who had linked his ideas to those of John Hunter and Humphry Davy), Lawrence advocated a materialist position that life was the result of the way in which matter was organized rather than a separate substance.

Organization means the peculiar composition, which distinguishes living bodies; in this point of view they are contrasted with inorganic, inert, or dead bodies. Vital properties, such as sensibility and irritability, are the means, by which organization is capable of exerting its purposes; the vital properties of living bodies correspond to the physical properties of inorganic bodies; such as cohesion, elasticity, &c. Functions are the purposes, which any organ or system of organs executes in the animal frame; there is of course nothing corresponding to them in inorganic matter. Life is the assemblage of all the functions, and the general result of their exercise. Thus organization, vital properties, functions, and life are expressions related to each other; in which organization is the instrument, vital properties the acting power, function the mode of action, and life the result. . . .

    Having thus proceeded, as far as we can, in ascertaining the nature of life by the observation of its effects, we are naturally anxious to investigate its origin, to see how it is produced, and to inquire how it is communicated to the beings in which we find it. We endeavour therefore to observe living bodies in the moment of their formation, to watch the time, when matter may be supposed to receive the stamp of life, and the inert mass to be quickened. Hitherto, however, physiologists have not been able to catch nature in the fact. Living bodies have never been observed otherwise than completely formed, enjoying already that vital force and producing those internal movements, the first cause of which we are desirous of knowing. However minute and feeble the parts of an embryo may be, when we are first capable of perceiving them, they then enjoy a real life, and possess the germ of all the phenomena, which that life may afterwards develop. These observations, extended to all the classes of living creatures, lead to this general fact, that there are none, which have not heretofore formed part of others similar to themselves, from which they have been detached. All have participated in the existence of other living beings, before they exercised the functions of life themselves. Thus we find that the motion proper to living bodies, or in one word, Life, has its origin in that of their parents. From these parents they have received the vital impulse; and hence it is evident, that in the present state of things, life proceeds only from life; and there exists no other but that, which has been transmitted from one living body to another, by an uninterrupted succession. . . .

In the science of physiology we proceed on the observation of facts, of their order and connexion; we notice the analogies between them; and deduce the general laws, to which they are subject. We are thus led to admit the vital properties, already spoken of, as causes of the various phenomena; in the same way as attraction is recognized for the causes of various physical events. We do not profess to explain *how* the living forces in one case, or attraction in the other, exert their agency. But some are not content to stop at this point; they wish to draw aside the veil from nature, to display the very essence of the vital properties, and penetrate to their first causes; to shew, independently of the phenomena, what is life, and how irritability and sensibility execute those purposes, which so justly excite our admiration. They endeavour to give a physical explanation of the contraction of a muscle, and to teach us how a nerve feels. They suppose the structure of the body to contain an invisible matter or principle, by which it is put in motion. . . .

To make the matter more intelligible, this vital principle is compared to magnetism, to electricity, and to galvanism; or it is roundly stated to be oxygen. . . .

The truth is, there is no resemblance, no analogy between electricity and life: the two orders of phenomena are completely distinct; they are incommensurable. Electricity illustrates life no more than life illustrates electricity. We might just as well say that an electrical machine operates by means of a vital fluid, as that the nerves and muscles of an animal perform sensation and contraction by virtue of an electric fluid. By selecting one or two minor points, to the neglect of all the important features, a distant similarity may be made out; and this is only in appearance. In the same way life might be shewn to be like any thing else whatever, or any thing else to be like life.

10.8 Baron Georges Cuvier, *A Discourse on the Revolutions of the Surface of the Globe, and the changes thereby produced in the Animal Kingdom. Translated from the French* (1825, translation 1829)

Drawing on his research into palaeontology and comparative anatomy, as well as on his study of fossils, the French scientist Georges Cuvier (1769–1832) became a leading advocate of catastrophism, the theory that the earth was formed by a series of catastrophic events (in Cuvier's version, a series of floods). Cuvier's ideas were a major influence on the catastrophic visions of a number of the poets of the later part of the Romantic period; for example, in the 'Preface' to Cain, *Byron wrote, 'The reader will perceive that the author has partly adopted in this poem the notion of Cuvier, that the world had been destroyed several times before the creation of man.'[12]*

FIRST APPEARANCE OF THE EARTH

When the traveller passes over those fertile plains where the peaceful waters preserve, by their regular course, an abundant variation, and the soil of which, crowded by an extensive population, enriched by flourishing villages, vast cities, and splendid monuments, is never disturbed but by the ravages of war, or the oppression of despotism, he is not inclined to believe that nature has there had her intestine war, and that the surface of the globe has been overthrown by revolutions and catastrophes; but his opinions change as he begins to penetrate into that soil at present so peaceful, or as he ascends the hills which bound the plain; they extend as it were with the prospect, they begin to comprehend the extent and grandeur of those events of ages past as soon as he ascends that more elevated chains of which these hills form the base, or, in following the beds of those torrents which descend from these chains, he penetrates into their interior.

FIRST PROOFS OF REVOLUTIONS

The strata of the earth, the lowest and most level, only show, even when penetrated to very great depths, horizontal layers of matter more of less varied, which contain countless marine productions. Similar layers and similar productions form the hills to very considerable heights. Sometimes the shells are so numerous that they form by themselves the entire soil; they are found at heights greatly above the level of the sea, and where at the present day no sea could reach from existing causes; they are not only imbedded in light sand, but the hardest stones often incrust them and are everywhere penetrated by them. Every part of the world, both hemispheres, all the continents, all the islands of any extent, afford the same phenomenon. The time is past when ignorance could

---

12 Lord Byron, *The Major Works*, ed. Jerome J. McGann (Oxford: Oxford University Press, 1986), p. 882.

assert that these relics of organic bodies were but freaks of nature, productions engendered in the bosom of the earth by its innate creative power; and the efforts of metaphysicians will not suffice to establish such assertions. A minute investigation of the formation of these deposites, of their contexture, even of their chemical composition, does not detect the least difference between the fossil shells and those produced from the sea; their conformation is not less perfect; we do not observe either the marks of friction or fracture, evincing violent removal; the smallest of them preserve their most delicate parts, their finest points, their most minute indications; thus they have not only lived in the sea, but have been deposited by the sea; the sea has left them in the places where they are found; but the sea has for a time remained in these places, it has remained there sufficiently long and undisturbedly to be enabled to form these deposites so regular, so thick, so extensive, and so solid, which compose these layers of aquatic animals. The basis of the sea has then experienced a change either in extent or situation. What a result from the first examination, and the most superficial observation!

The traces of revolution become more striking when we ascend higher, when we approach closer to the foot of the great chains of mountains. . . .

PROOFS THAT THESE REVOLUTIONS HAVE BEEN NUMEROUS

But the revolutions and changes which have left the earth as we now find it, are not confined to the overthrow of ancient layers, to this retreat of the sea after the formation of new layers.

When we compare in detail the various layers one with another, and the productions of nature which they comprise, we soon discover that this ancient sea has not always deposited stones exactly similar, nor the remains of animals of the same species, and that each of its deposites has not extended over the whole surface that it has covered. There have been successive variations there established, the first of which has been in great measure general, and the others appear to be less so. The more ancient the layers are, the greater their uniformity and extent; the more recent, the more limited and more subject are they to vary at short distances. Thus the displacing of the layers was accompanied and followed by alterations in the nature of the liquid and the materials which it held in solution: and when certain layers, raising themselves above the waters, had divided the surface of the sea into islands by projecting chains, there must have been various changes in many particular basins.

PROOFS THAT THE REVOLUTIONS HAVE BEEN SUDDEN

But, it is of great importance to note that these repeated irruptions and retreats have not all been gradual, not all uniform; on the contrary, the greater portion of these catastrophes have been sudden; and that is easily proved by the last of these events, that which by a twofold action inundated, and then left dry, our present continents, or at least a great portion of the soil which now composes them. It also left, in the northern countries, carcases of large quadrupeds frozen in the ice, and which have been preserved down to the present period with their skin, their hair and their flesh. If they had not been frozen as soon as killed, putrefaction would have decomposed them. And besides, this eternal frost did not previously exist in those parts in which they were frozen, for they could not have existed in such a temperature. The same instant that these animals were bereft of life, the country which they inhabited became frozen. This event was sudden, momentary, without gradation; and what is so clearly proved as to this last catastrophe, equally applies to that which preceded it. The convulsions, the alterations, the reversings of the most ancient layers, leave not a doubt in the mind but that sudden and violent causes reduced them to their present state; and even the powerful actions of the mass of waters is proved by the accumulation of relics and round flints which in many places intervene between the solid layers. Existence has thus been often troubled on this earth by appalling events. Living creatures without number have fallen victims to these catastrophes: some, the inhabitants of dry land, have been swallowed up by a deluge; others, who peopled the depth of the waters, their very race become extinct, and only a few remains left of them in the world, scarcely recognised by the naturalist.

These are the consequences to which the subjects which meet us at every step, and which we may find in almost every clime, necessarily conduct us. These overpowering and stupendous events are clearly imprinted everywhere, and are legible to the eye that knows how to trace their history in the monuments they have left. But what is yet more remarkable and no less certain is, that life has not always existed on the globe, and that it is easy for the observer to discover the precise point whence it began to deposit its productions.

10.9   Charles Lyell, *Principles of Geology, being an Attempt to Explain the Former Changes of the Earth's Surface, By Reference to Causes Now in Operation* (1830)

The major nineteenth-century proponent of 'uniformitarianism', the Scottish geologist Charles Lyell (1797–1875), rejected the catastrophism of Cuvier (extract 10.8) and provided a vindication of James Hutton's theories of the gradual formation of the earth (extract 10.2). In defending his methodology, Lyell emphasized the necessity of studying what could be observed in the present and using such observation as the basis of ideas about the past (as opposed to what he dismissed as the mere 'speculation' of many of the opposing theories). Such empirical research, Lyell argues, provides 'the alphabet and grammar of geology; not that we expect from such studies to obtain a key to the interpretation of all geological phenomena, but because they form the groundwork from which we must rise to the contemplation of more general questions relating to the complicated results to which, in an indefinite lapse of ages, the existing causes of change may give rise.'

All naturalists, who have carefully examined the arrangement of the mineral masses composing the earth's crust, and who have studied their internal structure and fossil contents, have recognized therein the signs of a great succession of former changes; and the causes of these changes have been the object of anxious inquiry. . . .

We hear of sudden and violent revolutions of the globe, of the instantaneous elevation of mountain chains, of paroxysms of volcanic energy, declining according to some, and according to others increasing in violence, from the earliest to the latest ages. We are also told of general catastrophes and a succession of deluges, of the alternation of periods of repose and disorder, of the refrigeration of the globe, of the sudden annihilation of whole races of animals and plants, and other hypotheses, in which we see the ancient spirit of speculation revived, and a desire manifested to cut, rather than patiently to untie, the Gordian knot.

In our attempt to unravel these difficult questions, we shall adopt a different course, restricting ourselves to the known or possible operations of existing causes; feeling assured that we have not yet exhausted the resources which the study of the present course of nature may provide, and therefore that we are not authorized, in the infancy of our science, to recur to extraordinary agents. We shall adhere to this plan, not only on the grounds explained in the first volume, but because, as we have above stated, history informs us that this method has always put geologists on the road that leads to truth, – suggesting views which, although imperfect at first, have been found capable of improvement, until at last adopted by universal consent. On the other hand, the opposite method, that of speculating on a former distinct state of things, has led invariably to a multitude of contradictory systems, which have been overthrown one after the other, – which have been found quite incapable of modification, – and which are often required to be precisely reversed. . . .

In our history of the progress of geology, in the first volume, we stated that the opinion originally promulgated by Hutton, 'that the strata called *primitive* were mere altered sedimentary rocks,' was vehemently opposed for a time, the main objection to the theory being its supposed tendency to promote a belief in the past eternity of our planet. Previously the absence of animal and vegetable remains in the so-called primitive strata, had been appealed to, as proving that there had been a period when the planet was uninhabited by living beings, and when, as was also inferred, it was uninhabitable, and, therefore, probably in a nascent state.

The opposite doctrine, that the oldest visible strata might be the monuments of an antecedent period, when the animate world was already in existence, was declared to be equivalent to the assumption, that there never was a beginning to the present order of things. The unfairness of this charge was clearly pointed out by Playfair, who observed, 'that it was one thing to declare that we had not yet discovered the traces of a beginning, and another to deny that the earth ever had a beginning.'

We regret, however, to find that the bearing of our arguments in the first volume has been misunderstood in a similar manner, for we have been charged with endeavouring to establish the proposition, that 'the existing causes of change have operated with absolute uniformity from all eternity'.[13]

It is the more necessary to notice this misrepresentation of our views, as it has proceeded from a friendly critic whose theoretical opinions coincide in general with our own, but who has, in this instance, strangely misconceived the scope of our argument. With equal justice might an astronomer be accused of asserting, that the works of creation extend throughout *infinite* space, because he refuses to take for granted that the remotest stars now seen in the heavens are on the utmost verge of the material universe. Every improvement of the telescope has brought thousands of new worlds into view, and it would, therefore, be rash and unphilosophical to imagine that we already survey the whole extent of the vast scheme, or that it will ever be brought within the sphere of human observation.

But no argument can be drawn from such premises in favour of the infinity of the space that has been filled with worlds; and if the material universe has any limits, it then follows that it must occupy a minute and infinitessimal point in infinite space. So, if in tracing back the earth's history, we arrive at the monuments of events which may have happened millions of ages before our times, and if we still find no decided evidence of a commencement, yet the arguments from analogy in support of the probability of a beginning remain unshaken; and if the past duration of the earth be finite, then the aggregate of geological epochs, however numerous, must constitute a mere moment of the past, a mere infinitessimal portion of eternity.

It has been argued, that as the different states of the earth's surface, and the different species by which it has been inhabited, have had each their origin, and many of them their termination, so the entire series may have commenced at a certain period. It has also been urged, that as we admit the creation of man to have occurred at a comparatively modern epoch – as we concede the astonishing fact of the first introduction of a moral and intellectual being, so also we may conceive the first creation of the planet itself.

We are far from denying the weight of this reasoning from analogy; but although it may strengthen our conviction, that the present system of change has not gone on from eternity, it cannot warrant us in presuming that we shall be permitted to behold the signs of the earth's origin, or the evidences of the first introduction into it of organic beings.

In vain do we aspire to assign limits to the works of creation in *space*, whether we examine the starry heavens, or that world of minute animalcules which is

13 Lyell's note: '*Quarterly Review*, No. 86, Oct. 1830, p. 464.'

revealed to us by the microscope. We are prepared, therefore, to find that in *time* also, the confines of the universe lie beyond the reach of mortal ken. But in whatever direction we pursue our researches, whether in time or space, we discover everywhere the clear proofs of a Creative Intelligence, and of His foresight, wisdom, and power.

As geologists, we learn that it is not only the present condition of the globe that has been suited to the accommodation of myriads of living creatures, but that many former states also have been equally adapted to the organization and habits of prior races of beings. The disposition of the seas, continents, and islands, and the climates have varied; so it appears that the species have been changed, and yet they have all been so modelled, on types analogous to those of existing plants and animals, as to indicate throughout a perfect harmony of design and unity of purpose. To assume that the evidence of a beginning or end of so vast a scheme lies within the reach of our philosophical inquiries, or even of our speculations, appears to us inconsistent with a just estimate of the relations which subsist between the finite powers of man and the attributes of an Infinite and Eternal Being.

Bibliography and Further Reading

General Studies of Romanticism

Abrams, M. H., *The Mirror and the Lamp: Romantic Theory and the Critical Tradition* (Oxford: Oxford University Press, 1953).

——, *Natural Supernaturalism: Tradition and Revolution in Romantic Literature* (New York: W. W. Norton, 1973).

Aers, David, Cook, Jon, and Punter, David, *Romanticism and Ideology* (London and Boston: Routledge, 1981).

Bate, Jonathan, *Romantic Ecology: Wordsworth and the Environmental Tradition* (London: Routledge, 1991).

——, *The Song of the Earth* (Cambridge, MA: Harvard University Press, 2000).

Bloom, Harold, *The Visionary Company: A Reading of English Romantic Poetry* (London and Ithaca, NY: Cornell University Press, 1971).

Bradley, Arthur and Rawes, Alan (eds), *Romantic Biography* (Aldershot: Ashgate, 2003).

Brewer, John, *The Pleasures of Imagination: English Culture in the Eighteenth Century* (London: HarperCollins, 1997).

Butler, Marilyn, *Romantics, Rebels and Reactionaries: English Literature and its Background, 1760–1830* (Oxford: Oxford University Press, 1981).

Buzard, James, *The Beaten Track: European Tourism, Literature, and the Ways to 'Culture', 1800–1918* (Oxford: Clarendon Press, 1993).

Carruthers, Gerrard and Rawes, Alan, *English Romanticism and the Celtic World* (Cambridge: Cambridge University Press, 2003).

Colley, Linda, *Britons: Forging the Nation, 1707–1837* (London: Vintage, 1996).

Curran, Stuart, *The Cambridge Companion to British Romanticism* (Cambridge: Cambridge University Press, 1993).

Everest, Kelvin, *English Romantic Poetry: An Introduction to the Historical Context and the Literary Scene* (Milton Keynes: Open University Press, 1990).

Gaull, Marilyn, *English Romanticism: The Human Context* (New York and London: W. W. Norton, 1988).

Jarvis, Robin, *The Romantic Period: The Intellectual and Cultural Context of English Literature, 1789–1830* (London: Pearson, 2004).

Keen, Paul (ed.), *Revolutions in Romantic Literature: An Anthology of Print Culture, 1780–1832* (Peterborough, Ont.: Broadview Press, 2004).

Larrissy, Edward, *Romanticism and Postmodernism* (Cambridge: Cambridge University Press, 1999).

McCalman, Iain et al. (eds), *An Oxford Companion to the Romantic Age: British Culture, 1776–1832* (Oxford: Oxford University Press, 1999).

McKusick, James, *Green Writing: Romanticism and Ecology* (New York: St Martin's Press, 2000).

Oerlemans, Onno, *Romanticism and the Materiality of Nature* (Toronto: Toronto University Press, 2002).

O'Neill, Michael, *Romanticism and the Self-Conscious Poem* (Oxford: Oxford University Press, 1997).

Pirie, David (ed.), *The Romantic Period* (Harmondsworth: Penguin, 1994).

Richardson, Alan, *Literature, Education and Romanticism: Reading as Social Practice* (Cambridge: Cambridge University Press, 1994).

Roe, Nicholas (ed.), *Romanticism: An Oxford Guide* (Oxford: Oxford University Press, 2005).

Ross, Marlon B., *The Contours of Masculine Desire: Romanticism and the Rise of Women's Poetry* (Oxford: Oxford University Press, 1989).

Sales, Roger, *English Literature in History, 1780–1830: Pastoral and Politics* (London: St Martin's Press, 1983).

Smith, Olivia, *The Politics of Language, 1791–1819* (London and New York: Oxford University Press, 1984).

Stabler, Jane, *Burke to Byron, Barbauld to Baillie: 1790–1830* (Basingstoke: Macmillan, 2001).

Williams, Raymond, *Culture and Society, 1780–1950* (Harmondsworth: Penguin, 1961).

Web links

BBC: British history: Empire and sea power
www.bbc.co.uk/history/british/empire_seapower/

Eighteenth-century collections online
www.gale.com/EighteenthCentury/

Internet Library of Early Journals: A digital library of 18th- and 19th-century journals
www.bodley.ox.ac.uk/ilej/

Internet Modern History Sourcebook
www.fordham.edu/halsall/mod/modsbook15.html

National Portrait Gallery
www.npg.org.uk/live/index.asp

Romantic Chronology
http://english.ucsb.edu:591/rchrono/

Romantic Circles
www.rc.umd.edu/

Romanticism On Line: A List of URLs
www.users.muohio.edu/mandellc/eng441/urllist.htm

Voice of the Shuttle: Romantics
http://vos.ucsb.edu/browse.asp?id=2750

Historical Events

Abrams, M. H., 'English Romanticism: the Spirit of the Age', in *The Correspondent Breeze: Essays on English Romanticism* (New York: W. W. Norton, 1984), pp. 44–75.

Bainbridge, Simon, *Napoleon and English Romanticism* (Cambridge: Cambridge University Press, 1995).

——, *British Poetry and the Revolutionary and Napoleonic Wars* (Oxford: Oxford University Press, 2003).

Barrell, John, *Poetry, Language, and Politics* (Manchester: Manchester University Press, 1988).

Bindman, David, *The Shadow of the Guillotine: Britain and the French Revolution* (London: British Museum, 1989).

Boulton, James, *The Language of Politics in the Age of Wilkes and Burke* (Westport, CT: Routledge & Kegan Paul, 1975).

Butler, Marilyn (ed.), *Burke, Paine, Godwin, and the Revolution Controversy* (Cambridge: Cambridge University Press, 1984).

Chandler, James, *England in 1819: The Politics of Literary Culture and the Case of Romantic Historicism* (Chicago and London: Chicago University Press, 1998).

Christie, Ian, *Wars and Revolutions: Britain, 1760–1815* (London: Edward Arnold, 1982).

Cookson, J. E., *The Friends of Peace: Anti-War Liberalism in England, 1793–1815* (Cambridge: Cambridge University Press, 1982).

——, *The British Armed Nation, 1793–1815* (Oxford: Clarendon Press, 1997).

Craciun, Adriana, *British Women Writers and the French Revolution: Citizens of the World* (Basingstoke: Palgrave Macmillan, 2005).

Cronin, Richard, *The Politics of Romantic Poetry: In Search of the Pure Commonwealth* (Basingstoke and New York: Macmillan and St Martin's Press, 2000).

Dickinson, H. T., *Britain and the French Revolution, 1789–1815* (Basingstoke and London: Macmillan Education, 1979).

Emsley, Clive, *British Society and the French Wars, 1793–1815* (Basingstoke and London: Macmillan, 1979).

Franklin, A. and Philp, Mark (eds), *Napoleon and the Invasion of Britain* (Oxford: Bodleian Library, 2003).

Goodwin, A., *The Friends of Liberty: The English Democratic Movement in the Age of Romanticism* (Cambridge, MA: Harvard University Press, 1979).

Hobsbawm, E. J., *The Age of Revolution: Europe, 1789–1848* (London: Weidenfeld & Nicolson, 1962).

Janowitz, Anne, *England's Ruins: Poetic Purpose and the National Landscape* (Oxford: Blackwell, 1990).

Levinson, Marjorie, *Wordsworth's Great Period Poems* (Cambridge: Cambridge University Press, 1986).

Liu, Alan, *Wordsworth: The Sense of History* (Stanford, CA: Stanford University Press, 1989).

McGann, Jerome J., *The Romantic Ideology: A Critical Investigation* (Chicago: Chicago University Press, 1983).

Mori, J., *Britain in the Age of the French Revolution* (London: Longman, 2000).

Paulson, Ronald, *Representations of Revolution (1789–1820)* (New Haven, CT: Yale University Press, 1983).

Roe, Nicholas, *Wordsworth and Coleridge: The Radical Years* (Oxford: Clarendon Press, 1990).

——, *John Keats and the Culture of Dissent* (Oxford: Clarendon Press, 1997).

——, *The Politics of Nature: William Wordsworth and Some Contemporaries* (Basingstoke: Palgrave Macmillan, 2002).

Shaw, Philip (ed.), *Romantic Wars: Studies in Culture and Conflict, 1793–1822* (Aldershot: Ashgate, 2000).

Shaw, Philip (ed.), *Waterloo and the Romantic Imagination* (Basingstoke: Palgrave Macmillan, 2002).

Watson, J. R., *Romanticism and War: A Study of British Romantic Period Writing and the Napoleonic Wars* (Basingstoke: Palgrave Macmillan, 2003).

Web links

British newspaper coverage of the French Revolution: a small archive of the British view of unspeakable events in the French Revolution
www.english.ucsb.edu/faculty/ayliu/research/around-1800/FR/

British War Poetry in the Age of Romanticism, 1793–1815
www.rc.umd.edu/editions/warpoetry/about.html

National Maritime Museum
www.nmm.ac.uk/index.php

A Web of English History: The Age of George III
www.historyhome.co.uk/c-eight/18chome.htm

Society, Politics and Class

Barrell, John, *The Idea of Landscape and the Sense of Place, 1730–1840: An Approach to the Poetry of John Clare* (Cambridge: Cambridge University Press, 1972).

——, *The Dark Side of Landscape: The Rural Poor in English Painting, 1730–1840* (Cambridge: Cambridge University Press, 1983).

Brewer, John, *The Common People and Politics, 1750–1790s* (Cambridge: Chadwyck Healey, 1987).

Daunton, M. J., *Progress and Poverty: An Economic and Social History of Britain, 1700–1850* (Oxford and New York: Oxford University Press, 1995).

Evans, E. J., *The Forging of the Modern State: Early Industrial Britain, 1783–1870* (London and New York: Longman, 1983).

Janowitz, Anne, *Lyric and Labour in the Romantic Tradition* (Cambridge: Cambridge University Press, 1998).

Landry, Donna, *The Muses of Resistance: Labouring-class Women's Poetry in Britain, 1739–1769* (Cambridge: Cambridge University Press, 1990).

McCalman, Iain, *Radical Underworld: Prophets, Revolutionaries, and Pornographers in London, 1795–1819* (Cambridge: Cambridge University Press, 1988).

Thompson, E. P., *The Making of the English Working Class* (Harmondsworth: Penguin, 1968).

Vincent, David, *Bread, Knowledge and Freedom: A Study of Nineteenth-Century Working Class Autobiography* (London: Routledge, 1982).

Web links

Labouring-class Writers
http://human.ntu.ac.uk/research/labouringclasswriters/

Making the Modern World
www.makingthemodernworld.org.uk/stories/ manufacture_by_machine/01.ST.01/

Revolutionary Players
www.revolutionaryplayers.org.uk/home.stm

Science Museum
www.sciencemuseum.org.uk/

Women

Butler, Marilyn, *Jane Austen and the War of Ideas* (Oxford: Clarendon Press, 1975).
Cracuin, Adriana, *Fatal Women of Romanticism* (Cambridge: Cambridge University Press, 2003).
Favret, Mary, *Romantic Correspondence: Women, Politics and the Fiction of Letters* (Cambridge: Cambridge University Press, 1993).
Fay, Elizabeth A., *A Feminist Introduction to Romanticism* (Oxford: Blackwell, 1998).
Feldman, Paula R. and Kelley, Theresa M. (eds), *Romantic Women Writers: Voices and Countervoices* (Hanover, NH, and London: University Press of New England, 1995).
Johnson, Claudia, *Jane Austen: Women, Politics, and the Novel* (Chicago: Chicago University Press, 1988).
Jones, Vivien (ed.), *Women in the Eighteenth Century: Constructions of Femininity* (London: Routledge, 1990).
—— (ed.), *Women and Literature in Britain, 1700–1800* (Cambridge: Cambridge University Press, 2000).
Keane, Angela, *Women Writers and the English Nation in the 1790s* (Cambridge: Cambridge University Press, 2000).
Kelly, Gary, *Women, Writing, and Revolution, 1790–1827* (Oxford: Oxford University Press, 1993).
Mellor, Anne K., *Romanticism and Feminism* (Bloomington, IN: Indiana University Press, 1988).
——, *Romanticism and Gender* (New York and London: Routledge, 1993).
——, *Mothers of the Nation: Women's Political Writing in England, 1780–1830* (Bloomington, IN: Indiana University Press, 2000).

Web links

Bluestocking archive
www.faculty.umb.edu/elizabeth_fay/archive2.html

British women playwrights around 1800
www.etang.umontreal.ca/bwp1800/

Corvey Women Writers on the Web
www2.shu.ac.uk/corvey/CW3/

Eighteenth-century England: Gender and sexuality
www.umich.edu/~ece/showcase/gender.html

The Orlando Project: a history of women's writing in the British Isles
www.ualberta.ca/ORLANDO/

Women Romantic-era writers
www.bbk.ac.uk/english/ac/wrew.htm

Religion and Belief

Canuel, M., *Religion, Toleration and British Writing, 1790–1830* (Cambridge: Cambridge University Press, 2002).

Clark, J. C. D., *English Society 1688–1832: Ideology, Social Structure and Political Practice during the Ancien Regime* (Cambridge: Cambridge University Press, 1985).

Harrison, J. F. C., *The Second Coming: Popular Millenarianism, 1780–1850* (New Brunswick, NJ: Rutgers University Press, 1979).

Hempton, D., *Religion and Political Culture in Britain and Ireland: From the Glorious Revolution to the Decline of Empire* (Cambridge: Cambridge University Press, 1996).

Hole, Robert, *Pulpits, Politics and Public Order in England, 1760–1832* (Cambridge: Cambridge University Press, 1989).

Hopps, Gavin and Stabler, Jane (eds), *Romanticism and Religion from William Cowper to Wallace Stevens* (Aldershot: Ashgate, 2006).

Knox, Ronald Arbuthnott, *Enthusiasm: A Chapter in the History of Religion with Special Reference to the XVII and XVIII Centuries* (New York: Oxford University Press, 1988).

McFarland, Thomas, *Coleridge and the Pantheist Tradition* (Oxford: Clarendon Press, 1969).

Mee, Jon, *Romanticism, Enthusiasm, and Regulation: Poetics and the Policing of Culture in the Romantic Period* (Oxford: Oxford University Press, 2003).

Prickett, Stephen, *Origins of Narrative: The Romantic Appropriation of the Bible* (Cambridge: Cambridge University Press, 1996).

Priestman, Martin, *Romantic Atheism: Poetry and Freethought, 1780–1830* (Cambridge: Cambridge University Press, 2000).

Ryan, Robert, *The Romantic Reformation: Religious Politics in English Literature, 1789–1824* (Cambridge: Cambridge University Press, 1997).

Ward, W. R., *Religion and Society in England, 1790–1850* (London: Batsford, 1972).

Philosophy and Ideas

Barker-Benfield, G. J., *The Culture of Sensibility: Sex and Society in Eighteenth-Century Britain* (Chicago: Chicago University Press, 1992).

Chandler, Alice, *A Dream of Order: The Medieval Ideal in Nineteenth-Century English Literature* (Lincoln, NE: University of Nebraska Press, 1970).

Ellis, Markman, *The Politics of Sensibility: Race, Gender, and Commerce in the Sentimental Novel* (Cambridge: Cambridge University Press, 1996).

Ellison, Julie, *Cato's Tears and the Making of Anglo-American Emotion* (Chicago: University of Chicago Press, 1999).

McFarland, Thomas, *Romanticism and the Heritage of Rousseau* (Oxford: Clarendon Press, 1995).

Mullan, John, *Sentiment and Sociality: The Language of Feeling in the Eighteenth Century* (Oxford: Clarendon Press, 1988).

Pinch, Adela, *Strange Fits of Passion: Epistemologies of Emotion, Hume to Austen* (Stanford, CA: Stanford University Press, 1996).

Todd, Janet, *Sensibility: An Introduction* (London: Methuen, 1986).

Whitney, L., *Primitivism and the Idea of Progress in English Popular Literature of the Eighteenth Century* (New York: Octagon Books, 1934).

Web link

The Dictionary of Sensibility
www.engl.virginia.edu/enec981/dictionary/

Aesthetics

Bohls, Elizabeth A., *Women Travel Writers and the Language of Aesthetics, 1716–1818* (Cambridge: Cambridge University Press, 1995).

Copley, Stephen and Garside, Peter (eds), *The Politics of the Picturesque: Literature, Landscape and Aesthetics since 1770* (Cambridge: Cambridge University Press, 1994).

Fulford, Timothy, *Land, Liberty, and Authority: Poetry, Criticism and Politics from Thomson to Wordsworth* (Cambridge: Cambridge University Press, 1996).

Hipple, W. J., *The Beautiful, the Sublime and the Picturesque in Eighteenth-Century British Aesthetic Theory* (Carbondale, IL: Southern Illinois University Press, 1957).

Hussey, Christopher, *The Picturesque: Studies in a Point of View* (London: Cass, 1967).

Webb, Timothy (ed.), *English Romantic Hellenism, 1770–1824* (Manchester: Manchester University Press, 1982).

Web links

The Elgin Marbles at the British Museum
www.thebritishmuseum.ac.uk/explore/highlights/article_index/w/what_are_the_elgin_
    marbles.aspx

The National Gallery
www.nationalgallery.org.uk/

Tate Online
www.tate.org.uk/

Popular Culture and Entertainment

Altick, Richard D., *The Shows of London* (Cambridge, MA: Harvard University Press, 1978).

Bolton, Betsy, *Women, Nationalism, and the Romantic Stage: Theatre and Politics in Britain, 1780–1800* (Cambridge: Cambridge University Press, 2001).

Burroughs, Catherine, *Women in British Romantic Theatre: Drama, Performance, and Society, 1790–1840* (Cambridge: Cambridge University Press, 2000).

Cave, Richard Allen (ed.), *The Romantic Theatre: An International Symposium* (Totowa, NJ: Barnes and Noble Books, 1986).

Donahue, Joseph W., *Dramatic Character in the English Romantic Age* (Princeton, NJ: Princeton University Press, 1970).

Harris, Tim, *Popular Culture in England, 1500–1800* (Basingstoke: Macmillan, 1995).

Hume, Robert D. (ed.), *The London Theatre World, 1660–1800* (Carbondale, IL: Southern Illinois University Press, 1980).

James, Louis (ed.), *English Popular Literature, 1819–1851* (New York: Columbia University Press, 1976).

Moody, Jane, *Illegitimate Theatre in London, 1770–1840* (Cambridge: Cambridge University Press, 2000).

Mullan, John and Reid, Christopher (eds), *Eighteenth-Century Popular Culture: A Selection* (Oxford: Oxford University Press, 2000).

Pascoe, Judith, *Romantic Theatricality: Gender, Poetry, and Spectatorship* (Ithaca, NY: Cornell University Press, 1997).

Richardson, Alan, *A Mental Theater: Poetic Drama and Consciousness in the Romantic Age* (University Park, PA: Pennsylvania State University Press, 1988).

Rogers, Pat, *Literature and Popular Culture in Eighteenth-Century England* (Brighton: Harvester Press, 1985).

Russell, Gillian, *The Theatres of War: Performance, Politics, and Society, 1793–1815* (Oxford: Clarendon Press, 1995).

Storch, Robert D., *Popular Culture and Custom in Nineteenth-Century England* (London: Croom Helm, 1982).

Web links

James Gillray: The Art of Caricature
www.tate.org.uk/britain/exhibitions/gillray/

Streetprint: Revolution and Romanticism
www.crcstudio.arts.ualberta.ca/streetprint/index.php

Literary Production and Reception

Altick, R. D., *The English Common Reader: A Social History of the Mass Reading Public, 1800–1900* (Chicago: University of Chicago Press, 1957).

Bate, Jonathan, *Shakespeare and the Romantic Imagination* (Oxford: Clarendon Press, 1986).

Clark, Timothy, *The Theory of Inspiration: Composition as a Crisis of Subjectivity in Romantic and Post-Romantic Writing* (Manchester: Manchester University Press, 1997).

Clery, E. J., *The Rise of Supernatural Fiction, 1762–1800* (Cambridge: Cambridge University Press, 1995).

——, and Miles, Robert (eds), *Gothic Documents: A Sourcebook, 1700–1820* (Manchester and New York: Manchester University Press, 2000).

——, Franklin, Caroline and Garside, Peter (eds), *Authorship, Commerce and the Public: Scenes of Writing, 1750–1850* (Basingstoke: Palgrave Macmillan, 2002).

Cox, Jeffrey N., *Poetry and Politics in the Cockney School: Keats, Shelley, Hunt and their Circle* (Cambridge: Cambridge University Press, 1998).

Davis, Leith, *Acts of Union: Scotland and the Literary Negotiation of the British Nation, 1707–1830* (Stanford, CA: Stanford University Press, 1998).

Dematta, Massimiliano and Wu, Duncan (eds), *British Romanticism and the Edinburgh Review* (London: Palgrave Macmillan, 2002).

Dyer, Gary, *British Satire and the Politics of Style, 1789–1832* (Cambridge: Cambridge University Press, 1997).

Ellis, Kate Ferguson, *The Contested Castle: Gothic Novels and the Subversion of Domestic Ideology* (Urbana, IL, and Chicago: University of Illinois Press, 1989).

Ellis, Markman, *The History of Gothic Fiction* (Edinburgh: Edinburgh University Press, 2000).

Fairer, David, *English Poetry of the Eighteenth Century 1700–1789* (Harlow and London: Pearson, 2003).

Gamer, Michael, *Romanticism and the Gothic: Genre, Reception, and Canon Formation* (Cambridge: Cambridge University Press, 2000).

Gilmartin, Kevin, *Print Politics: The Press and Radical Opposition in Early Nineteenth-Century England* (Cambridge: Cambridge University Press, 1996).

Hayden, John O., *The Romantic Reviewers, 1802–1824* (Chicago: University of Chicago Press, 1969).

Jones, Chris, *Radical Sensibility: Literature and Ideas in the 1790s* (London and New York: Routledge, 1993).

Jones, Steven E., *Satire and Romanticism* (New York: St Martin's Press, 2000).

—— (ed.), *The Satiric Eye: Forms of Satire in the Romantic Period* (New York: Palgrave Macmillan, 2003).

Kelly, Gary, *The English Jacobin Novel, 1780–1805* (Oxford: Oxford University Press, 1976).

——, *English Fiction of the Romantic Period, 1789–1830* (London and New York: Longman, 1989).

Kilgour, Maggie, *The Rise of the Gothic Novel* (London and New York: Routledge, 1995).

Klancher, J. P., *The Making of English Reading Audiences, 1790–1832* (Madison and London: University of Wisconsin Press, 1987).

McGann, Jerome J., *The Textual Condition* (Princeton, NJ: Princeton University Press, 1991).

——, *The Poetics of Sensibility* (Oxford: Clarendon Press, 1996).

Miles, Robert, *Gothic Writing 1750–1820: A Genealogy* (Manchester and New York: Manchester University Press, 2002).

Newlyn, Lucy, *'Paradise Lost' and the Romantic Reader* (Oxford: Clarendon Press, 1993).

——, *Reading, Writing, and Romanticism: The Anxiety of Reception* (Oxford: Oxford University Press, 2000).

Parker, Mark, *Literary Magazines and British Romanticism* (Cambridge: Cambridge University Press, 2000).

Price, Leah, *The Anthology and the Rise of the Novel from Richardson to George Eliot* (Cambridge: Cambridge University Press, 2003).

Punter, David, *The Literature of Terror: A History of Gothic Fictions from 1795 to the Present Day*, 2 vols (London and New York: Longman, 1996).

——, *The Blackwell Companion to the Gothic* (Oxford: Blackwell, 2000).

St Clair, William, *The Reading Nation in the Romantic Period* (Cambridge: Cambridge University Press, 2004).

Siskin, Clifford, *The Work of Writing: Literature and Social Change in Britain, 1700–1830* (Baltimore and London: Johns Hopkins University Press, 1998).

Spender, Dale, *Mothers of the Novel* (London: Pandora Press, 1986).

Stones, Graeme and Strachan, John (eds), *Satires of the Romantic Period*, 5 vols (London: Pickering & Chatto, 2003).

Taylor, John Tinnon, *Early Opposition to the English Novel: The Popular Reaction from 1760 to 1830* (New York: Folcroft, 1969).

Tompkins, J. M. S., *The Popular Novel in England: 1770–1830* (London: Methuen, 1969).

Trumpener, Katie, *Bardic Nationalism: The Romantic Novel and the British Empire* (Princeton, NJ: Princeton University Press, 1997).

Watson, Nicola, *Revolution and the Form of the British Novel, 1790–1825: Intercepted Letters, Interrupted Seduction* (Oxford: Clarendon Press, 1994).

Whale, John, *Imagination under Pressure: Aesthetics, Politics, and Utility, 1789–1832* (Cambridge: Cambridge University Press, 2000).

Wilson, Frances (ed.), *Byromania: Portraits of the Artist in Nineteenth- and Twentieth-Century Literature* (Basingstoke: Macmillan, 1999).

Wood, Marcus, *Radical Satire and Print Culture, 1790–1832* (Oxford: Clarendon Press, 1994).

Web links

British annuals and giftbooks
www.britannuals.com/mesp1-2.php?siteID=britannuals&pageref=1

The Corvey Project at Sheffield Hallam
http://extra.shu.ac.uk/corvey/

The Gothic Literature page
www.zittaw.com/gothicliterature.htm

The literary Gothic
www.litgothic.com/index_fl.html

Literary resources on the net (Jack Lynch)
http://andromeda.rutgers.edu/~jlynch/Lit/

A selective bibliography of British Romantic poetry and prose
http://faculty.washington.edu/nh2/biblio.html

Empire, Slavery and Exploration

Barrell, John, *The Infection of Thomas De Quincey: A Psychopathology of Imperialism* (New Haven, CT, and London: Yale University Press, 1991).

Bayly, C. A., *Imperial Meridian: The British Empire and the World, 1780–1830* (Cambridge: Cambridge University Press, 1989).

Carey, Brycchan, Ellis, Markman and Salih, Sara (eds), *Discourses of Slavery and Abolition: Britain and its Colonies, 1760–1838* (Basingstoke: Palgrave Macmillan, 2004).

Carretta, Vincent (ed.), *Unchained Voices: An Anthology of Black Authors in the English-Speaking World of the 18th Century* (Lexington, KY: University Press of Kentucky, 1996).

Chard, Chloe and Langdon, H. (eds), *Transports: Travel, Pleasure, and Imaginative Geography* (New Haven, CT: Paul Mellon Center, 1996).

Drayton, Richard, *Nature's Government: Science, Imperial Britain, and the 'Improvement' of the World* (New Haven, CT, and London: Yale University Press, 2000).

Drew, John, *British Romantics and India* (Oxford: Oxford University Press, 1987).

Ferguson, Moira, *Subject to Others: British Women Writers and Colonial Slavery, 1670–1834* (New York and London: Routledge, 1992).

Fulford, Tim and Kitson, Peter (eds), *Romanticism and Colonialism: Writing and Empire, 1780–1830* (Cambridge: Cambridge University Press, 1998).

—— (eds), *Travel, Exploration and Empires: Writings from the Era of Imperial Expansion, 1770–1835* (London: Pickering & Chatto, 2001).

Fulford, Tim, Lee, Debbie and Kitson, Peter J., *Literature, Science and Exploration in the Romantic Era: Bodies of Knowledge* (Cambridge: Cambridge University Press, 2004).

Hughes, William and Smith, Andrew (eds), *Empire and the Gothic: The Politics of Genre* (Basingstoke: Palgrave Macmillan, 2003).

Hulme, P. and Youngs, T. (eds), *The Cambridge Companion to Travel Writing* (Cambridge: Cambridge University Press, 2002).

Kitson, P. and Lee, Debbie (eds), *Slavery, Abolition and Emancipation: Writings in the British Romantic Period*, 8 vols (London: Pickering & Chatto, 1999).

Leask, Nigel, *British Romantic Writing and the East: Anxieties of Empire* (Cambridge: Cambridge University Press, 1992).

——, *Curiosity and the Aesthetics of Travel Writing, 1770–1840* (Oxford: Oxford University Press, 2002).

Lee, Debbie, *Slavery and the Romantic Imagination* (Philadelphia: University of Pennsylvania Press, 2002).

Majeed, Javeed, *Ungoverned Imaginings: James Mill's History of British India and Orientalism* (Oxford: Oxford University Press, 1992).

Makdisi, Saree, *Romantic Imperialism: Universal Empire and the Culture of Modernity* (Cambridge: Cambridge University Press, 1998).

Pratt, M. L., *Imperial Eyes: Travel Writing and Transculturation* (London: Routledge, 1992).

Richardson, Alan and Hofksoh, Sonia, *Romanticism, Race, and Imperial Culture, 1780–1834* (Bloomington, IN: Indiana University Press, 1996).

Said, Edward, *Orientalism* (Harmondsworth: Penguin, 1985).

——, *Culture and Imperialism* (London: Vintage, 1994).

Schwab, Raymond, *The Oriental Renaissance: Europe's Rediscovery of India and the East, 1680–1880* (New York: Columbia University Press, 1984).

Thomas, Helen, *Romanticism and Slave Narratives: Transatlantic Testimonies* (Cambridge University Press, 2000).

Wood, Marcus, *Slavery, Empathy, and Pornography* (Oxford: Oxford University Press, 2003).

Web links

BBC: British history: Abolition
www.bbc.co.uk/history/british/abolition/

The British Abolition Movement
www.users.muohio.edu/mandellc/projects/aronowml/

Slavery, abolition, and emancipation
www.brycchancarey.com/slavery/index.htm

South Seas: Voyaging and cross-cultural encounters in the Pacific (1769–1800)
http://southseas.nla.gov.au/

Transatlantic slavery: against human dignity
www.liverpoolmuseums.org.uk/maritime/slavery/

Science

Bewell, Alan, *Romanticism and Colonial Disease* (Baltimore, MD, and London: Johns Hopkins University Press, 1999).

Cadbury, Deborah, *The Dinosaur Hunters: A True Story of Scientific Rivalry and the Discovery of the Prehistoric World* (London: Fourth Estate, 2000).

Cunningham, A. and Jardine, N. (eds), *Romanticism and the Sciences* (Cambridge: Cambridge University Press, 1990).

Gascoigne, John, *Science in the Service of Empire: Joseph Banks, the British State and the Uses of Science in the Age of Revolution* (Cambridge: Cambridge University Press, 1998).

Golinsky, Jan, *Science as Public Culture: Chemistry and Enlightenment in Britian, 1760–1820* (Cambridge: Cambridge University Press, 1992).

Grabo, Carl, *A Newton among Poets: Shelley's Use of Science in 'Prometheus Unbound'* (Chapel Hill, NC: University of North Carolina Press, 1930).

Levere, Trevor H., *Poetry Realized in Nature: Samuel Taylor Coleridge and Early Nineteenth-Century British Science* (Cambridge: Cambridge University Press, 1981).

Lussier, Mark S., *Romantic Dynamics: The Poetics of Physicality* (New York: St Martin's Press, 2000).

Richardson, Alan, *British Romanticism and the Science of the Mind* (Cambridge: Cambridge University Press, 2005).

Ritterbush, Philip C., *Overtures to Biology: The Speculations of Eighteenth-Century Naturalists* (New Haven, CT, and London: Yale University Press, 1964).

Roe, Nicholas, *Samuel Taylor Coleridge and the Sciences of Life* (Oxford: Oxford University Press, 2003).

Ruston, Sharon, *Shelley and Vitality* (Basingstoke: Palgrave Macmillan, 2005).

Uglow, Jenny, *The Lunar Men: The Friends who Made the Future, 1730–1810* (London: Faber & Faber, 2002).

Wylie, Ian, *Young Coleridge and the Philosophers of Nature* (Oxford: Clarendon Press, 1989).

Web links

Literature, cognition and the brain
www2.bc.edu/~richarad/lcb/home.html

Romantic natural history
http://users.dickinson.edu/~nicholsa/Romnat/

Index

Page numbers in *italics* denote references to illustrations in the text.